WILLIAM MORRIS: THE CRITICAL HERITAGE

THE CRITICAL HERITAGE SERIES

GENERAL EDITOR: B. C. SOUTHAM, M.A., B.LITT. (OXON.)
Formerly Department of English, Westfield College, University of London

For a list of books in the series see the back end paper

WILLIAM MORRIS

THE CRITICAL HERITAGE

Edited by
PETER FAULKNER
Department of English, University of Exeter

ROUTLEDGE & KEGAN PAUL LONDON AND BOSTON

First published 1973
by Routledge & Kegan Paul Ltd
Broadway House, 68–74 Carter Lane,
London EC4V 5EL and
9 Park Street,
Boston, Mass. 02108, U.S.A.

ISBN 0 7100 7520 0
Library of Congress Catalog Card No. 72-93518

Printed in **Great** *Britain*
by Butler & **Tanner** *Ltd, Frome and London*

General Editor's Preface

The reception given to a writer by his contemporaries and near-contemporaries is evidence of considerable value to the student of literature. On one side we learn a great deal about the state of criticism at large and in particular about the development of critical attitudes towards a single writer; at the same time, through private comments in letters, journals or marginalia, we gain an insight upon the tastes and literary thought of individual readers of the period. Evidence of this kind helps us to understand the writer's historical situation, the nature of his immediate reading-public, and his response to these pressures.

The separate volumes in the *Critical Heritage Series* present a record of this early criticism. Clearly, for many of the highly productive and lengthily reviewed nineteenth- and twentieth-century writers, there exists an enormous body of material; and in these cases the volume editors have made a selection of the most important views, significant for their intrinsic critical worth or for their representative quality—perhaps even registering incomprehension!

For earlier writers, notably pre-eighteenth century, the materials are much scarcer and the historical period has been extended, sometimes far beyond the writer's lifetime, in order to show the inception and growth of critical views which were initially slow to appear.

In each volume the documents are headed by an Introduction, discussing the material assembled and relating the early stages of the author's reception to what we have come to identify as the critical tradition. The volumes will make available much material which would otherwise be difficult of access and it is hoped that the modern reader will be thereby helped towards an informed understanding of the ways in which literature has been read and judged.

B.C.S.

Contents

The Story of the Volsungs and Niblungs (1870)

Comments by contemporary men of letters

Love is Enough (1872)

Three Northern Love Stories (1875)

The Aeneids of Vergil (1875)

Sigurd the Volsung (1876)

CONTENTS

Hopes and Fears for Art (1882)

The Odyssey of Homer (1887–8)

Signs of Change (1888)

A Dream of John Ball (1888)

The House of the Wolfings (1889)

The Roots of the Mountains (1890)

News from Nowhere (1891)

Poems by the Way (1892)

Socialism: its Growth and Outcome (1893)

The Wood Beyond the World (1895)

Beowulf (1895)

Old French Romances (1896)

The Well at the World's End (1896)

The Water of the Wondrous Isles (1897)

The Sundering Flood (1897)

Preface

The Critical Heritage Series is concerned with literary reputations, while William Morris's activities took him well beyond literature. At the same time, his published works are enough in themselves to have called forth numerous reviews, which provide the main substance of this book. Some articles also concern his activities as a designer, and this aspect is also discussed briefly in the Introduction. The main emphasis is, however, on Morris's literary reputation.

The volume is not exhaustive: reviews and articles which simply repeat already accepted ideas have been omitted, and others of more interest have been excluded because of lack of space. But all stages of critical sophistication are represented in order to present a full historical account. Morris's wide range of interests ensures that a great variety of points of view is represented.

Acknowledgments

I should like to thank the publishers for permission to quote from the following books: the Oxford University Press for J. W. Mackail, *The Life of William Morris* and C. C. Abbott (ed.), *The Letters of G. M. Hopkins to Robert Bridges* and *The Correspondence of G. M. Hopkins and R. W. Dixon*; Rupert Hart-Davis for A. Wade (ed.), *The Letters of W. B. Yeats* and R. Hart-Davis (ed.), *The Letters of Oscar Wilde*; the Yale University Press for C. Y. Lang (ed.), *The Swinburne Letters*; and the Clarendon Press for O. Doughty and J. R. Wahl (eds.), *Letters of D. G. Rossetti.*

I am grateful to all who have helped in the preparation of this book, including the University of Durham for a term of sabbatical leave, the services of its University Library and its secretarial pool; the Cambridge University Library; the Fitzwilliam Museum, Cambridge; the British Museum; my colleagues for answering heterogeneous questions; and my wife for remaining serene.

Introduction

Despite the complications arising from his many-sidedness, the history of William Morris's reputation as a writer is reasonably clear. He began as a poet, and although his first volume, *The Defence of Guenevere* (1858), was poorly received, its successors, *The Life and Death of Jason* (1867) and *The Earthly Paradise* (1868–70) were successful with the reviewers and, even more markedly, popular with the public. Thus by 1870, at the age of only thirty-five, Morris was widely regarded as a major poet. It is as 'the author of *The Earthly Paradise*' that he appeared on the title pages of subsequent volumes. Morris himself considered his next poem, *Sigurd the Volsung*, to be his greatest literary work, but it did not achieve the popularity of its predecessors.

After its publication in 1876, Morris became more engaged in social issues. This led to his public lectures, later published in volume form, which have attracted more attention since his death than they did during his lifetime. The imaginative prose romances written during the last decade of his life also remained limited in their appeal. His later poetry consists only of the volume *Poems by the Way*, published in 1892, but his poetic reputation survived well enough for the young Yeats, for example, to think of Morris as the natural successor to Tennyson as Poet Laureate in that year, had not his politics ruled him out.[1] On his death in 1896 there were few who denied his greatness, but there was considerable disagreement as to where to locate it—a disagreement which has not yet been resolved.

REVIEWERS AND REVIEWING

The Victorian period is in many ways the golden age of reviewing: the journals of the time were able to give their contributors ample opportunities for the full discussion of contemporary publications. This sometimes led to garrulity and padding, but it meant that the able reviewer could develop his ideas much more fully than his modern counterpart. Morris's poetry was reviewed widely and at length by many of the most active literary journalists of the time, including Richard Garnett, Swinburne, Pater, Henry James, Alfred Austin,

Colvin, Gosse, Lang and Saintsbury. If Pater's review (No. 12) is out-standing in its probing articulacy, many of the others are thoughtful and well focused. Some of them, particularly Henry James's (No. 10), also reveal the limited function accorded to poetry at the time.

Reviewers tended to concentrate mainly on the two major literary forms of the century, poetry and the novel, so that Morris's later writings in the form of lectures and romances received less attention. Nevertheless, his later reviewers included Oscar Wilde, H. G. Wells and Yeats. Morris's engagement with the nascent Socialist movement in the eighties and nineties also ensured that his death should call forth tributes from such Radicals as Blatchford, Kropotkin and Edward Carpenter, who were less concerned about his poetry than his impact as a social critic.

MORRIS AND HIS CRITICS

Morris was not particularly communicative about his own creative processes, and it is hard to be sure of the effect of criticism on him. Mackail noted:[2]

It was part, and a very necessary part, of the Pre-Raphaelite creed to disregard both neglect and criticism: and Morris, of all persons in the world, was one who was only happy in his own content, and over whom the opinions of others slipped without leaving much impression. For professional literary criticism, beyond all, his feeling was something between amusement and contempt. 'To think of a beggar making a living by selling his opinion about other people!' he characteristically said: 'and fancy any one paying for it!' he added, in a climax of scorn.

Nevertheless Mackail also remarked that Morris stopped writing poetry soon after the publication of *Guenevere*, abandoning his *Scenes from the Fall of Troy*. An amusing letter from Swinburne in April 1858 describes Morris as giving 'no sign of life' at the time of publication of *Guenevere*, as if he wished to lie low until the criticism had been digested (No. 28b)[3] and May Morris recorded the pleasure he took in the two good reviews of the volume.[4] Morris's creative impulse could take many forms, and it seems likely that the generally poor reviews, together with his marriage and the necessity of furnishing a house, together with the success of Tennyson's *Idylls of the King* in 1859 treating Arthurian themes in a more polished style, all helped to lead Morris away from poetry for a time.

Morris's letters show that he read and responded to some of the reviews. Mackail prints a letter of June 1867 showing the encouragement Morris derived from the favourable early reviews of *Jason*:[5]

Naturally I am in good spirits after the puffs, but I reserve any huge delight until I see what the *Pall Mall* and *Saturday* say, one of which is pretty sure to act as Advocatus Diaboli. However I fancy I shall do pretty well now: last week I had made up my mind that I shouldn't be able to publish 'The Earthly Paradise' and was very low: I am as anxious as you are to get on with that work, and am going to set to work hard now.

In August 1869 he wrote thanking F. S. Ellis for sending him Austin's review in *Temple Bar* (No. 13), and commented that 'it did not excoriate my thin hide in spite of a tender contempt with which Mr Austin seemed to regard me.' He went on:[6]

Commercially I suppose I ought to be grateful to him and am so; from the critical point of view I think there is so much truth in his article as that we poets of today have been a good deal made by those of the Byron and Shelley time—however, in another sixty years or so, when it won't matter three skips of a louse to us (as it don't matter much more now), I suppose that we shall quietly fall into our places.

He sometimes sent reviews on to his wife, with brief comments.[7]

A letter to Sidney Colvin from Morris's great friend Edward Burne-Jones about a review by Colvin of Part 3 of *The Earthly Paradise* supports the view that Morris was sensitive to criticism: 'Morris seemed very pleased with the Gudrun article, so it must have been a tremendous puff (by this time you will have found out the poet's soul and how easily it is vexed and how you cannot fathom it).'[8] But Morris did not undertake elaborate precautions to ensure favourable reviews as did Rossetti, nor did he reply to the reviewers in the polemical fashion of Swinburne. His only letter to an editor about a review concerned what Morris held to be a question of fact—that *The Wood Beyond the World* (1895) was not, as the reviewer had suggested (No. 71), an allegory: 'I had not the least intention of thrusting an allegory in *The Wood Beyond the World*; it is meant for a tale pure and simple, with nothing didactic about it. If I have to write or speak on social problems, I always try to be as direct as I possibly can.'[9] He never contested reviewers' critical estimates. That he appreciated some reviews is shown by his remark to Theodore Watts, in connection with his review of *The Wood Beyond the World* (No. 70): 'I am so often praised for achieving what I never aimed at that it is quite refreshing to be criticized by a man like yourself who understands one's aim.'[10] Morris can hardly be called a Man of Letters; he did not read much contemporary poetry and he avoided reviewing other people's books, except when pressed into doing so in 1870 in the course of Rossetti's unsuccessful attempt to ensure a good press for his own *Poems*. Much of his energy went into the attempts of the firm of Morris, Marshall, Faulkner & Co. to improve standards of design. He had too many other activities for the literary field to have been crucial to him; but he was sensitive as well as robust, and the reviews no doubt affected his choices both within literature and between writing and other activities.

THE PUBLICATION OF MORRIS'S WORKS

The Defence of Guenevere was published by Bell and Daldy in 1858. According to Mackail, 'Some two hundred and fifty copies were sold or given away, and the remainder of the edition stayed long on the publishers' shelves. So late as 1871 there were still copies to be had.'[11] The second edition of 1875 was made possible only by the growth of Morris's reputation from his later volumes. *The Life and Death of Jason* was published in January 1867 by Bell and Daldy,[12] but in view of their earlier experience with his poetry they made Morris publish it at his own expense. A little earlier Morris had met the bookseller F. S. Ellis, whose advice helped him to obtain from Bell and Daldy 'a substantial sum'[13] for the right to print the second edition of *Jason*, which followed in December. After this, the copyright was transferred to Ellis, who published the lengthy *Earthly Paradise*. Sales were so high that a new contract was drawn up, giving Morris a larger share of the profits.[14] The success of this poem is reflected in the rapidity of the editions: for instance, there were five editions of the first volume between 1868 and 1870. No later work by Morris attained such success. *Love is Enough* (1872) appeared in only one edition; *Sigurd the Volsung* (1876), Morris's favourite poem, in two during Morris's lifetime (and also two in America). *The House of the Wolfings* had two editions, and *Poems by the Way* had three. *John Ball* was serialized in *Commonweal*, the magazine of the Socialist League, and published with *A King's Lesson* in 1888; it was reissued three times, and a second edition was published in 1892. There were four editions of *Hopes and Fears for Art* (1882) but *Signs of Change* (1888) was restricted to one. These books, therefore, did not reach a wide public, although Morris was becoming a prominent figure in these years.

Morris issued his later works in small editions through his own Kelmscott Press—*The Wood Beyond the World* (1895), *The Well at the World's End* (1896), *The Sundering Flood* and *The Water of the Wondrous Isles* all appeared in this way, the last two posthumously in 1897. The first two also received commercial publication. The most successful of his later works was the Utopian romance *News from Nowhere*, which originally appeared in *Commonweal* in 1890. Reeves and Turner published the book in 1891, with four reissues in Morris's lifetime, and there were also a Kelmscott edition in 1892 and two American issues. Only in *News from Nowhere* was the popularity of *The Earthly Paradise* approached, but in this case the reviewers were far less attentive, partly no doubt because of the fact that Morris was now working in a less orthodox literary form, as well as expressing less orthodox social views.

The Defence of Guenevere

Morris went up to Exeter College, Oxford, in 1853. His early writings include both poems and prose romances, some of which were published in 1856 in the *Oxford and Cambridge Magazine*[15]—despite its formal title, an enterprise of young university friends, largely financed by Morris, which (although praised by Ruskin and Tennyson) lasted only a year. Morris was fortunate throughout his life in the staunchness of his friends' belief in him; already in 1855 Edward Burne-Jones was writing to his cousin Maria Choyce with great conviction of his abilities:[16]

Watch carefully all that Morris writes. You will find one of the very purest and most beautiful minds on earth breathing through all he touches—sometimes I even regret that he is my friend, for I am open to the charge of partiality by praising him so, and if he were a stranger I know I should detect him in a heap of others' writings, and watch for something very great from him, as I do now.

Rossetti, seven years older than Morris, combined admiration and condescension in his account in a letter to William Allingham in December 1856: 'You would think him one of the finest little fellows alive—with a touch of the incoherent, but a real man' (No. 27a). In a letter to William Bell Scott in February 1857 Rossetti told of the arrival in London of Morris and Burne-Jones, 'now very intimate friends of mine', and remarked that 'Morris has written some really wonderful poetry' (No. 27b).

But the publication of *The Defence of Guenevere* in 1858 pleased

Morris's friends more than the reviewers. Swinburne, who had met Morris at Oxford, wrote to Edwin Hatch with good news in February: 'Morris's book is really out. Reading it, I would fain be worthy to sit down at his feet' (No. 28a). His enthusiasm seems to have aroused Hatch's criticism, for in September Swinburne wrote to say that he would take care to avoid 'Topsification'[17]—Topsy or Top being the nickname applied to Morris because of his close curly hair. Thomas Woolner, the Pre-Raphaelite sculptor, wrote acutely to Mrs. Tennyson in February 1858: 'Have you seen and do you like W. Morris's poems? I have not seen them to read yet, but long ago he read me some which I thought contained some original ideas and an extraordinary power of entering the far-back old knightly way of looking at things.'[18] Although it is impossible to ascertain which poems Woolner had heard Morris read, his sense of their imaginative power was shared by some sensitive readers. This imaginative power has increasingly been recognized as giving the poems their authority. That Ruskin felt it too may be seen from his letter to the Brownings in March 1858 in which Morris's poems 'about old chivalry' are found to be 'most noble —very, very great indeed—in their own peculiar way' (No. 24a). And Rossetti, writing to Mrs. Gaskell in July 1859, referred to Morris's 'truth to the dramatic life of the old romance' in the Arthurian part of the volume, which he found superior to Tennyson's recently published *Idylls of the King* (No. 27c).

But the reviewers in 1858 were certainly not indulgent to the new poet. They found the poems strange and difficult, and advised Morris, in tones varying from the indignant to the pained, to mend his ways. To account for the misunderstanding, and even hostility, it is necessary to recall that *The Defence of Guenevere* was the first volume of Pre-Raphaelite poetry to appear: neither Dante Gabriel nor Christina Rossetti, nor Swinburne, had yet published, except in magazines. Thus the widespread suspicion from which the Pre-Raphaelite painters were only gradually emerging readily transferred itself to Morris's poetry. Rossetti led his poetic army from the rear, while Morris paid the price of being in the van. The unpopularity of 'the Rossetti school' in the 1860s was attested by Sir John Skelton in his reminiscences, *The Table-Talk of Shirley* (1895). Skelton recalled how John Parker, the mild-mannered editor of *Fraser's Magazine*, had allowed him to 'extend recognition, more or less cordial, to a young writer named William Morris,'[19] but had felt it necessary to do so under protest, expressed in a letter of 14 May 1860:[20]

I saw Morris's poems in MS. He wanted us to publish them. I confess I could make nothing of them. Nor could a very able man who looked at the MS. for me. Surely 19/20ths of them are of the most obscure, watery, mystical, affected stuff possible. The man who brought the MS. (himself well known as a poet) said 'that one of the poems which described a picture of Rossetti was a very fine poem; that the picture was not understandable, and the poem made it no clearer, but that it was a fine poem nevertheless.' For myself, I am sick of Rossetti and his whole school. I think them essentially unmanly, effeminate, mystical, affected, and obscure. You ought really to say more as to Morris's obscurity and affectation.

The elderly Skelton remarked that Parker 'had a vast mass of authority on his side, and a grain of truth at least'.[21] The hostility towards what were regarded as the affectations of Pre-Raphaelitism was amusingly embodied in Du Maurier's satire 'A Legend of Camelot' in *Punch* in 1866.[22]

Writing in the same year, William Michael Rossetti remarked that Morris had not yet received the recognition he deserved:[23]

When he does so, he will be acknowledged as by far the most genially and subtly chivalrous and medieval of all modern English poets, and even transcending Victor Hugo in this particular department. A page of Morris is as rich as a painted window flooded with afternoon sun, and as dreamily sonorous as the choral chant from the further end of the cathedral. In the pitch and colour of his poems, Mr. Morris is almost unfailingly right; but, as an executive artist, he trusts too much to instinct and the chapter of accidents.

H. M. Hyndman (1842–1921), who was a man of wide interests as well as the founder of the Democratic Federation of which Morris was to be a member, also recalled in his autobiography that Morris's early poetry was little known:[24]

It shows how little was known of William Morris by the ordinary man who was deeply interested in literature, that it was not before 1865 that I became acquainted with his writings, though Swinburne, with his *Atalanta in Calydon* and other poems, had swept me away years before. I have never been able to understand this; for Morris was easily intelligible, the charm of his verse is attractive to all, and the fact that he was so closely associated with and so much admired by the men who were then so greatly influencing the world of art and letters ought to have secured for him a wide public. Yet it was not until Swinburne spoke of him as a great poet[25] that the majority even of reading men were aware that so fine a genius was living unappreciated among us.

He was much better known for his persistent revolutionary assaults upon the commonplace domestic decoration and furniture of the mid-Victorian period than for his delightful verse.

Hyndman has telescoped his reminiscences of Swinburne, whose *Atalanta* was not published until 1865, and he exaggerates the simplicity of Morris's early poems, but in view of the low sales of *The Defence of Guenevere* and the impact made on English taste by Morris's firm in the 1860s[26] this account is convincing.

The literary reminiscences of the art-critic J. Comyns Carr (1849–1916), however, seem to place the impact of Morris before that of Swinburne:[27]

Before I read *Atalanta in Calydon* my imagination had been deeply stirred by the first volume of Mr. Morris's verse, entitled *The Defence of Guenevere*. I found there, though in a form perhaps deliberately archaic, that deeper note of passion which Tennyson's poetry, even at its best, confessedly lacks; and its appeal was the more urgent because Morris too was attracted by the charm of medieval romance—romance which in Tennyson's hands had lost some of its primitive dramatic quality, and became, as he developed the Arthurian story, more and more material for setting forth a systematised body of ethical teaching. Morris at a single stroke seemed to restore the legend to its historical place, and to recapture a part of its passionate significance. I confess that no later work of his has ever affected me to the same degree, though there runs in them all that exquisite and ineffable charm of the born story-teller.

Carr must have been a precocious reader, but there is no need to doubt the substantial accuracy of his account. The experience he describes was, however, not widely shared. It is true that his judgment that Morris's poetry showed a decline from its early intensity was also that of some perceptive readers like Browning (No. 26c), Hopkins (No. 29c) and R. W. Dixon,[28] and of many modern readers; but it was not the view of most Victorians, as the enthusiastic reception of *Jason* and the *Earthly Paradise* suggests.

The Life and Death of Jason and The Earthly Paradise

Morris was clearly, and understandably, interested in the reception of *The Life and Death of Jason*, with which he broke his poetic silence in June 1867. According to May Morris's recollections: 'My father was in spirits over the reviews—a little cautious, too, and characteristically never over-sanguine until the success was an accomplished fact.'[29] She quotes a letter of Morris referring to Joseph Knight's review in the *Sunday Times* (No. 7): 'his notice is a handsome one, and so is his friend's in the *Athenaeum*, and there was another in the *Spectator* also following—so I am getting on pretty well.'[30] The reception of the poem by the reviewers was certainly encouraging. The *Athenaeum* had changed its view even of the earlier volume, though it still regretted that Morris showed no responsiveness to 'the creed of Christendom'. The monthlies were no less favourable; Swinburne wrote at enthusiastic length in the *Fortnightly* (No. 8), while two Americans, C. E. Norton and Henry James, praised the poem highly (Nos 9 and 10). Only the *Atlantic Monthly* argued that the poem was too derivative to be of much significance.[31]

The terms of the praise given to *Jason* help to clarify the appeal of the poem and its successor to a large Victorian public. Joseph Knight (No. 7) remarked, 'No single idea about it seems to have even the slightest reference to any modern thought or feeling.' Henry James concluded his review (No. 10): 'To the jaded intellects of the present moment, distracted with the strife of creeds and the conflict of theories, it opens a glimpse into a world where they will be called upon neither to choose, to criticise, nor to believe, but simply to feel, to look, and to listen.' It was a world which many enjoyed entering.

Reservations were nevertheless made by some of the reviewers. Swinburne, for instance, suggested that 'the river of romance' flowed rather too evenly, and that 'something of barrier or dam' might serve to increase the power of a future volume. Owen Meredith felt something similar, and his letter to Robert Browning of 24 June 1867 suggests:[32]

I think the book exceedingly clever, and much more than clever; but I don't know whether the unsatisfactory effect which it makes upon me is my own fault, or that of the Poet . . . But though my mind is not in harmony with it, I fancy it must be in harmony with a prevalent taste among poetry-readers and writers more cultivated and competent than myself.

Meredith's view of public taste proved correct, while Joseph Knight's belief that *Jason*, for all its merits, would prove 'caviare to the general', was remarkably inaccurate. Morris, recognizing and responding to the situation, proceeded confidently with a poem similar in mood though on a larger scale.

The Earthly Paradise achieved even greater popularity than *Jason*, perhaps because its division into a number of separate stories made it easier to assimilate. From the *Athenaeum's* enthusiastic welcome of the first part on 30 May 1868 ('Mr Morris is a marvel of imaginative fecundity'[33]) onward, the reviews hastened to celebrate the easy flow of the narrative and the pleasant scenic effects. The wide appeal of the poem to the ordinary reader is suggested in a letter from Mary Howitt to her friend Mrs. Alfred Watts in March 1869:[34]

I have vastly enjoyed Mr. Morris's poem: and thus it is a pleasure to me to think of him in his blue blouse and with his earnest face at 'The Firm' and to feel that he is a great poet . . . Morris is not before Tennyson, but he stands very near him in the living reality of his old-world pictures, and in his exquisite painting of scenery; the flowers, and the grasses, the 'brown birds', every individual object and feature in Nature is so lovingly and so faithfully portrayed. Tennyson's poetry is the perfection of art and truth in art. Morris's is Nature itself, rough at times, but quaint, fresh, and dewy beyond anything I ever saw or felt in language. I shall try to tell Mr. Morris what a joy and a refreshment it has been to me.

Even readers as intellectual as G. H. Lewes and George Eliot could enjoy the poem in the same spirit, as a letter to John Blackwood, written from Petersthal in the Black Forest in June 1868, indicates. 'We take Morris's poem into the woods with us and read it aloud, greedily, looking to see how much *more* there is in store for us. *If ever you have an idle afternoon, bestow it on the Earthly Paradise.*'[35] The undemanding charm of the poem pleased most of the reviewers and numerous readers.

But there were some with reservations. Lady Burne-Jones made her unconscious criticism, as she amusingly recorded in the *Memorials* of her husband, when Morris used to read the recently completed poems out loud. 'I remember, with shame, often falling asleep to the steady rhythm of the reading voice, or biting my fingers and stabbing myself with pins in order to keep awake.'[36] Browning, too, felt the lack of vitality in the poem, which he regarded as a grave shortcoming (No. 26c). It was Alfred Austin in *Temple Bar* for November 1869 who made the most severe criticisms of the lack of energy in the poem, though he rather condescendingly attributed this to the spirit of the age rather than the poet's own deficiencies (No. 13). Another serious criticism, that Morris's poetry was devoid of Christian morality, was made in the *Christian Observer* in March 1870[37] and by G. W. Cox in the *Edinburgh Review* in January 1871 (No. 18).

Their criticisms make it hard to see the grounds for Swinburne's amused comments about Morris's having become the 'Christian laureate' (No. 28e and f). The remark is perhaps due primarily to the contrast which many reviewers noted between Swinburne's exuberant celebration of pagan themes and Morris's restrained treatment of them. As Buxton Forman put it: 'These poems are such as no man need scruple to take home to his wife and leave within reach of his children; for if unimpregnated with modern doctrine, they are at least innocent of what is gross in ancient creeds.'[38] That Morris was aware of limitations in his own poetry is clear from his letter in reply to Swinburne's praise of the 'Lovers of Gudrun' in December 1869:[39]

I am delighted to have pleased you with the Gudrun. For the rest I am rather painfully conscious myself that the book would have done me more credit if there had been nothing in it but the Gudrun, though I don't think the others quite the worst things I have done. Yet they are all too long and flabby, damn it!

His involvement with Icelandic literature was an attempt to cope with this 'flabbiness'. Many reviewers noted that the 'Lovers of Gudrun' was the most vivid poem in the series.[40]

However, it was not vigour but charm and relaxation which most Victorian readers sought, and found, in the poem. Walter Crane, looking back in his autobiography *An Artist's Reminiscences* in 1907, recalled the atmosphere of the 'dream-world' in which he had been happy to lose himself as a young man:[41]

In such a mood I first read Rossetti's sonnets and *The Earthly Paradise* by William Morris, which was first published in 1870, and found in both a most congenial atmosphere. To read the latter seemed like entering one of the delightful houses or halls the poet himself helped to create and often described, stone-pillared, open-timbered, and hung with arras tapestries full of mythical histories and legends of races, and glowing in gold and colour.

Crane was to follow Morris into the Socialist movement in the 1880s, but meanwhile it was enough for the Earthly Paradise to be a pleasant dream.

In America Morris's reputation followed a similar course. *The Defence of Guenevere* was scarcely known, there being no American edition, but *Jason* and *The Earthly Paradise* achieved popularity. A particularly enthusiastic response is to be found in the letters of the minor Southern poet Paul Hayne (No. 30). Eventually, his correspondent Sidney Lanier, at first very fond of Morris, was to argue that Hayne's poetry suffered from Morris's influence, recommending Chaucer as healthier (No. 36). But Emerson was able to recommend Morris as a source of health in 1874, telling an interviewer[42]: 'Morris, the author of *The Earthly Paradise*, is just the opposite of Swinburne, and will help to neutralize his bad influence on the public.' A thorough and perceptive account of Morris's poetry in the *New Englander* in October 1871 (No. 22) acutely balanced the merits and limitations of the poem, but the common reader in America as in England seems to have been happy to come across a poetry so charming and undemanding.

The attack on Pre-Raphaelitism, which had died down for a decade, was renewed in some of the criticisms of Rossetti's *Poems* of 1870, and these criticisms were sometimes extended to Morris as well. The *North American Review* had some sharp words for the medieval enthusiasms of the group:[43]

Surely there is something wrong in the thinker or the poet—shall we say, too, the artist?—who can content himself with his fancies of the thoughts and feelings and views of times past, and who can better please himself with what after all must be more or less unreal phantasmagoria, than with the breathing life around him.

The strongest attack on Rossetti was the anonymous article in the *Contemporary Review* by Robert Buchanan entitled 'The Fleshly School of Poetry' in October 1871. This included some side-blows at Rossetti's associates, Swinburne and Morris. Buchanan laced praise with condescension most effectively in comparing Rossetti with the other two poets. 'He cannot tell a pleasant story like Mr. Morris, nor forge alliterative thunderbolts like Mr. Swinburne. It must be conceded, nevertheless, that he is neither so glibly imitative as the one, nor so transcendently superficial as the other.'[44] A much more subtle and telling criticism of the three poets was contained in W. J. Courthope's 'The Latest Developments of Literary Poetry' in the *Quarterly Review* in January 1872 (No. 23).

Morris's reputation may have been slightly affected by the association implied in the reference in a letter by the Earl of Lytton in 1871 to the 'Morris–Rossetti clique'.[45] Certainly Swinburne's enthusiasm for Morris's poetry was of doubtful value to Morris. The *Quarterly Review*'s account of Swinburne's *Essays and Studies* in April 1876 quoted as an example of his critical ineptitude Swinburne's praise of the scene in *Jason* in which Medea is about to slay her children.[46] On the other hand, a liberal reviewer like John Morley could refer enthusiastically in 1873 to the rise of the new school:[47]

Then Mr. Ruskin came, and the Pre-Raphaelite painters, and Mr. Swinburne, and Mr. Morris, and now lastly a critic like Mr. Pater, all with their faces averted from theology, most of them indeed blessed with a simple and happy unconsciousness of the very existence of the conventional gods.

Nor does it seem that Morris was totally identified with Pre-Raphael-itism. For instance, writing in 1876 a mainly unsympathetic account of the movement, Justin McCarthy paid a modest tribute to Morris's influence on domestic decoration in 'banishing the tawdry and un-meaning displays of white, and gold, and red, with which we used to plaster our walls, after certain fashions in France.'[48] He then remarked of the poetry:[49]

Some of Mr. Morris's descriptions, on the other hand, are, I am told, simply pre-Raphaelite pictures written out. I fancy, however, that Mr. Morris is hardly a thoroughly accepted poet of the school. He is considered, I believe, rather too decorative in style and perhaps not cheerless enough.

Few reviewers, however, found any excessive cheerfulness in Morris's poetry, and they sometimes contrasted him acutely with Chaucer on this account (Nos 22 and 36).[50]

Love is Enough and Sigurd the Volsung

In the early 1870s Morris became busier than ever. The Firm was developing well and gave him more and more to do; Walter Bagehot may be taken as an example of the kind of client who was becoming impressed by its work. Mrs. Russell Barrington records in her *Life* that in 1870 the Bagehots moved to Wimbledon Common. 'It was about this time that he became interested in the decorative art of William Morris and his School. He had a fine taste and a quick eye, and easily discerned in this work a distinguished quality which would be last-ingly satisfying.'[51] When Bagehot bought a house in Queen's Gate Place in 1874 he employed the Firm, writing in a letter: 'Wardle is doing most of the house, but the great man himself, William Morris, is composing the drawing room, as he would an ode.'[52] In addition to such work, Morris visited Iceland in 1871 and 1873, and began to pro-duce his translations with Magnússon, and he also wrote his most formally elaborate poem, *Love is Enough, or the Freeing of Pharamond.* Although the poem was well received in the *Athenaeum*,[53] the *Academy* (No. 31), the *Fortnighty Review* (No. 32), and the short-lived *Dark Blue*,[54] its elaboration precluded popular interest. Rossetti, who knew the poem before publication, considered it 'at a higher point of execu-tion than anything he has done' (No. 27i). Coventry Patmore was more equivocal in his remarks in a letter:[55]

I have lately read again Morris's poem, 'Love is Enough', which you gave me. It is a most lofty and delicate atmosphere of mystic tenderness and joy. I don't know that a poem can have higher praise. But it is one of those things which, as Lord Dundreary says, 'No fellow can be expected to understand'.

Meredith suggested that the poem reflected the unfortunate power of the reading public over its favourites:[56]

I have looked at Morris's poem 'Enough for Love',—'Love is Enough', I mean. Have you? I looked away. The look was enough. Our public seems to possess the fearful art of insensibly castrating its favourites. The Songs are of the species of Fitzball's Gossamer Tree; charming in melody, but there is no such thing as a gossamer tree.

It is more likely, however, that the elements of indulgence in the poem (described by Burne-Jones at the time as 'a pretty poem that is wondrously happy; and it has four sets of lovers and THEY ARE ALL WONDROUSLY HAPPY and it ends well'),[57] reflected the tensions of Morris's marriage and the relationship between Janey and Rossetti. Mackail is convincing when he remarks:[58]

Morris himself felt that this new poem was both tentative and difficult, and its failure to make any impression on a large audience was received by him with perfect equanimity. It was a thing he had done to please himself, and he thought highly of it, but he did not expect it to please other people to anything like the same degree.

At all events, it was not popular, and has remained little known. Morris's next work, the translation of Vergil's *Aeneid* in 1875, was not any more widely read, although it was praised in the *Athenaeum*, and by the classical scholar Henry Nettleship in the *Academy* (No. 35).

To the work which succeeded it, *Sigurd the Volsung*, Morris devoted his greatest effort, out of respect for what he regarded as a masterwork of Northern literature. There is an interesting problem over its reception. Mackail remarks that on its publication in late November 1876 'it was but languidly received'.[59] This is not, however, supported by a reading of the reviews. Theodore Watts (who was to review ten books of Morris in the *Athenaeum* in a manner both enthusiastic and confusing) hailed the poem as 'Mr. Morris's greatest achievement' (No. 37); Edmund Gosse in the *Academy* praised a style 'more spirited and more virile than that of any of his earlier works' (No. 38);[60] the *Saturday Review* called *Sigurd* 'his greatest and most successful effort' (No. 39). In America, the *North American Review* did argue that the poem was largely 'the outcome of a transient *vogue* in sentiment' (No. 41), but the *Literary World* found it 'at once the manliest and the loveliest work of Mr. Morris's genius' (No. 40), the *Atlantic Monthly* called it 'a great poem of almost solitary beauty' (No. 42) and the *International Review* regarded it as 'the crowning achievement of Mr. Morris's life' (No. 44), perhaps prematurely. Mathilde Blind (1841–96), the German bluestocking and friend of Swinburne, proclaimed its epic merits to Theodore Watts and Buxton Forman at William Bell Scott's: ' "I think," she said in her broad German-English—German only in the pronunciation, for she spoke and wrote the idiom perfectly, "I think it is quaïte as good as Baradaïse Lost!" '⁶¹ Swinburne was also enthusiastic, despite his dislike of Northern themes (No. 28h). Henry Hewlett certainly made some serious criticisms of the diffuseness of the poem and the monotony of the rhymed ballad metre, as well as suggesting that the barbaric morality of revenge was so alien to the nineteenth century that the poem could not be expected 'to be taken to the nation's heart' (No. 43). But Henry Morley, while himself moved to parody Morris's diffuseness, found this the only fault of a poem which had otherwise 'most deftly turned that ancient tale into a modern English poem which, when taken on its own terms, is full of charm'.⁶²

All these reviews appeared within a year of the publication of the poem and show that it was much more enthusiastically received by the reviewers than Mackail realized. But the fact that Morris wrote no other major poem (with the possible exception of the 'Pilgrims of Hope') in the next twenty years, having written three major poems in ten, suggests that he may have been disappointed with the reception of *Sigurd*. This is confirmed by Theodore Watts in his review of *The Water of the Wondrous Isles* in 1897 (No. 82). Watts knew Morris in the seventies, and summed up his attitude thus: 'He was far too good a critic not to know that all the qualities of a great epic are to be found in *Sigurd* . . . But the critics did not appreciate it. It made no impression on the public.' The first part of Watts's conclusion is not easy to accept in view of the evidence of the reviews; but the second is more convincing. Indeed, there was no second English edition of *Sigurd* until 1887, although there was a second American edition in 1879. It was not that the reviewers had turned against Morris's poetry, but that the general reading public, which had been so delighted by *Jason* and *The Earthly Paradise*, remained indifferent. For a man with Morris's belief in the proper usefulness of art (and his conviction of the value of the Nordic myths) this indifference was deeply disturbing. He was not the kind of writer to be sustained by the confidence of a clique, and he now developed his activities in directions which led him away from poetry. He could do this because his talents were so unusually diverse. His refusal of the Oxford Professorship of Poetry in February 1877 marked the virtual close of his career as a poet.[63]

LECTURES AND PROSE ROMANCES: *Hopes and Fears for Art* TO *The Sundering Flood*

The next decade was the least productive of Morris's career from the literary point of view. In October 1876 he made his first political act —a long letter to the *Daily News* protesting against English support of Turkey in the Balkans, and he threw himself with characteristic enthusiasm into the attempts of the Eastern Question Association to prevent Disraeli from going to war with Russia. Morris's increasing concern with social issues came out also in his campaign against the indiscriminate 'restoration' of medieval buildings, which led to the formation of the Society for the Protection of Ancient Buildings, following a letter to the *Athenaeum* in April 1877.

In 1877, too, Morris and Company opened their new showrooms at the corner of Oxford Street and North Audley Street. The business was developing well; Morris became interested in weaving, installing a tapestry loom in his bedroom at Kelmscott House (to which he moved in 1878), and producing carpets and rugs. The acquisition of Merton Abbey for the firm in 1881 gave the opportunity for further developments, including tapestry weaving: the works are described in two contemporary articles.[64] Interest in Morris was moving away from his poetry and focusing on his practical attempts to challenge the values of competitive industrialism.

The literary form which Morris gave to his increasing cultural and political concerns was the lecture. His first public lecture was 'The Decorative Arts: Their Relation to Modern Life and Progress', given to the Trades' Guild of Learning in December 1877. Under the title 'The Lesser Arts', it forms one of the five lectures published as *Hopes and Fears for Art* in 1882. Edith Simcox wrote sympathetically of the volume in the *Fortnightly* (No. 46), but it was not widely reviewed, though it was reprinted. The American *Century Magazine* found the social criticism symptomatic of the weaknesses of the English system, going so far as to write of 'these whimperings from Mr. Morris' (No. 47). In fact, on one level Morris was very successful. His ideas on decoration were becoming widely disseminated among the general public. Mrs. C. W. Earle may be taken as a representative witness: 'Mr. William Morris's *Lectures on Art*, published in 1881, helped me more than any other book I know; it cultivated my ideas and refined my taste.'[65] She quotes from 'The Beauty of Life' the advice about simplicity which Morris himself did not always follow. The young T. J. Cobden-Sanderson, who had recently been encouraged by Janey Morris to forsake office work for bookbinding, noted in his journal: 'I have been reading Morris's *Lectures on Art*. I read the first "On the Lesser Arts." It inspired me again with ardour, and made my own projected handicraft seem beautiful to me.'[66] The impetus of Morris's lectures helped to bring about the Arts and Crafts Movement of these years.

But for Morris, a concern for decoration was becoming inadequate when related to the vast squalor of industrial England as he saw it. His thinking became increasingly political, and he threw in his lot with the small group of early Socialists in the Democratic Federation, joining in January 1883. His lecture to the Russell Club at University College, Oxford, in November of that year, was a public challenge to his class. If the Master was dismayed, at least Ruskin approved (No. 24e). Morris devoted his time, money and energy to the propagation of Socialism, writing first in *Justice*, and then—after leaving Hyndman's organization to found the Socialist League—in *Commonweal* from February 1885.[67] An old friend like Burne-Jones might regret that Morris could no longer be 'busy only for the things he used to busy about', but he saw the profound significance of Socialism to Morris.[68] Tennyson was shocked (No. 25c), but younger men were inspired. Tom Mann, for instance, recorded in conversation: 'I was surprised to be in personal contact with so great a man; I wondered why he bothered to talk to scrappy, half-educated people like me, and to spend his time helping us.'[69] Edward Carpenter recalled Morris's inspiring personality on his visits to Sheffield and Chesterfield to lecture for the Socialist League,[70] and Bruce Glasier described Morris's day-long visit to the Glasgow Branch of the League as 'A Red-Letter Day'.[71] Across the Atlantic, W. D. Howells spent the winter of 1887 reading radical works, and recorded that he was 'greatly influenced by a number of William Morris's tracts'[72] (presumably the lectures); in the concluding section of his 'Criticism and Fiction' in 1891 Howells quoted from Morris's 1884 lecture 'Art and Socialism'.[73] Tom Mann went to the William Mitchell Library in Glasgow to read Morris's 'Revival of Architecture' in the *Fortnightly Review* for May

1888 and was deeply impressed: 'It was beautiful; it fed me.'[74] He could still quote it accurately in 1938.[75] Walter Crane was brought into the Socialist movement largely by Morris's influence, and remembered the effect on him of 'Art and Socialism'.[76]

In Vernon Lee's interesting early novel *Miss Brown* in 1884, the characters are already discussing the contribution art should make to society:[77]

'Oh papa, you know what I mean; and I'm sure art will gain ever so much. It's only what Mr. Ruskin has said over and over again, and what Mr. Morris is always talking about.'

'Anyone is free to give the lower classes the taste of beauty, as long as *I* am not required to see or speak to the noble workmen,' said Hamlin. 'I hate all that democratic bosh.'

The *Saturday Review* agreed with Hamlin, and became Morris's most consistent critic. Its sophisticated conservatism found Morris's ideas absurd—products of the Cloud-Cuckoo-Land at Hammersmith (No. 49). When Morris appeared in the Thames Police Court in September 1885 on charges arising from an open-air meeting at the corner of Dod Street and Burdett Road, he was discharged by the magistrate, there being insufficient evidence for the charges of disorderly conduct and striking a policeman. But the *Saturday* took the opportunity, in a comic poem, to advise Morris to return to his forsaken Muses.[78] Not surprisingly it was the *Saturday* which reviewed the political lectures of *Signs of Change* (1888) as 'The Earthly Inferno' (No. 54). A view similar to the *Saturday*'s was expressed by Amy Sharp in *Victorian Poets* in 1891; she praised Morris as 'the prince of modern story-tellers' and regretted the change in him:[79]

His songs have become Socialist Chants, and among its other responsibilities, modern civilization, with its imperfect control of the forces called by itself into play, has to answer for having drawn, or rather dragged, aside this poet from his ministry of beauty and refreshment.

Morris had made a decisive break with his own earlier reputation, like Ruskin and Dickens, and in all three cases the change attracted hostile criticism. To Engels, on the other hand, Morris seemed an unscientific kind of socialist, easily outmanoeuvred by anyone with political skill, though thoroughly well-intentioned. As he wrote to Laura Lafargue in September 1886:[80]

Morris is a settled sentimental socialist; he would be easily managed if one saw him regularly a couple of times a week, but who has the time to do it, and if we drop him for a month he is sure to lose himself again. And is he worth all the trouble even if one has the time?

Meanwhile, Morris was returning to 'literature', first in his translation of the *Odyssey* in 1887-8 (undertaken partly as a relaxation from his social concerns) and then in the series of prose romances, to which the politically significant *Dream of John Ball* (1888 in book form) provides a prelude. The first of the true romances, *The Tale of the House of the Wolfings and of all the Kindred of the Mark* was printed by Morris with special care, in a type based on an old Basel fount, appearing in December 1888. It was widely and on the whole favourably reviewed, although the archaisms were frequently criticized[81] and were parodied in the consistently hostile *Saturday Review*, which also objected to the type (No. 57). Wilde and Watts praised the book, as did Henry Hewlett (No. 58), the most severe critic of *Sigurd*.[82] The later romances attracted less attention, except from Theodore Watts, whose reviews in the *Athenaeum*, despite their formlessness,[83] earned the praise of Morris himself (No. 70) and of F. S. Ellis (No. 82). Yeats was a great admirer of the prose romances (No. 81).

The most popular of Morris's later works, *News from Nowhere* (1891 in book form) received little critical attention, although Maurice Hewlett contributed a thorough condemnation of the underlying feeling of the book as 'A Materialist's Paradise' to the anti-socialist *National Review* (No. 62). The letter in which Oscar Wilde thanked Morris for what was presumably a copy of the paper-covered edition of the romance might well have surprised Morris by its extravagance:[84]

How proud indeed so beautiful a gift makes me. I weep over the cover, which is not really lovely enough, nor nearly rich enough in material, for such prose as you write, But the book itself, if it is to have suitable raiment, would need damask sewn with pearls and starred with gold. I have always felt that your work comes from sheer delight of making beautiful things: that no alien motive ever interests you: that in its singleness of aim, as well as in its perfection of result, it is pure art, everything that you do. But I know you hate the blowing of trumpets. I have loved your work since boyhood: I shall always love it. That, with my thanks, is all I have to say.

Other aesthetes were less kindly disposed to Morris, because of his politics. A letter from Ernest Dowson to Victor Plarr in October 1892, soon after the death of Tennyson, shows this in an extreme form:[85]

But he was un grand poète, tout de même. Above all I love him because he did sacredly hate the mob—which whether it be the well dressed mob which Browning panders to, or the evil smelling mob to which William Morris does now, to the detriment of his art and of his own dignity still pander, I hold alike to be damnable, unwholesome and obscene.

Tennyson's death raised the question of the Laureateship. Most commentators on the subject felt that Swinburne and Morris were the two serious candidates, though their reputations and convictions would make the appointment of either improbable.[86] Yeats argued in the *Bookman* symposium on 'The Question of the Laureateship':[87]

Either would make a worthy successor to Wordsworth and Tennyson, Morris the worthier of the two, perhaps, for he is still producing work scarce a whit less moving than were the songs and stories of his youth, while Mr. Swinburne has been these many days, if we consider his verse alone, too careful of the sound, too careless of the sense.

In 1892 Morris published his first volume of poetry since *Sigurd*, a collection entitled *Poems by the Way* containing some of his contributions to *Commonweal* and other short pieces. It was quietly but favourably received, one reviewer being Richard Garnett (No. 64), who had welcomed *Guenevere* in 1858. Appointment of the Laureate was deferred until 1896, when the two principal candidates remained the same.[88] Mackail records that Morris had been sounded about the possibility of his acceptance but had politely refused;[89] the post went to Alfred Austin. A more detailed account of the affair would be of interest.

With the break-up of the Socialist League in 1890 because of increasing controversy with the anarchists, Morris and his friends founded the Hammersmith Socialist Society. The Sunday evening lectures continued in the coach-house beside Kelmscott House—occasions recalled in so many memoirs of the period, including Wells's review of *The Well at the World's End* (No. 79). Morris's most explicitly political work, *Socialism: its Growth and Outcome*, written with Belfort Bax, appeared in 1893 and was severely reviewed, especially in the American *Critic* (No. 67). But another American magazine, *Poet-Lore*, published O. L. Triggs's sympathetic account of 'The Socialist Thread in the Writings of William Morris' in 1893[90] and, a little later, in 1896, W. G. Kingsland's 'A Poet's Politics', which consisted mainly of extracts from Morris's letters on Socialism to the Rev. George Bainton of Coventry.[91]

On the continent, Morris was known rather as an associate of the Pre-Raphaelite group and a designer than as a poet. Indeed Taine, the principal French expert on English literature, shows no knowledge at all of Morris. Tennyson's representative status in English poetry, and Swinburne's flamboyant interest in French poetry, assured them of a European reputation that Morris did not achieve in his lifetime. It was not until after his death that some of his political writings and ideas on design began to be translated and known in Europe. Max Nordau knew enough of Morris's poetry to be able to include him among the less extreme examples of the universal decadence which he observed in late nineteenth-century European culture (No. 63), but Gabriel Mourey's attitude is more representative. Writing in the 1890s for a French audience about the London scene, he discussed Morris in the section of his book entitled 'Renaissance of Industrial Art', and particularly praised the work of the Kelmscott Press.[92]

Morris founded the Kelmscott Press in 1891, and there printed his last romances. The young George Sturt, who contributed occasionally to *Commonweal*, made a critical comment in his *Journal* in 1892:[93]

I cannot help thinking that Morris's admiration for ancient work (no doubt very admirable) has led him astray; and his passion for imitation has introduced into his books mannerisms that would be unendurable, were they going to become the fashion.

But the Press did encourage more interest in typography and set high standards of craftsmanship.

By this stage, Morris was often thought of as a designer rather than as a poet; in 1895, for example, George Saintsbury argued that Morris's poetry was still undervalued.[94] T. F. Plowman's article 'The Aesthetes' in the *Pall Mall Magazine* in 1895 also emphasized Morris's work in household decoration:[95]

By his work in this direction his name has become familiarized in thousands of households that his 'Earthly Paradise' had failed to penetrate. He it was who gave practical expression to the new-born desire of the modern householder to have his domestic surroundings more artistically fit and harmonious than they had hitherto been.

The publication of Morris's *Poetical Works* in ten volumes in 1896 by Longmans testifies to the continuing popularity of his work and led to Andrew Lang's appreciative review.[96] But by the time of his death in October 1896 Morris was felt to have been not so much a great poet as a major influence on many aspects of English life: the responses to his death of such writers as Robert Blatchford (No. 74), Kropotkin (No. 76) and Edward Carpenter (No. 77) show this. Morris would have valued such tributes more highly than those which referred solely to his achievements as an artist.

MORRIS'S REPUTATION IN THE TWENTIETH CENTURY

Morris's many-sidedness has ensured that he has never been completely neglected since his death in 1896, but interest in him has taken varied forms. Early in the century the Arts and Crafts Movement carried on his influence through people like Cobden-Sanderson, W. R. Lethaby and Walter Crane who had known Morris personally. But the change of emphasis towards the Bauhaus aesthetic led away from Morris, despite Professor Pevsner's attempt to present Morris as a pioneer of modern design in his basic honesty of approach.[97] In the last decade Morris patterns have again become fashionable and, in so far as this is more than tasteless eclecticism, it suggests a recognition of their fundamental vitality, unrelated to historical influence or importance. There is also increasing scholarly interest in the Victorian period, which has produced such perceptive studies as Dr Dixon Hunt's *The Pre-Raphaelite Imagination* of 1968.

It is as a poet that Morris's reputation has declined most seriously. The change of outlook associated with T. S. Eliot, the view that poetry should be intelligent and demanding rather than a form of relaxation or escape, worked against the author of *The Earthly Paradise*. Yeats had reached a similar position by his own course when he wrote 'Literature and the Living Voice' in 1906, making use of his recent reading of Chaucer for a contrast which previous critics had also made, but out of which Yeats was to make creative capital:[98]

Modern literature, above all poetical literature, is monotonous in its structure and effeminate in its continual insistence upon certain moments of strained lyricism. William Morris, who did more than any modern to recover medieval art, did not in his *Earthly Paradise* copy from Chaucer, from whom he copied so much that was naive and beautiful, what seems to me essential in Chaucer's art. He thought of himself as writing for the reader, who could return to him again and again when the chosen mood had come, and became monotonous, melancholy, too continuously lyrical in his understanding of emotion and of life. Had he accustomed himself to read out his poems upon those Sunday evenings that he gave to Socialist speeches, and to gather an audience of average men, precisely such an audience as I have often seen in his house, he would have been forced to Chaucer's variety, to his delight in the height and depth, and would have found expression for that humorous, many-sided nature of his.

A poetry expressive of a whole being was now Yeats's aim. Eliot's insistence on a unified sensibility has similar implications. In his seminal essay on Marvell in 1921, Eliot contrasted the definiteness and wit of Marvell's 'The Nymph and the Fawn' with the mistiness and vagueness of 'Morris's charming poem', 'The Nymph's Song to Hylas' in *Jason*. He concluded that Morris was the victim of an etiolated poetic tradition, which made its central effort 'to construct a dream world': 'Marvell is no greater personality than Morris; but he had something much more solid behind him: he had the vast and penetrating influence of Ben Jonson.'[99] Dr Leavis made a similar point in his influential plea for modernism, *New Bearings in English Poetry* in 1932:[100]

The further we go in *The Oxford Book* the more apparent does it become that the age did not make full use of its talent. Who for instance, would guess from his poetry that William Morris was one of the most versatile, energetic and original men of his time, a force that impinged decisively in the world of practice? He reserved poetry for his day-dreams.

The tradition of beautiful fantasy to which Morris's long poems belong is not acceptable to most modern readers of poetry:[101] our escapism takes less pretty forms. But there has been a rediscovery of the force and spontaneity of Morris's early poems, reflected in Geoffrey Grigson's selection[102] and in recent critical comments.

It is as social critic rather than designer or poet that Morris is most recognized today. G. D. H. Cole's centenary selection from Morris's writings in 1934 already showed this emphasis. Cole printed only two long narrative poems (one of them the Socialist 'Pilgrims of Hope'), but eleven of the lectures. He justified his choice in terms likely to be acceptable still: 'For I think Morris is alive even more on account of what he stood for and attempted than of what he accomplished; and in these occasional writings he gives a clear and telling presentation of what he was trying to do'.[103] Bernard Shaw's account of 'William Morris as I knew him,' contributed to the second volume of May Morris's 1936 collection of her father's social writings, had a similar emphasis: 'Morris's writings about Socialism . . . really called up all his mental resources for the first time. His verse, though it

23

cannot have been so effortless as it seemed, had not taken him to his limit.'[104] By the end, 'the idle singer of an empty day' had become, for Shaw, 'a prophet and a saint'.[105]

Interpretation of Morris along these lines was continued in Middleton Murry's *Heroes of Thought* (1938), Granville Hicks's *Figures of Transition* (1939), Margaret Grennan's *William Morris. Mediaevalist and Revolutionary* (1945), E. P. Thompson's splendidly detailed political biography *William Morris. Romantic to Revolutionary* (1955)—supplemented by his 1959 lecture 'The Communism of William Morris'—and Raymond Williams's influential account of a tradition, *Culture and Society* (1958). Williams argued: 'There is more life in the lectures, where one feels that the whole man is engaged in the writing, than in any of the prose and verse romances.'[106] Asa Briggs's selection from Morris in 1962 included two complete lectures and many extracts, with the same rationale interestingly developed. The introduction suggests:[107]

One of the reasons why his writings are relevant in the twentieth century—in some ways more relevant than they were in the late nineteenth century—is that they provide the material for a critique of twentieth century Socialism (and Communism) as much as for a critique of nineteenth century capitalism.

Detailed enquiry into Morris's social thinking has been facilitated by the recent publication of Professor E. D. LeMire's *Unpublished Lectures of William Morris*,[108] containing ten important lectures not included by May Morris in her edition or its supplements.

At a time of increasing public concern over the quality of life and the state of the environment, William Morris is likely to assume his main significance as one of those who strove to set the crooked straight, the quintessential human task. A recent editor of *News from Nowhere* claims that that romance 'more than any other single work of the period . . . relates the Romantic dream to the reality of contemporary life.'[109] It is probable that the works in which this is felt to have been achieved will be those on which Morris's future literary reputation will rest.

NOTES

1 W. B. Yeats in his contribution to a symposium on 'The Question of the Laureateship' in *Bookman*, iii, November 1892; see Allan Wade (ed.), *The Letters of W. B. Yeats* (London, 1954), 219–20.

2 J. W. Mackail, *The Life of William Morris* (1899), new impression, 2 vols (London 1920), I, 134.

3 Cecil Y. Lang (ed.), *The Swinburne Letters*, Yale Edition, 6 vols (New Haven, 1959–62), I, 19–20.

4 May Morris (ed.), *The Collected Works of William Morris*, 24 vols (London, 1910–15) I, xxi. But see also headnote to No. 2.

5 Mackail, *Morris*, I, 185; see also Introduction pp. 8–9.

6 P. Henderson (ed.), *The Letters of William Morris* (London, 1950), 28 (18 August 1869).

7 Ibid. 33 (15 March 1870); 37 (26 November 1870).

8 E. V. Lucas, *The Colvins and their Friends* (London, 1928), 35. The letter is not dated. If the review was the unsigned one in the *Pall Mall Budget* (No. 14), it was not adulatory.

9 *Spectator* 20 July 1895, lxxv, 81; see also Henderson, *Letters*, 371, and the preceding letter on the same subject to Lady Burne-Jones, 369–70.

10 T. Hake and A. Compton-Ricketts, *The Life and Letters of Theodore Watts-Dunton*, 2 vols (London, 1916), II, 98.

11 Mackail, *Life*, I, 130.

12 See C. E. Vaughan, *Bibliographies of Swinburne, Morris and Rossetti*, English Association Pamphlet No. 29 (London, 1914), 7. Most of the subsequent information about publication is from this source, but it is not complete.

13 Mackail, *Life*, I, 194.

14 Ibid. I, 195.

15 Morris's contributions to the *Oxford and Cambridge Magazine* include the tales 'The Story of the Unknown Church,' 'A Dream,' 'Frank's Sealed Letter,' 'Gertha's Lovers,' 'Svend and his Brethren,' 'Lindenborg Pool,' and 'The Hollow Land,' and the poems 'Winter Weather,' 'Riding Together,' 'Hands,' 'The Chapel in Lyonness' and 'Pray but One Prayer for Me'; see Mackail, *Life*, I, 92.

16 G. Burne-Jones, *Memorials of Edward Burne-Jones*, 2 vols (London, 1904), I, 123.

17 Lang, *Swinburne Letters*, I, 21 (15 September 1858).

18 Amy Woolner, *Thomas Woolner, R.A. Sculptor and Poet* (London, 1917), 143–4 (22 February 1858).

19 Sir J. Skelton, *The Table-Talk of Shirley* (London, 1895), 78. (The review appeared in *Fraser's Magazine*, June 1860, xi, 823–8.)

20 Ibid. 78–9. The poem 'based on' a Rossetti picture would be either 'The Blue Closet' or 'The Tune of Seven Towers'.

21 Ibid. 79.

22 The parody appeared in five numbers of *Punch* from 3 to 31 March 1866.

23 W. M. Rossetti, *Swinburne's Poems and Ballads* (London, 1866), 50–1.

24 H. M. Hyndman, *The Record of an Adventurous Life* (London, 1911), 348.

Joseph Campbell

25 Presumably in his *Fortnightly Review* (July 1867) article; see No. 8.
26 Especially with the move to Queen Square in 1865, and the appointment of George Warrington Taylor as business manager; see Mackail, *Life*, I, 174–7.
27 J. Comyns Carr, *Some Eminent Victorians* (London, 1908), 208–9. Evidence of the impact of Morris's early poems on some Oxford undergraduates is provided in an article by Andrew Lang (1844–1912) in *Contemporary Review*, August 1882, xlii, 200–17, entitled 'The Poetry of William Morris', and by George Saintsbury (1845–1933) in 'Mr. William Morris' in *Corrected Impressions* (London, 1895).
28 Cf. Mackail, *Life*, I, 135, for Dixon's regrets: 'His *Jason* was better than his *Earthly Paradise*, but the first flavour was gone from them both.'
29 May Morris, *Works*, I, xiv.
30 Ibid. I, xv. The *Athenaeum* review was in June 1867, no. 2068, 779–80, and the *Spectator* in June 1867, xl, 668–70.
31 *Atlantic Monthly*, November 1867, xx, 640.
32 A. B. Harlan and J. L. Harlan (eds), *Letters from Owen Meredith to Robert and Elizabeth Barrett Browning* (New York, 1936), 226.
33 *Athenaeum*, May 1868, no. 2118, 753.
34 Margaret Howitt (ed.), *Mary Howitt. An Autobiography*, 2 vols (London, 1889), II, 170 (17 March 1869).
35 G. S. Haight (ed.), *The George Eliot Letters*, 7 vols (New Haven, 1954–5), IV, 451. (June 1868).
36 G. Burne-Jones, *Memorials of Edward Burne-Jones*, 2 vols (London, 1909), I, 297.
37 *Christian Observer*, March 1870, lxix, 198–208.
38 H. Buxton Forman, *Our Living Poets* (London, 1871), 380.
39 Henderson (ed.), *Letters*, 30–1 (21 December 1869).
40 See especially *Atlantic Monthly*, June 1870, xxv, 750–2, which criticized Morris's diffuseness, and *Tinsley's Magazine*, November 1870, vii, 457–65 on 'The Later Labours of Mr. Morris'.
41 W. Crane, *An Artist's Reminiscences* (London, 1907), 102–3.
42 R. W. Emerson, an interview published in *Frank Leslie's Illustrated Newspaper*, 3 January 1874, 275.
43 *North American Review*, October 1870, cxi, 475.
44 *Contemporary Review*, October 1871, xviii, 337.
45 Lady Betty Balfour (ed.), *Personal and Literary letters of Robert First Earl of Lytton*, 2 vols (London, 1906), I, 281.
46 Unsigned review in *Quarterly Review*, April 1876, cxli, 519–20.
47 John Morley in *Fortnightly Review*, April 1873, lxxvi, 476. The review is of Pater's *The Renaissance*.
48 Justin McCarthy, 'The Pre-Raphaelites in England', *Galaxy*, June 1876, xxi, 728.

49 Ibid. 729.

50 See also 'Geoffrey Chaucer and William Morris,' *New Monthly Magazine*, September 1871, cxlix, 280–6.

51 Mrs. Russell Barrington, *The Life of Walter Bagehot* (London, 1918), 412.

52 Ibid. 442.

53 *Athenaeum*, November 1872, no. 2352, 657–8.

54 *Dark Blue*, January 1873, iv, 627–36.

55 B. Champneys, *Memoirs and Correspondence of Coventry Patmore*, 2 vols (London, 1900), II, 97. The letter is not dated.

56 C. L. Cline (ed.), *The Letters of George Meredith*, 3 vols (Oxford, 1970), I, 475. To Frederick Greenwood, 1 January 1873.

57 G. Burne-Jones, *Memorials*, II, 23; letter to C. E. Norton, 1871. An article by Henry Hewlett in the *Contemporary Review*, December 1874, xxv, 100–24, emphasized the lack of 'spiritual confidence' felt in Morris's later poetry.

58 Mackail, *Life*, I, 285.

59 Ibid. I. 330.

60 Gosse also wrote to Theodore Watts: 'It seems to me without question one of the noblest and best sustained poems in the language, and altogether beyond adequate praise.' Hake and Compton-Ricketts, *Watts-Dunton*, II, 97. (The reviewer is referred to as Theodore Watts throughout this volume.)

61 H. Buxton Forman, *The Books of William Morris* (London, 1897), 90.

62 H. Morley, *Nineteenth Century*, November 1877, ii, 704–12.

63 Mackail, *Life*, I, 336–7 gives his letter politely refusing the position.

64 'On the Wandle,' *Spectator*, November 1883, lvi, 1507–9; ' A Day in Surrey with William Morris' by Emma Lazarus, *Century Magazine*, July 1886, xxxii, 388–97.

65 Mrs. C. W. Earle, *Pot-Pourri from a Surrey Garden*, 3rd edition (London, 1900), 227. *Lectures on Art* was the title as given on the spine of *Hopes and Fears for Art*. Mrs Earl argued interestingly that 'in the Oxford Street shop Mr. Morris did not keep up entirely the high and simple standard of his early years'. *Pot-Pourri*, 278.

66 *The Journal of T. J. Cobden-Sanderson 1879–1922*, 2 vols (London, 1926), I, 97 (21 July 1882).

67 Hyndman, *Record of an Adventurous Life*, 348, points out how significant his commitment to Socialism was 'at the height of his great reputation. He had already succeeded in everything he had attempted.'

68 G. Burne-Jones, *Memorials*, II, 97.

69 Dona Torr, *Tom Mann and His Times* (London, 1956), I, 188.

70 E. Carpenter, *My Days and Dreams*, 2nd edition (London, 1920), 124; 216.

71 J. Bruce Glasier, *William Morris and the Early Days of the Socialist Movement* (London, 1921), ch. VIII.

72 E. H. Cady, *The Realist at War. The Mature Years 1865–1920 of W. D. Howells* (Syracuse, 1958), 81.

73 C. M. Kirk and R. Kirk (eds), *W. D. Howells, 'Criticism and Fiction' and Other Essays*, second printing (New York, 1965), 86: 'The men and women who do this hard work of the world have learnt from him (Ruskin) and from Morris that they have a right to pleasure in their toil, and that when justice is done they will have it.'
Howell's Utopian novel *A Traveller from Altruria* (1894) is pleasantly indebted to *News from Nowhere*.

74 Torr, *Tom Mann*, 191.

75 Ibid. 180.

76 Crane, *An Artist's Reminiscences*, 254–5.

77 'Vernon Lee' (Viola Paget), *Miss Brown* (London, 1884), II, 29.

78 'The Poet in the Police-Court', *Saturday Review*, September 1885, lx, 417.

79 Amy Sharp, *Victorian Poets* (London, 1891), 177–8.

80 *Frederick Engels to Paul and Laura Lafargue* (Moscow, 1959), I, 370; translated letter of 13 September 1886.

81 In the *Quarterly Review*, July 1889, clxix, 111–12, the classical scholar R. Y. Tyrell, condemning Morris's translation of Vergil, remarked on 'the sense of incongruity inspired by such Wardour-Street English as *eyen* and *clepe*.' Many critics of the romances have felt this awkwardness in the diction.

82 Oscar Wilde, *Pall Mall Gazette*, March 1889, xlix, 3; Theodore Watts, *Athenaeum*, September 1889, no. 3229, 347–50.

83 V. Rendall remarked of Watts's reviews, in the *Dictionary of National Biography*: 'Not lacking in good things and in generalizations of value, they are clogged with wise saws and ancient instances.'

84 R. Hart-Davis (ed.), *The Letters of Oscar Wilde* (London, 1962), 290–1; letter of March or April 1891.

85 D. Flower and H. Maas, *The Letters of Ernest Dowson* (London, 1907), II, 688.

86 On 11 October 1892 Morris wrote to Bruce Glasier: 'What a set of ninnies the papers are about the Laureateship, treating it with such absurd solemnity! Bet you it is offered to Swinburne. Bet you he takes it.' Henderson (ed.), *Letters*, 352.

87 W. B. Yeats, *Bookman*, November 1892, iii, 53.

88 A symposium in the *Idler* in 1895, vii, 400–19, shows Swinburne as the favourite candidate, with Morris next, but both generally held to be ruled out from the post for political reasons.

89 Mackail, *Life*, II, 288.

90 O. L. Triggs, *Poet-Lore*, March and April 1893, v, 113–22 and 210–18. A comparable article is F. Richardson's 'William Morris: Poet and Socialist,' *Primitive Methodist Quarterly Review*, July 1892, xxxiv, 414–29.

91 W. G. Kingsland, *Poet-Lore*, October and November 1896, vii, 473-7 and 543-6.

92 Gabriel Mourey, *Across the Channel* (London, 1895) is an English translation of a book of articles originally contributed to the 'Gil Blas' column of *Figaro* in the 1890s on English culture.

93 E. D. Mackerness (ed.), *The Journals of George Sturt*, 2 vols (Cambridge, 1967), I, 219 (6 November 1892).

94 G. Saintsbury, 'Mr. William Morris' in *Corrected Impressions: Essays on Victorian Writers* (London, 1895).

95 T. F. Plowman, 'The Aesthetes', *Pall Mall Magazine*, January 1895, v, 37.

96 Andrew Lang, *Longman's Magazine*, October 1896, xxviii, 560-73.

97 N. Pevsner, *Pioneers of Modern Design* (London, 1936). The work of Peter Floud, including the 1952 exhibition of Victorian and Edwardian Decorative Arts at the Victoria & Albert Museum, showed that Morris was by no means an innovating designer, simply a great one; see P. Floud, 'William Morris as an Artist: a New View', *Listener*, 7 October 1954, and the summary by Graeme Shankland in Asa Briggs's Pelican volume, *William Morris. Selected Writings and Designs* (London, 1962); and full discussions in Paul Thompson, *The Work of William Morris* (London, 1967) and R. Watkinson, *William Morris. Designer* (London, 1967).

98 W. B. Yeats, 'Literature and the Living Voice' in *Plays and Controversies* (London, 1923), 187-8.

99 T. S. Eliot, 'Andrew Marvell' in *Selected Essays* (London, 1961), 299, 301.

100 F. R. Leavis, *New Bearings in English Poetry*, 2nd edition (London, 1954), 21. *Scrutiny* did not follow up the implications of Dr. Leavis's comment about Morris's 'force'.

101 A critic who fails to give Morris a fair chance because of these presuppositions is Mr. W. W. Robson in the Pelican *From Dickens to Hardy* (London, 1958), 368. He quotes the opening of 'Golden Wings' as exemplifying the charm of Morris's 'beautiful world from which everything harsh or disagreeable is excluded', showing no awareness that the poem culminates in tragedy, reversing the initial mood.

102 G. Grigson (ed.), *A Choice of William Morris's Verse* (London, 1969).

103 G. D. H. Cole (ed.), *William Morris. Selected Writings*, 2nd edition (London, 1948), xix.

104 May Morris (ed.), *William Morris. Artist, Writer, Socialist*, 2 vols (Oxford, 1936), II, xxxvi.

105 Ibid. II, xxxix.

106 R. Williams, *Culture and Society 1780-1950* (London, 1958), 155.

107 Briggs (ed.), *William Morris*, 17.

108 E. D. LeMire, *Unpublished Lectures of William Morris* (Detroit, 1969).

109 J. Redmond (ed.), *News from Nowhere* (London, 1970), 192.

Note on the Text

The materials printed in this volume follow the earliest form of the original texts in all important respects, including the original footnotes. Numbered footnotes have been added by the present editor.

Lengthy quotations from Morris used simply to illustrate works under discussion have been curtailed, and passages in reviews and articles not directly relevant to Morris have been omitted. These curtailments and omissions are clearly indicated in the texts. Typographical errors in the originals have been silently corrected.

THE DEFENCE OF GUENEVERE,
AND OTHER POEMS

1858

---

1. Unsigned notice, *Spectator*

February 1858, xxxi, 238

For a discussion of these reviews, see Introduction, pp. 6–7.

The Poems of Mr. William Morris chiefly relate to the knights and ladies of King Arthur's time, and nearly all the rest of the pieces belong to the vaguely fabulous age of chivalry; though the author has introduced into his poems touches of what modern research or judgment has shown to be its real coarseness and immorality. To our taste, the style is as bad as bad can be. Mr. Morris imitates little save faults. He combines the mawkish simplicity of the Cockney school with the prosaic baldness of the worst passages of Tennyson, and the occasional obscurity and affectation of plainness that characterize Browning and his followers. Some of the smaller poems are less unpleasing in their manner than the bulk of the book, and a poetical spirit runs through the whole, save where it is unskilfully overlaid. We do not, however, augur much promise from this power; the faults of affectation and bad taste seem too deeply seated.

2. Richard Garnett, unsigned review, *Literary Gazette*

March 1858, xlii, 226-7

May Morris, in her Introduction to her father's *Collected Works* (London, 1910–15), IV, x, attributes this friendly review to Joseph Knight. But Knight was in Leeds until 1860 (see No. 7). The review was more probably the work of Richard Garnett (1835–1908), who had recently begun his career at the British Museum; it is attributed to him with convincing circumstantial detail in an article in the *Dublin University Magazine*, November 1878, n.s. ii, 557, entitled 'William Morris, M.A.', and in a later article by O. L. Triggs in *Poet-Lore*, March 1893, v, 116, entitled 'The Socialistic Thread in the Life and Works of William Morris' (when the date is given as 6 March 1859). May Morris refers to a review by Garnett of *The Defence of Guenevere* as 'cordial and discriminating' in *Collected Works*, I, xxi.

It might not be easy to find a more striking example of the indestructibility of anything truly beautiful, than the literary resurrection of King Arthur and his Knights, after so many centuries' entombment in the Avalon of forgetfulness. The Israfel of this revival was Mr. Tennyson, the first peal of whose awakening trumpet sounded some twenty-six years ago in his marvellous 'Lady of Shalott,' followed by utterances of no inferior beauty, some made public for our delight, others, it is whispered, as yet withheld from us. But the movement thus inaugurated has taken a direction which Mr. Tennyson cannot have anticipated. We are not alluding to Sir E. Bulwer's elegant but affected and artificial 'King Arthur,' nor to Mr. Arnold's lovely 'Tristram and Iseult.' These are remarkable poems, but not startling phenomena. But the pre-Raphaelite poets and painters have made the Arthurian cyclus their own, by a treatment no less strange and original than that which has already thrown such novel light on the conceptions of Shakspeare and the scenery of Palestine. Not long since our columns

32

contained a notice of certain fresco illustrations of Arthurian romance attempted at Oxford by painters of this school, who, being for the most part utterly unknown to fame, may be supposed to have been invented on purpose. One of these gentlemen has now enabled us to form some opinion of his qualifications for his task by the publication of the book before us; and we do not hesitate to pronounce, that if he do but wield the brush to half as much purpose as the pen, his must be pictures well worth a long pilgrimage to see.

In advocating the claims of an unknown poet to public attention, it is before all things necessary to establish his originality—a very easy matter in the present instance. It might almost have seemed impossible for any one to write about Arthur without some trace of Tennysonian influences, yet, for Mr. Morris, the Laureate might never have existed at all. Every one knows Tennyson's 'Sir Galahad'—Mr. Morris's exquisite poem on the same subject is unfortunately much too long for quotation, but our meaning will be sufficiently illustrated by a few of the initiatory stanzas:

> It is the longest night in all the year,
>   Near on the day when the Lord Christ was born;
> Six hours ago I came and sat down here,
>   And ponder'd sadly, wearied and forlorn.
>
> The winter wind that pass'd the chapel-door,
>   Sang out a moody tune, that went right well
> With mine own thoughts: I look'd down on the floor,
>   Between my feet, until I heard a bell
>
> Sound a long way off through the forest deep,
>   And toll on steadily; a drowsiness
> Came on me, so that I fell half asleep,
>   As I sat there not moving: less and less
>
> I saw the melted snow that hung in beads
>   Upon my steel-shoes, less and less I saw
> Between the tiles the bunches of small weeds:
>   Heartless and stupid, with no touch of awe
>
> Upon me, half-shut eyes upon the ground,
>   I thought; O! Galahad, the days go by,
> Stop and cast up now that which you have found,
>   So sorely you have wrought and painfully.

The difference between the two poets obviously is that Tennyson writes of mediæval things like a modern, and Mr. Morris like a contemporary. Tennyson's 'Sir Galahad' is Tennyson himself in an enthusiastic and devotional mood; Mr. Morris's is the actual champion, just as he lived and moved and had his being some twelve hundred years ago. Tennyson is the orator who makes a speech for another; Mr. Morris the reporter who writes down what another man says. Whatever mediævalists may assert, poetry flourishes far more in the nineteenth century than it ever did in the seventh; accordingly the Laureate is as superior in brilliance of phrase, finish of style, and magic of versification, as he is inferior in dramatic propriety and *couleur locale*. We might continue this parallel for ever, but shall bring the matter to a head by observing that Mr. Morris's poems bear exactly the same relation to Tennyson's as Rossetti's illustrations of the Laureate to the latter's own conceptions. We observed in noticing these designs that they illustrated anything in the world rather than Tennyson, and have certainly seen no reason to change our opinion. The more we view them, the more penetrated we become with their wonderful beauty (always excepting that remarkable angel in the Robinson Crusoe cap), but also the more impressed with their utter incompatibility with their text. Tennyson is the modern *par excellence*, the man of his age; Rossetti and Morris are the men of the middle age; and while this at once places them in a position of inferiority as regards Tennyson, it increases their interest towards ourselves, as giving us what it would be vain to expect from any one else. Who but Mr. Rossetti or his double could have written anything like this?—

> For these vile things that hem me in,
> These Pagan beasts who live in sin,
> The sickly flowers pale and wan,
> The grim blue-bearded castellan,
> The stanchions half worn-out with rust,
> Whereto their banner vile they trust—
> Why, all these things I hold them just
> Like dragons in a missal-book,
> Wherein, whenever we may look,
> We see no horror, yea, delight
> We have, the colours are so bright;
> Likewise we note the specks of white,
> And the great plates of burnish'd gold.
>
> Just so this Pagan castle old,
> And everything I can see there,
> Sick-pining in the marshland air,

I note; I will go over now,
Like one who paints with knitted brow,
The flowers and all things one by one,
From the snail on the wall to the setting sun.

Four great walls, and a little one
That leads down to the barbican,
Which walls with many spears they man,
When news comes to the castellan
Of Launcelot being in the land.

And as I sit here, close at hand
Four spikes of sad sick sunflowers stand,
The castellan with a long wand
Cuts down their leaves as he goes by,
Ponderingly, with screw'd up eye,
And fingers twisted in his beard—
Nay, was it a knight's shout I heard?

Other pieces are yet more characteristic; for example, 'Golden
Wings,' which seems to conduct us through a long gallery of Mr.
Rossetti's works, with all their richness of colouring, depth of pathos,
poetical but eccentric conception, and loving elaboration of every
minute detail. After all, those who have read the beautiful poems, contributed by the painter to the defunct *Oxford and Cambridge Magazine*,
will probably think this dissertation and Mr. Morris's dedication
equally superfluous.

Another influence, however, has done something towards making
Mr. Morris what he is. In spite of his having taken every precaution
that human foresight can suggest to render himself unintelligible, it
is impossible that so fine a poet and deep a thinker as Mr. Browning
should remain without influence on a generation so accessible as our
own to the fascination of genius. Accordingly his influence widens
day by day, and he already counts several disciples of unusual talent,
from Mr. Owen Meredith downwards. These, however, are too
undisguisedly imitators to earn a higher praise than that of considerable
adroitness. In Mr. Morris's volume we for the first time trace the
influence of Browning on a writer of real original genius, and the
result is very curious. 'Sir Peter Harpdon's End' shows that Mr. Morris
possesses considerable dramatic power, and is so far satisfactory,
otherwise it appears to us ultra-Browningian, unpleasant and obscure.
'The Judgment of God' reads exactly like Browning's dramatic lyrics,
but is, we think, better than any but the very best of them. By far the

best of these pieces, however, is 'The Haystack in the Floods,' where Mr. Morris's native romance and pathos unite with his model's passion and intensity to form a whole unsurpassed, we will venture to say, by any man save Tennyson, since the golden age of British poetry expired with Byron at Missolonghi. We regret that it is too long to quote here.

To describe any one as Rossetti *plus* Browning, is as much as to say that he is not a little affected and obscure. This, perhaps, is Mr. Morris's misfortune; his carelessness and inattention to finish is his fault, and a serious one. It has ruined the first two poems in his volume, which should have been the finest. A little trouble will, perhaps, make 'Queen Guenevere's Defence' what it ought to be, but 'King Arthur's Tomb' will never be fit for anything but the fire. We can only suppose Mr. Morris's frequent indifferent grammar, atrocious rhymes, and lines unscannable on any imaginable metrical system, to be the consequence of an entirely erroneous notion of poetry. Let him be assured that poetry is just as much an art as painting, and that the selfsame principle which forbids his drawing a lady with three feet ought to keep him from penning an iambic verse with six. All arts are but modifications of the one archetypal beauty, and the laws of any one, *mutatis mutandis*, bind all the rest.

No fleck, happily, mars the pure beauty of 'Sir Galahad' and 'The Chapel in Lyoness,' pieces in which the rough chivalry of the middle ages appears as it were transfigured, and shining with a saintly halo of inexpressible loveliness. Of 'Sir Peter Harpdon' we have already spoken. 'Rapunzel,' the next poem, will be a fearful stumbling-block to prosy people, and we must own that it is, if possible, too romantically ethereal in its wild, weird beauty. Like Shelley, Mr. Morris is often guilty of what we may call luminous indistinctness. We are delighted with his poetry, but cannot very well tell what it is all about; 'we see a light, but no man.' This is particularly the case with those very remarkable pieces, 'Golden wings,' 'The Blue Closet,' 'Spell-bound,' and 'The Wind,' in which it is true that something exciting happens, but, as the courier in *Little Dorrit* has it, there is no why. We return to 'Rapunzel,' to borrow two passages of perfect beauty:—

[quotes 'A Duel' and 'Guendolen']

The minor poems may be distributed into three classes, the Arthurian, the Froissartian, and the purely imaginative. Though bewildered

with a perfect *embarras de richesses*, we are fain to content ourselves
with a single example of each:—

[quotes 'Riding Together', 'The Eve of Crecy' and 'Summer Dawn']

The barbarous rhyme, *dawn* and *corn*, is but a sample of that carelessness of which the author must get the better if he is ever to rank
as a master of his art. Still his volume is of itself a sufficient proof that
it is not necessary to be a master in order to delight and astonish. Mr.
Morris is an exquisite and original genius, a poet whom poets will
love.

3. H. F. Chorley, unsigned review, *Athenaeum*

3 April 1858, no. 1588, 427–8

According to L. A. Marchand, *The Athenaeum. A Mirror of Victorian Culture* (Chapel Hill, 1941), p. 192, the reviewer was H. F.
Chorley (1808–72), of whom we are told 'he mirrored . . . truly
the average opinion of the readers of the journal' (p. 193).

Disposed, as we are, to recognize all who cultivate poetry honestly,
whatever be the style;—and admitting that Mr. Morris may be
counted among that choir,—we must call attention to his book of
Pre-Raphaelite minstrelsy as to a curiosity which shows how far
affectation may mislead an earnest man towards the fog-land of Art.
Of course, in rejoinder, we may be reminded how Wordsworth was
misunderstood, how Keats was misprized, when they set forth on
their original paths. We shall once more be invited to accept, wrapped
round with some delicate rose-leaf of sophistry, or locked up in some
casket of curious device, the fallacy that—

Naught is everything, and everything is naught.

—What matter? Truth is the same, poetry undying, from all time and in all ages,—but masquing is not truth, and the galvanism of old legend is not poetry. The justice of what has been said could be proved from every page of this provoking volume, to the satisfaction of the most enthusiastic lover of our Laureate's 'Lady of Shalott.' That strange dream, which, however beautiful, quaint, and touching it be, quivers on the furthest verge of Dream-land to which sane Fancy can penetrate, has been 'the point of departure' for Mr. Morris. While we were looking, a day or two since, at Mr. Egley's skilful, minute, yet barely intelligible, presentment of that magical ballad—something of sympathy, something of sadness, something of wonder, came over us, in consideration of time wasted and effort ill bestowed. This, however, the Pre-Raphaelite poets, apparently, do not perceive; otherwise, we should never have been bidden to look on so astounding a picture as Mr. Morris's 'Rapunzel.' How to express or make the subject of this clear, is not an easy task. The tale is one of enchantment. There is a Prince who is haunted by some mysterious desire. There is an enchanted damsel, whose 'web' (those familiar with 'The Lady of Shalott' will understand us) is her head of hair. This 'fair one of the golden locks' is under the power of wicked creatures. So much explained, let the Prince speak:—

[quotes from 'Rapunzel', ending with the Prince's song]

> If it would please God to make you sing again,
>   I think that I might very sweetly die,
> My soul somehow reach heaven in joyous pain,
>   My heavy body on the beech-nuts lie.
>
> Now I remember; what a most strange year,
>   Most strange and awful, in the beechen wood
> I have pass'd now; *I still have a faint fear*
>   *It is a kind of dream not understood.*
>
> I have seen no one in this wood except
>   The witch and her; have heard no human tones,
> But when the witches' revelry has crept
>   Between the very jointing of my bones.
>
> Ah! I know now; I could not go away,
>   But needs must stop to hear her sing that song
> She always sings at dawning of the day.
>   *I am not happy here, for I am strong,*

And every morning I do whet my sword,
Yet Rapunzel still weeps within the tower,
And still God ties me down to the green sward,
Because I cannot see the gold stair floating lower.

The italics are ours—Were we to continue the legend, stranger
mixtures of fantasy on stilts and common-place lying flat than even
the above could be shown; but such show would become painful,
not profitable. Let us only repeat that the 'Lady of Shalott's' loom was
not a *Jacquard* machine, into which, by cost and patience, a few more
perforated cards could be introduced, and her web, and its patterns
and devices be thereby complicated. Mr. Morris gives us a Manchester
mystery; not a real vision—stark, staring nonsense; not inspiration.

Has enough been shown concerning this volume—or are we still
open to the charge of having made extracts in an *ex parte* spirit,—of
having worried the author on some weak point, the defence of which
he would give up when in a lucid interval? To anticipate such objection, let us offer a complete ballad; and one of the best, to our thinking,
in the book:—

[quotes 'The Sailing of the Sword']

Mystical and pathetic the above looks, no doubt, as every picture
quaint in detail but possessing no real meaning, may be made to look.
But it is virtually as thin and theatrical as the veriest Arcadian or *Della-
Cruscan*[1] idyl, in which 'Cynthia wept by the urn which enclosed the
ashes of her *Adonis'*—the *Cynthia* dressed in the impracticable Greek
tunic, the urn well chiselled by sculptor,—neither *Cynthia*, nor *Adonis*,
nor tunic, nor urn, having one touch of nature. Greek academical
platitude is weak—Gothic traditional platitude is stiff:—both untrue
—neither strong. The Gothic is now in the ascendant. Shall we shortly
arrive at Chinese mysteries?—at the legend of the Willow Pattern?—
at the principle of the Pagoda?—at the '*nay*,' which shall protest against
barbarism, obesity, and cowardice being attributed to Yeh? Such things
may be; but the sooner that such possibility is made clear to those who
meditate verses, the better will it be for poetry; which belongs neither
to Basilica, Cathedral, Mosque, Italian dome, nor Indian wigwam,
but to air and sunshine, and hope and grief, shed down alike on the
just and the unjust—on Raphael and on the Pre-Raphaelites.

[1] Referring to the group of sentimental poets satirized by William Gifford in the *Baviad*
(1791).

4. Unsigned review, *Tablet*

April 1858, xix, 266

This favourable review was believed by Swinburne (No. 28b) to be by J. H. Pollen (1820–1902), who was Professor of Fine Art in Dublin, and participated in the painting of the Oxford Union ceiling in 1857. But the attribution is not supported by Pollen's biographer, Anne Pollen.

The final narrative section is omitted.

There are peculiarities both of thought and style in this volume which will not escape hostile criticism, but, in our judgment, it contains ample proof of the author's title to the privileges of a poet.

Now, the poet has this right, that, in consideration of the gift of poetry that he has received, and which he spends for our benefit, we must simply accept him as he essentially is, and forbear from requiring him to be something wholly different. We may reject his claims to the poet's wreath, or, granting that, we may point out faults and blemishes, the absence of which would be desirable. But our objections must not go to the very root and being of his nature and inspiration, for, had such objections prevailed, we should have been without his poem.

The dedication ('to my friend Dante Gabriel Rossetti, painter, I dedicate these poems') suggests already the Pre-Rafaelite sympathies of the author, and the book itself fully establishes them.

The 'conscientious rendering of the actual', in its minutest details, is observed not only in the description of gestures, attitudes, features, and garments, so that many passages read like descriptions of a Pre-Rafaelite picture, but the same 'fidelity to nature' is preserved in the language of the interlocutors (almost all the poems are in the first person singular), and we are free to admit that the result is in some few instances unsatisfactory. But *The Defence of Guenevere and other Poems* (as a statistical fact we may note that the 'Defence' is one poem out of thirty, and 17 pages out of 248), are poetry beyond all question, and we must e'en take them and be glad, for without their faults they would probably not have been in being. There is a grand roll in many of the verses, and a fine swing, which more than redeems a few bald lines and some which halt considerably; and if here and there the close copy of nature degenerates into caricature, in very many more instances the homely diction and quaint simplicity of the style not only satisfy the ear, but stir the heart.

Few volumes have been published of late years containing more passages which haunt the memory and constrain the tongue to unconscious repetition of them after one reading.

The first four poems are legends of King Arthur and the Knights of the Round Table. We pass over 'Guenevere' and 'Lancelot,' for 'Sir Galahad, a Christmas Mystery.'

[narrates the story, with quotations]

'The Chapel in Lyoness' is the legend of Sir Ozana le Cure Hardy—

> Ozana of the hardy heart
> Knight of the Table Round,
> Pray for his soul, Lords, of your part,
> A good knight he was found.

It is very beautiful, and not unworthy of the companionship of Tennyson's 'Morte d'Arthur' and 'Sir Galahad'.

The longest poem in the book is a drama, 'Sir Peter Harpdon's End'.

[narrates the story, with quotations]

'Rapunzel' and her golden hair will be a stumbling-block to those who did not know her in their nursery days, or who have not read her authentic history told by the Brothers Grimm.

There are many of the ballads in this book that must be set to music. On the eve of Crecy, Sir Lambert de Bois, a poverty-stricken knight, sings of Marguerite, and of the wealth tomorrow's fight may bring him by the ransom of the knights he means to overthrow:—

> Gold on her head, and gold on her feet,
> And gold where the hems of her kirtle meet,
> And a golden girdle round my sweet
> *Ah! qu' elle est belle La Marguerite.*

[quotes next three stanzas]

41

'The Judgment of God' is in a very different strain:—

> 'Swerve to the left, Son Roger', he said,
>> 'When you catch his eyes through the helmet-slit,
> 'Swerve to the left, then out at his head,
>> 'And the Lord God give you joy of it'.

Truly a grim ballad!

There is amazing variety in this volume, but there is power every-where, whether the poet recounts ancient legends or sings of knightly deeds, whether he deals with mystery or magic, love and joy, or sorrow and despair. We have quoted from it too largely, yet some of the best remains unnoticed. 'Golden Wings,' and 'Shameful Death,' and 'The Sailing of the Sword,' are favourites, but we must conclude with 'The Haystack in the Floods.' A terrible story, but Mr. Morris is frightfully in earnest.

[quotes and narrates the story]

5. Unsigned review, *Saturday Review*

20 November 1858, vi, 506–7

The review which is most directly hostile to Morris as a Pre-Raphaelite.

Did we choose to chronicle them, there would be no lack of materials for illustrating the current poetical literature. The volcano of poetry is not now in a state of eruption as in the good old days of the Pope school, the Lake school, and the Byron school; but there are always little jets and puffs of smoke, if not of flame, that serve to show the existence rather than the activity of the central fire. Annually there are produced, to the great benefit of paper-makers and printers, at least fifty little volumes of English poetry. They are curiously alike. They are all little thin volumes of about 200 pages. Every volume contains from twenty to a hundred little pieces, all about nothing in particular —not remarkably good nor remarkably bad—with just no character at all, like Pope's women. They give us very fair verse and generally correct imagery, not unpleasing nor yet striking, and yet we do not review them, simply because we cannot. When there is nothing to say, with Scriblerus we say 'We can no more.' What is the use either to the poet or to his reader, actual or possible, of saying that Mr. Jones has a correct ear, and has attained to certain smoothnesses in versification, and ripples out in a level current of poetical talk—or that Miss Brown has read Tennyson till she has acquired the same sort of likeness to her original that probably his colour-grinder had to Michael Angelo? If we select Mr. William Morris from the crowd, it is not for his surpassing merits, because we do not think that he has such, but partly because he has some real and substantial poetical merits—much of which, however, may be resolved into conceits and affectation and extravagance—and partly because he represents, we suppose for the first time, in one department of art, what has made a very great substantial revolution in another of its kingdoms—and partly because he writes upon a principle which, true enough in itself, he contrives wilfully and carefully to spoil by overdoing it.

Mr. Morris is the pre-Raffaelite poet. So he is hailed, we believe, by himself and the brotherhood. Now, in point of fact, if we trace the *genesis* of what is affectedly called pre-Raffaelitism, it is the offspring rather than the progenitor of a certain poetical school and principle. Pre-Raffaelitism is the product of the principle which was first preached by Wordsworth, and has culminated in Tennyson through Keats. The poet, prophet-like, preceded the painter—the plastic, or rather pictorial, development of art followed upon its poetical. Millais and Holman Hunt have but repeated the revolt against false taste which Wordsworth's Poetical Ballads inaugurated. It is odd enough that Wordsworth's personal influence with his friend Sir George Beaumont did not lead him to see—or if he saw, to repent of—the falsity of the conventional brown tree, for Wordsworth's was a life-long protest against the brown tree in poetry. But whether Wordsworth saw or did not see the application of his own principle, it is at the Laker's urn that pre-Raffaelitism first drank inspiration. If, therefore, Mr. Morris really wished to show us what pre-Raffaelitism in poetry was, he should have gone back to its beginnings, not to its recent developments. He has overlooked or neglected this truth; and because pre-

Raffaelitism has degenerated in many quarters into cant and affectation, he represents its absurdities and extravagances rather than its original aim and principle. In criticising Mr. Morris, we cannot but glance at the parallel development of art—in the poet we trace the painter. The later school of pre-Raffaelites and Mr. Morris seem to consider that all art is imitation—which Aristotle knew as well as they do—and further, that this imitation must be truthful and conscientious, which Cowper, without perhaps knowing much about it, and Words-worth upon principle, set themselves to show.

Now, great and true as this principle is, it is not quite so simple as it looks. An exact transcript of nature is impossible, and were it possible, would be false. Photography has shown us this. The light pictures are not likenesses, and mislead. Nature is made up of evanescent, com-bined, and shifting elements, and just as a landscape depends upon air, and aerial tint, and local colour, so a portrait depends upon mind, character, distance, and a thousand other nameless things, rather than on a set of features and complexion. The romantic school of poets and painters set themselves to work to get what they thought a general resemblance, with a thorough and insolent contempt for fact and details. But unquestionably they worked upon a knowledge of art and attained their end. No doubt of it, though every mountain of Claude's may be wrong in its 'cleavage,' and not a tree could be identified by Sir William Hooker, he could paint sunlight. So Alexander Pope does not give us Homer; but he has produced, in his *Iliad* and *Odyssey*, certain works of art which for general effect are unsurpassed and un-surpassable. Against the hazy and lazy impertinence which asked us to accept a blue blot for a man, and a scraggled scratch for a tree, or Mr. Mackenzie's Man of Feeling for a sample of human nature, it was a duty to protest: and art has every reason to be grateful to those painters and poets who told us that patient accuracy in details, and a con-scientious truthfulness in rendering the facts of the world either of matter or of mind, were the first duties of the artist, whether in letters or on canvas. But when painters think it their duty to work through a microscope, and to try to paint every stain on every leaf, as well as every leaf on every tree, they not only forget what art is, but are ignorant of what artistic imitation is. This extravagance is, we think, what Mr. Morris delights in. He works in the patient spirit of the illuminators, but then he is grotesque as well as minute and patient. All his thoughts and figures are represented on a solid plane; he has no notion of distance, or aerial perspective, or gradation of tints; or rather, of malice prepense, he neglects these things. He has abundance of vivid, positive colour, sharp outline, and great richness of word diaper, with a certain stiff, antique, cumbrous embroidery of diction; but it is all cold, artificial, and angular. It is, in words, just what Sir Isambras on the plum-coloured horse was two years ago.[1]

Mr. Morris has taken as his general groundwork the *Morte d'Arthur*, the British subject which Milton resigned in despair to the feebleness of Bulwer, or—may it be hoped?—to the fulness of Tennyson's powers. Of course he goes back to the *Morte d'Arthur*, for has not pre-Raffaelitism taken it under its special protection? His chief poem is the 'Defence of Guenevere'—a very tedious affair, as, in truth, the whole story of the Knights of the Round Table is; and, as far as we can understand what is hardly worth the understanding, it is a defence of the virtue of King Arthur's queen, a lady whose fair fame, like Helen's, it was reserved for our politeness to vindicate. The subjoined lines are in an ugly, disjointed series of unrhymed triplets, and present a very unfavourable specimen of Mr. Morris's powers, which are, in our judgment, considerable, though altogether spoiled and wasted by his devotion to a false principle of art. False principle, we say, because a poet's work is with the living world of men. Mr. Morris never thinks of depicting man or life later than the Crusades. With him, the function of art was at an end when people began, in decent life, to read and write. So all that he produces are pictures—pictures of queer, quaint knights, very stiff and cumbrous, apparently living all day in chain armour, and crackling about in cloth of gold—women always in mini-ver, and never in flesh and blood. The trees and flowers are very pro-nounced in colour, and exceedingly angular and sharp in outline; every building is a prickly castle, and every castle has its moat. Here it is, and the folks about it:—

[quotes seven stanzas from 'Golden Wings']

All this and the verses that follow are pretty in their way, though labouring under the slight disadvantage of having no story to tell, and of telling the no-story by broken hints and jerks of allusion, and what is meant to be suggestive. The title is 'Golden Wings', though what the wings are, and why golden, passes our wit to conjecture. And so throughout. Each poem is as hard to decipher as though it were written in black letter. It is crabbed, and involved, and stiff, and broken-backed in metre, but bright, sparkling, distinct, and pictorial in effect.

[1] The painting *Sir Isumbras at the Ford* was exhibited by J. E. Millais in 1857.

You cannot quite make out what it means, or whether it means anything taken altogether; but each touch is sharp, the colour is brilliant,
the costume picturesque. Still, the general effect is decidedly unpleasant. If the ages of faith and chivalry were this sort of thing, it must
have been a queer world to live in. We never knew any knights or
ladies of this class, but there must have been a great deal of blood as
well as lances and shields in these days; and though there was a great
amount of kissing, both according to the chronicles and Mr. Morris,
it appears that the kissers and kissed had but little respect for the marriage service. This, we are bound to say, is the general moral impression conveyed by Mr. Morris's very chivalrous little pictures. His men
and women, and trees and flowers, and castles and houses, are not like
anything we ever saw, except in illuminations; but they might, when
they did exist, be like Mr. Morris's delineations. Only it is a mercy to
have got rid of them. If this thing is to be reproduced, perhaps this
is the only way to do what is not worth doing. Mr. Morris could
employ himself better; and we regret that, with his gifts of colouring
and sense of force and beauty, he does not give us people and passions
with which we could sympathize. We have not the patience to go
through his anatomy—often a morbid study, of all the component
parts of forests or castles, or even of ladies' dresses or ladies' morals;
but he depicts these things by so many and so true touches, often with
such vivid realism, that if he would but consider that poetry is concerned about human passions and duties—with men of like moral
nature with ourselves, and with material nature where green and
white is not got up on the art principles of the mediæval miniaturists
—he might win a great place (which is not saying much) among his
contemporaries. But although aware that specimens will present neither
Mr. Morris's best nor worst points—neither his insufferable affectation
nor his command of language—we must let the poet of pre-Raffaelitism exhibit himself. The picture is a besieged knight waiting for
succour:—

> I cannot bear the noise
> And light out there, with this thought alive,
> Like any curling snake within my brain;
> Let me just hide my head within these soft
> Deep cushions, there to try and think it out.
>   *[Lying on the window-seat]*
> I cannot bear much noise now, and I think
> That I shall go to sleep: it all sounds dim

And faint, and I shall soon forget most things;
Yea, almost that I am alive and here;
It goes slow, comes slow, like a big mill-wheel
On some broad stream, with long green weeds a-sway,
And soft and slow it rises and it falls,
Still going onward.
           Lying so, one kiss,
And I should be in Avalon asleep,
Among the poppies and the yellow flowers;
And they should brush my cheek, my hair being spread
Far out among the stems; soft mice and small
Eating and creeping all about my feet,
Red-shod and tired; and the flies should come
Creeping on my broad eyelids unafraid;
And there should be a noise of water going,
Clear blue, fresh water breaking on the slates,
Likewise the flies should creep, &c.

And so long as they do not creep on canvas, and are not done in the brightest of verditer and ultramarine next year in Trafalgar-square, we may leave them creeping, creeping in Mr. Morris's poem.[1]

---

[1] The extract is from 'Sir Peter Harpdon's End' and in fact conveys the feelings of his lady, Alice.

6. J. H. Shorthouse contrasts Morris with Tennyson

1859

J. H. Shorthouse (1834–1903), best known for his historical romance *John Inglesant*, belonged at this period to the Friends Essay Society in Birmingham. Lectures were read to the Society, and afterwards circulated in manuscript. The undated lecture from which this passage is taken is concerned with Tennyson's *Idylls of the King*, of which the first group appeared in July 1859. Shorthouse's references to reviews of Morris (but not including that by 'Shirley' in 1860) suggest that it was probably written in 1859. The contrast he first drew was to be elaborated by many later critics.

Text from *Literary Remains of J. H. Shorthouse*, edited by S. Shorthouse (London, 1905), 108–9.

Those writers who have reproduced in a modern form the antique legends of the past have often enjoyed very great success, but it is plain that this success must depend on certain conditions—either they must preserve faithfully the spirit as well as the exterior form of the legends (in which case a wide success amongst modern readers is hardly to be promised them); or the age which gave birth to the legends must not be so distant that every trace of the leading idea of that age is lost; or, lastly, the subject of the legends must be simply one of the common wants and fears of humanity, which are alike in all ages, and which the animating spirit of every age, however different, suits and inspires equally. Mr. Tennyson has observed none of these conditions, and it is, as I take it, a natural consequence that he has failed.

The first of these conditions was observed by Mr. Morris in his *Defence of Guenevere*, which, speaking advisedly, is the most wonderful reproduction of the tone of thought and feeling of a past age that has ever been achieved. This book met, as was to have been expected, with the least possible success; the *Saturday* and the *Athenaeum*, with the rest of the reviews after them (with one honourable exception, the *Literary Gazette*), putting it on one side as a mass of rubbish that could not be understood. The author's most deadly enemy could not have invented a more condemnatory judgment on the book than that (as the reviewers understood the words) it *could* be understood. Did it never strike these gentlemen that, if a man opens a book written in the spirit and the manner, and influenced by the modes of thinking, of six or eight centuries ago, he is likely to find what he reads there rather different from a modern book on the electric telegraph, or the last new young ladies' novel, fresh from a nineteenth-century English village, with its classes at the school, and district visitors and the rector and his curate? Yet, what a hostile and contemptuous verdict was given against the book because the phrases and forms of expression were not exactly those to which the present century was accustomed, and because some of the poems really do require a careful study of the literature of the age of Chivalry to understand them at all! Mr. Morris, if we may judge him by his writings, is not a man to regret the course he took, or to consider his labour thrown away; and, even if he doubted it before, the publication of the *Idylls of the King* has proved that, if the Arthurian Romances ever are to be worthily rewritten in modern poetry, it will be as he has done it, and not otherwise.

THE LIFE AND DEATH OF JASON

1867

7. Joseph Knight, unsigned review, *Sunday Times*

9 June 1867, no. 2304, 7

This appreciative review was referred to by Morris in a letter; see Introduction, p. 8.

Joseph Knight (1829–1907) left Leeds in 1860 and became a literary journalist in London, concentrating mainly on the drama.

Since the appearance of *The Defence of Guenevere and other Poems*, two lustres have almost elapsed. That this time, long as it seems, has not been fruitlessly occupied by Mr. Morris, the publication of *Jason*, and the announcement of a second work of equal or superior pretensions, are enough to vouch. Very singular has been the fate of Mr. Morris's earlier work. As regards the general public it was a failure so complete that its author, if unsupported by self-knowledge and the promptings of genius, might well have retired in discouragement from the strife for fame. With a select few, however, comprising men of highest culture and those whose opinions upon poetry have most weight, it speedily became a remarkable favourite. Such a volume—so thoroughly imbued with antique spirit, so full of wonderful colour, so strange, mystical, and unearthly, yet withal so profoundly poetical— had seldom before been seen, and at its first appearance stamped its author a man of highest mark. A second volume from the same author has long been hoped for, and at length is here. The first feeling on glancing at its contents, or, indeed, at reading its title, is regret. So completely has the fame of Mr. Morris been associated with Gothic art that it is not without a twinge of pain we see him desert it for Classic. To the man who can write such poems as 'The Chapel in Lyoness,' 'Rapunzel,' 'Shameful Death,' or 'The Haystack in the Floods,' a mine of wealth is open which none but he can explore. If he leave its treasures unrevealed, they must remain for ever unknown. The wealth of classic subjects is opened out to us by many explorers, and the labours of the last comer might well, seeing what need there is of them elsewhere, have been spared. During a perusal of the work, however, such feelings as we have indicated rapidly disappear. Great as has been Mr. Morris's success in dealing with Arthurian legends and subjects drawn from mediæval life, it is not greater than that he has obtained in his treatment of one of the oldest and most character-istic of classical stories. *The Life and Death of Jason* is, indeed, one of the most remarkable poems of this or any other age. It claims the dignity of an epic having a 'dramatic fable,' and the 'revolutions, discoveries, and disasters,' on which, in the epic, Aristotle insists. The manner of Jason's death, moreover—for which Mr. Morris has classic warranty—is such as to bring the work within the limits of the Epopee, rendering it 'conversant with one whole and perfect action which has a beginning, middle, and end.' This action is, of course, the Argon-autic expedition, to undertake which Jason, unknown to himself, is divinely summoned. By this expedition and its results alone he is remembered, and his death is due to Argo, the vessel which has been the companion, and, in part, the means of his triumph. In structure, moreover, *The Life and Death of Jason* approaches closely the celebrated epics of antiquity. Its length is certainly epic. It consists of seven-teen books, whereof two contain over one thousand lines, the aggre-gate number of lines being almost identical with that of the *Paradise Lost*. An epic poem, then, in rhymed heroic stanza, is a truly remark-able experiment for a writer in modern days to attempt. Tried, how-ever, by the tests ordinarily applied to epic poetry, *Jason* would scarcely claim our praise. No previous work, in fact, resembles it in many important particulars, and it can scarcely be assigned to any class. Treatment of subject, and the nature of some of the episodes, recall the *Odyssey*—with which, indeed, the book has more in common than it has with any other work. In the manner in which the story is nar-rated we are at times reminded of some of the more than half-forgotten 'heroic' poems of the seventeenth century, such as the *Pharonnida* of William Chamberlayne. Ben Jonson, we know, on the testimony of Drummond of Hawthornden, projected an epic poem in rhymed couplets of ten syllables, but he never seems to have attempted to put his scheme into execution. This metre, he maintained, was best suited to the dignity of epic poetry. Mr. Morris's management of this metre is, however, so different from that of any writer past or present that it scarcely seems necessary to inquire who were his predecessors in its employment. No other verse has any likeness to it. The rhymed couplets of Pope have hardly more resemblance to it than the blank verse of Milton or the Alexandrines of Drayton. Mr. Morris's work, whatever its faults, is profoundly original, and bears the impress of the strongest conceivable individuality. It is not easy to give an idea of it by extracts, or, indeed, to judge of it by parts. Taken as a whole, it strikes us as one of the most beautiful, complete, and unearthly poems we have ever read. It is classical in thought and feeling, but its classicism is all unlike that of Swinburne, or Landor, or Tennyson, or Keats. No single idea about it seems to have even the slightest reference to any modern thought or feeling. In *The Defence of Guenevere* a noticeable charm was the utter unworldliness, so to speak, of the verse, its total divergence from all known models, and the manner in which its very metre carried the mind away from every-day life. Even stronger is this feeling as we read the passages of *Jason*. Its verse has a strange melody, the full sense and significance of which are not at first acquired. Its pictures are sharp, well-defined, and often of superlative beauty. The poem is full of colour, not such rich and glowing hues as belong to the early volume, but wonderful colour nevertheless. Pale opal-like tints it exhibits, such as on a spring morning the sky possesses an hour before sunrise, or such as are offered by a faint and distant vision of Northern Lights. The melody of the versification is perfect. A frequent use of particular words adds to the dreamy monotony which the author appears to have studied. Few works of equal pretensions have had less heat and passion. Here, in fact, is the most striking defect of the poem. It is too destitute of fire and glow. Strangely little is made of the dramatic opportunities offered. Yet if the poem does not rise it does not sink. It is as passionlessly beautiful as an antique bust. Its story follows so closely the common legends of Jason, it is needless to describe it. The birth of Jason and his nurture by Cherion occupy the first book. His return to Iolchos and his determination, after hearing the narration of Pelias, to go in quest of the Golden Fleece, are told in the second. The third contains an account of the various heroes whom desire to join the intended enterprise attracts, and is an imitation of the often-imitated catalogue of ships in the *Iliad*. Singularly beautiful is this part, the few lines in which the more-important characters, as Atalanta, Hercules, Orpheus, Theseus, or Pirithous, are described being admirable. After the departure of the heroes from Iolchos, the events that occur ere their arrival at Colchis are detailed at no great length; the famous episode of Hypsipylo and the Lemnian women being barely touched upon. Arriving at Æa, the capital of Colchis, the Argonauts are entertained by Æetes with feigned courtesy, and Jason learns the terrible conditions on which alone the fleece can be won. Aided by Medea, the sudden dawn of whose love for the hero is admirably described, Jason commences the enterprise. Æetes sees with dismay the taming of the two brazen bulls, the killing of the dragon, the sowing of its teeth, and the destruction by means of the stone which Medea had provided of the multitude of armed men which arose from the furrows. In the night Jason and Medea obtain the fleece and put to sea. The flaring of the beacon lights which follows is powerfully described. Then follow the murder of Absyrtus, the long journey northwards, the winter in the north, and the homeward journey in the spring. Circe is visited on her island and Medea learns the means by which alone she and Jason can be purified from the blood of Absyrtus. From the snares of the Sirens the travellers are preserved by the song of Orpheus. Arrived in Thessaly Medea first lands and causes the death of Pelias at the hands of his daughters, who think, under her direction to restore him to youth. Jason and his companions are received with applause and shouts of 'Jason for King! The Conqueror for King!' The journey to Corinth, Jason's love for Glauce, and Medea's terrible revenge are briefly narrated, and the poem ends with the death of Jason, by the falling of a beam of the ship Argo, under shade of which he was sleeping. To give an idea of the story of this poem is far easier than to describe its versification or explain the secret of its attractions. *Jason* is a work which can never enjoy a wide popularity, but its readers must include all cultivated lovers of poetry. Those parts of the poem which deserve special attention—we have left ourselves little space to quote—are the descriptions of the gathering of the Argonauts, their departure, the introduction of Medea, her gathering of the baneful drugs, and the scenes in the Islands of Circe and of the Sirens. Very little in literature is finer than the contrasted songs of Orpheus and the Sirens, the former proclaiming to the half-conquered mariners the glory of heroic deeds and the reception that awaits them at home; the latter, singing the joys of ease and sensual delight. A song of the golden days of Saturn, is like the famous 'Happy Age of

Gold,' in the *Pastor Fido* of Guarini. It is impossible to extract a stanza from the poem without seriously impairing its beauty. Some short specimen of the versification is, however, needed. Medea's entry to bear to Jason, sleeping, the magic preparations by aid of which his great deeds were to be accomplished, is by no means the best passage in the volume; it can, however, with least injury be separated from the context:—

> And last she reached the gilded water-gate,
> And though nigh breathless, scarce she dared to wait
> To fasten up her shallop to the stone,
> Which yet she dared not leave; so this being done,
> Swiftly by passages and stairs she ran,
> Trembling and pale, though not yet seen by man,
> Until to Jason's chamber-door she came.
> And there awhile indeed she stayed, for shame,
> Rose up against her fear; but mighty love
> And the sea-haunting, rose-crowned seed of Jove
> O'ermastered both: so, trembling on the pin,
> She laid her hand, but ere she entered in
> She covered up again her shoulder sweet,
> And dropped her dusky raiment o'er her feet,
> Then entering the dimly-lighted room,
> Where with the lamp dawn struggled through the gloom,
> Seeking the prince she peered, who sleeping lay
> Upon his gold bed, and abode the day
> Smiling, still clad in arms, and round his sword
> His fingers met; then she, with a soft word,
> Drew nigh him, and from out his slackened hand
> With slender rosy fingers drew the brand;
> Then kneeling, laid her hand upon his breast,
> And said: 'O Jason, wake up from thy rest,
> Perchance from thy last rest, and speak to me '

Many single lines and short stanzas have exceeding beauty, music, and picturesqueness. The description of the home of Erginus, son of Neptune, is very fine:—

>   Nigh the sea
> His father set him, where the laden bee
> Flies low across Meander, and falls down
> Against the white walls of a merchant town
> Men call Miletus.

Here are a few lines the beauty in which is of an altogether different order:—

> But far away the sea-beat Minyæ
> Cast forth the foam as through the growing night
> They laboured ever, having small delight
> In life all empty of that promised bliss,
> In love that scarce can give a dying kiss,
> In pleasure ending sweet songs with a wail,
> In fame that little can dead men avail,
> In vain toil struggling with the fateful stream,
> In hope, the promise of a morning dream.

Comment and quotation must, however, both cease. With no ordinary reluctance we take leave of this poem. Musical, clear, and flowing, strangely imaginative and suggestive, presenting pictures of almost incomparable beauty, it is a work of which an epoch may be proud. Its perusal leaves on the mind images of drowsy beauty, which are neither entirely recollections nor quite suggestions, but partake of the nature of each. Whoever loves poetry of the highest order will have this book on his shelves, will dip into it often, and will love it none the less that it will assuredly be 'caviare to the general.'

8. A. C. Swinburne, review, *Fortnightly Review*

July 1867, viii, 19–28

Algernon Charles Swinburne (1837–1909), the poet, was a friend of Morris and Rossetti. His enthusiastic but discriminating review includes a discussion of *The Defence of Guenevere*. That being praised by Swinburne—whose *Poems and Ballads* had attracted severe 'moral' criticism in 1866—was something of a liability for Morris is shown by Henry James's comment in his review of *Jason* (No. 10).

The review was reprinted by Swinburne in *Essays and Studies* (London, 1875).

The hardest work and the highest that can be done by a critic studious of the right, is first to discern what is good, and then to discover how and in what way it is so. To do this office for any man during his life is a task always essentially difficult, sometimes seemingly ungracious. We demand of the student who stands up as a judge, to show us as he best may, how and why this man excels that, what are the stronger and what the weaker sides of his attempted or achieved work when set fairly by the work of others. For if in some one point at least it does not exceed theirs, it is not work of a high kind, and worthy of enduring study. Who is to say this, who is to prove it, we have first to find out; and found out it must be, if criticism is to be held of more account than the ephemeral cackle of casual praisers and blamers; if it is to be thoughtful and truthful, worthy of an art, handmaid of higher arts. Now, as a rule, men are mistrustful of one who takes leave to judge the work of a fellow-workman. And not without reason or show of reason; for no verdicts more foolish or more false have been delivered than some of those passed by poet upon poet, by painter upon painter. Nor need this be taken as proof of anything base, or partial, or jealous in the speaker's mind. It is not easy to see at once widely and well. For example, could Byron and Wordsworth have judged better of each other's work, each might have lost something of fitness for his own. It is a hard law, but a law it is. Against this, however, a counter truth not less grave than this must be weighed. We do not appeal to men ignorant of politics for a verdict on affairs of state, to men unskilled in science on a scientific question. And no matter of science or state is more abstruse and hard to settle than a question of art; nor is any more needful to have settled for us in good time, if only lest accident or neglect, ignorance or violence, rob us unaware of some precious and irrecoverable thing, not known of or esteemed while safely with us. Consider what all men have lost already and for ever, merely by such base means as these; how much of classic work and mediæval, how much of Greece, of Italy, of England, has gone from us that we might have kept. For this and other reasons it may be permissible, or pardonable at least, for a student of art to speak now and then on art; so long only as he shall speak honestly and carefully, without overmuch of assumption or deprecation.

Over the first fortunes of a newly-born work of art accident must usually preside for evil or for good. Over the earliest work of the artist whom we are here to take note of, that purblind leader of the blind presided on the whole for evil. Here and there it met with eager recognition and earnest applause; nowhere, if I err not, with just praise or blame worth heeding. It seems to have been now lauded and now decried as the result and expression of a school rather than a man, of a theory or tradition rather than a poet or student. Those who so judged were blind guides of the purblind; reversing thus the undivine office of their god Accident. Such things as were in this book are taught and learnt in no school but that of instinct. Upon no piece of work in the world was the impress of native character ever more distinctly stamped, more deeply branded. It needed no exceptional acuteness of ear or eye to see or hear that this poet held of none, stole from none, clung to none, as tenant, or as beggar, or as thief. Not as yet a master, he was assuredly no longer a pupil.

A little later than this one appeared another volume of poems, not dissimilar in general choice of stories and subjects, perfect where this was imperfect, strong where this was weak; but strong and perfect on that side alone. All that was wanting here was there supplied, but all that was here supplied was wanting there. In form, in structure, in composition, few poems can be more faultless than those of Mr. Tennyson, few faultier than those of Mr. Morris, which deal with the legend of Arthur and Guenevere. I do not speak here of form in the abstract and absolute sense; for where this is wanting, all is wanting; without this there can be no work of art at all. I speak of that secondary excellence always necessary to the perfection, but not always indis-pensable to the existence of art. These first poems of Mr. Morris were not malformed; a misshapen poem is no poem; as well might one talk of unnatural nature or superhuman manhood; but they are not well clad; their attire now and then has been huddled on; they have need sometimes of combing and trimming. Take that one for example called 'King Arthur's Tomb.' It has not been constructed at all; the parts hardly hold together; it has need of joists and screws, props and rafters. Many able writers of verse whom no miracle could endow with competence to do such work, would have missed the faults as surely as the merits; would have done something where the poet has cared to do nothing. There is scarcely connection here, and scarcely composition. There is hardly a trace of narrative power or mechanical arrangement. There is a perceptible want of tact and practice, which leaves the poem in parts indecorous and chaotic. But where among other and older poets of his time and country, is one comparable for perception and expression of tragic truth, of subtle and noble, terrible and piteous things? where a touch of passion at once so broad and so sure? The figures here given have the blood and breath, the shape and step of life; they can move and suffer; their repentance is as real as their desire; their shame lies as deep as their love. They are at once remorseful for the sin and regretful of the pleasure that is past. The retrospective vision of Launcelot and of Guenevere is as passionate and profound as life. Riding towards her without hope, in the darkness and the heat of the way, he can but divert and sustain his spirit by recollection of her loveliness and her love, seen long since asleep and waking, in another place than this, on a distant night.

> Pale in the green sky were the stars, I ween,
> Because the moon shone like a tear she shed,
> When she dwelt up in heaven a while ago
> And ruled all things but God.

Retrospect and vision, natural memories and spiritual, here coalesce; and how exquisite is the retrospect, and how passionate the vision, of past light and colour in the sky, past emotion and conception in the soul! Not in the idyllic school is a chord ever struck, a note ever sounded, so tender and subtle as this. Again, when Guenevere has maddened herself and him with wild words of reproach and remorse, abhorrence and attraction, her sharp and sudden memory of old sights and sounds and splendid irrevocable days finds word and form not less noble and faithful to fact and life. The first words of Arthur bidding her cherish the knight 'whom all the land called his banner, sword, and shield;' the long first pressure of Launcelot's lips on her hand; the passionate and piteous course of love here ended (if ended at all) above the king's grave dug in part and unwittingly by their wrong-doing; the solitary sound of birds singing in her gardens, while in the lists the noise went on of spears and shouts telling which knight of them all rode here or there; the crying of ladies' names as men and horses clashed one against another, names that bit like the steel they impelled to its mark; the agony of anger and horror which gives edge and venom to her memory—

> Banner of Arthur—with black-bended shield
>
> Sinister-wise across the fair gold ground!
>   Here let me tell you what a knight you are,
> O sword and shield of Arthur! you are found
>   A crooked sword, I think, that leaves a scar
>
> On the bearer's arm so be he thinks it straight—
>   Twisted Malay's crease, beautiful blue-grey,
> Poisoned with sweet fruit—as he found too late,
>   My husband Arthur, on some bitter day!
>
> O sickle cutting harvest all day long,
>   That the husbandman across his shoulder hangs,
> And going homeward about evensong,
>   Dies the next morning, struck through by the fangs!*

—all these points and phases of passion are alike truly and nobly rendered. I have not read the poem for years, I have not the book at hand, and I cite from memory; but I think it would be safe to swear

---

* Perhaps in all this noble passage of poetry there is nothing nobler than this bitter impulse of irony, this fiery shame and rage of repentance, which here impels Guenevere to humiliate herself through her lover, and thus consummate the agony of abasement. 'False and fatal as banner, or shield, or sword, wherein is he better than a peasant's dangerous and vulgar implement, as fatal to him it may be, by carelessness or chance, as a king's weapon to the king if handled amiss?' And yet for all this she cannot but cleave to him; through her lover she scourges herself; it is suicide in her to slay him; but even so his soul must needs be saved—'so as by fire.' No poet about to start on his course ever saw for himself or showed to others a thing more tragic and more true than this study of noble female passion, half selfless and half personal, half mad and half sane.

to the accuracy of my citation. Such verses are not forgetable. They are not, indeed,—as are the *Idylls of the King*—the work of a dexterous craftsman in full practice. Little beyond dexterity, a rare eloquence, and a laborious patience of hand, has been given to the one or denied to the other.* These are good gifts and great; but it is better to want clothes than limbs.

The shortcomings of this first book are nowhere traceable in the second now lying before us. A nine years' space does not lie between them in vain; enough has been learned and unlearned, rejected and attained. Here, indeed, there is not the stormy variety, the lyric ardour of the first book; there is not the passion of the ballads, the change of note and diversity of power, all that fills with life and invigorates with colour the artist's earlier designs; for not all of this is here needed. Of passion and humour, of impulse and instinct, he had given noble and sufficient proof in manifold ways. But this *Jason* is a large and coherent poem, completed as conceived; the style throughout on a level with the invention. In direct narrative power, in clear forthright manner of procedure, not seemingly troubled to select, to pick and sift and winnow, yet never superfluous or verbose, never straggling or jarring; in these high qualities it resembles the work of Chaucer. Even against the great master his pupil may fairly be matched for simple sense of right, for grace and speed of step, for purity and justice of colour. In all the noble roll of our poets there has been since Chaucer no second teller of tales, no second rhapsode comparable to the first, till the advent of this one. As with the Greeks, so with us; we have had in lieu of these a lyric and a tragic school; we have also had the sub-ordinate schools, gnomic and idyllic, domestic and didactic. But the old story-singers, the old 'Saga-men,' we have no more heard of. As soon might we have looked for a fresh *Odyssey* from southward, a fresh *Njala* from northward. And yet no higher school has brought forth rarer poets than this. 'But,' it is said, 'this sort of poetry is a March flower, a child of the first winds and suns of a nation; in May even, much more in August, you cannot have it except by forcing; and forcing it will not bear. A late romance is a hothouse daffodil.' And so indeed it must usually be. But so it is not here; and the proof is the poem. It could not be done, no doubt, only it has been. Here is

---

* The comparison here made is rather between book and book than between man and man. Both poets have done better elsewhere, each after his kind; and except by his best work no workman can be fairly judged. A critic who should underrate either would be condemnable on both hands.

a poem sown of itself, sprung from no alien seed, cut after no alien model; fresh as wind, bright as light, full of the spring and the sun. It shares, of course, the conditions of its kind; it has no time for the subtleties and hardly room for the ardours of tragic poetry. Passion in romance is of its nature subordinate to action; the flowing stream of story hushes and lulls the noise of its gurgling and refluent eddies with a still predominance of sound. To me it seems that there has here been almost too much of this. Only by rare and brief jets does the poet let out the fire of a potent passion which not many others can kindle and direct. For the most part, the river of romance flows on at full, but keeping well to its channel, unvexed by rains and undisturbed by whirlpools. In a word, through great part of this poem there is no higher excellence attempted than that of adventurous or romantic narrative couched in the simplest and fittest forms of poetry. This abstinence is certainly not due to impotence, possibly not to intention, more probably to distaste. Mr. Morris has an English respect for temperance and reserve; good things as drags, but not as clogs. He is not afraid to tackle a passion, but he will not move an inch from his way to tackle it. Tragedy can never be more than the episode of a romance, and romance is rather to his taste than naked tragedy. He reminds us of the knight in Chaucer cutting sharply short the monk's tragic histories as too piteous for recital, or the very monk himself breaking off the detail of Ugolino's agony with a reference to Dante for those who can endure it.

The descriptive and decorative beauties of this romance of *Jason* are excellent above all in this, that, numberless though they be, they are always just and fit. Not a tone of colour, not a note of form, is misplaced or dispensable. The pictures are clear and chaste, sweet and lucid, as early Italian work. There are crowds and processions, battlepieces and merry-makings, worthy of Benozzo or Carpaccio; single figures or groups of lovers in flowery watery land, worthy of Sandro or Filippo. The sea-pieces are like the younger Lippi's; the best possible to paint from shore. They do not taste salt or sound wide; but they have all the beauty of the beach. The romance poets have never loved the sea as have the tragic poets; Chaucer simply ignores it with a shiver; even Homer's men are glad to be well clear of it. Ulysses has no sea-king's impulse; he fights and beats it, and is glad, and there an end; necessity alone ever drives him off shore. But Æschylus loves the Oceanides; and Shakespeare, landsman though he were, rejoices in the roll and clash of breakers.

For examples of the excellences we have noted—the chastity of colour and noble justice of composition, the fruitful and faithful touches of landscape incident—almost any page of the poem might be turned up. Compare the Hesperian with the Circean garden, the nameless northern desert lands with the wood of Medea's transformation, or the seaward bent where Jason 'died strangely.' No flower of the landscape is slurred, but no flower is obtrusive; the painting is broad and minute at once, large and sure by dint of accuracy. And there are wonderful touches on it of fairy mystery; weird lights pass over it and wafts of mystical wind; as here:—

> There comes a murmur from the shore,
> And in the place two fair streams are,
> Drawn from the purple hills afar,
> Drawn down unto the restless sea,
> *The hills whose flowers ne'er fed the bee,*
> *The shore no ship has ever seen,*
> Still beaten by the billows green,
> Whose murmur comes unceasingly
> Unto the place for which I cry.

All this song of a nymph to Hylas is full of the melody which involves colour and odour, but the two lines marked have in them the marvel and the music of a dream. Compare again this of Orpheus, in his contest with the Sirens:—

> O the sweet valley of deep grass,
> Wherethrough the summer stream doth pass,
> In chain of shallow, and still pool,
> From misty morn to evening cool;

[quotes next 16 lines]

Not more noble in colour, but more fervent, is the next picture:—

> Nigh the vine-covered hillocks green,
> In days agone, have I not seen
> The brown-clad maidens amorous,
> Below the long rose-trellised house,
> Dance to the querulous pipe and shrill,
> When the grey shadow of the hill
> Was lengthening at the end of day?

[quotes next 23 lines]

Nor is any passage in the poem pitched in a higher and clearer key than the first hymn of Orpheus as Argo takes the sea:—

> O bitter sea, tumultuous sea,
> Full many an ill is wrought by thee!
> Unto the washers of the land
> Thou holdest out thy wrinkled hand;
> And when they leave the conquered town,
> Whose black smoke makes thy surges brown,
> Driven between them and the sun
> As the long day of blood is done,
> From many a league of glittering waves
> Thou smilest on them and their slaves.

The rest is not less lofty in tone and sure in touch, but too long for an excerpt. As noble is the song of triumph at p. 217, which should be set by the side of this, to which it is in some sort antiphonal.

But the root of the romance lies of course in the character of Medea; and here, where it was needfullest to do well, the poet has done best. At her first entrance the poem takes new life and rises out of the atmosphere of mere adventure and incident. The subdued and delicate ardour of the scene in Jason's chamber, following as it does on the ghastly beauty of that in the wood of the Three-formed, is proof enough and at once with how strong and soft a touch the picture will be completed. Her incantations, and her flight with Jason, have no less of fanciful and tender power. The fifteenth book, where she beguiles Pelias to death at the hands of his daughters, is a sample of flawless verse and noble imagination unsurpassed by any here. For dramatic invention and vivid realism of the impossible, which turns to fair and sensible truth the wildest dreams of legend, there has been no poet for centuries comparable. But the very flower and crest of this noble poem is the final tragedy at Corinth. Queen, sorceress, saviour, she has shrunk or risen to mere woman; and not in vain before entering the tragic lists has the poet called on that great poet's memory who has dealt with the terrible and pitiful passion of women like none but Shakespeare since.

> Would that I
> Had but some portion of that mastery
> That from the rose-hung lanes of woody Kent
> Through these five hundred years such songs have sent
> To us, who, meshed within this smoky net
> Of unrejoicing labour, love them yet.

And thou, O Master!—Yea, my Master still,
Whatever feet have scaled Parnassus' hill,
Since like thy measures, clear, and sweet, and strong,
Thames' stream scarce fettered bore the bream along
Unto the bastioned bridge, his only chain—
O Master, pardon me, if yet in vain
Thou art my Master, and I fail to bring
Before men's eyes the image of the thing
My heart is filled with: thou whose dreamy eyes
Beheld the flush to Cressid's cheeks arise,
As Troilus rode up the praising street,
As clearly as they saw thy townsmen meet
Those who in vineyards of Poictou withstood
The glittering horror of the steel-topped wood.

Worthy, indeed, even of the master-hand is all that follows. Let the
student weigh well the slight but great touches in which the fitful fury
and pity and regret of the sufferer are given; so delicate and accurate
that only by the entire and majestic harmony of tragedy will he
discern the excellence and justice of every component note.

Ah! shall I, living underneath the sun,
I wonder, wish for anything again,
Or ever know what pleasure means, and pain?
And for these deeds I do; and thou the first,
O woman, whose young beauty has so cursed
My hapless life, at least I save thee this—
The slow descent to misery from bliss, &c.

To come upon this part of the poem is as the change from river to
sea (Book XII.), when wind and water had a larger savour in lip and
nostril of the Argonauts. Note well the new and piteous beauty of
this:—

Kindly I deal with me, mine enemy;
Since swift forgetfulness to thee I send.
But thou shalt die—his eyes shall see thine end—
Ah! if thy death alone could end it all!
But ye—shall I behold you when leaves fall,
In some sad evening of the autumn-tide?
Or shall I have you sitting by my side
Amidst the feast, so that folk stare and say,
'Sure the grey wolf has seen the queen to-day'?

[quotes next 14½ lines]

Rarely but in the ballad and romance periods has such poetry been written, so broad and sad and simple, so full of deep and direct fire, certain of its aim, without finish, without fault. The passion from hence fills and burns to a close; the verse for a little is as the garment of Medea steeped in strange moisture as of tears and liquid flame to be kindled by the sun.

> O sons, with what sweet counsels and what tears
> Would I have hearkened to the hopes and fears
> Of your first loves: what rapture had it been
> Your dear returning footsteps to have seen
> Amidst the happy warriors of the land;
> *But now—but now—this is a little hand,*
> *Too often kissed since love did first begin*
> *To win such curses as it yet shall win,*
> *When after all bad deeds there comes a worse,*
> *Praise to the Gods! ye know not how to curse.*
>   But when in some dim land we meet again
> Will ye remember all the loss and pain?
> Will ye the form of children keep for aye
> With thoughts of men? and 'Mother,' will ye say,
> 'Why didst thou slay us ere we came to know
> That men die? hadst thou waited until now,
> An easy thing it had been then to die,
> For in the thought of immortality
> Do children play about the flowery meads,
> And win their heaven with a crown of weeds.'
>   O children! that I would have died to save,
> How fair a life of pleasure might ye have,
> But for your mother:—nay, for thee, for thee,
> For thee, O traitor! who didst bring them here
> Into this cruel world, this lovely bier
> Of youth and love, and joy and happiness,
> That unforeseeing happy fools still bless.

It should now be clear, or never, that in this poem a new thing of great price has been cast into the English treasure-house. Nor is the cutting and setting of the jewel unworthy of it; art and instinct have wrought hand in hand to its perfection. Other and various fields await the workman who has here approved himself a master, acceptable into the guild of great poets on a footing of his own to be shared or disputed by no other. Strained clear and guided straight as now, his lofty lyrical power must keep all its promise to us. Diffusion is in the nature of a romance, and it cannot be said that here the stream has ever over-flowed into marshland or stagnated in lock or pool. Therefore we do not blame the length and fulness of so fair a river; but something of barrier or dam may serve to concentrate and condense the next. Also, if we must note the slightest ripples of the water-flies that wrinkle it, let us set down in passing that there are certain slight laxities or per-versities of metre which fret the ear and perplex the eye, noticeable only as the least shortcoming is noticeable in great work. Elision, for example, is a necessity, not a luxury, of metre. This law Chaucer, a most loyal versifier, never allows himself to slight after the fashion of his follower. But into these straits of technical art we need not now steer. So much remains unremarked, so much unsaid; so much of beauty slighted, of uncommended excellence; that I close these in-adequate and hurried notes with a sense of grave injustice done. To the third book of Mr. Morris we look now, not for the seal of our present judgment, but for the accomplishment of our highest hopes; for a fresh honour done to English art, a fresh delight to us, and a fresh memory for the future.

9. C. E. Norton, review, *Nation*

22 August 1867, v, 146–7

Charles Eliot Norton (1827–1908) was a distinguished American editor and academic, co-founder of the *Nation*, and correspondent of James and Morris.

No narrative poem comparable with this in scope of design or in power of execution has been produced in our generation. By this work Mr. Morris wins a secure place among the chief English poets of the age. The production of such a poem is not only proof of a rare individual genius, but the sign of the abiding vigor and freshness of our literature.

Mr. Swinburne has ventured in the *Fortnightly Review* to greet this work with the highest praise, but in doing so he unconsciously passes condemnation on his own poems. A sharper contrast could hardly be drawn than that presented by the methods of treatment of a classic theme followed by one and the other poet. The manliness, the straight-forwardness, the reserve of feeling which distinguish Mr. Morris's work are the very opposite to Mr. Swinburne's feminine passionate-ness, extravagance, and self-exposure. Mr. Morris is imbued not only with the form of the pagan legend, but in as great a measure with its spirit as is perhaps consistent with the modern intellectual temper. He has a strong sense of the dignity and proportion of art, and he treats his theme not as a Greek poet would have treated it, but as an artist aware of the impassable barrier set up between the ancient and the modern moods of feeling and manner of expression. Pouring his old wine into new bottles, he preserves the perennial freshness of its genuine flavor.

The Life and Death of Jason belongs to the same class as the *Odyssey*. Like that it is a poem of fable, romance, and adventure. In these days, to venture on a narrative poem of more than ten thousand lines is a bold undertaking. The art of story-telling grows more uncommon and more difficult as the world grows older. Stories belong to child-hood, and the youth of man. The inventions of later days fail in the essence of story. To tell a good story a man must choose an old one, with the outline of which he has himself long been familiar, and which other men heard first when they were first waking to the wonders of life. It is the twice-told tale that delights the old no less than the young. The poems which are in any real sense popular, the poems which have become a part of universal literature, are all either simple narratives or narratives in a dramatic form. The *Iliad* and the *Odyssey*, the *Divine Comedy*, the *Nibelungen Lied*, the old Ballads, *Paradise Lost*, are all illustrations of this fact, and Hamlet and Faust appeal to men as much through their story as through the delineation of character and experi-ence for which the story affords room. All men care to know what other men have done and suffered; it is but the few who are much interested in what other men have thought and felt. For the thoughts of men change from age to age, and feeling has different modes in each generation; but the deeds of men are the concrete forms in which their thoughts and feelings take shape, and awaken a sympathy such as cannot be aroused by the mere utterance of passion or reflection. The woes of Prometheus, the wanderings of Ulysses, the fury of

Orestes, the journey of Dante, are types or symbols of universal experience, and have an interest not limited by time or bounded by race.

The most popular poems of our own day show how strong this story-loving instinct still remains. 'The Lady of the Lake' has ten readers for one of the *Prelude*; 'Evangeline' and the *Idyls of the King* are read and re-read, and will be read long after 'Voices of the Night' and *In Memoriam* have taken their place among the purely literary records of the sentiment of an age that is gone.

But to tell an old story well is an art which few poets have possessed; and we doubt whether Mr. Morris has told so well the old story which he has chosen to repeat that his version of it will take its place among the everlasting works of the poets. The critic cannot absolutely forecast the verdict of the future; but even if Mr. Morris has failed to win the perennial fame which few poets succeed in winning, he has at least shown the possession of faculties such as few in any time surpass.

It is a great merit of his work that, in this period of self-consciousness, of morbid introversion, of exaggeration of the interest of individual feeling and experience, he has told his story, with but very slight exception, objectively, with simple regard to its own development, and with no direct expression of the emotions or thoughts its course awoke in himself. And he has, moreover, shown one of the highest qualities of the poet in the vividness of imagination by which he has reproduced scenes remote from experience with all the distinctness of reality, and invested imaginary characters with the natures of living men. The most marked characteristic of his poem is its picturesqueness; there is scarcely a page that does not give a picture to the eye; and this becomes at once a merit and a defect, for in the limited compass of his story the variety of pictures cannot be thus numerous without involving an occasional repetition not of details, but of what, in the language of pictorial art, is called motive. Mr. Morris's landscapes have frequently, underlying their diversity of detail, a general similarity of outline and of tone; his descriptions of persons and incidents might here and there be interchanged without apparent discordance. Every landscape, every description is clear, almost every one is finished and beautiful in itself, but there are too many which differ only in those minor points which, while they indicate the distinctness and truth of the poet's vision, yet do not serve to give a strong enough impression of absolute variety. There is in his poem something of the prolixity of a mediæval romance, and in this is its weakness. Though there is no single page to which, standing alone, praise might not belong, yet the general effect of the poem, and, we regret to believe, its permanent interest, would be increased by the omission of many of them, or at least by the condensation of many into a few. Each reader would, it is not improbable, select different passages as not adding to the effect of the work; the poet himself could alone determine what is least needful to the impression he has sought to produce.

Of Mr. Morris's general conception of his theme, his delineation of his characters, and of his picturing of special incidents, there is little to be said but praise. Only on one point does he seem to us to have failed to conceive justly the real condition of his story—this is the character of Medea, and the feelings of Jason towards her. Where he has followed most closely the original legend and its natural suggestions he has been most successful; where he has departed from it he has at best achieved only a doubtful success. It is dangerous to vary from a model set by such artists as the Greek poets from whom the story of Jason and Medea has come down to us. Although in Mr. Morris's Medea the union of the beautiful and lovely woman with the fell sorceress is occasionally admirably presented, yet, with a tendency easily explicable by the general direction of modern sentiment, he has been led to dwell too strongly on her lovely womanhood, and has not reproduced the awful and abiding sense of her magic art, and of her ruthless nature subdued to what it worked in, which alone can sufficiently account for the desertion of her by her lover, who owed to her both his life and his glory. In the mingling of fear with fascination, of loathing with love, are the secret of Jason's feeling to her and the explanation of her own misery. She loved as a woman, but even in her love she had the pitilessness of a sorceress. A poem such as this is not to be appreciated by such extracts as can be made from it in a brief notice, but we can at least give a specimen of the picturesqueness which makes its pages a gallery of fair scenes, colored by the hand of a master. Here is a description of the palace of King Æetes:

> The pillars, made the mighty roof to hold,
> The one was silver, and the next was gold,
> All down the hall; the roof, of some strange wood
> Brought over sea, was dyed as red as blood,
> Set thick with silver flowers, and delight
> Of intertwining figures wrought aright.
> With richest webs the marble walls were hung,

Picturing sweet stories by the poets sung
From ancient days, so that no wall seemed there,
But rather forests black and meadows fair,
And streets of well-built towns, with tumbling seas
About their marble wharves and palaces;
And fearful crags and mountains; and all trod
By many a changing foot of nymph and god,
Spear-shaking warrior, and slim-ankled maid.
  The floor, moreover, of the place was laid
With colored stones, wrought like a flowery mead;
And ready to the hand, for every need,
Midmost the hall, two fair streams trickled down
O'er wondrous gem-like pebbles, green and brown,
Betwixt smooth banks of marble, and therein
Bright-colored fish shone through the water thin.

The description of the island of Circe, with the fine imaginative conception of the victims of her magic arts and of the empty shades whom she made the agents of her enchantments, the description of the beach of the Sirens and of the garden of the Hesperides, might all be cited as instances of the full and easy power of the poet in picturing nature as she shows herself under various aspects of beauty. It is plain that he is a lover and student alike of nature and of art. There is nothing borrowed or at second-hand in his work, and his lines have often a simple freshness which recalls the charm of Chaucer, or a rich fulness which reminds one of the sweetness of Spenser.

The tragic interest of the story rises towards the end, and all the tender feeling and fancy of the poet are quickened into higher expression as the gloom cast by the shadow of impending and irresistible fate darkens round Jason and Medea. The exulting joy of Medea, having compassed the death of King Pelias, and secured the triumph of her love, is finely contrasted with the bitterness of her woe when deserted by him for whom she had dared so much. At first,

'O love!' she said, 'O love! O sweet delight!
Hast thou begun to weep for me this night?
Dost thou stretch out for me thy mighty hands—
The feared of all, the graspers of the lands?
Come, then, O love! across the dark seas come,
And triumph as a king in thine own home,
While I, the doer of this happy deed,
Shall sit beside thee in this wretched weed;
That folk may know me by thine eyes alone

Still blessing me for all that I have done.
Come, king, and sit upon thy father's seat,
Come, conquering king, thy conqueror love to meet.'

But when, long afterwards, she knows herself deserted of Jason, she
says:

'Would God that Argo's brazen-banded mast
'Twixt the blue clashing rocks had never passed
Unto the Colchian land! Or would that I
Had had such happy fortune as to die,
Then when I saw thee standing by the Fleece
Safe on the long-desired shore of Greece!
Alas, O Jason! for thy cruel praise!
Alas for all the kindness of past days!
That to thy heart seems but a story told
That happened to other folk in times of old;
But unto me, indeed, its memory
Was bliss in happy hours, and now shall be
Such misery as never tongue can tell.'

We have no disposition to point out the occasional carelessness of
rhythm and rhyme, the too frequent recurrence of certain epithets, and
other minor faults which injure here and there the structure of Mr.
Morris's verse. They are faults which a little care would remove,
leaving the poem remarkable among contemporary works for its
simplicity and strength of diction.

The American edition of the book is neat, but disfigured with errors
of the press which its publishers should hasten to correct. For instance,
on p. 43 a line seems to have dropped out after 'More than those
others whose crowned memories.' On pp. 49 and 51, Amphitryon is
four times misprinted Amphytrion. On p. 143, 'And round her panting side his fingers steal,' is travestied by the substitution of 'painting'
for 'panting.' On p. 254, the line in a passage quoted above, 'Still
blessing me for all that I have done,' is rendered unintelligible by
substituting 'him' for 'me.' There are other hardly less serious blunders.

Mr. Morris himself commits one curious anachronism, as we suppose. When, after the gain of the Golden Fleece, Medea urges Jason
to haste in their flight, the poet makes her say:

'Haste, then! No word! nor turn about to gaze
At me, as he who in the shadowy ways
Turned round to see once more the twice-lost face.'

But Orpheus was himself one of the Argonauts, and not till long after the return of the expedition was Eurydice lost to him.

10. Henry James, unsigned review, *North American Review*

October 1867, cvi, 688–92

Henry James (1843–1916), the American novelist, wrote a good deal of criticism in magazines in his early years.

The attribution of this favourable review to James is made by Leon Edel in his *Selected Letters of Henry James* (London, 1956), 50, note. In the related letter to T. S. Perry, 20 September 1867, James writes: 'For real and exquisite pleasure read Morris' *Life and Death of Jason*. It is long but fascinating, and replete with genuine beauty.'

In this poetical history of the fortunate—the unfortunate—Jason, Mr. Morris has written a book of real value. It is some time since we have met with a work of imagination of so thoroughly satisfactory a character,—a work read with an enjoyment so unalloyed and so untempered by the desire to protest and to criticise. The poetical firmament within these recent years has been all alive with unprophesied comets and meteors, many of them of extraordinary brilliancy, but most of them very rapid in their passage. Mr. Morris gives us the comfort of feeling that he is a fixed star, and that his radiance is not likely to be extinguished in a draught of wind,—after the fashion of Mr. Alexander Smith, Mr. Swinburne, and Miss Ingelow. Mr. Morris's poem is ushered into the world with a very florid birthday speech from the pen of the author of the too famous 'Poems and Ballads,'—a circumstance, we apprehend, in no small degree prejudicial to its success. But we hasten to assure all persons whom the knowledge of Mr.

Swinburne's enthusiasm may have led to mistrust the character of the work, that it has to our perception nothing in common with this gentleman's own productions, and that his article proves very little more than that his sympathies are wiser than his performance. If Mr. Morris's poem may be said to remind us of the manner of any other writer, it is simply of that of Chaucer; and to resemble Chaucer is a great safeguard against resembling Swinburne.

The Life and Death of Jason, then, is a narrative poem on a Greek subject, written in a genuine English style. With the subject all reading people are familiar, and we have no need to retrace its details. But it is perhaps not amiss to transcribe the few pregnant lines of prose into which, at the outset, Mr. Morris has condensed the argument of his poem:—

Jason the son of Æson, king of Iolchos, having come to man's estate, demanded of Pelias his father's kingdom, which he held wrongfully. But Pelias answered, that if he would bring from Colchis the golden fleece of the ram that had carried Phryxus thither, he would yield him his right. Whereon Jason sailed to Colchis in the ship Argo, with other heroes, and by means of Medea, the king's daughter, won the fleece; and carried off also Medea; and so, after many troubles, came back to Iolchos again. There, by Medea's wiles, was Pelias slain; but Jason went to Corinth, and lived with Medea happily, till he was taken with the love of Glauce, the king's daughter of Corinth, and must needs wed her; whom also Medea destroyed, and fled to Ægeus at Athens; and not long after Jason died strangely.

The style of this little fragment of prose is not an unapt measure of the author's poetical style,—quaint, but not too quaint, more Anglo-Saxon than Latin, and decidedly laconic. For in spite of the great length of his work, his manner is by no means diffuse. His story is a long one, and he wishes to do it justice; but the movement is rapid and business-like, and the poet is quite guiltless of any wanton lingering along the margin of the subject-matter,—after the manner, for instance, of Keats,—to whom, individually, however, we make this tendency no reproach. Mr. Morris's subject is immensely rich,—heavy with its richness,—and in the highest degree romantic and poetical. For the most part, of course, he found not only the great contours, but the various incidents and episodes, ready drawn to his hand; but still there was enough wanting to make a most exhaustive drain upon his ingenuity and his imagination. And not only these faculties have been brought into severe exercise, but the strictest good taste and good sense were called into play, together with a certain final gift which we hardly know how to name, and which is by no means common, even among very clever poets,—a comprehensive sense of form, of proportion, and of real completeness, without which the most brilliant efforts of the imagination are a mere agglomeration of ill-reconciled beauties. The legend of Jason is full of strangely constructed marvels and elaborate prodigies and horrors, calculated to task heavily an author's adroitness. We have so pampered and petted our sense of the ludicrous of late years, that it is quite the spoiled child of the house, and without its leave no guest can be honorably entertained. It is very true that the atmosphere of Grecian mythology is so entirely an artificial one, that we are seldom tempted to refer its weird, anomalous denizens to our standard of truth and beauty. Truth, indeed, is at once put out of the question; but one would say beforehand, that many of the creations of Greek fancy were wanting even in beauty, or at least in that ease and simplicity which has been acquired in modern times by force of culture. But habit and tradition have reconciled us to these things in their native forms, and Mr. Morris's skill reconciles us to them in his modern and composite English. The idea, for instance, of a *flying ram*, seems, to an undisciplined fancy, a not especially happy creation, nor a very promising theme for poetry; but Mr. Morris, without diminishing its native oddity, has given it an ample romantic dignity. So, again, the sowing of the dragon's teeth at Colchis, and the springing up of mutually opposed armed men, seems too complex and recondite a scene to be vividly and gracefully realized; but as it stands, it is one of the finest passages in Mr. Morris's poem. His great stumbling-block, however, we take it, was the necessity of maintaining throughout the dignity and prominence of his hero. From the moment that Medea comes into the poem, Jason falls into the second place, and keeps it to the end. She is the all-wise and all-brave helper and counsellor at Colchis, and the guardian angel of the returning journey. She saves her companions from the Circean enchantments, and she withholds them from the embraces of the Sirens. She effects the death of Pelias, and assures the successful return of the Argonauts. And finally —as a last claim upon her interest—she is slighted and abandoned by the man of her love. Without question, then, she is the central figure of the poem,—a powerful and enchanting figure,—a creature of barbarous arts, and of exquisite human passions. Jason accordingly possesses only that indirect hold upon our attention which belongs to the Virgilian Æneas; although Mr. Morris has avoided Virgil's error of now and then allowing his hero to be contemptible.

A large number, however, of far greater drawbacks than any we are able to mention could not materially diminish the powerful beauty of this fantastic legend. It is as rich in adventure as the *Odyssey*, and very much simpler. Its prime elements are of the most poetical and delightful kind. What can be more thrilling than the idea of a great boatful of warriors embarking upon dreadful seas, not for pleasure, nor for conquest, nor for any material advantage, but for the simple recovery of a jealously watched, magically guarded relic? There is in the character of the object of their quest something heroically unmarketable, or at least unavailable. But of course the story owes a vast deal to its episodes, and these have lost nothing in Mr. Morris's hands. One of the most beautiful—the well-known adventure of Hylas—occurs at the very outset. The beautiful young man, during a halt of the ship, wanders inland through the forest, and, passing beside a sylvan stream, is espied and incontinently loved by the water nymphs, who forthwith 'detach' one of their number to work his seduction. This young lady assumes the disguise and speech of a Northern princess, clad in furs, and in this character sings to her victim 'a sweet song, sung not yet to any man.' Very sweet and truly lyrical it is, like all the songs scattered through Mr. Morris's narrative. We are, indeed, almost in doubt whether the most beautiful passages in the poem do not occur in the series of songs in the fourteenth book. The ship has already touched at the island of Circe, and the sailors, thanks to the earnest warnings of Medea, have abstained from setting foot on the fatal shore; while Medea has, in turn, been warned by the enchantress against the allurements of the Sirens. As soon as the ship draws nigh, these fair beings begin to utter their irresistible notes. All eyes are turned lovingly on the shore, the rowers' charmed muscles relax, and the ship drifts landward. But Medea exhorts and entreats her companions to preserve their course. Jason himself is not untouched, as Mr. Morris delicately tells us,—'a moment Jason gazed.' But Orpheus smites his lyre before it is too late, and stirs the languid blood of his comrades. The Sirens strike their harps amain, and a conflict of song arises. The Sirens sing of the cold, the glittering, the idle delights of their submarine homes; while Orpheus tells of the warm and pastoral landscapes of Greece. We have no space for quotation; of course Orpheus carries the day. But the finest and most delicate practical sense is shown in the alternation of the two lyrical arguments,—the soulless sweetness of the one, and the deep human richness of the other. There is throughout Mr. Morris's poem a great unity and evenness of excellence, which make selection and quotation difficult; but of impressive touches in our reading we noticed a very great number. We content ourselves with mentioning a single one. When Jason has sown his bag of dragon's teeth at Colchis, and the armed fighters have sprang up along the furrows, and under the spell contrived by Medea have torn each other to death:—

> One man was left, alive but wounded sore,
> Who, staring round about and seeing no more
> His brothers' spears against him, fixed his eyes
> *Upon the queller of those mysteries.*
> *Then dreadfully they gleamed, and with no word,*
> *He tottered towards him with uplifted sword.*
> *But scarce he made three paces down the field,*
> *Ere chill death seized his heart, and on his shield*
> *Clattering he fell.*

We have not spoken of Mr. Morris's versification nor of his vocabulary. We have only room to say that, to our perception, the first in its facility and harmony, and the second in its abundance and studied simplicity, leave nothing to be desired. There are of course faults and errors in his poem, but there are none that are not trivial and easily pardoned in the light of the fact that he has given us a work of consummate art and of genuine beauty. He has foraged in a treasure-house; he has visited the ancient world, and come back with a massive cup of living Greek wine. His project was no light task, but he has honorably fulfilled it. He has enriched the language with a narrative poem which we are sure that the public will not suffer to fall into the ranks of honored but uncherished works,—objects of vague and sapient reference,—but will continue to read and to enjoy. In spite of its length, the interest of the story never flags, and as a work of art it never ceases to be pure. To the jaded intellects of the present moment, distracted with the strife of creeds and the conflict of theories, it opens a glimpse into a world where they will be called upon neither to choose, to criticise, nor to believe, but simply to feel, to look, and to listen.

11. A novelist's view of the Morrises

March 1869

A letter from Henry James to Alice James; from *The Letters of Henry James*, edited by Percy Lubbock, 2 vols (London, 1920), 16–19.

But yesterday, my dear old sister, was my crowning day—seeing as how I spent the greater part of it in the house of Mr. Wm. Morris, Poet. Fitly to tell the tale, I should need a fresh pen, paper and spirits. A few hints must suffice. To begin with, I breakfasted, by way of a change, with the Nortons, along with Mr. Sam Ward, who has just arrived, and Mr. Aubrey de Vere, *tu sais*, the Catholic poet, a pleasant honest old man and very much less high-flown than his name. He tells good stories in a light natural way. After a space I came home and remained until 4½ p.m., when I had given rendez-vous to C.N. and ladies at Mr. Morris's door, they going by appointment to see his shop and C. having written to say he would bring me. Morris lives on the same premises as his shop, in Queen's Square, Bloomsbury, an antiquated ex-fashionable region, smelling strong of the last century, with a hoary effigy of Queen Anne in the middle. Morris's poetry, you see, is only his sub-trade. To begin with, he is a manufacturer of stained glass windows, tiles, ecclesiastical and medieval tapestry, altar-cloths, and in fine everything quaint, archaic, pre-Raphaelite—and I may add, exquisite. Of course his business is small and may be carried on in his house: the things he makes are so handsome, rich and expensive (besides being articles of the very last luxury) that his *fabrique* can't be on a very large scale. But everything he has and does is superb and beautiful. But more curious than anything is himself. He designs with his own head and hands all the figures and patterns used in his glass and tapestry, and furthermore works the latter, stitch by stitch, with his own fingers—aided by those of his wife and little girls. Oh, ma chère, such a wife! *Je n'en reviens pas*—she haunts me still. A figure cut out of a missal—out of one of Rossetti's or Hunt's pictures—to say

77

this gives but a faint idea of her, because when such an image puts on flesh and blood, it is an apparition of fearful and wonderful intensity. It's hard to say whether she's a grand synthesis of all the pre-Raphaelite pictures ever made—or they a 'keen analysis' of her—whether she's an original or a copy. In either case she is a wonder. Imagine a tall lean woman in a long dress of some dead purple stuff, guiltless of hoops (or of anything else, I should say,) with a mass of crisp black hair heaped into great wavy projections on each of her temples, a thin pale face, a pair of strange sad, deep, dark Swinburnian eyes, with great thick black oblique brows, joined in the middle and tucking themselves away under her hair, a mouth like the 'Oriana' in our illustrated Tennyson, a long neck, without any collar, and in lieu thereof some dozen strings of outlandish beads—in fine complete. On the wall was a large nearly full-length portrait of her by Rossetti, so strange and unreal that if you hadn't seen her you'd pronounce it a distempered vision, but in fact an extremely good likeness. After dinner (we stayed to dinner, Miss Grace, Miss S. S. and I,) Morris read us one of his unpublished poems, from the second series of his un-'Earthly Paradise,' and his wife, having a bad toothache, lay on the sofa, with her hand-kerchief to her face. There was something very quaint and remote from our actual life, it seemed to me, in the whole scene: Morris reading in his flowing antique numbers a legend of prodigies and terrors (the story of Bellerophon, it was), around us all the picturesque bric-a-brac of the apartment (every article of furniture literally a 'specimen' of something or other,) and in the corner this dark silent medieval woman with her medieval toothache. Morris himself is extremely pleasant and quite different from his wife. He impressed me most agreeably. He is short, burly, corpulent, very careless and unfinished in his dress, and looks a little like B. G. Hosmer, if you can imagine B. G. infinitely magnified and fortified. He has a very loud voice and a nervous restless manner and a perfectly unaffected and business-like address. His talk indeed is wonderfully to the point and remarkable for clear good sense. He said no one thing that I remember, but I was struck with the very good judgment shown in everything he uttered. He's an extraordinary example, in short, of a delicate sensitive genius and taste, saved by a perfectly healthy body and temper. All his designs are quite as good (or rather nearly so) as his poetry: altogether it was a long rich sort of visit, with a strong peculiar flavour of its own.

THE EARTHLY PARADISE

1868–70

Volume I (consisting of Parts 1 and 2) appeared in 1868, Volume II (Part 3) in December 1869 (dated 1870), and Volume III (Part 4) in December 1870. Some of the reviews are therefore of parts of the poem; many of them also discuss Morris's earlier poems. For discussion, see Introduction, pp. 9–12.

12. Walter Pater, unsigned review, *Westminster Review*

October 1868, xc, 300–12

Walter Pater (1839–94) was a Fellow of Brasenose College, Oxford, and was to become the foremost English exponent of the aesthetic attitude. His review is of great interest both for its discussion of Morris's poems in the context of Romanticism, and for its expression of Pater's own preoccupations. The final section of the review is better known in its later use as the 'Conclusion' to *The Renaissance* (1873)—withdrawn from the second edition as likely to mislead the young, but later restored. Its form in the Morris review is rather more subversive of orthodox Victorian morality.

Pater published a revised form of the review, without the concluding section, as 'Aesthetic Poetry', in the first edition of *Appreciations* (1889), but it does not appear in later editions.

This poetry is neither a mere reproduction of Greek or mediæval life or poetry, nor a disguised reflex of modern sentiment. The atmosphere on which its effect depends belongs to no actual form of life or simple form of poetry. Greek poetry, mediæval or modern poetry, projects

79

above the realities of its time a world in which the forms of things are transfigured. Of that world this new poetry takes possession, and sublimates beyond it another still fainter and more spectral, which is literally an artificial or 'earthly paradise.' It is a finer ideal, extracted from what in relation to any actual world is already an ideal. Like some strange second flowering after date, it renews on a more delicate type the poetry of a past age, but must not be confounded with it. The secret of the enjoyment of it is that inversion of home-sickness known to some, that incurable thirst for the sense of escape, which no actual form of life satisfies, no poetry even, if it be merely simple and spontaneous. It is this which in these poems defines the temperament or personality of the workman.

The writings of the romantic school mark a transition not so much from the pagan to the mediæval ideal, as from a lower to a higher degree of passion in literature. The end of the eighteenth century, swept by vast disturbing currents, experienced an excitement of spirit of which one note was a reaction against an outworn classicalism severed not more from nature than from the genuine motives of ancient art; and a return to true Hellenism was as much a part of this reaction as the sudden pre-occupation with things mediæval. The mediæval tendency is in Goethe's *Goetz von Berlichingen*, the Hellenic in his *Iphigenie*. At first this mediævalism was superficial. Adventure, romance in the poorest sense, grotesque individualism—that is one element in mediæval poetry, and with it alone Scott and Goethe dealt. Beyond them were the two other elements of the mediæval spirit; its mystic religion at its apex in Dante and Saint Louis, and its mystic passion, passing here and there into the great romantic loves of rebellious flesh, of Lancelot and Abelard. That stricter, imaginative mediævalism which recreates the mind of the middle age, so that the form, the presentment grows outward from within, came later with Victor Hugo in France, with Heine in Germany.

The *Defence of Guenevere: and Other Poems*, published ten years ago, are a refinement upon this later, profounder mediævalism. The poem which gives its name to the volume is a thing tormented and awry with passion, like the body of Guenevere defending herself from the charge of adultery, and the accent falls in strange, unwonted places with the effect of a great cry. These Arthurian legends, pre-Christian in their origin, yield all their sweetness only in a Christian atmosphere. What is characteristic in them is the strange suggestion of a deliberate choice between Christ and a rival lover. That religion shades into

sensuous love, and sensuous love into religion, has been often seen;
it is the experience of Rousseau as well as of the Christian mystics.
The Christianity of the middle age made way among a people whose
loss was in the life of the senses only by the possession of an idol, the
beautiful idol of the Latin hymn-writers, who for one moral or
spiritual sentiment have a hundred sensuous images. Only by the
inflaming influence of such idols can any religion compete with the
presence of the fleshly lover. And so in these imaginative loves, in their
highest expression the Provençal poetry, it is a rival religion with a
new rival cultus that we see. Coloured through and through with
Christian sentiment, they are rebels against it. The rejection of one
idolatry for the other is never lost sight of. The jealousy of that other
lover, for whom these words and images and strange ways of sentiment were first devised, is the secret here of a triumphant colour and
heat. It is the mood of the cloister taking a new direction, and winning
so a later space of life it never anticipated. Who knows whether,
when the simple belief in them has faded away, the most cherished
sacred writings may not for the first time exercise their highest influence as the most delicate amorous poetry in the world?

Hereon, as before in the cloister, so now in the chateau, the reign of
reverie set in. The idolatry of the cloister knew that mood thoroughly,
and had sounded all its stops. For in that idolatry the idol was absent
or veiled, not limited to one supreme plastic form like Zeus at Olympia
or Athena in the Acropolis, but distracted, as in a fever dream, into a
thousand symbols and reflections. Quite in the way of one who handles
the older sorceries, the Church has a thousand charms to make the
absent near. Like the woman in the idyll of Theocritus—

$$\ldots\ldots\ \text{ἕλκε τὺ τῆνον ἐμὸν ποτὶ δῶμα τὸν ἄνδρα,}^{1}$$

is the cry of all her bizarre rites. Into this kingdom of reverie, and with
it into a paradise of ambitious refinements, the earthly love enters, and
becomes a prolonged somnambulism. Of religion it learns the art of
directing towards an imaginary object sentiments whose natural
direction is towards objects of sense. Hence a love defined by the
absence of the beloved, choosing to be without hope, protesting against
all lower uses of love, barren, extravagant, antinomian. It is the love
which is incompatible with marriage, for the chevalier who never
comes, of the serf for the chatelaine, the rose for the nightingale, of

---

1 Draw home to me that man of mine. *Idyll*, ii, 17.

Rudel for the Lady of Tripoli. Another element of extravagance came in with the feudal spirit: Provençal love is full of the very forms of vassalage. To be the servant of love, to have offended, to taste the subtle luxury of chastisement, of reconciliation—the religious spirit, too, knows that, and meets just there, as in Rousseau, the delicacies of the earthly love. Here, under this strange complex of conditions, as in some medicated air, exotic flowers of sentiment expand, the impression of this delirium been conveyed as by Victor Hugo in *Notre Dame de Paris*. The strangest creations of sleep seem here, by some appalling licence, to cross the limit of the dawn. The English poet too has learned the secret. He has diffused through 'King Arthur's Tomb' the maddening white glare of the sun, and tyranny of the moon, not tender and far-off, but close down—the sorcerer's moon, large and feverish. The colouring is intricate and delirious, as of 'scarlet lilies.' The influence of summer is like a poison in one's blood, with a sudden bewildered sickening of life and all things. In 'Galahad: a Mystery,' the frost of Christmas night on the chapel stones acts as a strong narcotic; a sudden shrill ringing pierces through the numbness; a voice proclaims that the Grail has gone forth through the great forest. It is in the 'Blue Closet' that this delirium reaches its height with a singular beauty, reserved perhaps for the enjoyment of the few:—

How long ago was it, how long ago,
He came to this tower with hands full of snow?
'Kneel down, O love Louise, kneel down,' he said,
And sprinkled the dusty snow over my head.
He watch'd the snow melting, it ran through my hair,
Ran over my shoulders, white shoulders, and bare.
'I cannot weep for thee, poor love Louise,
For my tears are all hidden deep under the seas.
In a gold and blue casket she keeps all my tears;
But my eyes are no longer blue, as in old years;
For they grow grey with time, grow small and dry—
I am so feeble now, would I might die.'
Will he come back again, or is he dead?
O! is he sleeping, my scarf round his head?
Or did they strangle him as he lay there,
With the long scarlet scarf I used to wear?
Only I pray thee, Lord, let him come here!
Both his soul and his body to me are most dear.
Dear Lord, that loves me, I wait to receive
Either body or spirit this wild Christmas-eve.

A passion of which the outlets are sealed, begets a tension of nerve, in which the sensible world comes to one with a reinforced brilliance and relief—all redness is turned into blood, all water into tears. Hence a wild, convulsed sensuousness in the poetry of the middle age, in which the things of nature begin to play a strange delirious part. Of the things of nature the mediæval mind had a deep sense; but its sense of them was not objective, no real escape to the world without one. The aspects and motions of nature only reinforced its prevailing mood, and were in conspiracy with one's own brain against one. A single sentiment invaded the world; everything was infused with a motive drawn from the soul. The amorous poetry of Provence, making the starling and the swallow its messengers, illustrates the whole attitude of nature in this electric atmosphere, bent as by miracle or magic to the service of human passion.

The most popular and gracious form of Provençal poetry was the *nocturn*, sung by the lover at night at the door or under the window of his mistress. These songs were of different kinds, according to the hour at which they were intended to be sung. Some were to be sung at midnight—songs inviting to sleep, the *serena*, or *serenade*; others at break of day—waking songs, the *aube*, or *aubade*.* This waking song is put sometimes into the mouth of a comrade of the lover, who plays sentinel during the night, to watch for and announce the dawn; sometimes into the mouth of one of the lovers, who are about to separate. A modification of it is familiar to us all in *Romeo and Juliet*, where the lovers debate whether the song they hear is of the nightingale or the lark; the aubade, with the two other great forms of love-poetry then floating in the world, the sonnet and the epithalamium, being here refined, heightened, and inwoven into the structure of the play. Those, in whom what Rousseau calls *les frayeurs nocturnes*[1] are constitutional, know what splendour they give to the things of the morning; and how there comes something of relief from physical pain with the first white film in the sky. The middle age knew those terrors in all their forms; and these songs of the morning win hence a strange tenderness and effect. The crown of the English poet's book is one of these songs of the dawn:—

> Pray but one prayer for me 'twixt thy closed lips,
> Think but one thought of me up in the stars.

---

* Fauriel's *Histoire de la Poésie Provençale*. Tome 2, ch. xviii.
[1] Nocturnal fears.

The summer-night waneth, the morning light slips,
Faint and grey 'twixt the leaves of the aspen,
betwixt the cloud-bars,
That are patiently waiting there for the dawn:
Patient and colourless, though Heaven's gold
Waits to float through them along with the sun.
Far out in the meadows, above the young corn,
The heavy elms wait, and restless and cold
The uneasy wind rises; the roses are dun;
Through the long twilight they pray for the dawn,
Round the lone house in the midst of the corn.
Speak but one word to me over the corn,
Over the tender, bow'd locks of the corn.

It is the very soul of the bridegroom which goes forth to the bride;
inanimate things are longing with him; all the sweetness of the
imaginative loves of the middle age, with a superadded spirituality of
touch all its own, is in that!

The *Defence of Guenevere* was published in 1858; the *Life and Death of
Jason* in 1867; and the change of manner wrought in the interval is
entire, it is almost a revolt. Here there is no delirium or illusion, no
experiences of mere soul while the body and the bodily senses sleep or
wake with convulsed intensity at the prompting of imaginative love;
but rather the great primary passions under broad daylight as of the
pagan Veronese. This simplification interests us not merely for the
sake of an individual poet—full of charm as he is—but chiefly because
it explains through him a transition which, under many forms, is one
law of the life of the human spirit, and of which what we call the
Renaissance is only a supreme instance. Just so the monk in his cloister,
through the 'open vision,' open only to the spirit, divined, aspired to
and at last apprehended a better daylight, but earthly, open only to
the senses. Complex and subtle interests, which the mind spins for
itself may occupy art and poetry or our own spirits for a time; but
sooner or later they come back with a sharp rebound to the simple
elementary passions—anger, desire, regret, pity and fear—and what
corresponds to them in the sensuous world—bare, abstract fire, water,
air, tears, sleep, silence—and what De Quincey has called the 'glory of
motion.'

This reaction from dreamlight to daylight gives, as always happens,
a strange power in dealing with morning and the things of the morning. Think of this most lovely waking with the rain on one's face—

(Iris comes to Argus as he sleeps; a rainbow, when he wakes, is to be
the pledge she has been present:—)

> Then he, awaking in the morning cold,
> A sprinkle of fine rain felt on his face,
> And leaping to his feet, in that wild place,
> Looked round and saw the morning sunlight throw
> Across the world the many-coloured bow,
> And trembling knew that the high gods, indeed,
> Had sent the messenger unto their need.

Not less is this Hellenist of the middle age master of dreams, of sleep
and the desire of sleep—sleep in which no one walks, restorer of
childhood to men—dreams, not like Galahad's or Guenevere's, but full
of happy, childish wonder as in the earlier world. It is a world in
which the centaur and the ram with the fleece of gold are conceivable.
The song sung always claims to be sung for the first time. There are
hints at a language common to birds and beasts and men. Everywhere
there is an impression of surprise, as of people first waking from the
golden age, at fire, snow, wine, the touch of water as one swims, the
salt taste of the sea. And this simplicity at first hand is a strange contrast to the sought-out simplicity of Wordsworth. Desire here is towards the body of nature for its own sake, not because a soul is divined
through it.

And yet it is one of the charming anachronisms of a poet, who,
while he handles an ancient subject, never becomes an antiquarian,
but vitalizes his subject by keeping it always close to himself, that
between whiles we have a sense of English scenery as from an eye
well practised under Wordsworth's influence, in the song of the brown
river-bird among the willows, the casement half opened on summer-
nights, the

> Noise of bells, such as in moonlight lanes
> Rings from the grey team on the market night.

Nowhere but in England is there such a nation of birds, the fern-owl,
the water-hen, the thrush in a hundred sweet variations, the ger-
falcon, the kestrel, the starling, the pea-fowl; birds heard from the field
by the townsman down in the streets at dawn; doves everywhere,
pink-footed, grey-winged, flitting about the temple, troubled by the
temple incense, trapped in the snow. The sea-touches are not less sharp
and firm, surest of effect in places where river and sea, salt and fresh
waves, conflict.

All this is in that wonderful fourteenth book, the book of the Syrens. The power of an artist will sometimes remain inactive over us, the spirit of his work, however much one sees of it, be veiled, till on a sudden we are *found* by one revealing example of it which makes all he did precious. It is so with this fourteenth book of *Jason*. There is a tranquil level of perfection in the poem, by which in certain moods, or for certain minds, the charm of it might escape. For such the book of the Syrens is a revealing example of the poet's work. The book opens with a glimpse of white bodies, crowned and girt with gold, moving far-off on the sand of a little bay. It comes to men nearing home, yet so longing for rest that they might well lie down before they reach it. So the wise Medea prompts Orpheus to plead with the Argonauts against the Syrens,—

> Sweetly they sang, and still the answer came
> Piercing and clear from him, as bursts the flame
> From out the furnace in the moonless night;
> Yet, as their words are no more known aright
> Through lapse of many ages, and no man
> Can any more across the waters wan,
> Behold those singing women of the sea,
> Once more I pray you all to pardon me,
> If with my feeble voice and harsh I sing
> From what dim memories may chance to cling
> About men's hearts, of lovely things once sung
> Beside the sea, while yet the world was young.

Then literally like an echo from the Greek world, heard across so great a distance only as through some miraculous calm, subdued in colour and cadence, the ghosts of passionate song, come those matchless lyrics.

In handling a subject of Greek legend, anything in the way of an actual revival must always be impossible. Such vain antiquarianism is a waste of the poet's power. The composite experience of all the ages is part of each one of us; to deduct from that experience, to obliterate any part of it, to come face to face with the people of a past age, as if the middle age, the Renaissance, the eighteenth century had not been, is as impossible as to become a little child, or enter again into the womb and be born. But though it is not possible to repress a single phase of that humanity, which, because we live and move and have our being in the life of humanity, makes us what we are; it is possible to isolate such a phase, to throw it into relief, to be divided against ourselves in zeal for it, as we may hark back to some choice space of our own individual life. We cannot conceive the age; we can conceive the element it has contributed to our culture; we can treat the subjects of the age bringing that into relief. Such an attitude towards Greece, aspiring to but never actually reaching its way of conceiving life, is what is possible for art.

The modern poet or artist who treats in this way a classical story comes very near, if not to the Hellenism of Homer, yet to that of the middle age, the Hellenism of Chaucer. No writer on the Renaissance has hitherto cared much for this exquisite early light of it. Afterwards the Renaissance takes its side, becomes exaggerated and facile. But the choice life of the human spirit is always under mixed lights, and in mixed situations; when it is not too sure of itself, is still expectant, girt up to leap forward to the promise. Such a situation there was in that earliest return from the overwrought spiritualities of the middle age to the earlier, more ancient life of the senses; and for us the most attractive form of classical story is the monk's conception of it, when he escapes from the sombre legend of his cloister to that true light. The fruits of this mood, which, divining more than it understands, infuses into the figures of the Christian legend some subtle reminiscence of older gods, or into the story of Cupid and Psyche that passionate stress of spirit which the world owes to Christianity, have still to be gathered up when the time comes.

And so, before we leave *Jason*, a word must be said about its mediævalisms, delicate inconsistencies which, coming in a Greek poem, bring into this white dawn thoughts of the delirious night just over and make one's sense of relief deeper. The opening of the fourth book describes the embarkation of the Argonauts; as in a dream the scene shifts and we go down from Iolchos to the sea through a pageant of the fourteenth century in some French or Italian town. The gilded vanes on the spires, the bells ringing in the towers, the trellis of roses at the window, the close planted with apple-trees, the grotesque under-croft with its close-set pillars, change by a single touch the air of these Greek cities and we are at Glastonbury by the tomb of Arthur. The nymph in furred raiment who seduces Hylas is conceived frankly in the spirit of Teutonic romance; her song is of a garden enclosed, such as that with which the glass-stainer of the middle ages surrounds the mystic bride of the song of songs. Medea herself has a hundred touches of the mediæval sorceress, the sorceress of the Streckelberg or the

87

Blocksberg; her mystic changes are Christabel's. Here again is an incident straight out of the middle age,—

> But, when all hushed and still the palace grew,
> She put her gold robes off, and on her drew
> A dusky gown, and with a wallet small
> And cutting wood-knife girt herself withal,
> And from her dainty chamber softly passed
> Through stairs and corridors, until at last
> She came down to a gilded watergate,
> Which with a golden key she opened straight,
> And swiftly stept into a little boat,
> And, pushing off from shore, began to float
> Adown the stream, and with her tender hands
> And half-bared arms, the wonder of all lands,
> Rowed strongly through the starlit gusty night.

It is precisely this effect, this grace of Hellenism relieved against the sorrow of the middle age, which forms the chief motive of *The Earthly Paradise*, with an exquisite dexterity the two threads of sentiment are here interwoven and contrasted. A band of adventurers sets out from Norway, most northerly of northern lands, where the plague is raging, and the host-bell is continually ringing as they carry the sacrament to the sick. Even in Mr. Morris's earliest poems snatches of the sweet French tongue had always come with something of Hellenic blitheness and grace. And now it is below the very coast of France, through the fleet of Edward III., among the painted sails of the middle age, that we pass to a reserved fragment of Greece, which by some θεία τύχη[1] lingers on in the Western Sea into the middle age. There the stories of *The Earthly Paradise* are told, Greek story and romantic alternating; and for the crew of the 'Rose Garland' coming across the sins of the earlier world with the sign of the cross and drinking Rhine wine in Greece, the two worlds of sentiment are confronted.

We have become so used to austerity and concentration in some noble types of modern poetry, that it is easy to mistake the lengthiness of this new poem. Yet here mere mass is itself the first condition of an art which deals with broad atmospheric effects. The water is not less medicinal, not less gifted with virtues, because a few drops of it are without effect; it is water to bathe and swim in. The songs 'The Apology to the Reader,' the month-interludes, especially those of April and May, which are worthy of Shakespeare, detach themselves by their

1 Divine chance.

concentrated sweetness from the rest of the book. Partly because in perfect story-telling like this the manner rises and falls with the story itself, 'Atalanta's Race,' 'The Man born to be King,' 'The Story of Cupid and Psyche,' and in 'The Doom of King Acrisius,' the episode of Danae and the shower of gold, have in a pre-eminent degree what is characteristic of the whole book, the loveliness of things newly washed with fresh water; and this clarity and chasteness, mere qualities here of an exquisite art, remind one that the effectual preserver of all purity is perfect taste.

One characteristic of the pagan spirit these new poems have which is on their surface—the continual suggestion, pensive or passionate, of the shortness of life; this is contrasted with the bloom of the world and gives new seduction to it; the sense of death and the desire of beauty; the desire of beauty quickened by the sense of death. '*Arriéré!*' you say, 'here in a tangible form we have the defect of all poetry like this. The modern world is in possession of truths; what but a passing smile can it have for a kind of poetry which, assuming artistic beauty of form to be an end in itself, passes by those truths and the living in-terests which are connected with them, to spend a thousand cares in telling once more these pagan fables as if it had but to choose between a more and a less beautiful shadow?' It is a strange transition from the earthly paradise to the sad-coloured world of abstract philosophy. But let us accept the challenge; let us see what modern philosophy, when it is sincere, really does say about human life and the truth we can attain in it, and the relation of this to the desire of beauty.

To regard all things and principles of things as inconstant modes or fashions has more and more become the tendency of modern thought. Let us begin with that which is without,—our physical life. Fix upon it in one of its more exquisite intervals—the moment, for instance, of delicious recoil from the flood of water in summer heat. What is the whole physical life in that moment but a combination of natural elements to which science gives their names? But those elements, phosphorus and lime, and delicate fibres, are present not in the human body alone; we detect them in places most remote from it. Our physical life is a perpetual motion of them—the passage of the blood, the wasting and repairing of the lenses of the eye, the modification of the tissues of the brain by every ray of light and sound—processes which science reduces to simpler and more elementary forces. Like the elements of which we are composed, the action of these forces extends beyond us; it rusts iron and ripens corn. Far out on every side of us these elements are broadcast, driven by many forces; and birth and gesture and death and the springing of violets from the grave are but a few out of ten thousand resulting combinations. That clear, perpetual outline of face and limb is but an image of ours under which we group them—a design in a web the actual threads of which pass out beyond it. This at least of flame-like our life has, that it is but the concurrence renewed from moment to moment of forces parting sooner or later on their ways.

Or if we begin with the inward world of thought and feeling, the whirlpool is still more rapid, the flame more eager and devouring. There it is no longer the gradual darkening of the eye and fading of colour from the wall, the movement of the shore side, where the water flows down indeed, though in apparent rest, but the race of the mid-stream, a drift of momentary acts of sight and passion and thought. At first sight experience seems to bury us under a flood of external objects, pressing upon us with a sharp, importunate reality, calling us out of ourselves in a thousand forms of action. But when reflection begins to act upon those objects they are dissipated under its influence, the cohesive force is suspended like a trick of magic, each object is loosed into a group of impressions, colour, odour, texture, in the mind of the observer. And if we continue to dwell on this world, not of objects in the solidity with which language invests them, but of impressions unstable, flickering, inconsistent, which burn, and are extinguished with our consciousness of them, it contracts still further, the whole scope of observation is dwarfed to the narrow chamber of the individual mind. Experience, already reduced to a swarm of impressions, is ringed round for each one of us by that thick wall of personality through which no real voice has ever pierced on its way to us, or from us to that, which we can only conjecture to be without. Every one of those impressions is the impression of an individual in his isolation, each mind keeping as a solitary prisoner its own dream of a world.

Analysis goes a step further still, and tells us that those impressions of the individual to which, for each one of us, experience dwindles down, are in perpetual flight; that each of them is limited by time, and that as time is infinitely divisible, each of them is infinitely divisible also, all that is actual in it being a single moment, gone while we try to apprehend it, of which it may ever be more truly said that it has ceased to be than it is. To such a tremulous wisp constantly reforming itself on the stream, to a single sharp impression, with a sense in it, a relic more or less fleeting, of such moments gone by, what is real in our life fines itself down. It is with the movement, the passage and dissolution of impressions, images, sensations, that analysis leaves off, that continual vanishing away, that strange perpetual weaving and unweaving of ourselves.

Such thoughts seem desolate at first; at times all the bitterness of life seems concentrated in them. They bring the image of one washed out beyond the bar in a sea at ebb, losing even his personality, as the elements of which he is composed pass into new combinations. Struggling, as he must, to save himself, it is himself that he loses at every moment.

Philosophiren, says Novalis, *ist dephlegmatisiren, vivificiren*.[1] The service of philosophy, and of religion and culture as well, to the human spirit, is to startle it into a sharp and eager observation. Every moment some form grows perfect in hand or face; some tone on the hills or sea is choicer than the rest; some mood of passion or insight or intellectual excitement is irresistibly real and attractive for us for that moment only. Not the fruit of experience but experience itself is the end. A counted number of pulses only is given to us of a variegated, dramatic life. How may we see in them all that is to be seen in them by the finest senses? How can we pass most swiftly from point to point, and be present always at the focus where the greatest number of vital forces unite in their purest energy?

To burn always with this hard gem-like flame, to maintain this ecstasy, is success in life. Failure is to form habits; for habit is relative to a stereotyped world; meantime it is only the roughness of the eye that makes any two things, persons, situations—seem alike. While all melts under our feet, we may well catch at any exquisite passion, or any contribution to knowledge that seems by a lifted horizon to set the spirit free for a moment, or any stirring of the senses, strange dyes, strange flowers and curious odours, or work of the artist's hands, or the face of one's friend. Not to discriminate every moment some passionate attitude in those about us and in the brilliance of their gifts some tragic dividing of forces on their ways, is on this short day of frost and sun to sleep before evening. With this sense of the splendour of our experience and of its awful brevity, gathering all we are into one desperate effort to see and touch, we shall hardly have time to make theories about the things we see and touch. What we have to do is

---

[1] To philosophize is to get rid of apathy, to bring to life.

to be for ever curiously testing opinion and courting new impressions, never acquiescing in a facile orthodoxy of Comte or of Hegel or of our own. Theories, religious or philosophical ideas, as points of view, instruments of criticism, may help us to gather up what might otherwise pass unregarded by us. '*La philosophie*,' says Victor Hugo, '*c'est le microscope de la pensée.*'[1] The theory or idea or system which requires of us the sacrifice of any part of this experience, in consideration of some interest into which we cannot enter, or some abstract morality we have not identified with ourselves, or what is only conventional, has no real claim upon us.

One of the most beautiful places in the writings of Rousseau is that in the sixth book of the *Confessions*, where he describes the awakening in him of the literary sense. An undefinable taint of death had always clung about him, and now in early manhood he believed himself stricken by mortal disease. He asked himself how he might make as much as possible of the interval that remained; and he was not biassed by anything in his previous life when he decided that it must be by intellectual excitement, which he found in the clear, fresh writings of Voltaire. Well, we are all *condamnés*,[2] as Victor Hugo somewhere says: we have an interval and then we cease to be. Some spend this interval in listlessness, some in high passions, the wisest in art and song. For our one chance is in expanding that interval, in getting as many pulsations as possible into the given time. High passions give one this quickened sense of life, ecstasy and sorrow of love, political or religious enthusiasm, or the 'enthusiasm of humanity.' Only, be sure it is passion, that it does yield you this fruit of a quickened, multiplied consciousness. Of this wisdom, the poetic passion, the desire of beauty, the love of art for art's sake, has most; for art comes to you professing frankly to give nothing but the highest quality to your moments as they pass, and simply for those moments' sake.

[1] Philosophy is the microscope of thought.
[2] Condemned (to death).

13. Alfred Austin, unsigned article, *Temple Bar*

November 1869, xxvii, 45–51

Alfred Austin (1835–1913) was a minor poet and literary journalist who was to become Poet Laureate in 1896.

Austin contributed a series of articles to *Temple Bar* under the title 'The Poetry of the Period,' stressing the weaknesses of contemporary poetry but attributing these to historical circumstance. The omitted first part of the present article dealt with Matthew Arnold. The articles were published in book form as *The Poetry of the Period* in 1870.

For Morris's comments on the article, see Introduction, p. 3.

Turn we to the singer of, perhaps, the most unvarying sweetness and sustained tenderness of soul that ever caressed the chords of the lyre. Whom can we mean, if not Mr. William Morris, the author of *The Life and Death of Jason*, and *The Earthly Paradise*? Even the critic, accustomed to grasp frail things firmly, almost shrinks from handling these exquisite poems with any but the lightest touch, and in turning them to the light, is fain to finger them as one does some beautiful fragile vase, the fruit of all that is at once simple and subtle in human love and ingenuity. Under a blossoming thorn, stretched 'neath some umbrageous beech, or sheltered from the glare of noon by some fern-crested Devonshire cliff, with lazy summer sea-waves breaking at one's feet—such were the fitting hour and mood in which—criticism all forgot—to drink in the honeyed rhythm of this melodious storier. Such has been our happy lot; and we lay before this giver of dainty things thanks which even the absence of all personal familiarity cannot restrain from being expressed affectionately. But if we are to persist in our task—if we are really to understand the 'Poetry of the Period,' we must needs lay aside for awhile the delicacy of mere gratitude, and attempt some more genuine estimate of Mr. Morris's poems than is implied in the fervent acknowledgment of their winsome beauty.

Delightful as a writer standing by himself and on his own merits, he is invaluable to us when considered along with the other writers whose precise station and significance in poetical literature we have striven to discover: invaluable when we apply to him the test already applied to them, and inquire how comes it that his muse is such as she is, and no other and no greater?

For in Mr. Morris is plain and obvious what in Mr. Tennyson, Mr. Swinburne, and Mr. Arnold has to be made so by some little examination, unravelling, and exegesis on the part of the critic. They halt infirmly and irresolutely between two currents, two influences, two themes. Mr. Morris's poetical allegiance is undivided. Now lured to sing of the Golden Year, now of Œnone—now fancying, as in Aylmer's Field, that a poem of value can be constructed out of the tritest and most threadbare of modern incidents, and now flying back across the centuries in the hope that King Arthur and his Knights may yield more enduring material for the texture of his strains—the Laureate has alternately courted the past and the future, without ever once being able to satisfy our, and, we presume, his own, ineradicable longings for a great contemporaneous poem. In Mr. Swinburne, endowed as he is with more fire and less skill, the results of these conflicting influences are far more apparent, and he is in turns coldly classical and effusively and erotically modern—modern, as of to-day. When we pass Mr. Arnold, we find him not only likewise a prey to this inevitable distraction—this sundering of the poet's soul in twain, this irreconcileable combat for it between the past and the future, because the present is not strong enough to hold it against the claims of either; but we see him conscious of the raging struggle of which he is the subject and the victim, and conscious whence is derived his impotence, and that of his peers, to wreak full undivided self on song, and produce a great poet linked for all time with a great period. In his own words, he

> Wanders between two worlds: one dead,
> The other powerless to be born.

Now, in Mr. Morris we have nothing of this. He too, like Mr. Arnold, has taken the measure of the age in which, whatever he will do this side the 'cold straight house,' must be done; but, unlike Mr. Arnold, he has cut himself off from all its active influences, compounded of disgust, sanguineness, impatience, and despondency, and has surrendered himself wholly to the retrospective tendency of his time, which, when taken by itself, is the most pathetic and poetical proclivity of which the time is capable. He ignores the present, and his eyelids close with a quiet sadness if you bid him explore the future. He has no power, he says, to sing of heaven or hell. He cannot make quick-coming death a little thing; neither for his words shall we forget our tears. His verses have no power, he candidly confesses, to bear the heavy trouble and bewildering care that weigh down the earners of bread. All he can do is to sing of names remembered, which, precisely because they are not living, can ne'er be dead. He finds no life in anything living, in anything around and about him; and he feels no impulse to strive vainly to vitalise them:

> Dreamer of dreams, born out of my due time,
> Why should I strive to set the crooked straight?
> Let it suffice me that my murmuring rhyme
> Beats with light wing against the ivory gate,
> Telling a tale not too importunate
> To those who in the sleepy region stay,
> Lulled by the singer of an empty day.

The realities of the latter half of the nineteenth century suggest nothing to him save the averting of his gaze. They are crooked; who shall set them straight? For his part, he will not even try. He knows that effort would be vain; and he warns us not

> To hope again, for aught that I can say.

He feels that he has wings, but all he can do with them is to beat against the ivory gate. He sings only for those who, like himself, have given up the age, its boasted spirit, its vaunted progress, its infinite vulgar nothings, and have taken refuge in the sleepy region. Not only conscious of, but vitally imbued with, the truth of Mr. Arnold's words, when applied to such a period as this, that

> He only lives with the world's life
> Who has renounced his own—

Mr. Morris refuses to renounce the latter, and throws over all the sights, sounds, and struggles of the former, such as they are, to quote Mr. Coventry Patmore, 'in these last days, the dregs of Time.' Having done so, he invites us to

> Forget six counties overhung with smoke,
> Forget the snorting steam and piston-stroke,
> Forget the spreading of the hideous town,

and to forgive him that he cannot ease the burden of our fears, but can only strive to build a shadowy isle of bliss in the golden haze of an irrevocable past. Again and again he repeats what it is he can and what it is he cannot do:

> Yet as their words are no more known aright
> Through lapse of many ages, and no man
> Can any more across the waters wan
> Behold those singing women of the sea—
> Once more I pray you all to pardon me,
> If with my feeble voice and harsh I sing,
> From what dim memories may chance to cling
> About men's hearts, of lovely things once sung
> Beside the sea, while yet the world was young.

A certain comparative feebleness there may be in his voice—must be, indeed, in any voice that is laden with the suppressed sobs of back-looking regret, as contrasted with one firmly charged with present messages or confident presages of a grand approaching future; but harshness is there none, here or ever, in the strains of this dulcet client of Apollo. But whether feeble or harsh, or whatever to men's ears it may fairly seem, his muse refuses to wander from the sleepy region:

> Alas! what profit now to tell
> The long unwearied lives of men
> Of past days—threescore years and ten,
> Unbent, unwrinkled, beautiful,
> Regarding not death's flower-crowned skull.
> But with some damsel intertwined
> In such love as leaves hope behind!
> Alas! the vanished days of bliss.
> Will no god send some dream of this,
> That we may know what it has been?

For all the unprofitable nature of reverting to these vanished days, he never quits them. But he is conscious all the while that it is a strange thing for a poet, a maker, a seer, to turn his back on his own time in order to dwell, through memory, in 'that flowery land, fair beyond words,' his love for which, he declares, no scorn of man can kill:

> Thence I brought away
> Some blossoms that before my footsteps lay,
> Not plucked by me, not over-fresh or bright;

> Yet since they minded me of that delight,
> Within the pages of this book I laid
> Their tender petals, there in peace to fade.
> Dry are they now, and void of all their scent
> And lovely colour; yet what once was meant
> By these dull stains, some men may yet descry,
> As dead upon the quivering leaves they lie.

What beautiful humility in the metaphor! Yet, we are constrained to add, what truth! What delicate loveliness, what rich hues, what lingering fragrance even, in the tales of *The Earthly Paradise*, and in the rhymed story of *The Life and Death of Jason*! But, for all that, the delicacy, the colour, the scent, are as of pressed flowers, 'not plucked by me.' How far short, then, of not being plucked at all, but still bright, dew-sprinkled, odorous, and blossoming

> In lovely meadows of the ranging land,
> Wherein erewhile I had the luck to stand!

Mr. Morris knows this, and says it. Still, be they what they may, these dry petals of a bygone world are better than any grown by a present world, that knows only

> Consuming love,
> Mother of hate, or envy cold,
> Or rage for fame, or thirst for gold,
> Or longing for the ways untried,
> That, raving and unsatisfied,
> Draws shortened lives of men to hell.

Therefore it is that he chooses his part, and his songs are all of

> Vain imaginings,
> And memories vague of half-forgotten things,
> Not true or false, but sweet to think upon.

If we turn from the details of *The Earthly Paradise*, and regard it in its entirety, we meet with the most remarkable confirmation of the view we are taking, and the view it is impossible not to take—for, just as in Mr. Browning's and Mr. Arnold's cases, it is the author's own—of the scope and limits of his genius. For what is the story, the 'argument' of the *Earthly Paradise*? Certain 'gentlemen and mariners of Norway, having considered all that they had heard of the Earthly Paradise, set sail to find it,' and after many troubles and sore disappointments, come to a 'peaceful and delicious land,' where they are tended and carried into a city whose denizens are 'seed of the Ionian race,' where there are 'pillared council-houses' and 'images of gold':

> Gods of the nations, who dwelt anciently
> About the borders of the Grecian sea.

We cannot say whether Mr. Morris consciously intended by this outline, and the way in which he fills it up, to typify the yearning shared by him with the age for some immortal poetry, art-production, his own, and its utter failure to find them, and their joint discovery in the poetry and art of the nations who dwelt about the borders of the Grecian sea, of their greatest and, indeed, their only refuge; or whether this be a light flung, as has so often before been the case, from the poet's page, without the poet being aware that he had set it there. The point, however, is immaterial, since the similitude, when once pointed out, is too obvious to be missed. We need not repeat what we have said already of the Greek turn of much of Mr. Tennyson's work; of Mr. Swinburne's entire enslavement, in the non-lyrical portions of his writings, to the Athenian dramatists; to Mr. Arnold's hankering after the Muse that has gone away; to the something astir which drives one Prime Minister to translate Homer, and another to publish volumes about the Homeric poems and theology, and which has, moreover, urged so many living men of letters to 'do' translations of the bards of Hellas. The facts are too notorious to require more detailed indication. Like Mr. Morris's 'gentlemen and mariners of Norway,' now that we see

> . . . . the land so scanty and so bare,
> And all the hard things men contend with there,
> A little and unworthy land it seems,
> And worthier seems the ancient faith of praise.

We have missed what we really wanted; we have not found for ourselves immortal verse in some hitherto unexplored region; but we are well content, or at least resigned, to find ourselves

> . . . . once more within a quiet land,
> The remnant of that once aspiring band,
> With all hopes fallen away, but such as light
> The sons of men to that unfailing night,
> That death they needs must look on face to face.

Who does not feel how strangely applicable, too, are the following lines to those who have turned from the unfruitful turmoil of the time to the calm study of the serene products of better days?

> Yet though the time with no bright deeds was rife,
> Though no fulfilled desire now made them glad,
> They were not quite unhappy: rest they had,
> And with their hope their fear had passed away.

★   ★   ★   ★   ★   ★

> In such St. Luke's short summer lived these men,
> Nearing the goal of threescore years and ten!
> The elders of the town their comrades were,
> And they to them were waxen now as dear
> As ancient men to ancient men can be.

So is it with Mr. Morris. So is it with Mr. Arnold. So is it with the age, or that in it and us which is alive to poetical impulse and dominion. The elders have waxen dear to us because we are ourselves ancient men, in all that concerns the soul, 'with all hopes fallen away.' The spiritual side of us can find nothing akin, nothing to assimilate, in 'six counties overhung with smoke,' in 'the spreading of the hideous town,' and all the mean vulgar passions which material civilisation calls into supreme play:

> Among strange folk they now sat quietly,
> As though that tale had nought with them to do.

★   ★   ★   ★   ★   ★

> Yet, since a little life at least was left,
> They were not yet of every joy bereft,
> For long ago was past the agony,
> Midst which they found that they, indeed, must die
> And now well-nigh as much their pain was past,
> As though death's veil already had been cast
> Over their heads—so, midst some little mirth,
> They watched the dark night hide the gloomy earth.

Could there be a more accurate picture of the real 'gentlemen and mariners' among ourselves? They have nursed a beautiful dream; they have passed through a series of disillusions; and now among strange folk, among the records and regrets associated with the past, they sit quietly

> Watching the dark night hide the gloomy earth.

But how can great poetry spring from such a mood or attitude as that? Impossible—for ever impossible! Great poetry is the growth of confident creed and fervent or settled passion combined. Great anything cannot be made out of beautiful regrets. What can be made out of them Mr. Morris has made; and we are inclined to think that his, after all, is the most valuable, as it is certainly the most definite, contribution to the Poetry of the Period. Mr. Ruskin, in his latest publication, 'The Queen of the Air,' speaks of Mr. Morris's poems as not quite so beautiful as those of Keats, but displaying a far more powerful grasp of subject. We think the criticism is sound; certainly the latter part of it is. Mr. Morris's grasp is complete—far more so, at least, than that of any other living poet. But that arises entirely from his freedom from that distraction on which we have dilated, and to which all the rest of them are subject. Mr. Morris has given the go-by to his age, and he has done wisely. But in doing so not only has he not produced great poetry—he has evaded the very conditions on which alone the production of great poetry is possible. Even in co-operation with an age—as the present one, for instance—it may be impossible to develop it: but without that co-operation all hope of such is bootless and vain. Exquisitely soothing strains, as of some sweet Æolian harp, may be borne about by the winds that have gently vexed some patient, passive soul; but they have nothing in common with the stirring notes swept by a living hand from the chords of a fresh-strung instrument. These are not for our day. The sweet sadness of things and inevitable death are the constant burden of Mr. Morris's strains, and he chants them with a childlike simplicity that, amid abominable literary affectation and artificialities has largely helped to deepen the cordiality with which hundreds of the weary have welcomed him. But when we had said all—and it might be much—of his precious contributions to the poetical literature of the time, we should, in justice, still have to estimate how far they were from being great; and less averse from saying it because he himself has said it in all sincerity, we should be compelled to pronounce him, not a great poet, not a mighty maker, not a sublime seer, but at most and at best—

The idle singer of an empty day;

the wisely unresisting victim of a rude irreversible current; the serene martyr of a mean and melancholy time.

14. Unsigned review, *Pall Mall Budget*

December 1869, iv, 26–7

A review of Part 3; perhaps the one by Sidney Colvin which Morris appreciated; see Introduction, p. 3.

Sidney Colvin (1845–1927) was an active journalistic critic of art and literature; he became Slade Professor of Fine Art at Cambridge in 1873.

A choice reading for the long dark of London winter evenings is offered us in this second instalment—or rather third instalment, as the fifth and latest edition of the work is divided—of Mr. William Morris's *Earthly Paradise*. That in our Victorian epoch of bustle and business overmuch, the popularity in which a fifth edition testifies should have been won by a poem outbidding most Elizabethan poems in its claims on the leisure and the patience of its readers, seems a fact not short of astounding. Certainly it is a fact that can scarcely be construed save as proof of some special and sterling excellence which the public has recognized in the work. We had great pleasure in ourselves acknowledging the presence of such excellence, and in attempting to analyze its character, when the first part of the *Earthly Paradise* was produced a year and a half ago. It now becomes our task to indicate to our readers to what extent and with what modifications such excellence seems to us to have been sustained by Mr. Morris in his new volume.

The first point that will strike every one on opening the volume in question is the increased length of the tales that are contained in it. Length of wind in the narrators waxes with length of days. The wanderers tell each other longer stories as they grow older. As the autumn grows into winter these tales develop into epics. And so, whereas the former volume of 676 pages traversed six months, and contained, besides the long general prologue, twelve separate stories, the present volume of only 150 less pages traverses no more than three months, and contains no more than six separate stories. And we are promised a third (or, according to the new division, a fourth) volume, which is to give us the six more stories that have to be told during the remaining three months of the cycle. It is obvious that to sustain the interest of the reader unabated through so vast a scheme of poetry as this is a task that might strain the power of any poet. The placid beauty, the unflagging vividness of realization, the easy fecundity of fancy and fresh simplicity of narration that have distinguished Mr. Morris's work, were just the qualities likelier than any other to effect their task, just the qualities to keep the reader always awake without ever stirring him into very strenuous excitement. The Mediterranean tidelessness, so to speak, of a poetry that seldom quite flowed to the high-water mark of sublimity, and never quite ebbed to the opposite line of dulness, was far less calculated to fatigue than a stormier flood alternating with a more languid reflux would have been. Every reader almost was glad to retire from the stress and the cares of his ugly work-aday English life and be entertained, for no matter how long, with that succession of gracious pictures and pleasant incidents of a remote romantic world—remote, but conceived and set forth with the inexhaustible detail of a loving eye-witness; romantic, but having its enchantments and its marvels realized into rational perspicuity, its personages and their supernatural ways controlled into definite loveliness and classical completion of form, by the imagination of a genuine artist, into which all the appearances of the actual world had penetrated with an amazing distinctness. Into this ideal world, however, there had passed at most a far-off echo of human passions. The ethical problems that vex our souls and bend our conduct this way and that had hardly made themselves felt there. There was one moving principle, the principle of love, which led these gracious figures hither and thither in search of each other through the delicate region in which they moved: but it was a love thwarted or prospered by outward hindrances and outward succours only; by gods hostile or auspicious, but human-hearted at the worst; by magical powers of which it was possible to defy the enmity or to propitiate the alliance. And in their commerce with these powers there arose no more than faint reminiscences and reverberations of the passions, far-off reflections and similitudes of the difficulties, among which we in the workaday world are hedged in. Therefore the charm and the interest which the figures of this poetical cosmos had for us lay not so much in their troubles or their joys, their love-sorrows and love-triumphs, their struggles and victories, as in the winning and delightful aspect of them as they moved about among their temples and gardens and magic forests, or sailed over their enchanted seas, or whispered among their watered orchards. It was not their souls but their bodies that we cared for; not their inward goings on that we sympathized with, but their outward shows that we delighted in. In a word, the world amidst of which Mr. Morris set us, in spite of the vividly realized physical beauty of it, was spiritually speaking a heterocosmic world (if we may without pedantry permit ourselves that phrase of the early German critics). Its personages were not of like passions with ourselves, or only so to a very partial degree, and under much easier circumstances than we are accustomed to. The dramatic interest was the weakest interest in the early tales of the *Earthly Paradise*—so far as dramatic interest signifies not the interest of the incidents in a tale but that of the passions that occasion or attend such incidents.

We have insisted on this point to an extent which the reader may think superfluous, but for which we have a reason. Our reason is that the chief difference between the former and the present portions of Mr. Morris's work lies in the increased prominence given in the present portion to passion and emotion. Either Mr. Morris has feared that his readers would weary of the mere description of beautiful scenes and incidents poetically entertaining; or else the passionate and dramatic aspect of things has taken a stronger hold than it had before upon his imagination; or else he has found the stories which he now narrates more suggestive than the others of a dramatic and passionate treatment. At any rate, and from whatever cause, the emotional elements are realized with a far greater intensity and expressed with a far greater vehemence in most of the present poems than in any of those of the former volume. The versified Saga of Gudrun, which forms the last and longest of the narratives here given, is in its intention a half tragic, half epic study of fate and passion, and that of the most highly strung and highly wrought kind, and having a quite modern subtlety and involution of emotion thrown into it, both where the characters speak for themselves and where the poet analyzes for them. For the moment we do not inquire whether this change does or does not constitute an improvement in a poem projected on the scheme of the *Earthly Paradise*; we merely point out that the change is there. Similarly, in the 'Death of Paris,' with which the volume opens, the scenery of Ida and visible details of the transaction, instead of being made paramount, are made quite subordinate, while the subtilized and involved repentance, jealousy, fury, despair of Paris and Œnone are studiously worked out. And even in such a fantastic Northern fairy tale (for such in its origin it is) as the 'Land East of the Sun,' and again even in such a fantastic piece of Oriental magic as the 'Man who never Laughed again,' we find psychology unexpectedly in the ascendant. Perhaps by accident, perhaps by an instinctive sympathy with the Greek spirit, two of the Greek stories of the book retain all, or nearly all, the old unreflecting simplicity, the old ascendancy of the object over the subject (to be pedantic for a second time); we mean the lovely stories of 'Rhodope' and of 'Acontius and Cydippe'—Acontius, we may remark in passing, being throughout unaccountably misspelt Acontius. In order to reassure the reader, lest we should have alarmed him concerning what seems to us a real change in Mr. Morris's manner, of the unimpaired persistence, nevertheless, of the poet's gift of gay and exquisite description, we quote from 'Acontius and Cydippe' the account of the lover's dream:—

> Now 'neath the tree he sank adown;
> Parched was the sward thereby and brown,
> Save where about the knotted root
> A green place spread. The golden fruit
> Hung on the boughs, lay on the ground;
> The spring-born thrushes lurked around
> But sang not. Yet the stream sang well,
> And gentle tales the sea could tell.

[quotes next 31½ lines]

In this passage the reader recognizes the familiar qualities of Mr. Morris's pleasant muse. In virtue of such qualities as are here displayed, and as were everywhere displayed and sustained in *Jason* and in the first part of *The Earthly Paradise*, Mr. Morris had appeared to us as the representative of the romantic movement proper in modern poetry, in its latest and probably its final stage; a stage in which as we have indicated already, romantic feeling coincided with classical expression in a manner altogether satisfying. The essence of romanticism, we take it, lies in this, that romanticism has sought to turn to the purposes of art all, instead of some only, of the material of the world and of imagination; that romanticism has held itself at liberty to handle every phase of being, past or present, natural or supernatural, to repeat or recast every construction of the mature or immature human imagination in which it can find beauty, be that construction never so irregular, never so unscientific, never so fantastic, wayward, 'heterocosmic:' whereas the school which opposes itself to romanticism, and for which there is no name that is not a misnomer, has preferred to deal with clear conceptions testable by rules of reason and canons of propriety, semi-scientific conceptions, not too remote from sight and handling, and clothed in forms of beauty not too wayward, fugitive, unstable, or hard to grasp and control. In England we have at no time witnessed a stand-up fight between these two schools such as raged in Germany and France at two distinct epochs of the present century. Romanticism in Germany ran into extravagance and excess; into the artistic error of indulging in vague, vaporous, 'moonshine-drunken' mysticism, and into the practical error of desiring to restore in life the feudal and Catholic conditions which were the theme of its art. Romanticism in France ran into rhetorical excess with its sophistical magniloquence, its inflated abstractions, its eager superlatives, and tumultuous melodramatic unrestraint; perhaps, also, into artistic error with its licence of form and licentiousness of matter. This latter-day romanticism in England, of which we have called Mr. Morris the representative, has scarcely been at any time in the militant position held by its predecessors, and has perhaps on that account avoided their extravagances. At any rate, Mr. Morris's attitude towards the fabulous, mythical, old-world, or romantic material of his art has been entirely simple, entirely without self-consciousness, the attitude, in a word, of *artistic credulity*—an attitude differing as little as possible from that of Chaucer and the true mediæval story-tellers. He has led us with all good faith into a delightful no-man's land, where nothing is improbable, where nature exists but has left her laws behind her, where the ideas of anomaly and anachronism never enter. And he has given to this romantic world the clear definition, the intelligible form and beauty that can be grasped and tested, which are demanded by the lovers of classical or 'plastic' work; he has done this by virtue of the vivid and fertile realism of his imagination and by the limpid flow and facility of his poetical style.

In that this world of his was only troubled, as we have said, by the faint reflex of human struggles and emotions, lay for many readers a great part of its charm. But that charm is now lost. A shadow has fallen upon that clear air. The equableness of Mr. Morris's manner makes it notoriously difficult to quote from his poetry with effect; but here is a passage from the 'Death of Paris,' showing the kind of tragic intensity which he continually seeks in this new set of tales: (Enone addresses the wounded Paris asleep:—

> Then spoke a sweet voice, close, ah! close to him:
> 'Thou sleepest, Paris? Would that I could sleep!
> On the hill-side do I lay limb to limb,
> And lie day-long watching the shadows creep
> And change till day is gone, and night is deep,
> Yet sleep not ever, wearied with the thought
> Of all a little lapse of time has brought.'

[quotes next 4 stanzas]

We seem to find something like a clue to the feeling which, consciously or unconsciously, has led the poet to this increased vehemence of sentiment, in these lines spoken by an elder before he tells his story, in one of the interludes which occur between each pair of stories (and of which the inexhaustible variety in monotony remains as wonderful as ever):—

> A dream it is, friends, and no history
> Of men who ever lived; so blame me nought
> If wonderous things together there are brought
> Strange to our waking world—yet as in dreams
> Of known things still we dream, whatever gleams
> Of unknown light may make them strange, so here
> Our dreamland story holdeth such things dear
> And such things loathed, as we do; else, indeed,
> Were all its marvels nought to help our need.

Now, in the exquisite 'Apology,' at the head of his first volume, Mr. Morris had almost in so many words deprecated his poem being regarded as 'ought to help our need.' In styling himself above all 'the idle singer of an empty day,' he seemed to promise that so long as he had us by the hand we should be exempt from the spectacle of disturbing passions and internal wrestlings. Inasmuch, however, as he has now, with or without intention, introduced a good deal of the disturbing element, a great intensity and complication of loathing and holding dear, the question to be asked is whether this has been done well or ill. Is or is not the emotional humanity of his personages right and true in its kind; first granting the poet, in order to be on common ground with him, his assumption of a world in which the passion of love is the be-all and the end-all, the only law? That the objective part of the work is done well, and singularly well, that every scene to be described is described as though the poet had been really there, is not a thing at this time of day to be doubted. Neither will any reader who knows the dramatic fragment called 'Sir Peter Harpdon's End,' in the author's early volume, doubt his possession of a strong dramatic faculty. But to weave the dramatic element, when this is carried at all far, into the narrative and analytic element is one of the most diffi-cult tasks that a poet can set himself. It is not given to every one to write the petition of Priam to Achilles or the agony of Dido before her death-fire. We think that Mr. Morris shows a signal but also a signally unequal power in this respect. We think that in the noble and melancholy story of Gudrun this power is well sustained through-out, that in versifying this saga Mr. Morris has added a genuine and pathetic vitality to the characters of the ill-starred heroine, of Olaf and Oswif, Kiartan and Bodli, Ingibiorg and Refna. This poem, taken altogether the most ambitious that Mr. Morris has yet produced, is well worth a careful analysis, which, however, we have no space to give it. Neither have we space to point out in detail, on the other hand, how sometimes here, oftener in 'The Land East of the Sun' and 'He who never Laughed again,' and even a little in 'Rhodope,' our author seems to err by dwelling on moods too fugitive and fluctuating, too little accountable, too little dependent on the action of the story, to chime in with the simplicity of the story-teller's method. Vague long-ings, reveries intermingled with reminiscence and foreboding, moods of languor half mental and half physical, the involved reluctations of the will and dreamy seizures of the spirit, these are not matters with which a modern Chaucer should too much occupy himself; and we think Mr. Morris does occupy himself with them too much in this volume. If this amount of psychology has been introduced to relieve the tedium of the narrative, it has not succeeded in its object; for our-selves, at least, although our author's mellifluous garrulity in simple narration has never seemed tedious for a moment, we must confess that the recital does seem to flag from time to time in the psychological passages. Dramatic work, in short, requires more concentration than Mr. Morris gives it here. For many readers, however, all this (and we feel that we have been disproportionately insisting on it) will only be a small set-off against the added interest which they will find in these poems by reason of their more pronounced and developed humanity.

15. G. A. Simcox, review, *Academy*

February 1870, i, 121–2

A review of Part 3.

Simcox (1841–1905) was a classical scholar, editor and Oxford eccentric.

Mr. Morris has always been the poet of moods rather than of passions, of adventures rather than of actions; and this characteristic is still to be traced in the third instalment of his great work; though there is a nearer approach to the familiar sources of human interest. Yet even now there is a curious abstractness and remoteness; for all the figures that move through the day-dream seem not so much to feel as to sympathise; they see themselves with other eyes, and feel for themselves as for strangers. It is without the least sense of effort or surprise that we follow Gregory's dream of the 'Land East of the Sun and West of the Moon' through its three stages. First the dreamer listens to the marvellous story, then he tells it, at last he acts it; and the change, we feel, is always natural, or rather we do not feel it to be a change at all. This subjective tendency has been asserted throughout the poem, not only in the framework, but in the tales. In more than one example the succession of moods is as important as the succession of incidents; in 'Cupid and Psyche,' and the 'Watching of the Falcon,' the incidents may be said to be governed by the moods. In the autumn tales a still greater development is given to the contemplative emotions which succeed each other, while the incidents to which they correspond are minimised in each of the tales except the last. Perhaps it may be thought that there is a conscious change of aim corresponding to this change of interest. In the introduction to the unearthliest of all the stories we are told that the personages hold such things dear,—

> And loathe such things as we do; else, indeed,
> Were all its marvels nought to help our need.

And in 'The Lovers of Gudrun' the narrator disclaims marvels altogether. But it would be a mistake to exaggerate the contrast between
such utterances and the prologue; the help that the narrator of the
'Land East of the Sun and West of the Moon' promises, is help for the
guidance of thoughts that may serve to fill and cheer a few inactive
years, the help that the prologue refuses is help to overcome the difficulties and perplexities of active life in the work-a-day world. After
all, though there is less of naïve adventure and blithe description in
these stories, and more of psychological analysis, we never cross the
invisible line which divides the poetry of dream from the poetry of
action. The passion of Œnone is as intense as the passion of Dido; but
it is far more unearthly. It is not that the forsaken love of Æneas is
a mortal, and the forsaken love of Paris is a river goddess; but Dido
is in conflict with Æneas; she appeals to him; she is under his influence;
she seeks to influence him in return. Œnone pities Paris; she complains
of him; she judges him; the tone in which she speaks to him in his
presence is the tone in which Ariadne appeals to Theseus in his absence.
Indeed, Mr. Morris is still further from the dramatic tone than the
vigorous and splendid idyll of Catullus; Ariadne's soliloquy represents
a progressive movement of passion; she passes through regret and
complaint to despair, and through despair to the fierce thirst of vengeance; Œnone unfolds with tender pitiless calm the fixed conditions
of a motionless resolve. It is the triumph of our author's art to admit
and use to the utmost the intensity of the situation, and yet to elude all
agitation and excitement to maintain one weird trance unbroken from
the first line to the last. For examples of a similar achievement, we
have to refer to such masterpieces as 'St. Agnes Eve,' the 'Bride of
Corinth,' and 'Francesca da Rimini;' and it is only in the last that the
situation is equally tragic. In 'The Lovers of Gudrun,' the reader is
still kept within 'the eventual element of calm' by a series of delicate,
almost imperceptible artifices. The narrator is made to pity his ancestors in Laxdale with the respectful pity of the poet. When we read of

> The man at Burg who sat
> After a great life, with eyes waxing dim,
> Egil the mighty son of Skallagrim,

it is easy to see where the modern sympathy blends with the simplicity
of the ancient recital. Besides, the habitual reticence and measured
speech of the North has its effect in maintaining this ideal repose; so
has the unadorned and scientific accuracy with which combats are

described. If Kiartan had had the unrestrained eloquence of Achilles to bewail and denounce a wrong of the same kind; if we had been told of the efforts of the fighters as well as the result of the fight, then 'The Lovers of Gudrun' would have been a poem of the same order as Homer's, a poem of purely human interest. As it is, we have a poem which is mystical without a single miracle; for the atmosphere of the story impresses us more than the figures which move through it. It was a harder task to undramatize the story of 'Acontius and Cydippe,' yet the task has been accomplished without loss of interest. In Ovid the stress of the story begins when Cydippe has been surprised into her promise, and is distracted between her deliberate pledge to a former lover and her engagement to the new comer, whose claims are enforced by the recurring chastisement of Diana. Mr. Morris throws his whole strength into the aimless, hopeless, pitying waiting and watching, as Acontius pines day after day for the maiden who, in this version of the story, is dedicated to the dreary honour of perpetual maidenhood. It is just the same in 'Rhodope': the poem is an analysis too tender to be tedious of the blameless selfishness of a maiden whose nature is destined to splendour and needs it, while she is doomed to be the child of parents who have bartered their comfort to escape the curse of childlessness. The story might be told in a page, without omitting one essential circumstance. It is spread over fifty by a crowd of delicious details, which derive all their importance from their harmony with the moods of Rhodope. This deliberate parsimony of incident, which contrasts so strongly with the rich inventiveness of the 'Man born to be King' or the 'Proud King,' serves to prevent any impression of sameness between the 'Land East of the Sun' and 'He who never laughed again,' though the two legends are substantially identical with each other, and with the still finer story of 'Ogier the Dane.' This last received, as it deserved, a fuller and more life-like development. The two tales in the present series are adequately differenced by the change of scene and of catastrophe, and by one or two variations of incident, which are quite sufficient to disguise the fundamental identity of subject where incidents are few. Before leaving the subject of Mr. Morris's relation to the sources which serve as food to his rare and peculiar inspiration, we may be permitted to express a doubtful regret that while he has dwelt with equal emphasis on each of the four stages of 'Gudrun's Dream,' he 'has dismissed the fourth stage of her life, which serves to interpret the dream, with only a hurried and per-functory mention. If this violation of obvious symmetry is really a fault, it may easily be forgiven to the poet who has transformed one of the least artistic of the Norse Sagas into one of the completest of English poems. It would require a very detailed analysis to show exactly how far Mr. Morris's manner has diverged as he has gone on writing from the manner of Chaucer, which he recalled so forcibly in *Jason*. We subjoin a few stanzas of the carol from the 'Land East of the Sun' to show how far the author has retained the power of reproducing the phantastic mediævalism of his earlier style:—

> News, news of the Trinity,
> > *The snow in the street, and the wind on the door.*
> And Mary and Joseph from over the sea!
> > *Minstrels and maids, stand forth on the floor.*
>
> For as we wandered, far and wide,
> > *The snow in the street, and the wind on the door.*
> What hap do ye deem there should us betide?
> > *Minstrels and maids, stand forth on the floor.*
>
> Under a bent when the night was deep,
> > *The snow in the street, and the wind on the door.*
> We saw three shepherds tending their sheep
> > *Minstrels and maids, stand forth on the floor.*
>
> 'O ye shepherds, what have ye seen
> > *The snow in the street, and the wind on the door.*
> To stay your sorrow, and heal your teen?'
> > *Minstrels and maids, stand forth on the floor.*
>
> 'In an ox-stall this night we saw,
> > *The snow in the street, and the wind on the door.*
> A babe and a maid without a flaw.'
> > *Minstrels and maids, stand forth on the floor.*

16. Unsigned review, *Spectator*

March 1870, xliii, 332–4

A review of Part 3.

Whither shall a reader turn in these days who longs to escape for a while from all the toil and clamour and strife of the world, and to roam at will in pleasant places, where nothing shall remind him of the doubtful battle-field where after a short breathing-space he must again bear his part? There are great masters who strengthen our sight to look at doubt and danger with steadfast eyes, and arm us for the fight with exalted hope and renewed faith in good: whether they speak to us in articulate words, or in parables of deathless music deeper than speech, or in the visible beauty of painting or sculpture. Their task is indeed the noblest of all; they are the mighty men of whom Mr. Morris has said that they slay the ravening monsters of the sea that beats around us. But we are not always in a mood to receive their gifts; there come times when we desire not their full light, but some cooler shadow; when we would learn not how to face cares, but how to forget them. And yet we must enjoy our short oblivion only so that after it we may the better remember; we shall gain no sweet or refreshing repose if we stupefy ourselves with scorn or indifference. He who can teach us the right and innocent forgetfulness has surely attained high praise, though not the supreme eminence of those others. Such an one is Mr. Morris, and though he has called himself 'the poor singer of an empty day,' his office is no idle nor empty one. His position is singular amongst our living writers; this new part of the *Earthly Paradise* has appeared almost at the same time with Mr. Tennyson's last poems, but no competition or comparison is possible. They belong to different worlds of thought, and the one cannot interfere with the other.

It is Mr. Morris's happy and peculiar faculty to cast utterly aside the complex questionings that vex our modern poetry. He carries us away to the days when men lived their life without overmuch thinking about it; he hardly ever touches on matters of speculation, and when he does so, it is with a very light hand. We have found no nearer approach to the modern introspective manner than this one stanza ('Story of Rhodope,' p. 315):—

> 'So is it now,' he said,
> 'With me as with a man soon to be dead.
> Wise is he all at once, and knows not why,
> And brave who erst was timorous; fair of speech,
> Whose tongue once stammered with uncertainty,
> Because his soul to the dark land doth reach.
> And is it so that love to me doth teach
> New things, because he needs must get him gone,
> And leave me with his memories all alone?'

Very few poets of our time would be content to leave the matter here. Mr. Tennyson would probably comment and explain in his own person. Mr. Browning would expand this man's speech into an analysis of all that the poet's subtle and exhaustive insight could find involved in the passing fancy. George Eliot might do, yet could and perhaps might abstain from doing, something in either kind; but one at any rate feels the speculative force struggling to escape. Indeed, the *Spanish Gypsy*, in the places where that force is put forth, seems to afford the extremest contrast that can be found to Mr. Morris's work in this respect. In such verses as these, where Duke Silva's character is described,—

> A spirit framed
> Too proudly special for obedience,
> Too subtly pondering for mastery;
> Born of a goddess with a mortal sire,
> Heir of flesh-fettered, weak divinity,
> Doom-gifted with long resonant consciousness
> And perilous heightening of the sentient soul,

every word carries a weight of elaborate thought, and strains the reader's attention to the utmost. The consideration of these magnificent lines, showing as they do the analytic tendency of modern poetry in its fullest development, may be a help to appreciating the difficulties Mr. Morris has had to overcome. A spirit is here exhibited which it might seem an almost hopeless task to reconcile with simple untroubled enjoyment. It has become a new thing that beauty should be offered to us without mystery, and apprehended without effort.

Mr. Morris, however, has given us an effectual antidote for the over-wrought self-consciousness of this generation; and the more we perceive the arduousness of his enterprise, the more we must value his success. He has established himself as an unrivalled master of the perfectly simple representation which gives us perfect repose. He never forces us to strain the inward vision, either directly or indirectly. For it should not be left out of account that poets have many powerful means of indirect compulsion, and often exercise them unmercifully. We say that they take us out of ourselves, but they often do so only to put us straightway into some other prison; for we lose our own personality only on the terms of realizing some other of the poet's creation; and then it may happen that we have to undergo a harder work of self-inspection for the poet's characters than they could do for themselves, or than we should like to do for ourselves. For instance, Mr. Browning's men and women do not appear to us as men and women would really know and disclose themselves, but transparent as it were with the light of the poet's fuller knowledge. They live by his magic in a Palace of Truth, where they speak out a great deal more of their minds than they could be expected, in fact, either to know or to utter. There is a preternatural definiteness about them that strains and dazzles the eye. And therefore we miss the feeling of acquiescence in solid reality which is given by the truest dramatic power, that which refuses to explain its own creations more minutely than life does actually explain itself. Such power we find, among our living writers, eminently in Henry Taylor's, and to a great extent also in the purely dramatic parts of George Eliot's work. Even so, however, we are led to a certain amount of pondering and explanation; we are not forced, but neither are we forbidden to seek farther than what we see. But Mr. Morris, as a purely narrative poet, goes beyond this; his business is to do away with explanations and questions altogether. The reader is not only taken out of himself, but allowed to remain an unattached and, as nearly as may be, an indifferent spectator; his sympathy is excited, but in a general and diffused way. He is not expected to identify himself with the poet who tells the story or with any of his creatures. The persons pass before him in their due order, as parts in a connected series of beautiful images, and the beauty of the whole is the sole and sufficient reason for each part existing and being what it is. We accept them and enjoy them, as we might gaze on figures completing the effect of an excellent landscape. There is no temptation to hunt for a hidden purpose, or to inquire curiously into probabilities and motives. That such is the effect advisedly sought by Mr. Morris may be concluded not only from the general tenor of his work, but from express declaration. He has shown in the 'Apology' prefixed to the first part of the *Earthly Paradise* how thoroughly he understands his object and his powers; and it is no small part of his merit that he has so clearly determined his course from the beginning, and has kept it without swerving. In this as well as the former volume the poet's firm adherence to his purpose has been, on the whole, amply rewarded. The new series of tales seems on the average somewhat less interesting than the first; but herein we cannot be sure of our judgment, till we have had time to become more familiar with these, and to view the whole work in an equal light. And whatever shortcomings there may be are at any rate far outweighed, as we shall presently see, by new achievements of no doubtful excellence. Certainly the path Mr. Morris has chosen has dangers as well as delights peculiar to itself; it is difficult in avoiding sharpness, excess of speed, and concentration, not to fall at times into a strain that wearies by very softness. We confess to certain misgivings about 'The Land East of the Sun and West of the Moon.' It is a region almost too dreamy and misty for living men to walk in; we lose ourselves in rambling melodies, and are oppressed with the vagueness of everlasting twilight. Yet Mr. Morris has to a great extent foreseen and disarmed this objection; for with a true instinct he has set forth this tale, and this alone, in the fashion of a dream; so that what might have been otherwise reproached as extravagant becomes in this place just and artistic. Whether or not this visionary show is exactly what we like best, we must admit that it is what we had to expect. A gradual change in the dream is finely conceived; the sleeper twice wakes and sleeps again, and whereas he began with dreaming of the tale as told by another, he dreams next that he is telling it himself, and in his third sleep it is no more a tale, but his own life. A singularly beautiful Christmas Carol is introduced (p. 86), and pleasantly relieves the rather monotonous flow of the story. It is too long to extract, and moreover we have no mind to save readers the trouble, or rather deprive them of the pleasure, of looking for it in the book. We know not if the shepherds' 'news of a fair and a marvellous thing' has been re-told by any modern poet with such a sweet antique simplicity.

Another comparatively weak portion of this volume is the story of 'The Man who never laughed again.' It fails to satisfy as much in the same way as the dream-piece; there is a similar want of substance and variety; a strange feeling, after we have heard the story out, that we cannot tell what it was all about. It is curious that the themes of these two poems are very much alike, though they seem to have come from sources widely apart, and differ in local colouring and catastrophe. In each case we have a dweller on the earth borne away to a cloudland of love and pleasure, and driven back to the common world, and losing his love, by his own perversity; and in each case we grow rather impatient of his selfish longings. Mr. Morris's characters, as we have said, are not capable of enlisting any strong or exclusive personal sympathy; rather it is essential to his method to prevent them from doing so. These solitary transports of desire and despair, relieved by no other interest, are too much for a shadow, and too little for a living soul.

But in 'The Death of Paris' and 'The Lovers of Gudrun' we find all, and more than all, that we looked for at Mr. Morris's hands. In the treatment of this last subject he has put forth new and unexpected strength. It is an Icelandic legend, terrible enough, one would think, in the original; at any rate, it demands a master's skill to make it beautiful in the telling. The abundance of incident, the length of time embraced, and the whole character of the story, have made it almost necessary to adopt a more rapid and direct style than usual. The result has been most happy; there is to some extent a return to the straightforward impetus of *Jason*, but with an increase of both power and refinement. The tale is broken up into several sections, and a careful judgment is shown in keeping the less important parts of the narrative at their proper level, as well as in handling and distributing the stronger effects. Mr. Morris had not hitherto shown himself capable of this reserve and discretion, which enhance the impression made by the exercise of an unwonted force. Here, too, is seen in free play that fresh and simple delight in life which contributes so much to the charm of both the *Earthly Paradise* and *Jason*. Elsewhere it is well nigh stifled at times in very luxuriance of description, for which there is here little or no place. But the tragic passages of this tale disclose powers of which the author's former work had given no sign. The events are brought on by the working of an inevitable doom, and they are told in a way to remind us of the horror subdued by divine awe that pervades the Æschylean drama. The whole effect of the poem is cumulative, and a short extract will therefore not do justice to it, though it will serve to illustrate the change of style. It is the morning when Gudrun's husband is going forth to slay the man who was her lover and his friend, and whom he has supplanted by treachery:—

Then she arose as one might in a dream
To clothe herself, till a great cloud did seem
To draw away from her; as in bright hell,
Sunless but shadowless she saw full well
Her life that was and would be, now she knew
The deed unmasked that summer day should do.

. . . .

But slowly now did fade
All will away from her, until the sun
Risen higher, on her nerveless body shone,
And as a smitten thing beneath its stroke
She shrank and started, and awhile awoke
To hear the tramp of men about the hall.
Then did a hand upon the panel fall;
And in her very soul she heard the ring
Of weapons pulled adown, and everything,
Yea, even pain, was dead a little space.

We come to speak last of 'The Death of Paris.' In this, as well as in
'The Lovers of Gudrun,' there is more than usual fire and passion; but
there is no marked variation from the writer's general manner. There
is an especial felicity in his treatment of the Greek heroic legends, and
the stories of Atalanta, Perseus, and Alcestis were those we cared for
most in the former volume; here he has equalled, if not surpassed, his
success with those themes, and this is the piece we should on the whole
select by preference as a specimen of his best workmanship. The
argument runs as follows:—

Paris, the son of Priam, was wounded by one of the poisoned arrows of
Hercules that Philoctetes bore to the siege of Troy; wherefore he had himself
borne up into Ida that he might see the nymph Œnone, whom he once had
loved, because she, who knew many secret things, alone could heal him: but
when he had seen her and spoken with her, she would deal with the matter in
no wise, wherefore Paris died of that hurt.

We give this at length, partly to explain the stanzas about to be quoted,
partly to call attention to these short arguments generally. They are
very short and unobtrusive, but not less cunningly and delicately
wrought than the poems they introduce. The meeting of Paris and
Œnone is thus brought about; and it will be no wonder if these lines
are found hard to reconcile with our opinion as to the passionless and
impersonal mood in which Mr. Morris's poetry ought to be enjoyed:

Then looked she towards the litter as she spake,
And slowly drew anigh it once again,

And from her worn tried heart there did outbreak
Wild sobs and weeping, shameless of its pain,
'Till as the storm of passion 'gan to wane
She looked and saw the shuddering misery
Wherein her love of the old days did lie.

[quotes next stanza]

He opened hollow eyes and looked on her
And stretched a trembling hand out; ah, who knows
With what strange mingled look of hope and fear,
Of hate and love, their eyes met! Come so close
Once more, that everything they now might lose
Amid the flashing out of that old fire,
The short-lived uttermost of all desire.

It is almost a matter of course that the short intermediate pieces which form a sort of connecting thread, and at the same time give a relief to the longer narratives, are as full of natural and refreshing beauty as the corresponding parts of the first volume. No doubt can remain on this point after reading the lines headed 'October' and 'November.' As for pure description, there is in 'Rhodope,' a picture of a June day, and in 'The Lovers of Gudrun,' one of a winter morning, both quite perfect in their kind.

One quarrel, however, we are inclined to have with Mr. Morris; why will he bring out his poems in winter? So many independent observers have found that they ought to be read in summer, and out of doors if possible, that their combined experience must have sufficient truth in it to deserve the regard of all persons concerned. It may be answered that the second reading of poetry is the best, and that it is, therefore, fit and proper to use the winter for a first reading, and reserve the pleasures of summer and open air for the second. To which argument we have not at present any satisfactory reply.

17. Sidney Colvin, review, *Academy*

December 1870, ii, 57–8

A review of Part 4.

Mr. Morris, in the verses to the reader which opened the first volume of his long poem, as well as in the 'Envoi,' which closes its last volume now before us with an accent the most intimate and winning, has on his own account disclaimed alike ambition and prowess for the deeds that befit heroes. For other people, however, it will be difficult to avoid thinking of him as the hero in truth of a notable material exploit; inasmuch as he has in little more than three years carried his great undertaking safely through, and beyond all danger of falling, like so many poetical undertakings, into the category of things unaccomplished.

Another risk proper to the work of art which grows slowly, and takes long from projection to completion, is the risk of losing unity through change of sentiment in the artist, or through new modes of treatment or conception growing upon him unawares. It seems as if this contingency might be traced as having, within certain limits, actually befallen the progress of the *Earthly Paradise*. There is much, certainly, to maintain in the book from end to end a prevailing harmony of impression. Above all there is one never-forgotten key-note; there are the conscious love of life for living's sake, and the realized detestation of death because it puts an end to life, which at all moments of imagined festivity or delight recur with wistfulness to deplore that such things must pass away, and to desire for them immortality in the midst of denying it. All this indeed takes, if possible, a greater explicitness and importunity in the last than in the earlier volumes. In this lay the lure which first drew the Northern voyagers from their homes, and in this lies the sadness of their latter days. After the last tale of the twelvemonth's cycle is told out, the epilogue dealing with their remaining life is very short, and is addressed chiefly to their vindication against a conjectured charge of vain hope and cowardice, in seeking to escape from fate:—

> Cry out upon them, ye who have no need
> Of life to right the blindness and the wrong!
> Think scorn of these, ye who are made so strong
> That with no good-night ye can loose the hand
> That led you erst thro' love's sweet flowery land!
> Laugh, ye whose eyes are piercing to behold
> What makes the silver seas and skies of gold!
> Pass by in hate, ye folk who day by day
> Win all desires that lie upon your way!
> Yet 'mid your joyous wisdom and content,
> Methinks ye know not what those moments meant
> When ye, yet children, 'mid great pleasure stayed,
> Wondering for why your hearts were so downweighed;
> Or if ye ever loved, then, when her eyes
> In happiest moments changed in suddenwise,
> And nought ye knew what she was thinking of;
> Yet, O belike, ye know not much of love
> Who know not that this meant the fearful threat,
> The End, forgotten much, remembered yet
> Now and again, that all perfection mocks.

Again, and in a vein less intense than the above, where in the 'Envoi' the author personifies his book—despatching it, in a half-laughing manner of delightful simplicity, on its dubious journey towards 'the land of Matters Unforgot,' and dictating a discourse which it is to hold with the shade of Chaucer on the road—one of the first things it is instructed to say of itself and its writer is this:—

> Death we have hated, knowing not what it meant;
>   Life we have loved thro' green leaf and thro' sere.
> Tho' still the less we knew of its intent.

And once more, in the story of 'Bellerophon in Lycia,' where Philonoe urges her lover to leave her father's city because of plots laid against life, her last resort of persuasion is to a passionate amplification of the question—

> *Of the dead* what hast thou heard
> That makest thee so rash and unafeared?
> *Can the dead love?* &c.

But it would be endless to complete the tale of instances in which this dominant sentiment asserts itself. And it remains to signify what

are the points of change, and what the novelty of strain, of which we
have spoken as perceptible beneath this spiritual unity, and notwithstanding the further and technical unity of a style easy and voluble in
one place as in another, and calling for little castigation if perhaps it
gets less, of a diction always appropriate in simple fecundity, a versification neither aiming at finish nor missing music and variety. At the
beginning, then, it seemed that this story-teller was going to content
himself, for sources of interest, with the primary and simplest elements
of story-telling; moving his figures through incidents foreknown in
the main to all of us, and, although with deliberate pause and affectionate delay devising and filling in such visible details as the mind loves
to linger among, yet not working up the turns of his narrative or the
inward processes of his characters to any advanced pitch of dramatic
or human intensity. The work thus conceived was a new thing in
modern literature, an inspiration carried out to clear and admirable
success. But by degrees there have come other elements into some of
the tales told,—deeper poetical motive, greater complexity of incident,
greater force and subtlety of emotion, more of the conscious and sensitive modern self mingling with the ancient direct nature and all-
adorning fancy. And with these has come the loss of something of the
old melodious equality, and gentle maintenance of delightfulness. The
fuller and more intense poems, like those of 'Gudrun' or 'Bellerophon,'
are both better and worse than the quieter and more external or
pictorial poems, like those of 'The Man born to be King' or 'Acontius
and Cydippe.' They are full of strokes and passages that indicate ample
command over whatever lies deepest, ample knowledge of passion
and the heart, full imaginative and rhetorical mastery. But these things
seem to need for their expression a poetical medium more concentrated and more highly wrought than this is, except now and then for
some half-dozen lines; they do not, I think, lend themselves with complete propriety to that method of descriptive *cataloguing* (if one may
use so ugly a word for so pleasant a thing) which is full of charm when
employed on matters of lighter import.

The tale of Bellerophon is the leading one of this last volume, and
is divided into two parts told by two different elders, and with a
Northern tale coming between them. The former part has most of
tragic intensity, dealing with the difficult subject of the passion of
Sthenobœa:—

> Ut Proetum mulier perfida credulum
> falsis inpulerit criminibus nimis

casto Bellerophonti
maturare necem refert.*

The latter part has most of narrative complexity and suspense, dealing with the love of Bellerophon for Philonoe, daughter of Jobates, his victories over the Solymi, the Amazons (conceived not as Attic art conceived them, but as grimly hags by mere hideousness a terror to their enemies), and the Chimæra; and some further adventures, invented in the spirit of the most vivid modern romance, in which the conqueror with the help of his love frustrates the wiles of a jealous captain of Lycia. This is a poem in its author's very best manner, full not only of sentiment and action, but of all that is most his own in sustained sweetness and minute visionary veracity, and equal affection for things homely and heroic. The poem placed between these two tells a version of the well-known tale of the bronze Venus closing her finger on the ring meant for the finger of a mortal bride—a tale employed, among others, by M. Prosper Mérimée for his *Venus d'Ille*. Note in it admirable loveliness of the following passage of nature; where Laurence, the spell-bound bridegroom of the bronze, instead of the mortal lady, is on his way to an appointed encounter with a nightly train of heathen spirits:—

> At first on his left hand arose
> Great cliffs and sheer, and, rent from those,
> Boulders strewn thick across the sand,
> Made weary work for foot and hand;
> But well he knew the path indeed,
> And scarce of such light had he need
> As still the summer eve might shed
> From the high stars of sunset dead.

[quotes next 24 lines]

But note also a certain vagueness and dreaminess of the senses coupled with a certain exaltation of the spirit, and constituting a subjective state for the reception of the landscape impression in this case, such as is alien from the ordinary temper of the writer. Ordinarily his landscape is the precise and delicate record of observation by perfectly alert senses free from all preoccupation, trouble, or impediment; and of this there is no better instance than the return of fishing-boats at morning seen by Laurence after his adventure is over:—

---

* Tells how a treacherous woman drove credulous Proetus with false charges to hasten death for chaste Bellerophon; Horace, *Odes*, III, vii, 13–16.

Then from that drear unhallowed place
With merry heart he set his face.
A light wind o'er the ocean blew,
And fresh and fair the young day grew;
The sun rose o'er the green sea's rim,
And gave new life and joy to him;
The white birds crying o'er his head
Seemed praising all his hardihead,
And laughing at the worsted foe;
So, joyous, onward did he go.

[quotes next 16 lines]

In this poem we find a weakness at a critical point, in the shape of somewhat indistinct and dubious narration of that upon which the story hinges, the misadventure of the bridal night under the curse of the goddess: and in the 'Bellerophon' what seems a similar lapse makes a little shadowy the fight of the hero with the Chimæra. The other tales of the volume are of Aslaug and Ragnar, of Hercules and the Hesperides, and of Tannhäuser. Of these the Scandinavian story of Aslaug, the child of Sigurd and Brynhild, and her evil fostering by a carle and carline until Ragnar comes sailing to woo and win her, is full of the brightest grace and freshness; that of the Venusberg, I think, is again a little too vague in its most critical enchantments, and upon the whole falls perhaps into something of tediousness and surfeit. The intervening three-stanza lyrics of December, January, and February, are as full as their predecessors of tender and various pathos; and so the whole delightful book comes to an end, and leaves all readers the richer for itself.

18. G. W. Cox, unsigned review, *Edinburgh Review*

January 1871, cxxxiii, 243–66

G. W. Cox (1827–1902) was a divine and historian. His review is of *Jason* and the whole *Earthly Paradise*. The review is unusual in doubting the likely popularity of the poems, and in the severe morality of its judgment of the characters in 'The Lovers of Gudrun'.

Not many men have been more richly endowed with the gift of song than the author of the beautiful poems which are here woven together as a garland of flowers gathered in an earthly Paradise. Not many poets have so successfully schooled themselves to rest content with the mere appearances of things; and hence it is that, while he professes to seek only to draw forth sweet music from a harp which could scarcely be swept by more skilful fingers, he has succeeded in impressing on all his utterances the character of the philosophy, which regards the outward aspect of things as all that may be known about them. This success he has achieved, not by any efforts to fathom the depths and measure the varying currents of human thought. His purpose is rather to watch the movements or the calms on the surface of the waters, without an answer to the question of that inner life which dwells beneath it. Thus while his words flow on in streams soft as any which might come from the lyre of Hermes or the reed of Pan, they carry with them the burden of a strange weariness and sadness.

In truth, the exquisite simplicity and grace of Mr. Morris's poems are the fruit of consummate art and skill. The subjects which he has chosen are with few exceptions subjects which have been already handled by the Homeric and Orphic poets, by Pindar and Stesichorus, by Sophocles and Euripides. They are, in other words, the stories with which the bards of the Greek heroic age charmed their countrymen, and which in the hands of the tragic and lyric poets were made vehicles of the highest lessons of political or ethical wisdom, or means

of imparting the purest and most intense delight. These stories Mr.
Morris has told again, professedly with the latter of these two purposes
only. He speaks of himself emphatically as 'the idle singer of an empty
day;' and, as we read tale after tale, it would be vain to attribute to
him the fixed design by which Mr. Tennyson has worked the several
parts of the Arthurian story into one magnificent whole. But as our
thoughts rest on the Medea and Alcestis of Mr. Morris, we cannot
banish from our minds the images of the Medea and Alcestis of
Euripides, and we are led to contrast the atmosphere in which these
creatures of Greek imagination move, with that in which the same
forms are exhibited to us by the modern poet. Probably none have
sought more earnestly to relate these stories simply as stories, and certainly none have imparted to them a more touching charm. The
Arthur of Mr. Tennyson is manifestly the embodiment of the highest
Christian chivalry, and the Prometheus of Shelley is the man who
strives against injustice and wrong in all ages and in all countries;
these poems may therefore be regarded from a point of view lofty
and immutable. Mr. Morris's tales can be submitted to no such criticism. They are put before us as 'murmuring rhymes;' insensibility to
their delightful melodies would argue a strange coldness to versification. Yet, while we give up ourselves to the spell of the enchanter as
at the waving of his wand the scenes change and each creation of
his plastic power comes before us, it is impossible to rest under it. It
may not be fair to compare a poet with other poets, but it can scarcely
be unfair to compare him with himself; and if Mr. Morris's purpose has
been only to charm away the hours when 'feeling kindly unto all the
earth,' we

> Grudge every minute as it passes by,
> Made the more mindful that the sweet days die,

we cannot help marking the signs which seem to show the channel
in which the thoughts of the poet have been running, or sometimes
pausing to reflect how far it may be wise to follow in the same path.

The melody of Mr. Morris's verse is so sweet, the movement so
smooth, that we care as little to assume the attitude of critics towards
these poems as to analyse our feelings while we watch the light playing
on calm waters beneath a cloudless summer sky. Some flaws may
doubtless be found—a few false rhymes, a few sentences which differ
from prose only in the recurrence of the same sound at the end of
each couplet, and, more frequently, a certain ruggedness and faultiness

of scanning. With Mr. Morris, 'real' is invariably a monosyllable, and 'really' a dissyllable. But we need not give instances of defects which, after all, are little more than the purposed discords of the musician. While we accompany Mr. Morris we roam through an enchanted land; and we are too much contented with the beauty of the scenes before us to dwell on the neutral tints or the few unshapely objects which in no way mar their loveliness.

The tales related in the *Earthly Paradise* are strung together on a very simple framework. The horrors of a wasting plague at Micklegarth give strength and shape to the vague dreams of a happier land far away to the West, with which some of its people had been wont to solace themselves while serving among the Varangian guards at Byzantium; and the learned squire Nicholas, whose betrothed is ready to follow him over the world, makes a vow with the Swabian Lawrence and others, that they will at once set out and never give up their search for this land,

> Till death or life have set their hearts at rest.

In the English Channel they fall in with the fleet of Edward III and the Black Prince, who gives them some lines of writing, lest they should find it hard to deal with some of his people

> who pass not for a word
> Whate'er they deem may hold a hostile sword.

But the story of the voyage, until they descry a new land, differs little, if at all, from the story of Columbus and his men, or of others who have wandered through unknown seas led on chiefly by their hopes and fancies. It is the old tale of eager anticipation and wild enjoyment, followed by blank depression and dismay; but when, after surmounting dangers not less terrible than those which Ulysses encountered in the land of the Læstrygonians or the dwelling of Circe, after escaping from an ocean of misery, in which they had grown to be like devils and learnt what man sinks to

> When every pleasure from his life is gone,

they come at last to a land where the simple folk, taking them to be gods, treat them as kings, we may well doubt whether the insane yearning for an earthly home where there is no death can live on in the hearts of men who had already numbered their threescore years and ten. But this passion to escape from Death is the burden of Mr.

Morris's poems. From the Prologue to the Epilogue of the *Earthly Paradise*, which concludes the fourth and last part, his ancient mariners are described as men who

> deemed all life accurst
> By that cold overshadowing threat—the end.

If the delights of a life not without some likeness to that of the Lotos-eaters still left, as it might well leave, them dissatisfied, the longing would surely be rather for the old home, where they might once again hear the old familiar speech. But though after a time their life seemed to them once more 'trivial, poor, and vain,' not a thought is given to Norway; and the one desire is still to find the country where the old may become young again, and the young may not die. They would be fools and victims, and the veiled prophet was not wanting to lure them on to their destruction. From the horrible captivity which follows they escape at last, only to see their numbers dwindle quickly away from sickness of body and mind, until Nicholas, the most learned and the most besotted of them all, dies and is left beneath the trees upon the nameless shore, and the scanty remnant is at length brought to a shining city in a distant sea, where they hear not the language of Norway, but the softer sounds of that Greek tongue to which they had listened long ago in Byzantium. Here, kindly welcomed by the grey-haired elders, they feel that their earthly wanderings are done, and their journey to the grave must now be

> like those days of later autumn-tide,
> When he who in some town may chance to bide
> Opens the window for the balmy air,
> And seeing the golden hazy sky so fair,
> And from some city garden hearing still
> The wheeling rooks the air with music fill,
> Sweet hopeful music, thinketh, Is this spring,
> Surely the year can scarce be perishing?
> But then he leaves the clamour of the town,
> And sees the withered scanty leaves fall down,
> The half-ploughed field, the flowerless garden-plot,
> The dark full stream by summer long forgot,
> The tangled hedges where relaxed and dead
> The twining plants their withered berries shed,
> And feels therewith the treachery of the sun,
> And knows the pleasant time is well-nigh done.

The mournful sound of autumn-tide runs as a keynote through all the tales which the city elders and these storm-tossed men relate to each other, and which are here woven into the chaplet of the *Earthly Paradise*. They may be tales which tell of high hopes and heroic deeds; they may paint the joys of the young and the mighty achievements of fearless men; but the shadow of death is on these 'murmuring rhymes' which

> Beat with light wing against the ivory gate,
> Telling a tale not too importunate
> To those who in the sleepy region stay;

and the touch of the very fingers of death alone stirs within us whatever sense of life there may be left. If it be hard to say whether the music of Mr. Morris's song carries with it more of pleasure than of pain, the pleasure must at the least be that of men who sit at the banquet-table in the presence of the veiled skeleton, and the enjoyment that of the youth who is bidden to rejoice because all is vanity and vexation of spirit, and because the hour will soon come when the bowl shall be broken at the fountain. That 'the idle singer of an empty day,' who has here woven together some blossoms which lay before his footsteps 'in a flowery land, fair beyond words,'

> Not plucked by him, not overfresh or bright,

has given us melodies of exquisite sweetness, it would be mere ingratitude to deny; but the music of this Earthly Paradise is mournful because it is so earthly. Whether the tale be that of Perseus victorious over every enemy who seeks to bar his way, or of Alcestis going forth in all the freshness of youth to the dark land whither her husband should have gone, or of Ogier the Dane, who rises from his charmed sleep to strike a blow for the land where the great Karl had reigned; whether it be the legend of Jason turning deliberately from the old love to the new, or of Psyche toiling on with the very sickness of hope deferred in her search for the glorious being on whom her eyes had but for one moment rested, there is everywhere the same thought that gladness is only gladness because it is dogged by decay and change. The lesson may be true; but the penalty for the iteration of it is a monotony which disposes rather for drowsiness than enjoyment; and the words by which it is enforced leave on the mind the impression of a faith altogether less hopeful than that of the poets who told these tales long ago in their old land, and of whom we are wont to speak as heathens.

The truth is that Mr. Morris never cares to lift his eyes from the earth, except to the visible heaven in which we may see the glories of dawn and sunset; and only on this earth and under this heaven is there any real hope and any real joy for man. For the agonies involved in the constant flux and reflux of human affairs the only remedy lies in the 'crucible of time,'

> that tempers all things well,
> That worketh pleasure out of pain,
> And out of ruin golden gain.

But for the individual man the language of the poet throughout is not only that of resignation to a doom of absolute extinction after a short sojourn here, but of the philosophy which makes this extinction the one justification of merriment. The cornel-wood image stands in the city of Rome

> For twice a hundred years and ten,
> While many a band of striving men
> Were driven betwixt woe and mirth
> Swiftly across the weary earth,
> From nothing unto dark nothing;

and the fact that a log of wood will last

> While many a life of man goes past,
> And all is over in short space,

is a reason for not fearing what any son of man can do, and for being

> merry while we may,
> For men much quicker pass away

than the tablet on which a tale is written. It is true that it is a wicked sorcerer who asks

> who knoweth certainly
> What haps to us when we are dead?

and answers

> Truly, I think, by likelihood,
> Nought haps to us of good or bad.
> Therefore on earth will I be glad
> A short space, free from hope or fear.

But everywhere the signs are manifest that to the mind of the poet the future presents the same utter blank, and that life is not merely a mystery but an unsubstantial and wearisome dream. This is the cold comfort administered by Phœbus Apollo to Admetus, when he tells him

> The times change, and I can see a day,
> When all thy happiness shall fade away.
> And yet be merry. Strive not with the end,
> Thou canst not change it;

and when the end comes, it swallows up the thought of all other things. Trust or reliance in a loving Father, or even in a guiding Mind, there had been none; and with the fading away of hope the last props give way,

> When death comes to stare
> Full in men's faces and the truth lays bare,
> How can we then have wish for anything
> But unto life that gives us all to cling?

Hence, although great things are said of the power of love, it is not easy to think of a love stronger than death. Love is bounded by the limits of time, and derives its strength from the certainty of coming separation which shall last for ever. In the words of Admetus to Alcestis,

> O love, a little time we have been one,
> And if we now are twain, weep not therefore;

or of Cupid to Psyche,

> Time will go
> Over thine head, and thou mayest mingle yet
> The bitter and the sweet, nor quite forget,
> Nor quite remember, till those things shall seem
> The wavering memory of a lovely dream.

There is nothing solid, nothing real anywhere; and life itself is but a mirage which lasts a little longer than the mocking paradise of the desert. It is not here and there only that the same chords are struck. The one burden runs through all. We have it in the beautiful song in Ogier the Dane:—

> By the white-flowered hawthorn brake,
> Love, be merry for my sake;
> Twine the blossoms in my hair,
> Kiss me where I am most fair;

> Kiss me, love, for who knoweth
> What thing cometh after death?

The placid resignation of the lover passes into something like the impassiveness of the mystic:—

> Shall we weep for a dead day,
> Or set sorrow in our way?
> Hidden by my golden hair,
> Wilt thou weep that sweet days wear?
> Kiss me, love, for who knoweth
> What thing cometh after death?

Rejoicing in the love of the Icelander Kiartan, the beautiful sister of the Norwegian Olaf still casts not away

> From out her heart thought of the coming day,
> When all should be as it had never been,
> And the wild sea should roll its waves between
> His grey eyes and her weary useless tears;

and the same lesson is preached still more pointedly when Perseus rescues Andromeda from the dragon:—

> Love while ye may; if twain grow into one,
> 'Tis for a little while: the time goes by,
> No hatred 'twixt the pair of friends doth lie,
> No troubles break their hearts,—and yet, and yet—
> How could it be? we strove not to forget;
> Rather in vain to that old time we clung,
> Its hopes and wishes round our hearts we hung:
> We played old parts, we used old names,—in vain,
> We go our ways, and twain once more are twain;
> Let pass,—at latest when we come to die,
> Then shall the fashion of the world go by.

This cold consolation, couched in words whose music is sweet as that of a dream, is introduced somewhat gratuitously into a myth which, unlike those of Phœbus, Theseus, Dionysos, Heracles, or Jason, knows nothing of inconstancy or forgetfulness. From first to last Perseus is bent on avenging his mother's wrong; and with him Danaê returns in glory to the land from which she had been cast forth with her babe into the unpitying sea. From first to last his love is given unvaryingly to the maiden whom he had rescued on the Libyan sands from the jaws of the merciless monster.

131

How thoroughly the same strain pervades these poems we may see by comparing almost any one portion of them with another. When Jason, in the full exultation of early manhood, undertakes the quest of the Golden Fleece, he still thought

> When sixty years are gone at most,
> Then will all pleasure and all pain be lost,
> Although my name indeed be cast about
> From hill to temple, amid song and shout;
> So let me now be merry with the best.

When, at the beginning of March, the poet rejoices in the outburst of a new spring, he asks

> Ah! what begetteth all this storm of bliss,
> But death himself, who, crying solemnly
> E'en from the the heart of sweet forgetfulness,
> Bids us, 'Rejoice, lest pleasureless ye die;
> Within a little time must ye go by.
> Stretch forth your open hands, and while ye live
> Take all the gifts that death and life may give.'

It is the old maxim, 'Let us eat and drink, for to-morrow we die.' Hence, although almost every story is a tale of love, whether happy or unrequited, all exhibit the same type. In each case it is the armed Eros who pierces his victim, and holds him as the captive of his bow and spear. If we have ecstatic unions and unimaginable bliss, this joy is the fruit of a glance or a touch. The love, in short, is both sudden and physical; and we look in vain for anything more. While Medea, at her father's bidding, is telling Jason of the perils to be surmounted before he can win the Golden Fleece,

> Love came unseen, and cast his golden yoke
> About them both, and sweeter her voice grew
> And softer ever, as betwixt them flew
> With fluttering wings the new-born strong desire;

and, when coming to offer him her aid in the quest, she expresses her dread of the wrath of Æetes after the departure of the Argonauts, the words rush to the lips of Jason,

> By this unseen delight
> Of thy fair body, may I rather burn,
> Nor may the flame die ever, if I turn
> But to my hollow ship, and leave thee here,

Who in one minute art become so dear,
Thy limbs so longed for, that at last I know
Why men have been content to suffer woe
Past telling, if the gods but granted this
A little while such lips as thine to kiss,
A little while to drink such deep delight.

So it is again when, sated with the exacting love of the wise Colchian
woman, Jason first sees the brilliant Glauce. No sooner have her
fingers touched his than he forgets

all the joys that he had ever known;
And when her hand left his hand with the ring
Still in the palm, like some lost stricken thing
He stood and stared, as from his eyes she passed;
And from that hour all fear away was cast,
All memory of the past time, all regret
For days that did those changed days beget;
And there withal adown the wind he flung
The love whereon his yearning heart once hung.

So is it with Accontius when first he sees the Delian maiden whom
he is to win as his bride:—

Then standing there in mazed wise,
He saw the black-heart tulips bow
Before her knees, as wavering now
A half step unto him she made,
With a glad cry, though half afraid,
He stretched his arms out, and the twain
E'en at the birth of love's great pain,
Each unto each so nigh were grown,
That little lacked to make them one,
That little lacked that they should be
Wedded that hour, knee touching knee,
Cheek laid to cheek.

So, again, when, in the story of the 'Lovers of Gudrun,' Thorgerd,
Kiartan's sister, seeks to excite his love for Refna, she can think of no
other way of attaining her end than by saying

if I were a man, not old or wise,
Methinks I should remember wide grey eyes,
Lips like a scarlet thread, skin lily white,
Round chin, smooth brow 'neath the dark hair's delight,

Fair neck, slim hands, and dainty limbs well hid,
Since unto most of men doth fate forbid
To hold them as their own.

In all this there is not much in harmony with the thought and feelings, perhaps even with the ethics, of our own day; and as we are compelled in some degree to measure humanity by our own standard, we may fairly say that such words as these possess no great human interest. It is for this reason that although Mr. Morris is already one of the most voluminous of poets, and has a marvellous power of imagery and diction, we question whether his works will attain great popularity or pass to lasting fame. They lack entirely the divine element, which touches in its power the human heart, and makes the poet, like itself, immortal. Yet of all the old stories which Mr. Morris has related again in the *Earthly Paradise*, and not a few of which may be resolved even into grotesque absurdities, there is probably not one which fails to exercise over us an indescribable fascination. They are tales which have been told for ages on ages in almost every land, and on which have been built the great fabrics of the epic and tragic poets of old time. They are tales which mingle possible events with things impossible, and exhibit characters which we can conceive as those of real men by the side of others which must be to us simply unmeaning. But, although the possible and the impossible elements of the story are so mingled together that no attempt to separate or decompose them can be successful, we cannot say that our interest is excited only by the words and deeds of those who are manifestly represented as of our own flesh and blood, and not at all by the joys and sufferings of beings who, if they have any existence, belong to another sphere of life. We do feel moved by the sorrow of Zeus when he mourns that Sarpedon, his bright and beautiful child, must die; and we smile no smile of contempt when the poet tells us how the tears, great as drops of blood, fell from the sky when the brave Lycian chieftain was smitten by the spear of Patroclos, how Phœbus bathed the body in the stream of Simoeis, and how, as the first flush of dawn lit up the sky, the Powers of Sleep and Death laid him on the threshold of his Eastern home nigh to the banks of the golden river. We can feel the woes of Psyche, as she wanders on in all but hopeless misery in her search for the beautiful being whom her envious sisters had slandered to her as an unsightly monster; and if the story of Aphrodité weeping for the lovely Adonis done to death by the wild-boar's tusk be too sensuous for northern taste, no such flaw mars the pathos of the tales which tell us how

Baldur and the heroic Helgis, smitten down in the fulness of youth and beauty, rise again to a renewed life and strength which should never waste away. But, if we would raise our enjoyment of these stories to the highest point, we must take them simply as they are. Any attempts to define sharply the boundaries which separate the human from the divine are as wise as the efforts of the man who might think to heighten the butterfly's beauty by brushing the down from its wings.

There can be no doubt that the attempt to treat the actors in the old tales as specimens of human character has done much towards blinding us to the real beauty of the tales themselves, and that this attempt in the case of legends which we are in the habit of regarding as nearer to our time and as framed by men whose thoughts were more akin to our own, can be made only at the cost of more or less serious moral mischief. Mr. Morris is well aware of this, and he is careful before beginning some of his stories to warn us that they are dreams and no histories of men who ever lived; but he touches on doubtful ground when he adds—

> Yet as in dreams
> Of known things still we dream, whatever gleams
> Of unknown light may make them strange, so here
> Our dreamland story holdeth such things dear,
> And such things loathed, as we do: else, indeed,
> Were all its marvels nought to help our need.

If we follow the beautiful rhymes in which 'the idle singer of an empty day' introduces us to his fairy garden, we must believe that we have no needs to help; but if we have, then it may fairly be doubted whether some or any of the poet's legends will stand the test which he has himself laid down. Taken in its bare outlines, few myths are more repulsive than that of the maiden who stakes her person on the issue of a race in which the penalty for the unsuccessful lover is instant death by the headsman's axe, and who day by day sees human blood poured out with eyes unmoved and heart untroubled. Nor can the magic of the poet's verse at all reconcile us to the thought of the pitiless being who, armed with superhuman powers, can see brave men die for her sake, until one comes who wins her only because he has the special aid of a god. It is of little use to tell us of her beauty as, standing at the starting-post,

> She seemed all earthly matters to forget,
> Of all tormenting lines her face was clear;

Her wide grey eyes upon the goal were set,
Calm and unmoved as though no soul were near;

Or again how, when she had reached the goal, she stood

breathing like a little child
Amid some warlike clamour laid asleep,
For no victorious joy her red lips smiled,
Her cheek its wonted freshness did but keep:
No glance lit up her clear grey eyes and deep,
Though some divine thought softened all her face,
As once more rang the trumpet through the place.

We remember that this divine thought is no thought of pity for the victim whose head falls at the trumpet blast; and if we judge by any human standard, we turn aside from the maiden as we should from the ferocious rites which marked the devil-worship of Artemis Tauropola or the Spartan Iphigeneia. But although the poet speaks of Atalanta as reared up, like Helen, to be 'a kingdom's curse,' and as making her

city's name accurst
Among all mothers for its cruelty,

he does not wish us so to dwell upon this thought as to kill all our sympathy for her when the warm human feeling wakes up in her heart as Milanion, by the help of a god, and by this help alone, at last outruns her. Neither do we wish it. But we can avoid this only by ceasing to look upon her as human at all. The beauty of the tale cannot be questioned, but neither can we question the beauty of those many other tales in which we find the two thoughts that furnish the framework of the story of Atalanta—the idea, namely, of the maiden whom hundreds stake their lives to win, and the idea of the suitors who meet their death until in due time comes the man destined to win her. Some of these stories have been wedded to verse by modern as well as by ancient poets; and if the beauty of their work must be measured by the degree of their fidelity to the ideas which lie at the root of these stories, we can but wonder at the magic power which those ideas have exercised on poets who seem to have scarcely felt a temptation even to modify them.

In the 'Doom of King Acrisius' Mr. Morris handles a subject which might furnish materials for many epics, and which is handled by himself more than once in other poems. The child Perseus is also 'the Man

born to be King'; and none will read the two tales as the one follows
the other, without seeing that the framework in both is the same and
that not a few of the incidents correspond. No beauty can exceed that
of Danaê, no grace surpass that of her child Perseus, the pure hero,
whose office it is to redress wrong and punish the evil-doers. Here then
is the chord struck which excites our human sympathy; but we cannot
rest on this or on the love of Perseus for the Libyan maiden, as we
wander along in the midst of wonders, marvellous as any in Arabian
story, which tempt us continually to stray into the many other regions
where we may survey the same scenes and hear the same sounds. The
temptation is the stronger, because the points of likeness between the
several tales heighten their charm; and thus we may follow the 'idle
singer' through his 'murmuring rhymes,' being well assured that the
imagery of his stories will at each step recall other scenes in the
enchanted land.

We feel ourselves in the old and well-known paths as we read

> There on the sill she laid her slender hand,
> And, looking seaward, pensive did she stand,
> And seemed as though she waited for the Sun
> To bring her news her misery was done;
> At last he came, and over the green sea
> His golden road shone out right gloriously,
> And into Danae's face his glory came
> And lit her softly waving hair like flame.
> But in his light she held out both her hands,
> As though he brought her from some far off lands
> Healing for all her great distress and woe.

In the incidents that follow, Mr. Morris adheres more strictly to the
old legend, which shows with singular clearness how thoroughly the
elements of European folk lore were known to the nurses and poets of
ancient Hellas.

In the rescue of Andromeda we approach the true work of all
heroes; and Mr. Morris's dragon, which is very well described, may
serve excellently as a type of all the monsters slain by Theseus, Heracles,
Bellerophon, or Jason, by Cadmus, Œdipus, St. George, or Feridun.
True to himself, Mr. Morris closes the scene in which Perseus first sees
and wins his bride by words which, put into the mouth of Andromeda,
throw over it the shadow of future darkness:—

> O love, to think that love can pass away,
> That soon or late to us shall come a day

When this shall be forgotten! e'en this kiss
That makes us now forget the high God's bliss,
And sons of men with all their miseries.

Mr. Morris introduces us into a very garden of delights when he tells us again the often-told story of Psyche—the history of lovers severed by the malice of others almost as soon as they are wed, and retaining no other consolation than the thought that it is 'better to have loved and lost than never to have loved at all.' If to explain the hatred of Aphroditê for Psyche Mr. Morris has departed from the ordinary story, his language still shows that her jealousy of the fair maiden is but another form of the jealousy of Eos in the story of Procris. Psyche is receiving at all hands the worship which should be reserved for the Queen of Beauty only: she is a maid

> Whom any amourous man this day would kiss
> As gladly as a goddess like to me;
> And though O known an end to this must be,
> When white and red and gold are waxen grey
> Down on the earth, while unto me one day
> Is as another, yet behold, my son,
> And go through all my temples one by one,
> And look what incense rises unto me;
> Hearken the talk of sailors from the sea
> Just landed, ever will it be the same,
> 'Hast thou then seen her?'

The Love-God promises obedience; but his cruel purpose gives way to a feeling of absorbing rapture when he comes upon the desolate Psyche, who has sunk to sleep beneath the weight of her sorrow. The god kneels beside her as she slumbers, and the picture, sensuous, though it may be, is full of beauty:—

> From place to place Love followed her that day,
> And ever fairer to his eye she grew,
> So that at last, when from her bower he flew,
> And underneath his feet the moonlit sea
> Went shepherding his waves disorderly,
> He swore that of all gods and men, not one
> Should hold her in his arms but he alone;
> That she should dwell with him in glorious wise,
> Like to a goddess in some paradise;
> Yea, he would get from Father Jove this grace,
> That she should never die, but her sweet face

And wonderful fair body should endure
Till the foundations of the mountains sure
Were molten in the sea.

After a long and grievous pilgrimage—after tasks wholly beyond
human powers, in which, like the wandering princes and maidens of
folk lore in like case, she is aided by birds and beasts whom she has
befriended, this consummation is at last brought about: but although
to do full justice to the way in which Mr. Morris has told the story,
we should have to quote the whole of it, we must pause for awhile to
look on the picture of the beautiful maiden who leaves the abode of
lost love and happiness, with a weight of misery not to be described
in words, yet nerved by a purpose which no earthly power could
conquer or turn aside:—

> Thenceforth her back upon the world she turned,
> As she had known it; in her heart there burned
> Such deathless love, that still untired she went;
> The huntsman dropping down the woody bent
> In the still evening saw her passing by,
> And for her beauty fain would draw anigh,
> But yet durst not; the shepherd on the down,
> Wondering, would shade his eyes with fingers brown,
> As on the hill's brow, looking o'er the lands,
> She stood with strained eyes and clasped hands,
> While the wind blew the raiment from her feet;
> The wondering soldier her grey eyes would meet,
> That took no heed of him, and drop his own;
> Like a thin dream she passed the clattering town;
> On the thronged quays she watched the ships come in.
> Patient, amid the strange outlandish din;
> Unscared, she saw the sacked town's miseries,
> And marching armies passed before her eyes.
> And still of her the god had such a care,
> None did her wrong, although alone and fair
> Through rough and smooth she wandered many a day,
> Till all her hope had well-nigh passed away.

From this image of purely spiritual beauty, the loveliness of Una
which the touch of neither man nor beast may mar, the poet takes us
with consummate art to the sensuous home of the Paphian Queen,—

> Whose beauty sole had lighted up the place,

where the maidens danced in the house made beautiful with gold.

A crown there was upon her glorious head,
A garland round about her girdlestead,
Where matchless wonders of the hidden sea
Were brought together and set wonderfully.
Naked she was of all else, but her hair
About her body rippled here and there,
And lay in heaps upon the golden seat,
And even brushed the gold cloth where her feet
Lay amid roses,—ah! how kind she seemed,
What depths of love from out her grey eyes streamed.

But the kindness and the love are not for those who approach her too nearly in their beauty; and her unconscious rival bleeds beneath her cruel scourges, until the time comes when Psyche must drink the draught which after her grievous sorrows is to render her immortal.

We must hasten through the other scenes of the *Earthly Paradise*. We must not be tempted to linger amidst the beauties of the legend of the brave Ogier, some portion of whose story Mr. Morris tells again in his charming poem of the 'Land East of the Sun.' But the simple hero of the 'Land East of the Sun' comes back, not like Ogier, to the scenes of his ancient glory and renown, but like Psyche for a long and agonizing quest, which lasts until the spell is broken by the utterance of the magic name of the land where he finds again the love whom he had lost. In the fourth part of the work, recently published, the legend of Bellerophon appears again, in Argos and in Lycia; but in our judgment the 'Ring given to Venus' is the most attractive portion of this volume, and one of the most perfect of Mr. Morris's compositions, for he avoids in it his two besetting sins of despondency and prolixity.

From this banquet in the halls of Fairyland we turn to the most powerful of the stories told in the *Earthly Paradise*, and the most human. In the poem which tells the story of Gudrun and her lovers we have the working only of human passions; but of the result we are bound to say plainly that it is more repulsive and more shocking to our moral sense than any incidents of the stories which professedly carry us out of the region of human ethics. The Gudrun of this terrible drama is not the Gudrun of the Volsung and Niblung legend, although she is one

Whose birth the wondering world no more would blame
Than hers who erst called Tyndarus her sire,
What hearts soe'er, what roof-trees she might fire,

> What hearts soe'er, what hearths she might leave cold,
> Before the ending of the tale be told.

If we choose to sup on horrors, knowing them to be impossible or unreal, it may perhaps be well. If we take these horrors as in any sort true pictures of the society of an historical age, it is not well; and the claim which Mr. Morris has put forward for the substantially historical character of the Grettir Saga, a story of like complexion, justifies some further comments on a poem, to the beauty and power of which we can have no wish to shut our eyes.

The course of Gudrun's future life is revealed to her, while she is yet a girl, by Guest the Wise; but our concern is not with the predictions but with the incidents of her strange career. The first is her marriage with Thorvald, whom she weds without feeling for him a spark of affection, but only because it was too much trouble to say 'no' for ever. The man is coarse; but his coarseness must of itself reflect on the choice of a maiden who had grown up to 'perfect womanhood.' He is also rough and passionate, and

> As she ever gloomed before his eyes,

he is moved by some not altogether unnatural or inexcusable anger against the woman who, at the first, was at the least as much to blame as himself, and far more so in the end, when on a time it fell

> That he, most fain indeed to love her well,
> Would she but turn to him, had striven sore
> To gain her love, and yet got nothing more
> Than a faint smile of scorn, 'neath eyes whose gaze
> Seemed fixed for ever on the hoped-for days
> Wherein he no more should have part or lot.

All other feelings are now overpowered by resentment, and smiting her on the face in his despair, he rushes out and rides away furiously over hill and moor. Gudrun after this behaves more kindly to Thorvald, whose wife she continues to be for several months, till, when he is gone to the Thing, she rides over with one man to Bathstead to tell her tale:—

> And as in those days law strained not to hold
> Folk whom love held not, or some common tie,
> So her divorce was set forth speedily,
> For mighty were her kin.

This is plain speaking; and the thought may be pardoned that, it Gudrun, on subsequent occasions, had chosen to set in motion the simple machinery which she had shown herself so competent to use, she needed not to have undergone the miseries of her life, or the poet to have related the horrors of her history. Freed from Thorvald, she soon marries Thord, a man of whom nothing more can be said than that he was 'brisk, and brave, and fair;' and the fact would seem to imply that with Gudrun marriage was the end of life rather than marriage with true love. We are, however, told that 'she deemed she loved him well;' and that things might perhaps have continued to run smoothly had not her husband been drowned in a summer gale. Her eyes are next turned to Kiartan, a man who is described as the bravest of the brave and the fairest of the fair—a man worthy of the love of the noblest and best of women. But Gudrun, who had thus far shown no unwillingness to run into marriage, now betakes herself to other ways; and when her father hints that she might do well to take Kiartan as her third husband,

> She answered nought, but drew her hand away,
> And heavier yet the weight upon her lay
> That thus men spake of her. But, turning round,
> Kiartan upon the other hand she found
> Gazing upon her with wide hungry eyes
> And parted lips; then did strange joy surprise
> Her listless heart, and changed her old world was;
> Ere she had time to think, all woe did pass
> Away from her, and still her life grew sweet,
> And scarce she felt the ground beneath her feet,
> Or knew who stood around, or in what place
> Of heaven or earth she was; soft grew her face;
> In tears that fell not yet, her eyes did swim,
> As, trembling, she reached forth her hand to him,
> And with the shame of love her smooth cheek burned,
> And her lips quivered, as if sore they yearned
> For words they had not learned, and might not know
> Till night and loneliness their form should show.

This is very pretty; but when we remember what she had done before, and what she did afterwards, we may well think that she might have married him at once, and so made an end of the business. Instead of this, when Kiartan suggests to his bosom friend and foster-brother Bodli Thorleikson that he should get him a wife, and when

Bodli, who in secret loves Gudrun, says that his sword must bring home a bride, Gudrun urges that all three should take a voyage up the Thames or Seine. Kiartan, taking up the thought, says that he will go with Bodli, and will wed Gudrun when he comes back to Iceland full of fame. The next scene shows Kiartan and his friend in the court of the sainted Olaf, whose faith they would have been willing to adopt, but that they

> knew not how their forefathers to call
> Souls damned for ever and ever.

Olaf, however, is less peremptory with them than it was his wont to be; but when they fail to be convinced by the exposition of a German bishop, 'that seemed both dull and long,' they bring themselves into some jeopardy, from which they are delivered by the noble and chivalrous candour of Kiartan. At length, both the friends are hallowed at the font, and Kiartan, while he says that 'nought at all may move his heart from Gudrun,' allows Ingebjorg, Olaf's sister, to fall in love with him, until the king, pleased with the affection growing up between them, has in heart to raise Kiartan so that he too should be a king. A ship is now to sail for Iceland; but Kiartan will not go, the reason given being that he 'passed his life, fulfilled of praise and love and glory.' Bodli, whom Kiartan charges with a cold message to Gudrun that he had won great honour and bliss, and that they should meet again, tells Gudrun, in answer to her importunate questionings, that Kiartan sits ever by Ingebjorg's side, and that men said that he should wed her and be king; and in so saying he spoke but the plain truth. If he thought that Gudrun might now turn from his friend to himself, her former history might pardon, or even justify, the hope. Kiartan tarries three years in Norway, sending no tidings of himself to Gudrun; but at the end of this time he determines to return to Iceland, and goes to bid farewell to Ingebjorg, whom

> He loved with a strange love very sore,
> Despite the past and future.

We are at a loss to know what name is to be given to this kind of love, however great may be our sympathy with the gentle Ingebjorg, who, seeing the tears streaming down his cheeks, says in all simplicity—

> Weep, then!
> If thou, who art the kindest of all men,
> Must sorrow for me, yet more glad were I

To see thee leave my bower joyfully
This last time; that when o'er thee sorrow came,
And thought of me therewith, thou might'st not blame
My little love for ever saddening thee.
Love! let me say Love once—great shalt thou be,
Beloved of all, and dying ne'er forgot.

Kiartan, on reaching Iceland, learns from his sister Thurid that Gudrun,
incapable, it would seem, of abstaining from marriage for more than
a few months, is the wife of his friend Bodli, and bursts into the cry—

O Gudrun, Gudrun,
Have I come back with all the honour won
We talked of, that thou saidst thou knewest well
Was but for thee—to whom then shall I tell
The tale of that well-doing? And thou, friend,
How might I deem that aught but death should end
Our love together? Yea, and even now,
How shall I learn to hate thee, friend, though thou
Art changed into a shadow and a lie?

The words sound much like rhodomontade, and we can but ask how
he can speak of Gudrun as his love, when he had but a little while
before confessed that despite the past and future he loved Ingebjorg
with a strange love very sore, and in what way Bodli had become to
him a shadow and a lie. If fault there were anywhere, it lay now, as
before, with Gudrun; and if Kiartan had particularly wished to tell her
of his exploits, he might have returned with Bodli for this purpose;
for it does not appear that he added greatly to his achievements after
his friend's departure, his time being chiefly taken up with furnishing
fuel for the fire which was to consume the heart of Ingebjorg.

At this point a new lover of Kiartan is brought on the stage; nor is
it to be wondered at that the beautiful Refna should be drawn towards
Kiartan, or that Kiartan should speak kindly to her. Meanwhile, at
Bathstead, Gudrun had received the tidings of Kiartan's return to
Iceland, and late in the night she leaves her chamber to hold forth to
her husband after the following fashion:—

Night hides thee not, O Bodli Thorleikson,
Nor shall death hide from thee what thou hast done.
What, thou art grown afraid, thou tremblest then,
Because I name death, seed of fearless men?
Fear not, I bear no sword, Kiartan is kind;

He will not slay thee because he was blind,
And took thee for a true man time agone.
  My curse upon thee! Know'st thou how alone
Thy deed hath made me? Dreamest thou what pain
Burns in me now when he has come again?
Now, when the longed-for Sun has risen at last
To light an empty world, whence all has passed
Of joy and hope—great is thy gain herein!
A bitter broken thing to seem to win,
A soul the fruit of lies shall yet make vile,
A body for thy base lust to defile,
If thou durst come anigh me any more,
Now I have curst thee, that thy mother bore
So base a wretch among good men to dwell,
That thou might'st build me up this hot-walled hell.

It has been said of Cranmer, that it is difficult to speak our mind of
the lessons given by him to Edward VI in the art of persecution
without calling foul names; but without thus assailing Gudrun, the
answer to this furious and unseemly outburst is, briefly, that Bodli had
done nothing but speak the truth; that if she felt dissatisfied with his
report, her business was to ascertain the real state of things by writing
to Kiartan, or, if need be, by going herself to Norway; that instead
of doing this, she had chosen to repeat in Bodli's case what she had
done twice already, and married for the third time without real love;
that her words meant nothing, for at a later time she bore children to
Bodli, and that all the difficulty might have been settled at once by a
resort to that court whose aid she had effectually invoked for a far
smaller matter, even if her words were true, in the case of her first
husband, Thorvald. It seems almost idle to waste words on this
wretched medley of unnecessary miseries. Kiartan, we are told, would
now sit and watch the weary sun go by,

> Feeling as though his heart in him were dead.

He had already made the voyage to Norway once; he had only to
make it again to find there a true and devoted woman whose love
would be worth that of a thousand Gudruns. But in Ingebjorg there
is no further count taken; and because Gudrun will not divorce herself
from Bodli, Kiartan weds not Ingebjorg but Refna. It would not be
easy to find a parallel to this mingled baseness and absurdity, unless
perhaps we look for it to the confessions of Augustine, who sends
away the long-loved mother of his child because he wishes to marry a

Milanese lady, and because this lady is still too young, enters into another unlawful connexion until she should be old enough to marry him. To make the matter even worse, when his sister Thurid has told Kiartan the truth about Refna, Kiartan with a certain feeling of relief lays himself on his bed, thinking of Ingebjorg

> And all the pleasure her sweet love had brought
> While he was with her; and this maid did seem
> Like her come back amidst a happy dream:

and Kiartan now called himself a Christian. 'Ah, well! what will you have?' asks Mr. Morris.

> This was a man some shreds of joy to save
> From out the wreck, if so he might, to win
> Some garden from the waste and dwell therein.
> And yet he lingered long, or e'er he told
> His heart that it another name might hold
> With that of the lost Gudrun.

This is intolerable. What we would have is the plain duty of a Christian man—which in such a case would be, either that he should remain as he was, or that, as he could not marry the woman whom he had first loved, he should betake himself to her whom he professed to love with a strange love great and sore. In strict truth, there was no wreck and no waste except such as he had chosen to make. According to the Icelandic ethics of the day, all might be settled on Gudrun's part by an appeal to the divorce court; on his own part, he was bound to make Ingebjorg happy and not to make Refna miserable. But in point of fact, he had allowed another name to hold his heart along with that of Gudrun, if there was but a grain of truth in the words which he had spoken of Ingebjorg; nor can we shut our eyes to these glaring inconsistencies in an awkwardly constructed story.

We need all our patience to go through the sequel of the tale. It is enough to say that a feud is made to spring up between the house of Bathstead and Kiartan's house of Herdholt—that Kiartan finds it consistent with his Christian profession to harry his neighbour's house and steal his cattle, and that in the issue

> Gudrun's five brethren, and three stout men more,

valiantly attack Kiartan and his single attendant in a desolate pass, and at length succeed in slaying him, their luck being better than that of the eighty assailants of Grettir, who are vanquished by that hero as

easily as the thousand Philistines were smitten by Samson when armed
with the jaw-bone of an ass. The rest may be told in few words, but
these are not the less noteworthy. Refna dies soon of a broken heart;
and three years later Bodli is slain by Kiartan's kinsfolk. As to Gudrun,

> when Bodli's sons were men,
> And many things had happed, she wed again;

and when Thorkel in his turn had been dead for a long while, she
discourses to one of the sons of Bodli on the merits of her several
husbands. If we allow, as well we may, when she came to speak of one
who had not been her husband, that she told no more than the bare
truth in saying,

> I did the worst to him I loved the most,

we must also allow that, if these words imply blame to herself, that
blame was most fully deserved; but as we can see nothing to praise or
to love in her life, we can find little that is wholesome in the chronicle
of her self-inflicted miseries.

It may, indeed, be said that if there are horrors here, there are
horrors also in the story of Jason. But when we get among fire-
breathing bulls, and men springing up after the sowing of dragon's
teeth, and the marvels wrought by the wise Colchian maiden, our
thoughts pass at once into another channel, where the contrast of the
tale of Gudrun with the laws which underlie all our social life is not
forced upon us; and in the story of Jason Mr. Morris has found a
subject which he has handled with even greater skill than the most
beautiful of the legends selected for the poems of the *Earthly Paradise*.
That this poem is tinged with the same tones of thought and feeling
which pervade all the others, we have already seen; but here, as elsewhere, the lines in which these feelings are expressed are among the
most melodious of Mr. Morris's rhymes. The Argonautic legend itself
is worked up into a tale of absorbing interest; and from the moment
when the Olympian Queen reveals her loving purpose respecting
Jason to the hour when he lies down to take his last sleep beneath the
divine Argo, we are carried on with the art of the bard whose strains
drive away all sleep from the eyes of his hearers. The contrast between
the earlier scenes of the story and those in which the career of Jason
is brought to the end, is drawn with singular force. The great work of
Medea is done, and she sits a queen beside her crowned king:—

> Yet surely now, if never more again,
> Had she and all these folk forgotten pain,

And idle words to them were Death and Fear;
For in the gathering evening could they hear
The carols of the glad talk through the town
The song of birds within the garden drown:
And when the golden sun had gone away,
Still little darker was the night than day
Without the windows of the goodly hall.
  But many an hour after the night did fall,
Though outside silence fell on man and beast,
There still they sate, nor wearied of the feast;
Yea, ere they parted, glimmering light had come
From the far mountains, nigh the Colchian's home,
And in the twilight birds began to wake.

The golden light rests on all,

    And there in happy days, and rest and peace,
    Here ends the winning of the Golden Fleece.

But the winning of the Golden Fleece is not the end of the story;
and, as though to nerve himself for the great catastrophe, Mr. Morris
breaks off into one of the few passages in which he speaks of himself;
nor will his readers think that in these lines he advances a claim which
savours in the least of presumption.

    So ends the winning of the Golden Fleece,
    So ends the tale of that sweet rest and peace,
    That unto Jason and his love befell.
    Another story now my tongue must tell,
    And tremble in the telling. Would that I
    Had but some portion of that mastery
    That from the rose-hung lanes of woody Kent
    Through these five hundred years such songs have sent
    To us who, meshed within this smoky net
    Of unrejoicing labour, love them yet.
    And thou, O master!—yes, my master still,
    Whatever feet have scaled Parnassus' hill,
    Since like thy measures, clear and sweet and strong,
    Thames' stream scarce fettered, bore the bream along
    Unto the bastioned bridge, his only chain.
    O master, pardon me, if yet in vain
    Thou art my master, and I fail to bring
    Before men's eyes the image of the thing
    My heart is filled with; thou, whose dreamy eyes
    Beheld the flush to Cressid's cheeks arise,

When Troilus rode up the praising street,
As clearly as they saw thy townsmen meet
Those who in vineyards of Poitou withstood
The glittering horror of the steel-topped wood.

Chaucer himself might regard with complacency the work of his disciple throughout this poem, and, most of all, in that closing scene in which Jason thinks with tenderness of his first love and with more than tenderness of the later-won maiden,

Whose innocent sweet eyes and tender hands
Made [him] a mocking unto distant lands,

and with high purpose nerving his heart, can still say

with the next returning light will I
Cast off my moody sorrow utterly,
And once more live my life as in times past
And 'mid the chance of war the die will cast.

So, thinking of great deeds still to be done in other lands, and

gazing still across the sea,
Heavy with days and nights of misery,
His eyes waxed dim, and calmer still he grew,
Still pondering over times and things he knew,
While now the sun had sunk behind the hill,
And from a white-thorn nigh a thrush did fill
The balmy air with echoing minstrelsy,
And cool the night-wind blew across the sea,
And round about the soft-winged bats did sweep.

The next day a shepherd of the lone grey slope finds crushed under the ruined stem of Argo all dead of Jason that here can die; and amid the funeral rites of the great king and hero the divine ship is offered

to the Deity
Who shakes the hard earth with the rolling sea.

We turn reluctantly from this noble poem as from the charming tales which Mr. Morris has gathered from the great storehouse of Greek tradition. Of the *Earthly Paradise* we need only say that if, as in the story of Gudrun, there may be some thorny plants in its beautiful garden, and if the songs which tell us of its glories and its pleasures rather add to than lighten the burden of life, we are not blind to the loveliness of its flowers, or deaf to the music which is heard amidst its groves.

19. Unsigned notice, *Westminster Review*

April 1871, xcv, 581

A notice of Part 4, approving of Morris's frequently criticized diction.

The quick appearance of the second edition of the fourth volume of Mr. Morris's *Earthly Paradise* proves that there is a public which welcomes genuine poetry. Mr. Morris's popularity has, however, something remarkable about it. He is, we have noticed, appreciated by those, who as a rule, do not care to read any poetry. To our personal knowledge, political economists and scientific men to whom Shelley is a mystery and Tennyson a vexation of spirit, read the *Earthly Paradise* with admiration. We do not pretend fully to explain this phenomenon. One of the causes, however, obviously is the excessively easy flow and simple construction of Mr. Morris's verse. The rhyme, too, is never forced. It seems to fall into its place in the most natural way possible. Then again, those wonderfully simple photographic touches of Mr. Morris's reveal, without any trouble on the reader's part, the whole scene in a moment bright and vivid. It is this direct painting, which in a great measure has made Mr. Morris such a favourite with that highly cultivated class of readers and thinkers, who shun anything like vagueness and thinness of treatment. We must remark, too, in noticing the second edition, the way in which Mr. Morris, like Mr. Rossetti, has enriched our language by drawing upon the stores of our old and forgotten words. Reading his poem is like reading a fresh and more vigorous style of English than that to which we are daily accustomed. We have probably the richest language in the world, and yet we do not know how to use it effectively. Mr. Morris has evidently made our older authors his especial study. If we look at merely the first tale in the volume—'Golden Apples'—we shall see how many noble words he has rescued. First there comes in the third line, that fine old word 'rack,' for cloud, used by Shakspeare and his contemporaries, and which has never gone out of use probably in any part of England, certainly in none with which we are acquainted, among the peasantry. Then immediately after follows 'foredone,' destroyed, another Shakspearian word, but which, like 'forespent,' has long been forgotten. And these words, like all the others which follow, 'fell' for skin, 'worm' for dragon, 'ness' for headland, still locally retained in Devonshire, are never forced upon us, but fall naturally, and almost we would say, lovingly into their places. Lastly, we would especially call attention to the beauty and freshness with which all natural objects are described. As long as there are fields and flowers, and sea and sky, Mr. Morris's *Earthly Paradise* will be read for the beauty and truth with which he has described them all.

THE STORY OF THE VOLSUNGS AND NIBLUNGS

1870

20. G. A. Simcox, review, *Academy*

August 1870, ii, 278–9

Acknowledgment is made to G. Vigfússon, the Icelandic scholar, for the 'philological criticisms in this article'.

The translators challenge attention to their work as the great Epic of the North as the tale of Troy is the great Epic of the South, and certainly there are points of contact. The tale of Troy was the property of the whole Greek race, and the tale of the Volsungs and Niblungs is the property of the whole Teutonic race. Both introduce the heroes of many divisions of the race which subsequently became separate states. In both, mythical and legendary elements are inextricably entangled. We are sure that Sigurd slaying Fafnir is the same as Apollo slaying Python; we are sure that Briseis and Chryseis must be cosmical impersonations of some kind, for they appear in India as well as in Greece. But when we try to carry the cosmical interpretation through, we find the same difficulty in both; the story is rooted in geography, and in the tale of the Volsungs and Niblungs the proper names coincide with those of historical characters so often that it is hard to believe that all the coincidences are accidental. It is not surprising that the ethnographical patriotism of the translators has made them overlook the reasons why stories which have such a similar place in the history of the Greek and Teutonic race have such a dissimilar place in the history of Greek and Teutonic literature; why Homer, as represented by Dictys and Dares, has been so much more to Englishmen than the Edda and *Nibelungenlied*. It is probable that the Greek race was more

152

highly gifted for artistic purposes than the northern; it is certain that the society of the Homeric age was artistically richer than the society of the Icelandic sagas, for it was more complex and more regular. These Icelandic compositions are largely influenced by a spirit of *naïve* 'historical veracity, a desire to get as quickly as possible through all that is remembered of the traditional facts. This tendency is not without its value; it excludes inartistic loitering,' and sobriety is always impressive. But a literature of this kind is not suggestive, it does not germinate; it begins and ends in ballads, and the compilations that come between are scarcely epical—even in dimensions. *Volsunga Saga* is constructed like all Icelandic stories on the principal of beginning the Trojan War with Leda's Egg, and the Return of Diomed with the Death of Meleager, yet it is not a quarter of the length of either the *Iliad* or the *Odyssey*, which deal each with a single episode of the tale of Troy.

And the Sagaman was not a Homer, he was not even a Sir Thomas Mallory. The quaint archaic English of the translation with just the right outlandish flavour, does much to disguise the inequalities and incompletenesses of the original. No one can trace in the translation the difference of style between the equable prose of chapters 1-8, 10, 40-41, with part of 43 (according to the division of the translators) where the compiler seems to have followed the lost *Sigurd's Saga*, quoted by old writers,—and the clumsy paraphrases of lays which make up the rest of the work, except chapter 22, which together with a few phrases elsewhere is taken, with little variation, from Wilkina Saga. The translators are aware of this coincidence between a work of the thirteenth century and one which they assign to the twelfth; but they give no explanation of this point, and no grounds for the date they assign. We have reason to be grateful to the awkwardness of the compiler for continually allowing poetical phrases to crop up in his prose, so that they can sometimes without trouble be turned back into verse, for the original of chapters 23-30 belonged to the lost leaves of our only MS. of Saemunds Edda; but this circumstance, which is an attraction to the student, is a difficulty, perhaps a temptation to the translator, who is led by literary interests to claim a liberty not always compatible with fidelity.

When a clumsy and unequal writer is to be brought up to an empirical standard of archaic elegance, it is easy to see how Vala-ript (which means quite literally Welsh cloth or Welsh stuff) comes to be translated 'cloth dyed red by the folk of the Gauls.' The same tendency to prettiness invades the notes; we are actually told that Valkyrja means 'Chooser of the Elected,' and Valhall 'Hall of the Elected,' instead of 'Chooser of the Slain,' and 'Hall of the Slain.' On the other hand, while 'Battle-apple tree' of a warrior is paraphrased 'Fair fruit of the byrnie's clash,' other uncouth and difficult phrases like 'Helmstaffe' for 'warrior,' or 'Windhelm,' *i. q.* 'helmet of the wind,' for 'sky,' or 'sharp steel's root and stem,' for 'warrior,' and the like, are left not only unadorned but unexplained, and where an explanation is given it is not always adequate. It is quite true that an outlaw was a *wolf's head*, but there is a difference between this and a *wolf in holy places*. This last condition surely answers rather to excommunication and to the profanation of the holy places than to outlawry. It would have been as well also to explain that the verse in Fjolnis's song translated 'Great is the trouble of foot ill tripping' refers to the omen of stumbling before going into a battle or beginning a war, which Harold Hardrada vainly endeavoured to elude at Stamford Bridge. The last line of the same song is positively mistranslated, 'And base to fall before fate grovelling,' which has no connection with what goes before, and contradicts Norse sentiment into the bargain, for there 'old age bends all knees, and fate and death lays all prostrate, rich and poor, weak and mighty.' The real meaning is 'it is ill to rush headlong before (a man's) luck,' which coincides admirably with the precepts of cheerful prudence just before. The notion is, the headlong fool rushes into destruction, leaving his luck behind him; while the wise man is wary and gives good luck time to go before and prepare his way. In the same spirit we are told that a 'fey'-man's fylgja or 'fetch' follows behind, whereas the fylgja of a man in health and wealth walks before him and heralds his coming.

The translators have not been able to efface the gaps and discrepancies of their story as completely as they have effaced its inequalities of style. The ballads which the compiler tried, or did not try, to work into narrative, were written at different times and places; they sometimes represent incompatible traditions, and to appreciate them we ought to remember that, for the most part, they were intended to stand alone. The old poets are not responsible for the difference of tone between the scenes where Brynhild and Gudrun are contrasted as lioness and lamb, and those where Gudrun outdoes the ferocity of Medea, first in defence and then in revenge of her brother. They are not responsible for the way in which Sigurd's son disappears from the story, leaving his murder, among so many, to be a matter of inference,

alluded to, but never stated. They are not responsible either for the
omission of the love passages between Gunnar and Oddrun, which
would be some excuse for the treachery of Atli, or for the identification of Sigrdrifa, the companion of Odin and the goddess of victory,
with Brynhild. This last identification gives a thoroughly sophistic look
to the commandments of the goddess, and makes the portion of the
lay, which the translators have called Sigrdrifa Mal, appear a mere
marvel of science and courtesy for Norse gentlemen; a rhetorical
exercise of the same order as Nestor's advice to Neoptolemus, composed by Hippias. The translators have aided the identification by
omitting Sigrdrifa, which is given as the name of the sleeping shield-
may in the birds' song. We notice, by the way, that the exigencies of
alliteration have produced a fresh variation of every stanza of Sigrdrifa's
song of the formula ('Thou shalt know' such and such 'runes'), which
opens all. Nor are the old poets to blame for the astonishing chrono-
logical confusion of the story as we have it, where Sigurd's widow
marries a king of the fifth century, her daughter marries Jormunrek
or Ermanrik, a king of the third, while his other daughter marries
Raguar, a king of the eighth or ninth. The legend lived on in many
lays, and it fitted itself to many historical names; but while it was alive
it never fitted itself to all at once. It is hard to see why the translators
have omitted the story of Heimir and Aslaug, Brynhild's daughter,
which has as much to do with the main story as the tale of Erp and
Hamdir, and serves, besides the beautiful legend of the harp child, to
connect the cycles of Sigurd and Raguar. But unanswerable questions
were sure to multiply when the translators decided to use the lays as
a supplement to the compilation, instead of using the compilation
as a key to the lays. The worst consequence of this mistake is, that as
we read the Saga continuously, the principal incidents are all anticipated
before the birth of Sigurd. Sigi is betrayed like Sigurd by his brothers-
in-law, Atli like Siggeir betrays, and Signy's vengeance is an anticipation of Gudrun's, both in its treachery and its ferocity of self-sacrifice.
Sigrun's invocation to Helgi is just like Gudrun's invocation of Sigurd.

Still, with all its defects even the prose Saga abounds with beauties
which justify the praise of Mr. Morris's lovely 'Prologue in Verse.'
There are touches of pathetic elevation, like the last words of Signy; 'All
these things have I done that vengeance might fall on him, and that
I too might not live long; and merrily will I die with King Siggeir,
though I was nought merry to live with him.' And all the situations
of the lays, where Brynhild is the heroine, are too lofty to be spoilt by

paraphrase. Where she expounds Gudrun's dream, which is a prophecy of all that is to pass between them; where she meets Sigurd for the last time, and sacrifices her love to duty and revenge, and refuses his offer to undo what has been done by mistake; where she forbids any to be driven by hand or word to follow her to her wedding with Sigurd on the funeral pile, while she offers wealth to be enjoyed beyond the grave to all who will follow her of their own accord,—the story is on the highest level of artistic tragedy. Gudrun's lament is later and more literary; it turns like Mr. Tennyson's well-known lines, 'Home they brought her warrior dead,' on the difficulty of winning tears. Each of her women in turn recounts her own greatest sorrow, till the wisest uncovers the face of the dead, and bids her embrace him once more. Then the tears come, and the words; and it is an unimpeachable testimony to the power that they gain from the situation that St. Gertrude sang the Low Dutch version of Gudrun's lament daily as a lamentation for her beloved. The story falls where the story of the *Nibelungenlied* rises, when it comes to the death of the Giukungs. The way in which Gunnar receives the tokens, feigned and true, of Hogni's death, is of course very lofty; but the effect is marred by the motionless self-distrust with which he provokes his brother's death. The murder of Erp is grimly told by Sorli, and Hamdi's is grimly told; but it is almost too silly to be tragical; and it is hard after all to care for the deaths of men who did not care for their own lives. Norse literature, when all is said, must still be left to students. When will the author of *Jason* give us the final perfect English *Odyssey*?

21. Unsigned review, *Spectator*

13 August 1870, xliii, 983–4

A debt of gratitude is owing to Messrs. Magnússon and W. Morris for this translation of what they term 'the most complete and dramatic form of the great lyric of the North,'—though indeed they have improved the actual Saga by inserting into it passages of or even the whole of several of those poems of the older Edda on which it is mainly founded, whilst they have added others in their second part. Perhaps the permanent value of the work would have been greater if each original had been left untouched, *i.e.*, the Saga on the one hand, and the Edda poems relating to its subject on the other; but in its present shape it is both shorter and more readable.

It is strange to remember that an island lying far away from the great fields of human activity, and well nigh lost amid the Northern ice, should have been, if not the well-spring, yet the chief focus and the last shrine of one of the literatures of the world. For the Eddas and Sagas of the Norse form a literary type as distinct as the Greek, the Hebrew, the Sanskrit,—a type which, mingling in Western Europe with the Latin, itself but a derivation of the Greek, and with what may be called the Christian, the final flowering of the Hebrew, has evolved the whole variety of modern literatures. It is impossible, from the study of all other literary types put together, to imagine either such poetry as that of the older Edda, or such prose as that of the 'Story of Burnt Njal;' both are imperishable monuments of a race, a state of being, unlike all others. Perhaps the most remarkable peculiarity of the early Norse literature is this,—that there is none other worthy of the name which exhibits to us so low a stage of civilization and moral development. Its heroes and heroines are the most ferocious set of savages that ever inspired poetry of a really high order. Bloodshed has elsewhere been the theme of song; witness Bertrand de Born's *Sirventes*, celebrating the joys of battle, when the blood flows in streams, and the limbs of men fall asunder beneath the sword; but such themes are only exceptional in Provençal literature. Crimes of the most fearful character are not wanting in the legends of early Greece. But demi-fiends like Medea, if they may be so exhibited as to arouse our pity, are yet invariably set forth primarily as objects of horror to us. Tales of incest may be frequent, but the crime, even when unintentional, is always pursued by the most dread retribution. On the other hand, the *Völsunga Saga* in one place exhibits to us a queen named Sogny, to revenge her family, encouraging her brother Sigmund to kill her two sons by a husband whom she disliked, then voluntarily bearing a son to the former, that by his prowess her husband may 'get his bane at last,'— in another, a still more renowned personage, Gudrun, Sigurd's widow, killing her two sons by her second husband, Atli, making him eat their flesh and drink their blood out of their skulls, and then helping to murder him. In the former tale, indeed, Sogny, after she has brought destruction to her husband by the means of her brother and son, refuses life and honour, that she may 'merrily' die with her husband, though she was 'naught merry to wed him,' and after kissing brother and son, goes back into the fire, where he 'and all his good men' are burning, and there dies. But Gudrun, though after murdering sons and husband, she 'has no wish to live longer,' yet lives to marry a third husband and have other sons. And so little does the narrator discern any real moral horror in tales like these, that his judgment on the Volsungs and Giukings, the two races forming the subject of his work, is simply that they were 'the greatest-hearted and the mightiest of all men.'

And yet this literature, in which the moral sense plays so secondary a part, and in fact scarcely exhibits itself otherwise than in the shape of relentless vengeance, is one unsurpassed in breadth of pathos, when it deals with the common affections of humanity. In what language has the grief of a widow over her slain husband been portrayed with more life-like power and simplicity than in the 'First Lay of Gudrun'?:—

> Gudrun of old days
> Drew near to dying
> As she sat in sorrow
> Over Sigurd;
> Yet she sighed not,
> Nor smote hand on hand,
> Nor wailed she aught
> As other women.
>
> .   .   .   .   .   .
>
> Bright and fair
> Sat the great earls' brides,

Gold-arrayed,
Before Gudrun.
Each told the tale
Of her great trouble,
The bitterest bale
She erst abode.

Then spake Giaflaug,
Giuki's sister,
'Lo! upon earth
I live most loveless
Who of five mates
Must see the ending,
Of daughters twain
And three sisters,
Of brethren eight,
And abide behind lonely.'

Naught gat Gudrun
Of wail or greeting,
So heavy was she
For her dead husband,
So dreadful-hearted,
For the King laid dead there.

Then Herborg, Queen of Hunland, tells of the loss of her seven sons
and her husband in battle, of her father and mother and four brothers
'on the wide sea,' all 'in one season's wearing,' and none was left for
love or solace; tells of her own captivity, and of the 'cruel lashes'
laid on her by her mistress; 'but naught gat Gudrun of wail or
greeting.' . . . .:—

Then spake Gullrond,
Giuki's daughter,—
'O foster-mother!
Wise as thou mayst be,
Naught canst thou better
The young wife's bale.'
And she bade uncover
The dead King's corpse.

[quotes next three stanzas]

We can hardly, however, say, with the translators of the *Völsunga
Saga*, that this 'great story of the North. . . . . . should be to all our

race what the "Tale of Troy" was to the Greeks.' To say nothing of
the different magnitudes of the two themes,—on the one hand, a
struggle between two races, on the other, a mere blood feud between
two families,—there is one ineradicable fault in the Norse story,—want
of internal unity. Both the prose work and the collection of poems in
the older Edda, on which it is founded, represent a hopeless attempt
to weave into one thread of story two or more absolutely opposed
traditions. Who would suppose that the Gudrun whom we have seen
thus agonized beside a husband, the victim of her brothers' treachery,
and cursing them for the breaking of their bounden oaths, would be
shown to us further on, at her second husband's court, putting on
armour of mail and taking sword in hand to fight for those same
brothers, and finally killing her sons and her husband in revenge for
their deaths? The later poet or poets who composed the great German
epic of the *Nibelungenlied* on the same theme, though that work also
is full of minor inconsistencies, avoided at least this glaring one, and
made the slaughter of the Niblungs to be the work of Kriemhilt's own
revenge (Kriemhilt in the German legend taking the place of Gudrun
in the Norse). But the true 'Tale of Troy' has no such blot as this.
No doubt, the marvellous power of human sympathy in the Greek
poet has made many a reader take sides rather with Hector than with
Achilles, with the conquered than with the conquerors. But we are
never called upon to view the same personages successively under two
entirely opposite aspects, to reverse our sympathies wholly, to forget
the past half of the narrator's story in order to enter fully into the half
which he has yet to tell. And since the incongruity thus produced is
far more apparent in a continuous prose tale like the *Völsunga Saga*
than in a series of separate poems, we cannot altogether agree with
Messrs. Magnússon and Morris in viewing the *saga* as the most
'dramatic' as well as the most 'complete' form of the 'Epic of the
North.' A drama without internal unity is surely no drama at all.

The name of the author of the *Earthly Paradise* is a guarantee of
the beauty of the language into which the *Völsunga Saga* has been
translated. One observation, however, it seems time to make on his
diction, which it would not have been fair to do in respect of a work
so entirely fanciful as that collection of tales in verse of which the last
volume is promised to us. There are certain archaisms which become
intolerable when made a practice of. 'Maid' or 'maiden' is as good and
honest an English word as 'may,' and we warn Mr. Morris that of his
'mays' we are heartily tired. 'Adrad' may pass muster in verse; but

when we find it wilfully inserted in prose, we long for the simpler 'afeared', or even 'afraid.' We may not quarrel with 'letted' for its own sake, but when it occurs in the next line to 'impassable' it is simply incongruous. Perhaps, as a rule, it is never safe to attempt in prose narration more archaic English than that of the authorized version of the Bible, as being the oldest recognized model in this branch of literature which is familiar to a sufficiently large number of readers. In poetry one may go further back, though scarcely in any case beyond Chaucer; nor will it ever do to *Chaucerize* altogether, under pain of being unintelligible to by far the greater number of readers.

One word more. We lay no claim to Norse scholarship, but we have remarked that in several passages of the Edda poems the sense given departs from that of the old Latin version, which is itself sufficiently close to make the text generally intelligible to an Englishman somewhat familiar with the older forms of German. We presume Mr. Magnússon has good authority for his renderings.

22. An American view of the limitations of Morris's poetry

1871

Unsigned article, *New Englander*, October 1871, xxx, 557–80.

This perceptive article uses the comparison with Chaucer to give some clear insights into Morris's poetry.

Two things—both of which we might have guessed—Mr. Morris has chosen to tell us about himself; that he is a pupil of Chaucer; and that into that company of poets 'heroically fashioned,' whose conscious or unconscious aim it is to interpret to us an otherwise unintelligible world, he has neither power nor will to enter. Unskilled, he tells us, out of the discord and confusion of actual life to charm a music strong enough to over-power and reconcile it to itself, he deliberately with-draws into the 'sleepy region,' to which all the outer noises of the waking world, which hopes and fears and longs and seeks and suffers and enjoys and loses and despairs, come blended into a lulling, mur-muring sound, whose origin is now half forgotten, and now only enough remembered 'to convey a melancholy into all his day;' a vague and voluptuous melancholy, which soothes more than it saddens, and is chiefly valued as a proof and portion of repose. To build for us this

> Shadowy isle of bliss,
> 'Mid most the beating of the steely sea
> Where tossed about all hearts of men must be,

has been Mr. Morris's work as a poet, and to these pleasures he invites us,—in the pauses of our labor or our warfare,—to rest and forgetful-ness and the dreaming of dreams.

In an age like this, which has had so much to say about the mission of the poet as a teacher, a thinker, a prophet, an apostle of humanity, and so forth, it may seem strange to some to hear a considerable poet declaring frankly that his chief aim is to give pleasure; but if they will consider how many and various things are included in the giving of pleasure, and will call to mind that the undoubted first object which two of our greatest poets, Chaucer and Shakespeare, had in view, was the amusement of their contemporaries, it need no longer excite sur-prise. But what does excite surprise, and what seems to place Mr. Morris in a peculiar position, is the close limitation to which he de-liberately commits himself in his choice of subjects and means of treatment. Not only does he say to us, my object is simply to amuse you by telling you stories, but he adds also that these stories shall be essentially of only one class; ministering to only one kind of pleasure; and built up of only certain materials to which he confines himself, neglecting or ignoring others, many of them the very ones which we should have expected of a follower of Chaucer, that he would seek out and attempt to use among the very first. And when considering his poems together, we note the effect of this limitation upon them, it is impossible to avoid wishing, perhaps an idle wish, that the poet had either not found it necessary to be content to keep within such bounds, or else that he had more clearly recognized and more zealously guarded against the almost inevitable prolixity and monotony to which writings of such a length attempted under such conditions, must always be most dangerously exposed.

But, except as regards some few, and these generally minor, points of technical treatment, it is idle to lament or blame an artist's limitations. A man can do only his own work; and such limitations as we find in any one's whole work must be regarded for the most part as characteristic and necessary. And yet because to know what a man's work is not, is to be on the way to discover what it is, and because Mr. Morris, though too reverent and careful a student of his master to make for himself any claim to be compared with him, is yet professedly the pupil of Chaucer, and has been called by some Chaucerian, it is natural and will probably be useful, to consider in what the two poets are alike and in what respects they differ.

And the truth is that in all essentials the difference between them is so great and so evident that it seems almost absurd to compare them. Chaucer, a man of his age, keenly alive to the political and religious significance of the time; so human, so English, so full of common sense, so social, buoyant, humorous, gay; what has he, so real, so credulous, so confident, so full of faith, in common with the 'dreamer of dreams, born out of his due time?' To Chaucer's many sided nature such a philosophy of life as that of Mr. Morris would have been an impossibility, but in Mr. Morris it is his very genius, coloring all his work and defining it. Differing from each other so widely as they do in their ideas of life, it is to be expected that this difference should be communicated to their styles. And thus it is. The two styles are very different. Read one of Chaucer's tales and then one of Mr. Morris's, and there is seen to be a resemblance, a certain resemblance in the movement of the lines, in the pauses, in the rhymes, and to some extent in the choice of words; but this resemblance is not deep, it is superficial; enough to remind us in a general way of Chaucer, but unfortunately it reminds us also that in Chaucer's style there is a good deal that is not here; we miss the fullness, the variety, the flexibility, the directness, the boldness, the animation, the very life and soul of his verse, and realize that however excellent for his own purposes Mr. Morris's style may be, and however much it may have benefited by his loving study of Chaucer's, its likeness to it is very far from being that of kinship and inheritance. A poet who sees so many things, and sees into them so quickly and clearly as Chaucer, who has such various and such deep sympathies, and is so heartily interested in so many and such different persons, must have and cannot help having such a style as Mr. Morris neither has nor wants for his expression. He has needs for utterance that the other never feels. This is not said in disparagement of Mr. Morris, for, as hereafter will be seen, it is no less true that he too has for his own needs his own fit and admirable expression. What we wish to insist upon is simply that Mr. Morris's style, though formed upon it, is not akin to Chaucer's, and that for the reason that it is merely impossible that two men with such different thoughts about God and man and nature, should have styles resembling each other in any but the most superficial way.

Look at their descriptions of scenery and persons. Evidently what Mr. Morris, as an artist, regards especially in the master is his objectivity, his love of natural objects for their own sakes; his fondness for the outside of things; for color and form and sound and motion; for things rich and splendid, as well as those that are common and plain; for those qualities, in short, which make a painter of him, a painter whose eye loves rather to dwell upon the object itself than to wander off in search of any moral or spiritual significance which may perhaps be associated with it. But here we wish to call attention to the fact that while Chaucer is almost constantly showing this fondness for the appearances of things, yet in his mention or description of them, it is none the less quite as frequently his characteristic habit to convey with them something more than the things themselves. Often in the most delicate and inexplicable way something of his own personality is infused into these descriptions, giving an indescribable charm to the simplest lines; and his eminent skill in the art of making the mention of one thing, without metaphor, the suggestion of another or of many others, is known to all his readers. Let us take a few well-known examples; and first, of the way in which his own personal delight in the things he sees and hears enters into his style, and gives a peculiar character to the verse. Of birds singing, from the 'Cuckow and the Nightingale':—

> Some songë loudë as they had yplainëd,
> And some in other manner voice yfainëd,
> And some all outë with the fullë throte.

How direct the style is here, how full of animation, how glad! and how strong and light and flexible the verse! And now take these well known lines (of which Coleridge is said to have been fond), about sunlit trees in spring:—

> With branches brodë, laden with levës newe
> That sprongen out agen the sunnë shene
> Some very redde and some a glad light green.

There is very little description here, but there is a magical something about the verse that brings all the fresh beauty of the scene before us even more vividly perhaps than the actual sight of it could do for most of us. We have not only the scene itself, but Chaucer's delight in it besides. No amount of detail could have given it to us so perfectly and so happily. Shakespeare in the great moonlight scene in the *Merchant of Venice*, with hardly any, even the slightest description, manages to convey all the unutterable charm of moonlight and the clear, still night to us, by simply bringing us in sympathy with Lorenzo and Jessica, whose souls are steeped in its delight. Of the same kind is Chaucer's brief and simple mention of the nightingale and the moon.

> A nyghtyngale upon a cedre grene,
> Under the chambre wal ther as she lay,
> Ful lowdë song agen the moonë shene.

And now see how he speaks of the grass, English grass, as Marsh has noticed:—

> ——the grenë grass
> So smale, so thicke, so short, so fresh of hewe.

This is simplicity itself, the simplicity of pure, unreflecting delight. The verse seems to move over the grass in which the poet has such joy as if it were his hand stroking it,—

> So smale, so thicke, so short, so fresh of hewe!

Again, take this from the 'Legende of Goode Women':

> Upon the smalë, softë, swotë grass
> That was with flowrës swote embrouded al.

Once more, take this for straightforwardness about the flying hart:—

> Ther was the hert y-wont to have his flight,
> And over a brook, and so forth in his weye,

and this for its fullness and strength,—

> With knotty knarry bareyn treës olde.

And now take some examples of that other characteristic of Chaucer's style just spoken of, its way of indirectly or covertly suggesting one thing by another. For instance: sailors are proverbially bad riders, and Chaucer says in his direct way of his Schipman, that,

> He rood upon a rouncy, as he couthe.

He had hired a hackney horse and rode him 'as he could.' Of the
Monk, a full fed, rosy, well-dressed man of the world, fonder of the
hunt than of the cloister, he says:—

> And when he rood, men might his bridel heere
> Gyngle in a whistling wind so cleere,
> And eek as lowde as doth the chapel belle,

implying not only that the monk was a man of fashion, who decorated
his horse's bridle with 'bells and bosses brave,' but hinting good-
naturedly also that he had a quicker ear for these than for the chapel
bell. And with all this how delightful only for itself is that second line,

> Gyngle in a whistling wind so cleere!

In the Sompnoure's tale, a lazy, impudent, begging friar comes into
Thomas's house and makes himself at home:—

> And fro the bench he drof away the cat
> And layd adown his potent and his hat,
> And eek his scrip, and set him soft adown.

Another famous passage, without the humor, is that in which he says
of the Schipman,

> Hardy he was and wise to undertake;
> With many a tempest had his berd ben schake.

These are a few convenient examples of Chaucer's large way of
dealing with the things he sees and hears, enough however to show
that his style is himself and his verse inseparable from the spirit that
informs it and makes it move.

And now recall Mr. Morris's way of looking at similar things, and
notice the effect upon his style. Passing over his very characteristic
song of May, take this from the narrative:—

> Now must these men be glad a little while
> That they had lived to see May once more smile
> Upon the earth; wherefore, as men who know
> How fast the bad days and the good days go
> They gathered at the feast:

[quotes next 14½ lines]

This is a good specimen of Mr. Morris's style when he is describing or
narrating generally. And now read a specimen of Chaucer's style, in
general description, of a similar scene:—

> Forgeten had the erthe his pore estate
> Of wynter, that him naked made and mate,
> And with his swerd of colde so sorë grevëd;

[quotes next 20 lines]

In one the smooth, even flow of a pensive willowy stream; in the other the rippling animation of a running brook. The difference is radical. But now let us try to get at Mr. Morris's method in dealing with particular scenes. No one can help seeing that he is a very careful and minute observer, and very skillful and patient in the use of his materials, and no one, it seems to us, turning from Chaucer to Mr. Morris, can help seeing also that while Chaucer's way is to make his pictures serve chiefly for illustrations of his text, it is Mr. Morris's tendency to make pictures for the picture's sake. Not that Chaucer does not indulge in long descriptions, as in his account of the temples in the Knight's Tale; and dwell upon minute particulars, as in his descriptions of the pilgrims in the Prologue; but in such cases it is his habit mainly to bring forward and insist upon such details only as are significant of the persons and things which he wishes us to see, and help to interpret them to us. His Yeoman has a nut head; his Plough-man rides upon a mare; his Monk has a bald head which shines like glass; his Prioress has a straight nose, gray eyes, and a little mouth, she leaves not a bit of grease to be seen on her cup after she has drunk, and is very seemly in her way of reaching after food; his Squire is embroidered like a flowery mead, and so on; all these particulars are vital and to the point. Now compare with any of Chaucer's descriptions of men and women, Mr. Morris's. Take one of the best, the beautiful first description of Gudrun. Here are details in abundance; hair, eyes, cheeks, brow, bosom, hands, lips, chin, neck, dress, all these are mentioned, and yet after all what do we know about Gudrun, except that she was a beautiful young girl? When Chaucer wishes to tell us no more than that he says, 'Emilie the brighte,' or

> Emelie that fairer was to seene
> Than is the lilie on hire stalkës grene,
> And fresscher than the May with flowrës newe.

And now turn to Mr. Morris's description of houses and gardens and temples; there are several of them. Read the elaborate description of the Gardens of the Hesperides, in the XIVth Book of *Jason*; the description of the house in the 'Cupid and Psyche,' and that in the

'Lady of the Land,' and others; and notice what a fondness he has for the accumulation of details. He loves to enumerate. He has a Pre-raphaelite's longing to give everything—everything external. In his first book, the *Defence of Guenevere and other Poems*, this tendency of his may be seen exercising itself almost without restraint.*

[quotes stanzas 2 to 5 of 'Golden Wings']

> White swans on the green moat
> Small feathers left afloat
> By the blue painted boat;
> Swift running of the stoat;
> Sweet gurgling note by note
> Of sweet music.†

'The Praise of my Lady' is too long to quote; but his lady's hair, her forehead, her eyelids, her eyelashes, her eyes, her chin, her neck, her slim body, her long hands, have each a separate mention, and after eighteen stanzas about these, hear the nineteenth and the first line of the twentieth:—

> God pity me though, if I missed
> The telling, how along her wrist
> The veins creep, dying languidly
>   Beata mea Domina.
> Inside her tender palm and thin.

That is the bent; to miss nothing that the eye can take in as it slowly, pensively passes, without passion either of joy or grief, from object to object, liking one apparently as much as another, and enumerating all. To such a mood and such a method as this Chaucer's straightforward

---

* With an abandonment indeed, which has in it something so willful that the book seems full of such airs and attitudes and affectations as strike one with amazement, and is as hard reading almost as a 13th Century metrical romance.

† In some of this early work it is curious to see what a disposition there is to distinguish things by their colors, rather than by their forms even, or by any inherent qualities; 'I sit on a purple bed, outside the wall is red;' 'The red-billed moor-hen;' scarlet shoon, red lips, gold hair, red-gold hair, gown of white and red, green covered bosoms, &c.; and in 'The Tomb of King Arthur,' Night is the extinguisher of colors, and Twilight the changer of them:

> Upon my red robe, strange in the twilight
> With many unnamed colours—
>   ——there were no colours then
> For near an hour, and I fell asleep.
>   ——so that the sun
> Had only just arisen from the deep
> Still land of colours.

and various style is a thing alien and unattainable. And though from
the *Defence of Guenevere* to the *Earthly Paradise*, the distance is immense,
yet the last work is animated by the same artistic spirit as the first,
only corrected, trained, and furnished. But now let us have a specimen
of this later work. Here is a picture which one cannot help admiring,
in which one can take pleasure again and again.

> Most fair to peaceful heart was all,
> Windless the ripe fruit down did fall,
> The shadows of the large grey leaves
> Lay grey upon the oaten sheaves
> By the garth-wall as he passed by;
> The startled ousel cock did cry
> As from the yew-tree by the gate
> He flew; the speckled hen did wait
> With outstretched neck his coming in,
> The March-hatched cockerel gaunt and thin
> Crowed shrilly, while his elder thrust
> His stiff wing-feathers in the dust
> That grew aweary of the sun:
> The old and one-eyed cart-horse dun
> The middenstead went hobbling round
> Blowing the light straw from the ground.
> With curious eye the drake peered in
> O'er the barn's dusk, where dust and din
> Were silent now a little space.

And now after this take one more, the last, quotation from Chaucer,
his description of Chaunteclere:—

> He lokith as it were a grim lioun;
> And on his toon he rometh up and down,
> Him deyneth not to set his foot to grounde.
> He chukkith, whan he hath a corn ifounde,
> And to him rennen than his wifes alle.

In what we have had to say of Mr. Morris's relation to Chaucer, it
has not been our intention to make any closer comparison between
them than was immediately necessary to the purpose of illustrating, in
a general way, what was meant by the assertion that two poets differing so widely in spirit, could not be like each other in poetic expression,
even when dealing with similar materials and endeavoring to produce
a similar result. For this purpose it was unnecessary to take account of
much more in the writings of either than of those portions, and of but a

few of those, in which it seemed likely that they would resemble each other, if in any, those namely in which the chief object of either poet was to describe. But it is time to go further in Mr. Morris's case and try to get a less imperfect notion of his position as a poet. We know pretty well already what his aim is as an artist, and under what conditions, either chosen by himself or imposed upon him by necessity, he has undertaken to do his work. If we could be satisfied to ask only, what has the poet attempted, and, on the whole, how has he succeeded in his attempt, it would be enough to speak in general terms of the result, and say no more. But in the case of any considerable work it is impossible to stop there. We need to know more about the work itself, its character and relative position; we want to ask—if voluntarily chosen, was it wise to choose such an aim and to accept such limitations? Or, if imposed upon the poet by necessity, it remains to consider their effect upon his work.

The chief limitations of Mr. Morris's work are imposed upon it by his philosophy, and his philosophy is the expression of his temperament. And though one may be pardoned, perhaps, for sometimes wondering, if there may not be a very little affectation in so complete an abandonment to the conditions of such a philosophy; still it is so evident upon the whole, that it is the best fitted to the peculiar temperament and needs of Mr. Morris as an artist, that it will hardly be so well worth while to discuss the wisdom of his acceptance of it, as to consider the effects of it upon his work.

From even so partial an examination as has been made already of his poetry, it has resulted, that a good deal has been said and implied about his ideas on art and nature, and it is plain enough that Mr. Morris has little or no practical sympathy with any theories which represent it as their chief aim and peculiar glory to refer to something beyond themselves. On Mr. Morris, nature never makes such an impression as she does on Wordsworth, for example, or on Shelley; nor to him does the aspiration of the artist appear the same thing that it does to Mr. Browning. His is a philosophy that encourages no reference to anything beyond and is unwilling to inquire; and in him, therefore, the love of nature is the love of her outward beauty, and the aim of the artist to minister to an ephemeral pleasure or console a transitory grief. Other poets have thought it enough for them often to ask no more of nature than the pleasure of the present sight, but none of them, not Chaucer, nor Wordsworth, nor Keats, nor Scott, nor Byron, seem ever able to avoid the intrusion of an emotion—

communicating itself to the verse—which is strange to Mr. Morris; and for none of these—not even Wordsworth or Scott with all their fondness for details—was it ever possible to remain so long contented with the comparatively inferior portions of a landscape as Mr. Morris. Scott, in some points of artistic intention the most like to Mr. Morris of any of them, without seeking anything beyond the joy of the moment, will thrill with delight when Mr. Morris feels only a pensive pleasure; and, while he loves the garden and the flowers of the meadow, loves better the mountain brook and the wild flowers of the hills, and prefers the sunset to the twilight, and the daybreak to the afternoon. But in all these men there was an instinctive love of freedom undreamt of in Mr. Morris's philosophy, and another love of life and the beauty of life, than that which moves the tears of the dwellers in the Earthly Paradise.

And yet, if to such pleasure as the freer and more active and more inquiring spirits seek out and find for us in nature, Mr. Morris has little or nothing of the same kind to contribute, still to him also, many things have been revealed; things which less patient eyes than his would never have remarked, and which more eager natures could never have obtained. And, in the midst of our regret that his range should be so limited, it is impossible not to see that after all it is under and because of these very limitations that he has been enabled to do some of his best work. As in the dreamy hero of the 'Land East of the Sun,' his inability to do some things that we wish he could, is his power to do some others that no one else can do. With more passion, with more earnestness, with a wider view and a deeper insight, with greater intellectual force and larger sympathies, he would have been a greater poet, but his most characteristic work would probably never have been done. Wordsworth with as attentive a gaze, and even a keener eye than Mr. Morris for the minutest details of the landscape, was too much engaged in trying to get at the heart of things, too sensitively conscious of the life of the things about him, to be often at liberty to look at them and describe them as if they were mere pictures. But Mr. Morris has the painter's eye. To him things are as parts of pictures, and made to be painted. Where Wordsworth notices that 'every flower enjoys the air it breathes,' Mr. Morris remarks that it is small and as 'red as blood,' or that it 'flames' in 'grey light,' or that it has a black or a yellow centre and takes a certain curve in bending. To know such facts as these about flowers, and similar facts about all natural objects, is of more importance to his purpose than to be impressed with a belief that they are alive and enjoying the life they feel; and to the observation and report of such facts as these, accordingly it is his instinct and his habit to confine himself. The range is narrower, of course. Of what Matthew Arnold calls 'the grand power of poetry, its interprative power,' there will be little if any manifestation; but of its pictorial power, its power of naming and arranging the details of a scene so as to bring its outward appearance like a picture before the mind of the reader, of this power there will be many remarkable examples. In fact it is in the exercise of this power that Mr. Morris excels, excelling because, in the first place, as we have just said, it is his instinct to see things rather as pictures or as parts of pictures than as if they were alive and conscious of their life; and, in the second place, because it is possible for him with his temperament, to be a deliberate and accurate observer of details, little disturbed by a consciousness of anything more in what he sees than can be apprehended by the senses, and unvexed by any longing to suggest much more in his descriptions than the very things themselves which he describes. Thus it is that he makes his limitations serve him; what he describes he seems to have seen, and his best descriptions make very nearly the same impression on us as if we had stood before a painting of an actual scene, and been enabled easily, quietly, and at leisure to look at each separate object, passing lightly from this to that, sometimes tempted to linger, but never forced to try to 'see into the life of things,' or stand surprised before

> A presence that disturbs us with the joy
> Of elevated thoughts.

How well such a kind of pictorial description is adapted to some of Mr. Morris's needs, as a teller of tales, pure and simple, need not be said. To read 'The Man Born to be King,' is almost like taking the walks and rides that the persons of the story take, going on with them from place to place, talking little, thinking little, doing little, but seeing many things, among others such a scene as this:

> Then downward he began to wend,
> And 'twixt the flowery hedges sweet
> He heard the hook smite down the wheat,
> And murmur of the unseen folk;
> And when he reached the stream that broke
> The golden plain, but leisurely
> He passed the bridge, for he could see

The masters of that ripening realm,
Cast down beneath an ancient elm
Upon a little strip of grass,
From hand to hand the pitcher pass,
While on the turf beside them lay
The ashen-handled sickles grey,
The matters of their cheer between:
Slices of white cheese, specked with green,
And greenstriped onions and ryebread,
And summer apples faintly red
Even beneath the crimson skin;
And yellow grapes well ripe and thin,
Plucked from the cottage gable-end.

This is not seeing things deeply, but it is seeing them with surprising accuracy and clearness. He seems to fix his eye exactly upon the objects which he wishes us to notice, and to resign himself without reserve to the simple, single task of reporting faithfully what he sees and no more. The verse omits to be musical, but it pictures like a glassy pool, even to the green specks in the white cheese, and the stripes upon the onions; and that is what Mr. Morris meant that it should do; that is what Mr. Morris means that the greater portion of his poetry shall chiefly do, it shall make pictures. Even his songs do it; the interpolated songs in the *Earthly Paradise* are almost all descriptions, and here is a song that Orpheus sings in contention with the Sirens:—

O the sweet valley of deep grass
Wherethrough the summer stream doth pass,
In chain of shadow, and still pool,
From misty morn to evening cool;
Where the black ivy creeps and twines
O'er the dark-armed, red-trunked pines,
Whence clattering the pigeon flits,
Or, brooding o'er her thin eggs, sits,
And every hollow of the hills
With echoing song the mavis fills.
There by the stream, all unafraid
Shall stand the happy shepherd maid,
Alone in first of sunlit hours;
Behind her, on the dewy flowers,
Her homespun woollen raiment lies,
And her white limbs and sweet grey eyes
Shine from the calm green pool and deep,

> While round about the swallows sweep,
> Not silent; and would God that we
> Like them, were landed from the sea.

So strong is this tendency in him, and so great a part of his genius
is it, that he cannot be satisfied to let us imagine a thing for ourselves;
he sees what he describes and will make us see it as he sees it. He sees
even in his dreams, his 'eyes make pictures when they are shut.' Even
his monsters, his dragons, his chimaera have all their share of description, and where he so far restrains himself as to confuse the outline,
he still cannot resist the temptation to color them with care, or to
indulge in some such detail about them as makes it plain that the things
are conceived of by him as objects to be seen and not merely to be felt.
And as for faeries, and gods, and goddesses, he looks at them generally
as if they were men and women, and draws, and drapes and colors
them as such. And see how he realizes the ghostly procession in the
latter part of 'The Ring Given to Venus,' deliberately describing, as if
from actual sight, shape after shape as it passes by, till he comes to the
'Lord of all':

> Most like a mighty king was he,
> And crowned and sceptred royally;
> As a white flame his visage shone,
> Sharp, clear-cut as a face of stone;
> But flickering flame, not flesh it was;
> And over it such looks did pass
> Of wild desire, and pain, and fear,
> As in his people's faces were,
> But tenfold fiercer; furthermore,
> A wonderous steed the Master bore,
> Unnameable of kind or make,
> Not horse, nor hippogriff, nor drake,
> Like and unlike to all of these.

And his men and women he sees as pictures, and like to pictures.

> But with him was a boy, right fair
> Grey-eyed and yellow haired, most like
> Unto some Michael who doth strike
> The dragon on a minster-wall,
> So sweet-eyed was he and withal
> So fearless of all things he seemed.

Gudrun's first appearance is as a complete picture in a frame; and
here is Cydippe among the tulips:

And his heart stopped awhile, for there
Against a flowering thorn-bush fair,
Hidden by tulips to the knee,
His heart's desire his eyes did see,
Clad was she e'en as is the dove
Who makes the summer sad with love;
High girded as one hastening
In swift search for some longed-for thing;
Her hair drawn by a silken band
From her white neck, and in her hand
A myrtle-spray.

And to him their actions even are as pictures. His description—in 'The Ring Given to Venus'—of the games in the garden is a picture of astonishing distinctness, and indeed, 'lovely to look on:'

Lovely to look on was the sway
Of the slim maidens 'neath the ball
As they swung back to note its fall
With dainty balanced feet; and fair
The bright outflowing golden hair,
As swiftly, yet in measured wise
One maid ran forth to gain the prize;
Eyes glittered and young cheeks glowed bright,
And gold-shod foot, round limb and light,
Gleamed from beneath the girded gown
That, unrebuked, untouched, was thrown
Hither and thither by the breeze.

There others on the daisies lay
Above the moat and watched their quill
Make circles in the water still,
Or laughed to see the damsel hold
Her dainty skirt enwrought with gold
Back from the flapping tench's tail,
Or to his close-set dusky mail
With gentle force brought laughingly
The shrinking finger tip anigh.

This is charming, and an excellent specimen of the wonderful things that can be effected within the limits of the pictorial style. And now as a general illustration of Mr. Morris's dominant tendency, note finally how fond all his women and goddesses are of contemplating their own beauty; how they are always lifting their long skirts when they move, and letting them fall when they stop; what a loosening and letting down there is of long gold hair; what a putting on and putting off of raiment; what a fluttering of gowns, and what a clinging of them to slim bodies and round limbs. His painter's eye seems never to have enough of these appearances. But for us, remembering how frequent they are in his poems, we begin to feel the pressure of the limitations and to ask ourselves if this fondness for the outside of things is not excessive, if there is not a little too much 'pointing out,' if things are not often made a little too plain to us, and if we are not forced often to see some things which we would rather feel; if, in short, Mr. Morris in so bountifully providing for the senses is not in danger of cloying the appetite he feeds. And withal there is so very little bread to all this immeasurable deal of nectar. There is as little plain living as high thinking; as little sensuality as spirituality; it is all sensuousness. And certainly it is curious to notice, with all Mr. Morris's realism, how little reality we get after all. He pictures things to us so effectually, that we cease to care for them except as pictures; and his men and women become little more than pictures and statues, pleasant to the eye, but little dear to the heart. In even the poems that have the most of humanity in them, in which he attempts to answer the inevitable demand for a more continuous recognition and fuller treatment of human interests—the Jason—the Gudrun—the two Bellerophons—he still, it seems to us, relies too much upon the picture-making method, and from lack of concentration and speed, and from want of penetrative power, fails to interest us deeply in Medea, and Gudrun, and Bellerophon themselves; and with all his skill, is unable to give the characters individual force and life enough, to make Bellerophon seem to differ much from Perseus, or Medea from Gudrun. In fact, 'the human heart by which we live,' is not Mr. Morris's first consideration, for he really, we think, cares very little for actual men and women, and is constitutionally rather shy of them than otherwise. But certain of its joys and sorrows he sympathizes with, and some of its tendernesses, he can represent with a peculiar grace. Indeed, to us, one of the most interesting things to notice in Mr. Morris's work, is the connection that exists between his fondness for the outside of things, his liking to see clearly and accurately what he paints, and to paint little else than he can see; and his natural choice of what emotions he shall deal with, and of the manner in which he shall treat of them. The one tendency is the legitimate offspring of the other. For such emotions and such moods of mind as have their birth and abode in the debateable land between the possible and the impossible, between sleeping and waking, Mr. Morris has a regard which seems like fascination. Devoted to things visible, and striving to fix his attention on these, and not to slip off and go beyond the object itself, practically believing that it is useless to try to go beyond it, it follows of course, that whatever he cannot clearly apprehend, whatever is doubtful, and obscure, and mysterious in nature and human life, disturbs and pains him more or less. He cannot help seeing and feeling that there are secrets, but he cannot and will not attempt to discover and possess them; he takes no pleasure in speculating about them; where he cannot see, he will not venture far; all beyond, is to him an unknown country, which affects him somewhat, if one may say so, as darkness affects children. The result is, that for the representation of moods of unending reverie and states of dreamy half-consciousness; and for the expression of such visionary fears and nameless dreads, such sudden and inexplicable sinkings of the heart, such vague regrets and inefficient longings, such strange emotions of self-pity and the like as are natural to those who are fond of things clear and simple, and hence sensitive to things obscure and complicated, for the representation and expression of these he has a peculiar aptitude and ability. Hatred and dread of death, not knowing what it means, except that it is an end of life and its pleasures had or hoped for, and love of life for the mere life's sake; this, it is unnecessary to say, is the prevailing sentiment which he never lets us lose sight of from the beginning of the *Jason* to the end of the *Earthly Paradise*. And with this too goes a conviction of the vanity of all things done or attempted, seldom so fully expressed in any poetry, and probably never in so even a tone of quiet, helpless, merely pensive melancholy; and a vague, vain, passive pity for the sum of human suffering, so vague and vain as apparently never to feel any need of the relief of indignation or of the consolation of hope. There is no desperate cursing of the gods, no passionate hoping against hope, 'till hope creates, from its own wreck, the thing it contemplates;' the acquiescence is complete, and the pity that results little more than the self-pity of pleasure-loving natures devoid of will, and incapable of despair. See what an utter abandonment to the most self-regarding and most incapable melancholy there is in such a passage as this:

> Sirs, ye are old, and ye have seen perchance
> Some little child for very gladness dance
> Over a scarcely-noticed worthless thing,
> Worth more to him than ransom of a king,

177

Did not a pang of more than pity take
Your heart thereat, not for the youngling's sake,
But for your own, for man that passes by,
So like to God, so like the beasts that die.—
Lo sirs, my pity for myself is such
When like an image that my hand can touch
My old self grows unto myself grown old.★

This is fine in its way; but a deeper pathos is in the timid question, that John's old mother asks him tearfully after his return from Faeryland.

Fair art thou come again, sweet son,
And sure a long way hast thou gone
I durst not ask thee where; but this
I ask thee by the first sweet kiss,
Wherewith I kissed thy new-born face
Long since within the groaning place—
If thou hast been so far, that thou
Canst tell to me—grown old, son, now,
Through weary life, unsatisfied
Desires, and lingering hope untried—
If thou canst tell me of thy ruth,
What thing there is of lies or truth,
In what the new faith saith of those
Great glories of the heavenly close,
And how that poor folk twinned on earth
Shall meet therein in joy and mirth.

Indeed, this whole story of 'The Land East of the Sun,'—to us, in spite of its diffuseness and its too great length, one of the most suggestive and winning of all his poems—is full of examples of a very delicate perception of the unacknowledged fears, the incommunicable doubts of one's own identity, the indefinable longings, and strange regrets, the bewilderment and loneliness, and all the shadowy emotions that haunt the borderland of sleep, to which we have already alluded. The mixture of forgetfulness and memory, the loneliness and the

★ Compare his 'Master,' Chaucer's noble and affecting lines:

That thee ys sent receyve in buxomnesse,
The wrasteling of this world asketh a falle;
Hēr is no home, hēr is but wyldyrnesse.
Forth pilgrimë! forth, best out of thy stalle!
Loke up on hye, and thankë God of alle;
Weyvë thy lust, and let thy goste thee lede,
And trouthe shal thee delyver, hit is no drede.

yearning for more human companionship that clouds John's bliss in Faeryland; the confusion of mind, the feeling of estrangement that fears to look upon the future;

> I love thee so, I think upon the end.

a love whose ideal is, exempt from death and change, to live forever in a sweet forgetfulness of all the troubles of the world and all its fears, prolonging love's first day to all eternity. There is humanity in this certainly. But so sadly fond is Mr. Morris of brooding over the inevitable nature of death and change, and so much and yet so little does he value life and love, that he cannot resist the temptation, in season and out of season, here, there and everywhere of impressing his favorite belief upon us, even to satiety. At first it is pleasant enough to see two lovers, waked up for the first time to a quick consciousness of the value of life and time, grow shudderingly aware of the possibility of death and change, and 'weep to have that which they fear to lose;' and in Shakespeare's sonnet and in Mr. Morris's 'How can I have enough of life and love,' the thought comes home to us as natural and appropriate. But Mr. Morris is continually going further, and filling the whole atmosphere of love with such a scent of mortality and such sighs of self-pity, and tears of voluptuous pain, that it becomes heavy and hard to breathe. It is a mistake in art if nothing more, it is too frequent and too obtrusive, it fails of its intended effect and becomes part of the too much that helps the poems to some of their monotony. There is a dramatic propriety in Medea's forebodings as she leaves her father's palace, but consider the case of Andromeda, whose love, so far as we know, was happy to the end. To us it seems that the beauty of the first part of the love scene is considerably lessened by the unneeded melancholy of its ending.

> There on a rock smoothed by the washing sea
> They sat, and eyed each other lovingly.
> And few words at the first the maiden said,
> So wrapped she was in all the goodlihead
> Of her new life made doubly happy now:
> For her alone the sea-breeze seemed to blow,
> For her in music did the white surf fall,
> For her alone the wheeling birds did call
> Over the shallows, and the sky for her
> Was set with white clouds, far away and clear;
> E'en as her love, this strong and lovely one,
> Who held her hand, was but for her alone.

This is beautiful. But when Andromeda says afterward,

> O love, to think that love can pass away,
> That soon or late, to us shall come a day
> When this shall be forgotten! e'en this kiss
> That makes us now forget the high God's bliss,
> And sons of men with all their miseries,

is it not a little overmuch for Mr. Morris to make Perseus answer in such words as these:

> And if thou needs must think of that dull night
> That creepeth on no otherwise than this,
> Yet for that thought hold closer to thy bliss,
> Come nigher, come! forget the more they pain.

If this be a reproduction of Greek sentiment, if these be the manners of the early world,★ O, how much good a little of Chaucer's 'frank anachronism' would have done Mr. Morris!† And how much too, a little of Byron's passion would have helped to reconcile us to this worship of the body! Let any one compare Mr. Morris's love-makings with one that this scene with Andromeda partly resembles, the magnificent love-scene between Juan and Haidee, in the second canto of the *Don Juan*, and see the difference between describing a thing as if it had been seen as a picture, and describing it as if it had been seen as an event. In Mr. Morris's pictures, his persons take graceful attitudes and are beautifully draped and colored, but they seem as if fixed in position; there is no progression in the scene. To Byron, his lovers are alive, beings of flesh and blood, and soul, and in continual motion; he sees them doing something and is interested chiefly in the action. But to Mr. Morris the attitude is dearer than the action, and the curves and colors by which the emotion is manifested more than the emotion

★ Of the manners of the past, especially as shown in its art—Grecian, and of the Middle Age—Mr. Morris has evidently a good deal of knowledge. And he would like apparently to keep more or less close to the time of his story. In the *Defence of Guenevere, etc.*, he becomes almost pedantic in his treatment of some subjects drawn from the times of the Black Prince. In his later poems, however, he wisely allows himself greater freedom, though still intending to be generally true to the manners of the age with which he has to do. But he is truer, we think to his own nature,—as indeed he should be, for that matter, —as an artist, and as he cannot help being, as a genuine part really of the 19th century, with all his preference for the past. And hence, though there may be and is a certain amount of truth to Grecian sentiment (one side of it) in his versions of the Grecian stories, the prevailing sentiment, we think, belongs, and is to be criticized as belonging, not so much to the Greek as to the Dream-World of Mr. Morris, and to Mr. Morris himself.
† Chaucer makes Troilus, like a mediæval knight, talk of his unworthiness, and his hope of being made a nobler and better man through virtue of his love for Cressida.

itself. For his love of beauty is a love of the outward beauty of persons and things. He has so much pleasure in lines and colors that his natural tendency is to be satisfied with these, and to dwell upon them. For the hidden beauty and the soul of things, he has no such regard. These are not to be seen with bodily eyes, they are revealed to earnest thought and to passionate feeling. But Mr. Morris is 'seeking still the pleasure of his eyes,' as he tells us; he can hardly have enough of looking at things; he loves to see better than to think, and to dream better than to feel. Hence, his devotion to detail, his preference of the foreground to the remoter and larger, and higher portions of the landscape; hence, his greater liking for objects of external nature, than for men and women; hence too, his comparative want of concentration and speed in narration, and hence, its evenness and its sameness. More dreamy than intellectual, more inclined to melancholy than to passion, less imaginative than clear-sighted, more patient than penetrating, Mr. Morris, it seems to us, is insufficiently provided for a great narrative or lyric poet. A great narrative poet should be various, he should be thoughtful and sympathetic, he should have humor and passion, and pathos, he should be in short, what Chaucer is, a great dramatic poet. He should be deeply and chiefly interested in life, and in the minds, and hearts of living men, he should have faith and hope, for the great poetry is not the poetry that soothes but the poetry that stirs, that elevates, that makes alive. But to Mr. Morris art is dearer than life, and the body more than the spirit that it hides from him. In his own field, however, and with his own materials, he has done some of the best work of the day, work which at times, one wonders at himself for criticizing at all, remembering gratefully how much pleasure it has given, and how much hearty praise and admiration it deserves.

23. An English view of the limitations of Morris's poetry

1872

Unsigned article by W. J. Courthope, *Quarterly Review*, January 1872, cxxxii, 75–81.

The article, entitled 'The Latest Developments of Literary Poetry', discussed Swinburne's *Songs before Sunrise* and Rossetti's *Poems* with the complete *Earthly Paradise*. Only the section referring to Morris is printed here.

Courthope (1842–1917) was a civil servant, active literary journalist and editor of Pope.

Without in any way affecting the character of a mystic, Mr. Morris withdraws himself, perhaps, even farther than Mr. Rossetti from all sympathy with the life and interests of his time:—

> Of Heaven and Hell I have no power to sing,
> I cannot ease the burden of your fears,
> Or make quick-coming death a little thing.
> Or bring again the pleasures of past years,
> Nor for my words shall ye forget your tears,
> Or hope again for aught that I can say,
> The idle singer of an empty day.

[quotes next two stanzas]

Such is Mr. Morris's apology for taking us back to a kind of mediæval legend for the scheme of his *Earthly Paradise*. 'Certain gentlemen and mariners of Norway having considered all that they had heard of the "Earthly Paradise" set sail to find it, and, after many troubles, and the lapse of many years, came old men to some western land of which they had never before heard: there they died when they had dwelt there certain years much honoured of the strange people.' The narrative of their wanderings is told with much grace and pathos. A propo-

sal by a priest of the strange people that feasts should be instituted, for
the wanderers to hear some of the tales of their Greek ancestors,
connects the stories of the poem with the introduction. Mr. Morris
ascribes his inspiration to Chaucer, but we think that the design of
The Earthly Paradise bears much more resemblance to the *Decameron*
than to *The Canterbury Tales*. The characters are far more like the
colourless ladies and gentlemen who left Florence during the plague,
and serve so conveniently as narrators and audience of the Tales in the
Decameron, than Chaucer's vivacious company of pilgrims. At the end
of each of Boccaccio's stories, his ladies 'praise the tale,' or 'laugh very
pleasantly', or 'feel their cheeks suffused with blushes'. In like manner
Mr. Morris's wanderers 'watch the shades of the dead hopes pass by,' sit
'silent, soft-hearted, and compassionate,' or are 'wrapped up in soft
self pity.' We are never interested in their actions, as in the quarrel
between the Frere and the Sompnoure; indeed it is clear that the racy
incidents of real life would be out of place among his legendary
shadows. The symmetrical division of the Tales by periods of time is
after the manner of the *Decameron*; but the institution of monthly
feasts for the mere purpose of telling stories is a somewhat clumsy
contrivance for connecting the tales with the introduction, and for
giving the poet an excuse for a graceful prelude to every month of the
year. In spite, however, of small blemishes, there is a beauty and completeness in the design of the *Earthly Paradise*, which gives it a fine
distinction among the crowd of chaotic fragments that darken modern
literature.

Of the manner in which Mr. Morris has executed his task we cannot
speak with unmixed praise. In the first place it is clear that he has
expended his whole skill upon investing his poems with an antique air.
The closeness with which he reproduces the effect of the old romance
style in his loosely constructed verse is often surprising as a poetical
tour de force. A passage in the 'Lovers of Gudrun,' where Guest the seer
watches the sons of Olaf bathing, strikes us as particularly noticeable,
but there are many parts of his tales, and especially the openings, where
the ancient simplicity has been imitated with great fidelity. In his
description of nature, also, the out-of-door freshness and *naïveté* of the
romances has been very happily caught.

His command of the ancient style has, however, been acquired at the
cost of other qualities far more essential to real success in narrative. In
delineation of character, vivacity of incident, and energy of versification, Mr. Morris shows himself either negligent or incapable. His

poetical method may be contrasted not unfairly with that of Ariosto. Like the great poet, he professedly appears 'in raiment clad of stories oft besung.' Ariosto's style, however, is extremely idiomatic, and generally ironical. Yet, though no revivalist, and while looking on the marvels of Turpin's Chronicle with the eye of a humourist, he had a poet's appreciation of all that was noble in the idea of chivalry. Mr. Morris, on the other hand, while trying above all things to tell his stories in the language of romance, often misses the romantic spirit; indeed, so far is he from feeling it, that he is for ever breathing into his Neo-Gothic verse the expression of that decrepit love-longing, which is the peculiar product of modern poetry. There is nothing heroic about his heroes. They perform great deeds, it is true, because the old stories so represent them; but the only adventures in which Mr. Morris shows any interest are their love affairs. Thus when Perseus falls in with Andromeda, several pages are taken up with a recital of all that they felt and said, but when the sea-monster appears, he is despatched in as many lines. Perseus is armed with the Gorgon's head, a weapon of such tremendous power, that he ought to have felt it should be used only on great occasions; yet he employs it on the least provocation, and against the most ignoble foes, merely, as it appears, that Mr. Morris may have the pleasure of conducting him back as quickly as possible to the embraces of Andromeda. Ruggiero, in the *Orlando Furioso*, has a similar enchanted shield, but he keeps it carefully under cover, and when on one occasion he gains the victory, by the accidental removal of the case, he flings the shield into a well. Even the lovers in Mr. Morris's stories do not command our respect. In the 'Lovers of Gudrun,' perhaps the best story of the collection, our sympathy is claimed for Kiartan, who is deprived of his mistress by the treachery of his friend. In the old story we should probably feel compassion for such a man, for, though the knights of romance are by no means immaculate, their infidelities are generally lightly passed over in the *naïve* simplicity of the narrative. But how can we waste our sympathy on Mr. Morris's soft-hearted lover, who loiters in Norway, scarcely sending a meagre message to Gudrun, while he amuses himself with the king's sister Ingibiorg, who

> More than well
> Began to love him, and he let her love,
> Saying withal that nought at all might move
> His heart from Gudrun; and for very sooth
> He might have held that word; and yet for ruth

And a soft pleasure that he might not name
All unrebuked he let her soft eyes claim
Kindness from his.

More tiresome still is Acontius. This youth having fallen in love with
a lady whom he has just seen 'through half-shut eyes,' learns to his
horror that she is to be sacrificed to Diana. Yet though he afterwards
sees her twice, he has never the heart to speak to her, much less to effect
her escape. It is characteristic of Mr. Morris, that after a thousand lines
filled with languishing and lamentation, without one act of courage or
ingenuity on his part, this most detestable of lovers, through the intervention of Venus, is rewarded by the hand of the beautiful Cydippe.

The heroines of the tales, on the other hand, are as forward as the
heroes are languid. We have no objection to their falling in love at
first sight—though the occasional appearance of some shrewish
Katharine would certainly be a relief—but it appears to us that their
unconcealed complaisance would have disenchanted any lovers more
particular than Mr. Morris's. Even Aslaug, fostered in the rudest retire-
ment, on the appearance of a ship off her coast, speculates whether 'the
great lord' to whom it belongs will fall in love with her. Mr. Morris, in
fact, seems to think that shame and reserve are qualities incompatible
with simplicity. Yet he might remember that Homer's Nausicaa, on
approaching her father's town with Ulysses in her waggon, bids him
leave her, lest she should provoke comment by appearing in the company of a stranger.

Again, the author has the very slenderest appreciation of the value of
incident. This is not the fault of his originals. Both the Greek and the
Norse legends have their full complement of the marvellous, but for
the marvellous Mr. Morris cares nothing. We confess that we approached
these stories with delighted expectation. The reappearance of the
dragon in poetry, and in the face of a sceptical age, is an event which
all readers of poetry should welcome. We recalled the spirit-stirring
combat between Ruggiero and the Ork, and the magnificent description of the dragon in the first book of the *Faery Queen*. But Mr. Morris
cannot 'see' a dragon, much less can his dragons fight. When the
Chimæra appears, the messenger who reports it to King Jobates
confesses to having been so frightened as to be unable to say what it was
like. When Mr. Morris himself has to describe the sea-beast killed by
Perseus, this is all he has to say of him:—

He beholding Jove's son drawing near
A huge black fold against him did uprear,

Maned with a hairy tuft, as some old tree
Hung round with moss *in lands where vapours be!*

It excites neither surprise nor admiration that this most feeble and incapable monster should succumb beneath one whisk of the hero's magic sword.

Lastly, the natural languor of Mr. Morris's style makes his verse at once diffuse and tedious. An incurable habit of gossipping causes him to loiter in his narratives, when he should be swift and stirring. If one of his heroes, say the man born to be a King, sets out on a journey of life and death, we are told all that he thought about, whether the apples that he saw were ripe, and how many old women he passed, going to market. If a princess has occasion to look out of a window, Mr. Morris peeps to see what sort of a carpet she is standing on; and when he has married a pair of lovers in the middle of a story, he pauses to breathe a tearful blessing after them, telling them to make the most of their time, as they will probably some day grow tired of each other's company and at any rate they will have to die.

This tendency to diffuseness is encouraged by the metre of the poems. The heroic couplet, properly so called with all its proved capacities, is set aside in favour of the elementary style of Chaucer, who, if he were now alive, would be the first to own that the noble metre which he invented had received its last development from later hands. But Mr. Morris is far more diffuse than Chaucer himself. The latter, though he does not observe the couplet, rarely makes a break in the middle of a line, so that his rhymes are clearly marked, Mr. Morris, on the other hand, writes by sentences, and, as his chief aim is to give each sentence an archaic turn, his verse resembles old prose with incidental rhymes. In this way his rhymes become useless not only as points of rhetoric, but as points of limitation. We select a passage at random to illustrate our meaning.

So Bodli nothing loth went every day
When so they would to make the lovers gay,
When so they would to get him gone, that these
Even with such yearning looks their souls might please
As must be spoken, but sound folly still
To aught but twain, because no tongue hath skill
To tell their meaning. Kinder, Kiartan deemed,
Grew Bodli day by day, and ever seemed
Well nigh as happy as the happy twain,

> And unto Bodli life seemed nought but gain,
> And fair the days were.

The octosyllabic metre, with its inherent facility, does not become vigorous in the hands of Mr. Morris, nor can we approve of his revival of the seven-line stanza, after its long supersession by the Spenserian stanza. It is in this measure, however, we think, that Mr. Morris writes best; indeed, when obliged to consider the ways and means of metre, he shows that he can be concise and forcible enough. The following stanza describes the feelings of Atalanta at her first interview with Milanion before the race:—

> What mean these longings, vague, without a name,
> And this vain pity never felt before,
> This sudden languor, this contempt of fame,
> This tender sorrow for the time past o'er,
> These doubts that grow each minute more and more?
> Why does she tremble as the time draws near,
> And weak defeat and woeful victory fear?

In the graceful epilogue to *The Earthly Paradise*, Mr. Morris sends forth his book to find the spirit of Chaucer, who, he says, will understand and sympathize with his attempt

> to lay
> The ghosts that crowd about life's empty day.

We confess we do not think that Chaucer, however gratified he might be with Mr. Morris's preference and real appreciation, would at all sanction his method of laying ghosts. Of all poets Chaucer shows the most vigorous enjoyment of the activity and incident of life, from which his fastidious scholar so delicately withdraws himself. With his quick perception of character and his genial humour, we believe that the father of our poetry would never have found the present a mere 'empty day.' Such a phrase might characterize the society that existed at Rome under the latter empire, where all the springs of political and social life were dried. But a nation like England, whose historical fame is still recent, and whose liberties are not extinct, does not subside at once into such a state of torpor as the expression indicates. It is true that the picturesqueness of life that marked the period of Chaucer, has almost entirely disappeared; it is true also that other arts like those of journalism and novel-writing have done much to supersede poetry in the representation of national manners; yet after all deductions, enough remains of passion in politics, and individuality in character to give opportunities to the poet who knows how to seize them. That the opportunities have not been seized argues, we think, less the emptiness of the day, than the incapacity of the poets.

COMMENTS BY CONTEMPORARY
MEN OF LETTERS

24. John Ruskin on William Morris

1858–83

Ruskin, from whom Morris learned so much, was largely in sympathy with Morris both as poet and social critic.

(a) From a letter to Mr. and Mrs. Browning, 29 March 1858 (Ruskin, *Works*, edited by Cook and Wedderburn, 39 vols (1903–12), xxxvi, 280):

I haven't seen those poems of W. Morris's you speak of, but I've seen his poems, just out, about old chivalry, and they are most noble—very, very great indeed—in their own peculiar way.
[The Brownings must have seen Morris's contributions to the *Oxford and Cambridge Magazine*.]

(b) From *The Queen of the Air. A Study of the Greek Myths of the Cloud and Storm* (1869) in *Works*, xix, 309:

For all the greatest myths have been seen, by the men who tell them, involuntarily and passively . . . for it belongs exclusively to the creative or artistic group of men . . .

So that you may obtain a more truthful idea of the nature of Greek religion and legend from the poems of Keats, and the nearly as beautiful, and, in general grasp of subject, far more powerful, recent work of Morris, than from frigid scholarship, however extensive.

(c) From a letter to Miss Joan Agnew, at Mrs Cooper-Temple's ('Isola's'), 21 January 1870 (*Works*, xxxvii, 3):

Has Isola got Morris's last—3rd book of the *Earthly Paradise*? I can't understand how a man who, on the whole, enjoys dinner—

and breakfast—and supper—to that extent of fat—can write such lovely poems about Misery. There's such lovely, lovely misery in this Paradise. In fact, I think it's—the other place—made pretty, only I can't fancy any Paradise today but a Paradise of rug.

Ruskin quotes from 'The Land East of the Sun,' adding, 'It's not one of the best bits at all, but it's nice.'

(d) From a letter to Morris, refusing from incapacity an invitation to address the Society for the Preservation of Ancient Buildings, 27 May 1880 (*Works*, xxxvii, 315):

You younger men must found a new dynasty—the old things *are* passed away.

(e) From *The Art of England*, lectures given in Oxford in 1883 by Ruskin as Slade Professor of Art, and referring to a controversial lecture recently given by Morris to the Russell Club of University College (*Works*, xxxiii, 390):

The significant change which Mr. Morris made in the title of his recent lecture, from Art and *Democracy*, to Art and *Plutocracy*, strikes at the root of the whole matter; and with wider sweep of blow than he permitted himself to give his words. The changes which he so deeply deplored, and so grandly resented, in this once loveliest city, are due wholly to the deadly fact that her power is now dependant on the Plutocracy of Knowledge, instead of its Divinity.

25. Alfred Tennyson on William Morris

1867–84

Tennyson seems to have 'acknowledged' Morris as a poet, though he was totally unable to follow Morris in his later political views.

(a) From a letter from F. T. Palgrave to W. M. Rossetti, 25 October 1867 (*Rossetti Papers*, edited by W. M. Rossetti (London, 1903), 273–4):

I am delighted to see that *Jason* reached a second edition. I heard very favourable things about it from A. Tennyson (who came with me for three weeks last autumn into Devonshire), but I have seen no other judge of poetry who knew it except Woolner. I reckon much—indeed more—on his Tales; because *Jason* appears too long and weak a fable for effect, however skilfully treated.

[The 'Tales' is no doubt a reference to the projected *Earthly Paradise*.]

(b) From a letter of FitzGerald in 1876 (*More Letters of Edward Fitz-Gerald* (London, 1901), 186):

He (Tennyson) still admires Browning, for a great, though unshapen, Spirit; and acknowledges Morris, Swinburne, and Co., though not displeased, I think, that I do not.

(c) From *William Allingham—A Diary*, edited by H. Allingham and D. Radford (London, 1907), 326 (26 July 1884):

T. was shocked to hear of William Morris's Democratic Socialism, and asked to see a copy of *Justice* (Morris's *Justice*, I partly agree with and partly detest. It is incendiary and atheistic and would upset everything).

[*Justice* was the journal of the Democratic Federation.]

(d) From *William Allingham*, 339 (25 December 1884):

We spoke of William Morris (from whom I had just had a long

letter). T. said, 'He has gone crazy.' I said I agree with many of Morris's notions. Labour does not get its fair share.

T.—'There's brain labour as well as hand labour.'

W.A.—'And there are many who get money without any labour. The question, how to hinder money from accumulating into lumps, is a puzzling one.'

T.—'You must let a man leave money to his children. I was once in a coffee-shop in the Westminster Road at 4 o'clock in the morning. A man was raging "Why has so-and-so a hundred pounds, and I haven't a shilling?" I said to him, "If your father had left you £100 you wouldn't give it away to somebody else." He hadn't a word to answer. I knew he hadn't.'

26. Robert Browning on William Morris

1868–70

Browning appears to have been among those who preferred Morris's earliest verse—which in fact was said by several critics to show Browning's influence; Morris wrote one of his very few critical essays, on Browning's *Men and Women*, in the *Oxford and Cambridge Magazine* in March 1856.

(a) From Mackail, *Life of William Morris*, I, 133:

Browning himself, it may not be without interest to know, was one of the earliest and most enthusiastic admirers of this volume [*The Defence of Guenevere*]. 'It has been my delight,' he said of it many years afterwards, 'ever since I read it.' When the first volume of *The Earthly Paradise* was published, he wrote to Morris a letter of warm and finely-appreciative phrase. 'It is a double delight to me,' he added, 'to read such poetry, and know you of all the world wrote it,—you whose songs I used to sing while galloping by Fiesole in old days,—"Ho, is there any will ride with me."'

(b) From W. M. Rossetti's diary, 13 February 1868, (*Rossetti Papers* edited by W. M. Rossetti, 299):
Browning expresses (as I had before been told) a very high opinion of Morris's *Jason*.

(c) From Browning's letter to Isabel Blagden, 19 January 1870 (*Letters of Robert Browning*, edited by T. L. Hood (London, 1933), 134):
Morris is sweet, pictorial, clever always—but a weariness to me by this time. The lyrics were 'the first sprightly runnings'—this that follows is a laboured brew with the old flavour but no *body*.

27. Dante Gabriel Rossetti on William Morris

1856–71

Morris was something of a protégé of Rossetti in his early years, and throughout the period of their intimacy—up to the mid-seventies—Rossetti always showed a warm though not uncritical appreciation of Morris's work.

(a) From a letter to William Allingham, 18 December 1856 (*Letters of D. G. Rossetti*, edited by O. Doughty and J. R. Wahl, 2 vols (Oxford, 1965), I, 311–12):
Morris, besides writing those capital tales, writes poems which are really much better than the tales, though one or two short ones in the Mag were not of his best ... Morris' facility at poetizing puts one in a rage. He has been writing at all for little more than a year, I believe, and has already poetry enough for a big book ... To one of my water-colours called 'The Blue Closet,' he has written a stunning poem. You would think him one of the finest little fellows alive—with a touch of the incoherent, but a real man.

(b) From a letter to William Bell Scott, February 1857 (*Letters*, I, 319):
[Morris] has written some really wonderful poetry too, and as I happen to have a song of his in my pocket I enclose it to you.

(c) From a letter to Mrs. Gaskell, 18 July 1859 (*Letters*, I, 354):
I will not ask you how you like the *Guenevere* book, for I know for certain you must like it greatly by this time. It is a book, as you say, made for quiet places. With all its faults of youth, I must say I think the Arthurian part has much the advantage (in truth to the dramatic life of the old romance) over Tennyson's *Idylls of the King*, just out; wonderful as of course these last are, in rhythm, in finish, in all modern perfections.

(d) From a letter to John Skelton, 7 February 1869, about his favourable review of Morris in *Fraser's* (*Letters*, II, 688):
I think all you say of Morris is very completely and excellently said. It indicates, I should say, on the whole, the same estimate of him which I have long entertained, as being—all things considered—the greatest literary identity of our time. I say this chiefly on the ground of that highest quality in a poet—his width of relation to the mass of mankind; for, in inexhaustible splendour of execution, who can stand beside Swinburne?—not to speak of older men.

You know Morris is now only 35, and has done things in decorative art which take as high and exclusive a place in that field as his poetry does in its own. What may he not yet do? The second volume of the *Earthly Paradise* is getting forward, but will not be ready, I should think, till the spring of next year. In some parts of it the poet goes deeper in the treatment of intense personal passion that he has yet done. After the work is finished, I trust his next step will be in dramatic composition, in which I foresee some of his highest triumphs.

(e) From a letter to Miss Losh, 16 July 1869 (*Letters*, II, 708):
One day lately, working from 10 one morning to 4 in the morning after (with intervals of meals etc) he produced 750 lines!—and this of the finest poem he has yet done.

(f) From a letter to Swinburne, 21 December 1869 (*Letters*, II, 778):
By the bye, I am very glad you take so much my own view of the surprising merits of 'Gudrun,' and am quite of your opinion on the other hand about 'Acontius,' which I told Topsy was below his mark . . .

'The Man Who Never' etc. is also a very fine poem, I think, of its kind (from hearing it read) but really Topsy's very titles are almost too much for a Gillott's Magnum Bonum.

(g) From a letter to C. E. Norton, 22 January 1870 (*Letters*, II, 784):
Of course you know how great a success Morris's new *Earthly Paradise* is; and no doubt you agree with all the most reliable opinions, that there is some real advance as to strength and human character in this volume even over the former one. The 'Gudrun' is surely on the whole one of the finest poems in the English language.

(h) From a letter to Alexander Macmillan, 3 December 1870 (*The Rossetti–Macmillan Letters*, edited by L. M. Packer (Berkeley, 1963), 91–2):
Why does your magazine resolutely ignore the best things going? It's no business and no meaning of mine to speak for myself—let anyone do that who pleases—but why in the world has Morris been left in the lurch till now?

(i) From a letter to William Bell Scott, 2 October 1871, about *Love is Enough* (*Autobiographical Notes of the Life of William Bell Scott*, edited by W. Minto, 2 vols (London, 1892), II, 161):
The poem is, I think, at a higher point of execution than anything he has done,—having a passionate lyric quality such as one found in his earlier poems, and of course much more mature balance in carrying out. It will be a very fine work.

28. Algernon Charles Swinburne on William Morris

1858–95

Swinburne and Rossetti were Morris's two closest literary friends, and their names were often linked by critics of their poetry. Although Swinburne denied the similarity in a well-argued letter to John Nichol in 1876 (*The Swinburne Letters*, Yale edition, edited by C. Y. Lang, 6 vols (New Haven, 1959–62), III, 168–9), he and Morris remained on good terms to the end—Swinburne was sent copies of many of the Kelmscott Press books. In addition to his reviews of *Jason* (No. 8) and *The Well at the World's End* (No. 74) Swinburne made a number of references to Morris throughout his lively correspondence. He dedicated his 1898 volume to the memory of Morris and Burne-Jones.

(a) From a letter to Edwin Hatch, 17 February 1858 (*Swinburne Letters*, I, 15):
Morris's book is really out. Reading it, I would fain be worthy to sit down at his feet.

(b) From a letter to Edwin Hatch, 26 April 1858 (*Swinburne Letters*, I, 19–20):
Item: a review of *Guenevere* in *The Tablet*—I believe by Pollen: certainly the best as well as most favourable review Morris has had. That party has given us no signs of life as yet; in vain has the *Oxford County Chronicle* been crammed with such notices as the following:
'If W.M. will return to his disconsolate friends, all shall be forgiven. One word would relieve them from the most agonizing anxiety—why is it withheld?'
'If the Gentleman who left an MS. (apparently in verse) in George Street will communicate with his bereaved and despairing Publishers, he will hear of something to his advantage. Otherwise the

MS. will be sold (to pay expenses) as waste paper, together with the stock in hand of a late volume of poems which fell stillborn from the press.'
Even this latter—a touching effusion of the creative fancy and talented pen 'which now traces these imperfect records with a faltering hand'—has failed to move him. The town-crier is to proclaim our loss to-morrow. 'Lost, stolen, or strayed, an eminent artist and promising littérateur. (The description of his person is omitted for obvious reasons.) Had on when he was last seen the clothes of another gentleman, much worn, of which he had possessed himself in a fit or moral—and physical—abstraction. Linen (questionable) marked W. M. Swears awfully, and walks with a rolling gait, as if partially intoxicated.'

(c) From a letter to W. M. Rossetti, 7 December 1869 (*Swinburne Letters*, II, 65):
I want to read the 'Gudrun's Lovers'—a part I once heard of it seemed to me the most grateful exhalation that has of late emanated from the expanding jaws of that prudential 'allegory on the banks of the Nile'.

(d) From a letter to D. G. Rossetti, 10 December 1869 (*Swinburne Letters*, II, 68):
I have just received Topsy's book; the Gudrun story is excellently told, I can see, and of keen interest; but I find generally no change in the *trailing* style of work; his Muse is like Homer's Trojan women ἐλκεσίπεπλους—drags her robes as she walks; I really think a Muse (when she is neither resting nor flying) ought to tighten her girdle, tuck up her skirts, and step out. It is better than Tennyson's short-winded and artificial concision—but there is such a thing as swift and spontaneous style. Top's is spontaneous and slow; and especially, my ear hungers for more force and variety of sound in the verse. It looks as if he purposely avoided all strenuous emotion or strength of music in thought and word: and so, when set by other work as good, his work seems hardly done in thorough earnest. The verses of the months are exquisite—November I think especially.

(e) From a letter to W. M. Rossetti, 28 December 1869 (*Swinburne Letters*, II, 78):
I wrote to Topsy my congratulations on his promotion by the

reviews to the post of Christian laureate, and he responded with much unction and proper feeling.

(f) From a letter to D. G. Rossetti, 12 February 1870 (*Swinburne Letters*, II, 89):
... Watts, Morris or Keble—the three Christian singers of England (*vide* press *passim*).

(g) From a letter to Morris, 9 November 1875, thanking him for his *Aeneids* (*Swinburne Letters*, III, 85):
Whenever I have dipped into the book your version seems to me wonderful for grace & ease & strength. I wish you would give us a Homer, or at least an Odyssey: I am certain no poet was ever born who could do his country that service better or so well.

(h) From a letter to Edward Burne-Jones, 28 December 1876, referring to *Sigurd* (*Swinburne Letters*, III, 249):
What a feast shall I make of his glorious book when once I fairly tackle it!

(i) From a letter to Theodore Watts, 3 October 1882 (*Swinburne Letters*, IV, 307):
Your account of Morris gives me at once joy and apprehension. Let him build—and burn—as many halls or homesteads after the pattern of Burnt Njal's as he pleases—but for any sake withhold him from more metrication à la Piers Ploughman. I always foresaw that he would come to reject Chaucer at last as a modern. It is my belief that you encourage all this dashed and blank Volsungery which will end by eating up the splendid genius it has already overgrown and encrusted with Icelandic moss.

(j) From a letter to A. H. Bullen, thanking him for an anthology of Christmas carols, including Morris's 'Masters, in this hall', 19 January 1885 (*Swinburne Letters*, V, 96):
No more welcome present than this of your Christmas Garland could have reached me at this still seasonable time of year. I only wish my under-graduate imitation of an old carol was worthier of a place so near my friend Mr. Morris's perfect and incomparable examples; but no one can come within a thousand miles of him in any such field of work.

(k) From a letter to William Morris, thanking him for the Kelmscott *Wood Beyond the World*, 4 November 1894 (*Swinburne Letters*, VI, 76):

The Wood Beyond the World makes my mouth water—I only wish I had had it to read a month or two ago at Dursley, when I was spending some weeks with my mother and sisters in one of the most delicious corners of England.

(l) From a letter to Theodore Watts, 25 August 1895 (*Swinburne Letters*, VI, 110):
I have just read the *Well at the World's End*. The living charm of its loveliness is wonderful.

29. Gerard Manley Hopkins on William Morris

1877–81

Hopkins's letters to Robert Bridges and R. W. Dixon show his acute critical sense. He does not seem to have been aware that Dixon (whose letter of reply has its own interest) had been a friend of Morris at Oxford; he married Morris to Jane Burden at St Michael's, Oxford, in April 1859. Dixon also supplied his reminiscences to Mackail for incorporation into *The Life of William Morris*.

(a) From a letter to Robert Bridges, 13 June 1877 (*The Letters of G. M. Hopkins to Robert Bridges*, edited by C. C. Abbott (London, 1935), 41):
His Vergil is very likely a failure but it cannot be said that Wm. Morris is an ass, no.

(b) From Hopkins's first letter to R. W. Dixon, expressing his admiration for Dixon's poems, 4 June 1878 (*The Correspondence of G. M. Hopkins and R. W. Dixon*, edited by C. C. Abbott (London, 1935), 2):
Your poems had a medieval colouring like Wm. Morris's and

the Rossetti's and others but none seemed to me to have it so unaffectedly . . . And the Tale of Dauphiny and 'It is time to tell of fatal love' (I forget the title) in the other book are purer in style, as it seems to me, and quite as fine in colouring and drawing as Morris's stories in the *Paradise*, so far as I have read them, fine as those are.

(c) From letters to Bridges, 14 August and 22 October 1879 (*Letters to Bridges*, 89, 96): For it seems to me that the poetical language of an age shd. be the current language heightened, to any degree heightened and unlike itself, but not (I mean normally: freaks and graces are another thing) an obsolete one. This is Shakespeare's and Milton's practice and the want of it will be fatal to Tennyson's *Idylls* and plays, to Swinburne, and perhaps to Morris . . .

Since I must not flatter or exaggerate, I do not claim that you have such a volume of imagery as Tennyson, Swinburne or Morris, though the feeling for beauty you have seems to me pure and exquisite; but in point of character, of sincerity or earnestness, of manliness, of tenderness, humour, melancholy, human feeling, you have what they have not and seem scarcely to think worth having (about Morris I am not so sure: his early poems had a deep feeling).

(d) From a letter of Hopkins to Dixon about his poems, 29 October 1881 (*Correspondence*, 82–3):
The language is a quaint medley of Middle-Ages and 'Queen Annery,' a combination quite of our age and almost even our decade, as we see in Morris and that school (to which you, I suppose, belong), and having a charm of its own that I relish and admire, but as a thing alien to me.

(e) From Dixon's letter of reply, 4 November 1881 (*Correspondence*, 92):
I do not think I belong to the school of Morris. I have seen very little of his poetry: only three tales of the *Earthly Paradise*, and a little of *Jason*. Also that immense work *Sigurd*. So far as I can judge his touch is entirely different from mine: very powerful, even sledge-hammery: but not over subtle, by no means intellectual, and what I call desolately limited. His creed, that is, his ideas of life, is to me monstrous and insupportable. His method, his mingling of the couplet measure and the old stanza in his tales—not mingling in the same tale, but using either one or the other—looks somehow like

writing in ruins: gives a very different impression from what it gives when Chaucer does the same. His couplets in *Jason*, when I saw it last, seemed to have an immense deal of mere tagging. He very lawlessly intersperses it with lyric songs, brought in in the midst of these couplets and interrupting it. I could no more do that than introduce a passage of prose: the one is as unjustifiable as the other. In short he has not (as I think) a high feeling for form. If he had, he would be a very great poet: which he just misses being.

(f) From Hopkins's answering letter, 1 December 1881 (*Correspondence*, 98):

I must hold that you and Morris belong to one school, and that though you should neither of you have read a line of the other's. I suppose the same masters, the same models, the same tastes, the same keepings, above all, make the school . . . I used to call it the school of Rossetti: it is in literature the school of the Pra-raphaelites.

30. Southern American views of William Morris

1868–84

The correspondence between the two Southern poets Paul Hayne (1830–86) and Sidney Lanier (1842–81) shows that some American readers were enthusiastic about Morris's poetry as early as 1868. Lanier shared Hayne's admiration of Morris for a while, but after reading Chaucer acclaimed him and Shakespeare as 'the Masters'; in a thoughtful critical article on Hayne's poetry in 1875 Lanier argued that Hayne should turn from Morris to Chaucer as a source of poetic inspiration (No. 36).

(a) From a letter from Paul Hayne to Sidney Lanier, 7 September 1868 (*Sidney Lanier. Centennial Edition* (Baltimore, 1945), vii, *Letters 1857–1868*, 395):

As for *Wm. Morris*, I—for one, consider him as beyond doubt, the *purest, sweetest, noblest narrative* poet, Great Britain has produced since *Chaucer*. This may sound exaggerated, nevertheless it is simply *true*! By all means, procure his books, *Jason* and *The Earthly Paradise*.

(b) From a letter from Lanier to Virginia Hankins, 7 July 1869, saying that he had given a copy of the *Earthly Paradise* to his wife as a birthday present (*Lanier*, viii, *Letters 1869–1873*, 37):

She has been reading some of it to me, in my sick moments. It is very *great*. It is good for *you* to read. It is simple, *toned down*, strong, unstrained, dreamy, real, sensuous, pure, and *good*. Read all the stories. You will like them better, the more you know them.

(c) From a letter from Hayne to Lanier, 30 October 1869 (*Lanier*, viii, 43):

Wm. Morris I am ready to swear by. I like him a thousand times better than *Swinburne*—Indeed, often in reading his marvellous tales the question *involuntarily* arises, 'has *Chaucer* come back to Earth'?—Just think of his 'Pysche,' his '*Doom* of King Acrisius'! ! A healthful, noble, picturesque poet is this Wm. Morris! How *Keats* would have loved him! ! and Charles Lamb, and Coleridge! !

(d) From a letter from Virginia Hankins, 15(?) September 1870 (*Lanier*, viii, 106, note):
You do not like 'this Babylon'—William Morris, whose poetry . . . brings to one so forcibly the sense of flowers—birds—long green shadows—lives in London and is an upholsterer,—most commonplace calling.

(e) From a letter from Lanier to Hayne, praising his poetry (*Lanier*, viii, 347):
It is so rarely *musical* . . . It is, in this respect, simply unique in modern poetry: Wm. Morris comes nearest to it, but Morris lives too closely within hearing of Tennyson to write unbroken music.

(f) From a letter from Virginia Hankins to Lanier, 5 August 1875 (*Lanier*, ix, *Letters 1874–1877*, 232, note):
The truth is, I have not been able to watch the slow, gradual onward-moving of Art. I still believe in the mastery of Tennyson and William Morris.

(g) From Lanier's reply, 15 August 1875 (*Lanier*, ix, 233):
No, Tennyson and William Morris are not the masters; indeed, My Child, they never were . . . Chaucer and Shakespeare—these are the Masters.

(h) From Lanier's *Poems* (1884); the brief 'Poem Outline' points to the romantic escapism of Morris's poetry (*Lanier*, i, *Poems and Poem Outlines*, 260):
William Morris. He caught a crystal cup-full of the yellow light of sunset, and, persuading himself to dream it wine, swallowed it with a sort of smile.

LOVE IS ENOUGH

1872

31. G. A. Simcox, review, *Academy*

December 1872, iii, 461-2

The conception and arrangement of Mr. Morris's last poem are singularly refined and perfect; and it is written throughout with an intensity and seriousness which many readers will be inclined to contrast favourably with the half querulous half indolent *insouciance* which runs through much of the *Earthly Paradise*, and finds a definite expression in the *Apology* and *L'Envoi*. The poem begins with a conversation between Giles and Joan, who are two married peasants, in a crowd at the pageant of an emperor's marriage. They speak in octosyllabic couplets, and the imagery of their speeches is homely, and Joan mistakes the marshal's sergeant for a knight: otherwise it may be doubted whether any peasants out of Arcadia ever expressed themselves with such elegant simplicity and propriety. Then after a short song, which, like all in the poem, begins with the words, 'Love is Enough,' the emperor and empress appear and exchange lofty courtesies about their love in heroic triplets, each of which is followed by a burden. Then we have the mayor in alliterative lines begging leave to present a play. He feels called to apologize for the subject, which seems to depreciate rank and prosperity; as equally of course he regards the rank of the emperor and empress with loyal complacency; equally of course they give a gracious dispensation for the play to proceed.

The story of the play deals with familiar elements; but they are treated in an abstract passionate way that is anything but familiar. Pharamond succeeds his father, who is killed in battle, and for five years works wonders in defence of his kingdom. Through all these years he has been haunted by the vision of a maiden in a valley shut in by mountains, over which the only pass lies through a yew wood. At last he breaks down under his longing; and, after passing nine days in lethargy, sets off with his foster-father to find the reality of the vision. It seems they met with many adventures in their search; but these are only used for a scene of dreamy reminiscences; it is hardly worth while to enquire which come from Calprenède, which were invented for a story which upon reflection the poet did not care to tell. It is not till the search has lasted for years, and hope has failed, that Love reveals himself, and then withdraws to make way for the beloved in the very valley of the vision where Pharamond has lain down in a mist to die. While Pharamond has been longing for her, Azalais has been longing, not yet for him, but for love; and so when she sees him, she too recognizes that she has been longing for the meeting.

After the first raptures are over, Pharamond, to please his foster-father, and to gratify his natural self, or what is left of it, goes back to his kingdom to resume it if he can. He finds that Theobald the constable (whose *lâches* did much to aggravate his early difficulties) has usurped the throne to the general satisfaction. Accordingly he goes back to his love under the impression that he is too good for a king, and that there would be little pleasure in conquering his subjects after conquering their enemies. The emperor and empress are much pleased with the play, and wish in vain that they could make friends with the players; but they are cut off by their rank from a felicity which is reserved for Giles and Joan. After each scene there is a musical interlude, which becomes more and more like a hymn; and Love delivers an address to the audience, which becomes more and more like a sermon by a saint; and the talk of Giles and Joan as they go home from the show lets the reader down gently and happily to common life again.

When we pass from the conception to the execution, it is impossible to speak too highly of the rich rapturous melody of the songs, which are all in long anapaestic stanzas with double rhymes, that have an echo here and there of Mr. Swinburne—perhaps inevitable, but hardly welcome. We extract the last and the sweetest:—

LOVE IS ENOUGH! Ho ye who seek saving,
  Go no further; come hither; there have been who have found it,
And these know the House of Fulfilment of Craving;
  These know the Cup with the Roses around it;
  These know the World's Wound and the balm that hath bound it,
Cry out, the world heedeth not, 'Love, lead us home!'

He leadeth, He hearkeneth, He cometh to you-ward;
  Set your faces as steel to the fears that assemble
Round his goad for the faint, and his scourge for the forward;

Lo his lips, how with tales of last kisses they tremble!
Lo his eyes of all round that may not dissemble!
Cry out, for he heedeth, 'O Love, lead us home!'

O hearken the words of his voice of compassion:
'Come, cling round about me, ye faithful who sicken
Of the weary unrest and the world's passing fashion!
As the rain in mid-morning your troubles shall thicken,
But surely within you some Godhead shall quicken,
As you cry to me heeding, and leading you home.

'Come—pain ye shall have, and be blind to the ending!
Come—fear ye shall have, mid the sky's overcasting!
Come—change ye shall have, for far are ye wending!
Come—no crown ye shall have for your thirst and your fasting,
But the kissed lips of Love and fair life everlasting!
Cry out, for one heedeth who leadeth you home.'

Is he gone, was he with us?—ho ye who seek saving,
Go no further; come hither; for have we not found it?
Here is the House of Fulfilment of Craving;
Here is the Cup with the Roses around it,
The World's Wound well healed, and the balm that hath bound it:
Cry out! for he heedeth, fair Love, that led home.

The following lines are perhaps as fair a sample as can be isolated of
the tone and doctrine of Love's discourses:—

Have faith, and crave and suffer, and all ye
The many mansions of my house shall see
In all content: cast shame and pride away,
Let honour gild the world's eventless day,
Shrink not from change, and shudder not at crime,
Leave lies to rattle in the sieve of Time!
Then, whatsoe'er your work-day gear shall stain,
Of me a wedding-garment shall ye gain
No God shall dare cry out at, when at last
Your time of ignorance is overpast;
A wedding-garment and a glorious seat
Within my household, e'en as yet be meet.

The last line seems hardly finished; and there are other indications
here and there that Mr. Morris has lost something of his easy mastery
in abandoning the ruder form of the heroic couplet which he inherited
from Chaucer. The writer himself seems to be aware of a more serious

fault: with all his gracious delightful fervour, Love argues and insists too much; his discourses are not merely a commentary on the poem, they are a defence of it, almost a criticism; and it is only a very youthful literature which is ingenuous enough to permit itself such confidences. Perhaps too, it might be said that the several disguises of Love, who sometimes appears as a maker of images, sometimes as a maker of pictured cloths, have little value for the reader; though, if there could be found worthy actors and a fit audience, they would add another grace to the pageant.

It is hard to pronounce upon a single trial whether the revival of alliterative rhythm will be a permanent addition to our poetical resources. We are inclined to think that Mr. Morris himself has gained by it a greater directness and energy of expression, and consequently more of the eloquence of passion, and this without any sacrifice of delicacy; but after all he has not yet shaken our impression that the harmony of regular metre was a decided artistic progress.

Here is an extract from the speech of Azalais, as she sees Pharamond asleep:—

> As one hearkening a story, I wonder what cometh,
> And in what wise my voice to our homestead shall bid him.
> O heart, how thou faintest with hope of the gladness
> I may have for a little if there he abide,
> Soft there shalt thou sleep, love, and sweet shall thy dreams be,
> And sweet thy awaking amidst of the wonder
> Where thou art, who is nigh thee—and then, when thou seest
> How the rose-boughs hang in o'er the little loft window,
> And the blue bowl with roses is close to thine hand,
> And over thy bed is the quilt sewn with lilies,
> And the loft is hung round with green Southland hangings,
> And all smelleth sweet as the low door is opened,
> And thou turnest to see me there standing, and holding
> Such dainties as may be thy new hunger to stay—
> Then well may I hope that thou will not remember
> Thine old woes for a moment in the freshness and pleasure,
> And that I shall be part of thy rest for a little.

Perhaps the anapaestic movement is here as elsewhere too unbroken, indeed there are whole paragraphs that only want rhymes to remind us of Mr. Swinburne when he writes in a minor key. But we feel it is ungracious to criticize music at once so rich and so simple: the idyllic grace of Azalais' awaking shyly to the consciousness of love furnishes the ideal relief after the passionate scene in which Pharamond's hushed intense expectation passes through sweet music into the trance in which she finds him.

The charm of the *Earthly Paradise* was that it gave us the picturesqueness of earth with the atmosphere of fairyland; we drifted along a swift current of adventure under a sky heavy with sweet dreams, through which the dew of death fell without dimming the sunshine: we were amused and yet enthralled. In his new work Mr. Morris demands more of the reader; instead of abandoning himself to a passive fascination, he has to be penetrated with a profound and earnest passion: we have to live in the poem, not to dream of it. Consequently it will not be surprising if *Love is Enough* attracts fewer readers than the *Earthly Paradise*; though those who are attracted will be held longer under a deeper spell. Those outside the charmed circle will perhaps complain that the figures which move within are shadowy, because their own desire does not burn within them.

32. Sidney Colvin, review, *Fortnightly Review*

1 January 1873, xiii, 147–8

That he clothes modern thoughts in modern words, is not the definition of Mr. Morris's work. Rather it has been made an accusation against him that he occupies himself exclusively with old stories, and goes back to old sources of language for words to put them in: 'Remote subjects—archaic manner,' grates every now and then the note of a criticism respectable if only for rustiness; while the mind susceptible to literature, and awake to poetry, is enjoying itself in the sense of a delightful possession, and acknowledging that no subject is too old, and no style too primitive, when the one is made to fit the other with a result so true, so fresh, so living, so full of brightness and colour, so rich in lovely inventions and amplifications of the renovating and realizing fancy, as this is. That, I say, is the feeling towards the *Earthly*

Paradise series of every one who cares for poetry, except (as George Eliot's Tom cared for animals) in the sense of caring to throw stones at it. Modern thoughts are certainly valuable; but every thought can be made to have the value of modernness for the imagination of every age, when it is repeated in this loving, this sincere, this caressing and revivifying spirit. And about the vividiness, the limpid simplicity and bright reality of Mr. Morris's versions of ancient stories, there could be no two opinions. Whatever else could be urged against them, it was not obscurity. That is not quite equally the case with the small new volume which is before us. *Love is Enough* is more difficult to follow, it is a little vaguer in its incidents, and more puzzling in its motives, than other poems of Mr. Morris. It consists mainly of the adventures of a prince of romance, Pharamond, in search of his love, Azalais. Pharamond is a victorious king, haunted and troubled by the love of a lady whom he has seen in a dream, and who he knows is to be found in some enchanted foreign land. Presently his love grows so strong upon him that he quits his kingdom, with a faithful foster-father for chief attendant, to wander over the world in search of his dream. At last, almost spent with adventures and disasters, he finds her, and finds her ready to be his. Next, he is back in his kingdom, and discovers a usurper in possession. He decides that it is not worth while to make war for his own re-instatement—that 'love is enough;' and so goes back to unknown days with Azalais in the far country. That is the story; and that is acted by a pair of masquers who have had their own experiences of love, at the marriage festivities of an emperor and empress who have had theirs, and in the presence of a certain Giles and Joan who have had theirs. So that we have three pairs of live lovers, as well as the pair of personated lovers in the play. That of itself is a complication; and the figure of the god Love coming in and playing the part of Chorus under various disguises, does not diminish the complication. Then I think some of the actual adventures of the fable, as they are described or assumed in the representation, are a little too vague and shadowy. Altogether the poem is not limpid at first sight, and requires that you should read yourself into it. Reading yourself into it, you find much loveliness and a singular originality. There is the originality of using a metrical system of anapaests without rhyme, and with an irregular alliterative tendency, roughly resembling the common form of early English verse. That at first is rather uncomfortable, and I do not know that even at last one becomes quite converted to it; but it is certainly proved capable of effects of great metrical charm and dignity. Then there is the originality of an exquisitely tender, profound, and brooding sentiment—a sentiment which is almost a philosophy—of love and its predominance, and the worthlessness of everything else in the world along side of it. And that is put in, both in the body of the acted fable, in the comments of Love as Chorus, and the lyric interludes of the musicians, with a much greater aim at concentration and fulness of thought than has been common in any other of Mr. Morris's work. And, taken together with the picturesqueness of his imagination, it produces, in some places, a result which, new as it is in form, less clear as it is than one would have fully desired, leaves yet an impression most delicate and enchanting. Some strokes of the lyric interludes, some passages like that where Azalais comes upon Pharamond in his sleep are of an almost perfect poetry.

33. Unsigned review, *Athenaeum*

17 July 1875, no. 2490, 75

Much vexation of spirit arises from seeing work ill done, and as ample cause for it is provided by translators as by any class of literary men. Usually, indeed, translations are either depressing or exasperating. The fatuity of some, the criminality of others, weighs heavily upon the reader's mind or painfully disturbs his liver. Now and then, however, a most agreeable exception to the rule presents itself, and a version from some foreign tongue appears which is in itself a work of art, not only satisfying the just demands of the foreign original, but also gratifying the ear and the taste of the native reader. Of such a nature are the versions from the Icelandic for which we are indebted to Mr. Eiríkr Magnússon and Mr. William Morris, the most recent of which is now before us. Of it, as of its predecessors, too high praise cannot be spoken, both as regards the grace and vigour of its own language and its fidelity to that which it interprets.

These Northern love-stories are deserving of the pains which have been taken with them. Not only do they contain a series of trustworthy pictures of the old times to which they refer, but they are rich in scenes of romantic as well as historic interest, through which move with unaffected dignity the forms of brave men and fair women. He who has read them feels the better for having done so, as one who has been transferred from a relaxing to a bracing air. From the tropical raptures and languors of so many modern love-stories it is good to turn to these simple but vigorous records of ancient warrings and wooings in the North.

The oldest is, perhaps, the best, telling how Gunnlaug the Worm-tongue, so called because he was a great skald 'somewhat bitter in his rhyming,' loved Helga, 'the fairest woman in Iceland, then or since,' and she was 'vowed, but not betrothed,' to him, on condition that he should 'go abroad and shape himself to the ways of good men,' returning at the end of three winters to claim his bride. So he set forth on long wanderings, visiting many lands and gaining much honour. But, mean time, another warrior and skald, Raven by name, claimed the hand of Helga, and was promised it if Gunnlaug did not return by the appointed time. And Gunnlaug was detained in England by King Ethelred until the third winter was past, so when he arrived in Iceland he found that Helga was Raven's wife. So one day at the Althing, when men had gone thronging to the Hill of Laws, and the matters of the law had been done there, he challenged his supplanter to meet him in the holm of the Axe water, for 'at that time it was lawful for him who thought himself wronged by another to call him to fight on the holm.' A drawn battle took place between the rivals, and thereupon 'it was made law in the law-court that, henceforth, all holmgangs should be forbidden,' so Gunnlaug and Raven had to settle their quarrel in Norway. There on Dingness they met in mortal conflict, and Gunnlaug killed Raven outright, but received a mortal wound, of which, after three nights, he died. Time passed by, and Helga was married to one Thorkel, 'a doughty man, and wealthy of goods, and a good skald.' But Helga loved him little, 'for she cannot cease to think of Gunnlaug, though he be dead,' and her chief joy was to pluck at the threads of a rich cloak, which her first lover had given to her.—

So one Saturday evening Helga sat in the fire-hall, and leaned her head upon her husband's knees and had the cloak, Gunnlaug's gift, sent for; and when the cloak came to her she sat up and plucked at it, and gazed thereon awhile, and then sank back upon her husband's bosom, and was dead. Then Thorkel sang this:—

> Dead in mine arms she droopeth,
> My dear one, gold-rings bearer,
> For God hath changed the life-days
> Of this Lady of the linen.
> Weary pain hath pined her,
> But unto me, the seeker
> Of hoard of fishes highway,
> Abiding here is wearier.

As fresh and spirited as the story of Gunnlaug the Worm-tongue is that of Frithiof the Bold, a tale which bears manifestly true witness to the hardy and adventurous nature of the people among whom it was composed, to whose sympathies it appealed. One of its chapters is indeed magnificent, that which relates how Frithiof sails for the Orkneys, and all but suffers shipwreck from the violence of a storm brewed by two 'witch-wives,' at the instigation of Halfdan and Helgi, the false brothers of the fair maiden Ingibiorg, whom Frithiof desires to wed. For when his ship, Ellidi, is come out far into the main, the sea waxes wondrous troubled, and a storm arises with so great drift of snow that none may see the stem from the stern, and they ship seas so that they must be ever a-baling. But even when the sea breaks over the bows, so that the water comes in 'like the in-falling of a river,' and 'liker to huge peaks and mountains than to waves' seem the sea-breakers that crash on all sides against the ship, the courage of her crew suffers no change, and the voices of their leaders sing steadily in response to the howl of the blast such staves as Frithior's:—

> So come in the West-sea
> Nought see I the billows,
> The sea-water seemeth
> As sweeping of wild-fire.
> Topple the rollers,
> Toss the hills swan-white,
> Ellidi wallows
> O'er steep of the wave-hills.

Even when Frithiof begins to admit that death seems to be at hand when 'none might see the stem or stern from amidships, and therewith was there great drift of spray amid the furious wind, and frost, and snow, and deadly cold,' his chief care is that each of his men 'should have somewhat of gold on him,' so as to reach the house of Ran in glorious array; so he smites asunder a golden circlet, the gift of Ingibiorg, and shares it among them. At this point the story loses much of its interest for us, since supernatural machinery, when suddenly introduced upon the stage in a piece apparently representing scenes of real life, is apt to subject the illusion of a modern beholder to a strain too great for endurance. But the Saga man's contemporaries in the fourteenth century probably listened with rapt attention as he described how Frithiof saw from the masthead that a great whale was circling round the ship, bearing two women on its back; so he made straight for it, and with the aid of his good ship Ellidi, which 'knew the speech of man,' he broke the backs of those witches, and the whale disappeared, the gale sank, and the weather-tossed mariners came safe to land.

A similar witch-storm occurs in the tale of 'Viglund the Fair,' but it is not of equal interest, except in so far as it makes us acquainted with a melody, which is 'an old traditional one in Iceland, and may be taken as an example of the sort of tune to which the staves of verse in the Sagas were sung.' The words to which it is mated form one of the most attractive specimens of the songs, which have been most skilfully rendered, but which, depending as they do on alliteration, will scarcely succeed in charming the ears of hearers unaccustomed to that species of poetic cunning:—

> No more may my eyen
> Meet the sea ungreeting,
> Since the day my speech-friend
> Sank below the sea banks.
> I loathe the sea-flood's swartness
> And the swallowing billow,
> Full sore for me the sorrow
> Born in sea-wave's burden.

In the story of Hogni and Hedinn, which is 'a later and amplified version of the mythological tale given in the "Skáldskarparmál" (or Treatise on Poetic Diction),' there are two fine scenes, the one in which Hedinn sees 'the ghostly shadow,' vast and dark, of the being whom he had taken for a fair and true woman, and by whom he had been led into evil courses, and the other that which shows him and his foster-brother Hogni, with their several hosts, engaged in endless warfare day after day, and night after night, and year after year, till at last 'a christened man' breaks the spell which Odin laid upon them, and looses them 'from this woeful labour and miserable grief of heart.' In the short tale of 'Thorstein Staff-smitten,' which is 'a kind of hanger-on to the more important story of "The Weapon-firth Men,"' there are not many striking incidents, though it is full of pictures of Icelandic life in old times, and ' "Roi the Fool," in spite of its very characteristic Northern colouring, is a version of an Eastern story,' rendered remarkable by its antiquity, having been found 'in the ancient Icelandic MS. commonly called the "Flateyjarbók," and in that part of it which was written before 1380.' But the whole volume, like the rest of the work which we owe to the joint labours of Mr. Magnússon and Mr. Morris, is full of lively interest, and with respect to its literary merits we may use the words which they employed in their Preface to *The Story of the Volsungs and Niblungs*:—'We think we may well trust the reader of poetic insight to break through whatever entanglement of strange manners or unused element may at first trouble him, and to meet the nature and beauty with which it is filled.'

THE AENEIDS OF VERGIL

1875

34. Unsigned review, *Athenaeum*

13 November 1875, no. 2507, 635–7

This appreciative review is entitled 'A New Translation of the *Aeneid*'.

We have never seen any attempt made to account for the fact that while, for some time past, every two or three years' interval has seen a new translation of the *Iliad* or the *Odyssey*, there should have been published, so far as we know, within anything like recent times, only two translations of the *Æneid*. Of these, that by Mr. Rickards was the praiseworthy effort of a man occupied in other business to find a 'humane' employment for his leisure hours, and probably gained but few readers beyond the circle of the author's friends, if, indeed, it ever reached any other than a private circulation; it was, if we remember right, in ten-syllable couplets. The second, on the other hand, as the work of a scholar by profession, and one who had given much attention to Vergil in particular, was looked for with some interest, all the more so as the author, after balancing the claims of various metres to represent the Vergilian hexameter, and deciding, perhaps with reason, that the heroic couplet challenged too close a comparison with the sonorous verse of Dryden, while blank verse was an instrument only to be wielded by a consummate poet, selected the metre rendered familiar by Scott as giving 'the best chance of imparting to his work that rapidity of utterance which is indispensably necessary to a long narrative poem.' The experiment can hardly be said to have succeeded, and Prof. Conington's translation is, we fear, by this time almost forgotten, except by those whom his eminence as a scholar induced at the time to possess themselves of the book. In reading his Preface, however,

216

one thing strikes us as remarkable, namely, that among the metres
which he discusses that one should be entirely omitted which has the
oldest claim of all to represent the epic hexameter. It is more strange,
too, that it should not have suggested itself to him in the course of
his work. When we read such a passage as the following—

> King Anius, king and priest in one,
> With bay-crowned tresses hoar,
> Hastes to accost us, and is known
> Anchises' friend of yore.
> We grasp his friendly hand in proof
> Of welcome, and approach his roof.
> The sacred temple I adored.
> Of immemorial stone:
> 'O grant us, Thymbra's gracious lord,
> A mansion of our own.'

we see at once that the metre of the 'Lay of the Last Minstrel' is, after
all, merely a modification of the true English heroic metre known as
common measure, and consisting of alternate eight and six-syllable
lines, or, more accurately, couplets of fourteen-syllable lines. This, as
all the world knows, is the metre which George Chapman, the father
of English translation in verse, used in that noble attempt to render
the *Iliad* into English, which, with all its defects, has yet more vitality
than any of its successors, and bids fair to make the name of its author
outlast, as a translator of Homer, all subsequent ones, from Pope to
Lord Derby. Such being the case, it seems curious that no one, as far
as we know, before Mr. Morris should have bethought him of the
possibility of employing the same metre in rendering the *Æneid*. We
can only say that the experiment has been fully justified by the results:
Whether for elegance of verse or accuracy of translation, Mr. Morris's
Æneids of Virgil (the plural form is apparently suggested by Chapman's
Iliads) must be pronounced the most satisfactory attempt that has yet
been made to present the greatest of Roman poets to English readers.
Let our readers judge, for Christopher North's opinion that the secret
of reviewing was plentiful quotation certainly holds in the case of
a long poem; still more when that poem is a translation, which must
be estimated from a double point of view. We will first give Mr.
Morris's version of a beautiful and well-known bit of description in
the first Book:—

> There goes a long firth of the sea, made haven by an isle,
> Against whose sides thrust out abroad each wave the main doth send

Is broken, and must cleave itself through hollow lights to wend
Huge rocks on this hand and on that, twin horns of cliff, cast dread
On very heaven; and far and wide beneath each mighty head
Hushed are the harmless waters; lo, the flickering wood above
And wavering shadow cast adown by darksome hanging grove:
In face whereof a cliff there is of rocks o'erhung made meet
With benches of the living stone, and springs of water sweet,
The house of nymphs: a riding there may way-worn ships be bold
To lie without the hawser's strain or anchor's hooked hold.

We are at once struck by the exceeding literalness which Mr. Morris has been able to attain. With the exception of the '*horns* of cliff,' there is hardly a word in this whole passage which has not its corresponding word in the Latin. 'The flickering wood' gives no less than the *silvis coruscis* of the original, the play of the sunlight through the boughs on the top of the cliff, contrasting with the *atrum nemus* in the shaded part below the edge. While on this subject, we cannot refrain from giving our readers a French translator's rendering of the three lines 163–165. They are a good specimen of the translation, which aims at elegance, somewhat to the neglect of accuracy:—

Balancés par les vents, de bois aigrent son front;
A ses pieds le flot dort dans un calme profond;
Et des arbres touffus l'amphithéâtre sombre
Prolonge sur les flots la noirceur de son ombre.[1]

M. Delille has, indeed, rendered, though he has transposed it, the *scena* which Mr. Morris has rather shirked; but the last line, lovely as it is, introduces an idea of which there is no trace in the original.

We proceed to give another, and this time a longer, extract. We should say that we have not selected it for any special excellence, rather because it is a well-known passage, containing a vivid picture, and complete in itself:—

Far mid the sea a rock there is, facing the shore-line's foam,
Which beat by overtoppling waves, is drowned and hidden oft,

---

[1] The quotation is from Jacques Delille's translation of the *Aeneid*, published in 1804. There are three errors in the quotation: the first line concludes, 'des bois ceignent son front', and the last line refers to 'les eaux' rather than 'les flots':

Moved by the winds, trees encircle its brow;
At its feet the sea sleeps in a profound calm;
And the dark ampitheatre of the leafy trees
Prolongs the darkness of its shadow upon the waves.

All translations here and in the next review are by the present editor.

What time the stormy North-west hides the sun in heaven aloft:
But otherwhiles it lies at peace, when nought the sea doth move,
And riseth up a meadow fair that sunning sea-gulls love.

[quotes next 54 lines]

We cannot give the conclusion of this famous boat-race, but the
passage we have quoted is a very fair specimen of Mr. Morris's work.
The flow of the verse must strike the most casual reader; and in order
to see the advance in mere technical skill made by the last 280 years,
it is sufficient to read aloud first a page of Chapman, and then a page
of the Victorian poet. There is a fine excitement in galloping a good
horse over rocks: but smooth turf is preferable for a continuance. Yet
Mr. Morris's verse is not singsong or monotonous; a short inspection
will show the art with which the pauses are arranged. The literalness
is almost more exact here than in our former extract; the only fault
that we can suggest being the rendering, twice repeated, of 'lævus' by
'lee.' The sound of the Latin may have suggested a word which is out
of place in a rowing-match, though no doubt if Gyas and Cloanthus
had been at Cowes it would have properly described the situation.
In the second case at least, 'left-hand' might have been retained without
much detriment to the verse. Some may possibly object to Mr.
Morris's use of archaic words, such as 'twiyoke' here, and others in
other places; but, as Mr. Conington pointed out, they are at least as
defensible as Vergil's own 'faxo,' 'aulai,' or 'olli.' One word, however
which occurs in this passage, reminds us to find fault. We must demur
to the translator's perpetual use of 'dight' as a present. Surely it is the
past tense and participle of 'to deck,' so that such a phrase as 'the feast
she dights again' is a mere solecism. May we remind Mr. Morris of the
good word 'busk,' with which his study of the Sagas must have made
him familiar? While we are in a censorious frame, let us specify one
or two other points which a second edition may correct. 'Stored' and
'broad,' is a very bad rhyme; 'fierce' and 'ears' not much better. Then
'from everywhither' is surely not English, nor, as far as we can make
out, are the following: 'Her whom the Fates would ne'er be moved';
'Rumour, of whom nought swifter is of any evil thing.' As to renderings of the Latin, we have already said that Mr. Morris seems to us to
surpass, both in fidelity and accuracy, all Vergilian translators, 'quot
sunt quotque fuere,'[1] but even he slips now and then. 'Panthus, how
fares it at the worst?' 'Fearing where no fear was,' do not, we believe,

_____
[1] As many as there are, and as many as have been.

represent 'Quo res summa loco, Panthu?'[1] or, 'Omnia tuta timens';[2] and, in Book VII., 1. 467, Mr. Morris is, to make a poor joke, very much at sea. 'Unda' is no doubt the sea sometimes, but hardly when it is a brazen cauldron. The whole passage in which this occurs is indeed perhaps the weakest in the entire volume: 'furit intus' is poorly rendered by 'within comes rage to pass.' Once only, throughout the whole 10,000 lines or so, is Mr. Morris guilty of a real cacophony. In VII., 300-2, we have these grand lines:—

> Absumptæ in Teucros vires cælique marisque.
> Quid Syrtes, aut Scylla mihi, quid vasta Charybdis
> Profuit?[3]

which are thus rendered:—

> Against these Teucrians sea and sky have spent their strength for nought:
> Was Syrtes aught, or Scylla aught, or huge Charybdis aught?

We can only hope that Mr. Morris, after the manner of poets, does not regard the second of these as the best line he has ever written, and that we may not be visited with Mr. Swinburne's scathing satire for our bad taste in thinking it ugly.

No review of a translation of the *Æneid* is, we suppose, complete without a reference to its most famous passage. We will, therefore, give Mr. Morris's version of Bk. VI. 869-887, premising, however, that he hardly seems to us quite to rise to the occasion; but that is only saying that the highest poetry cannot be moved out of its own words without injury:—

> Then midst the rising of his tears father Anchises spoke:
> 'O son, search not the mighty woe and sorrow of thy folk!
> The Fates shall show him to the world, nor longer blossoming
> Shall give. O Gods that dwell on high, belike o'ergreat a thing
> The Roman tree should seem to you. Should this your gift endure,
> How great a wail of mighty men that Field of Fame shall pour
> On Mavor's mighty city walls: what death rites seest thou there,
> O Tiber, as thou glidest by his new wrought tomb and fair!
> No child that is of Ilian stock in Latin sires shall raise
> Such glorious hope; nor shall the land of Romulus e'er praise
> So fair and great a nursling child mid all it ever bore.

---

[1] Panthus, where is the main action?

[2] Fearing everything even when it was safe.

[3] The strength of sky and sea were spent against the Trojans. What use to me were the Syrtes, Scylla, or vast Charybdis?

Goodness, and faith of ancient days, and hand unmatched in war,
Alas for all! No man unhurt has raised a weaponed hand
Against him, whether he afoot had met the foeman's band,
Or smitten spur amid the flank of eager foaming horse.
O child of all men's ruth, if thou the bitter Fates mayst force,
Thou art Marcellus. Reach ye hands of lily-blooms fulfilled;
For I will scatter purple flowers, and heap such offerings spilled
Unto the spirit of my child, and empty service do.'

One more short quotation and we have done. Mr. Morris has, to our thinking, written no finer line than that with which the whole work closes; and we give it, with the two preceding:—

Deep in that breast he driveth sword e'en as the word he saith;
But Turnus,—waxen cold and spent, the body of him lies,
And with a groan through dusk and dark the scornful spirit flies.

Whether any Keats of the twenty-second century will immortalize Mr. Morris by his gratitude we cannot say; but we predict that our great-great-grandchildren will consider not the least claim to remembrance possessed by the author of the *Earthly Paradise* to be that he was the translator of Vergil.

35. Henry Nettleship, review, *Academy*

November 1875, x, 493–4

Nettleship (1839–93) was a classical scholar; he became Professor of Latin Literature at Oxford in 1878.

The very long quotations have been abbreviated.

Few things are more interesting than to study a poet's translation of a poet (now unhappily a rare phenomenon), and to observe how the translator in reading, as it were, the heart of his brother, breathes a new spirit into his utterances, recasts his work in another mould, and enables men to enjoy it afresh in another aspect and in the feeling of a living inspiration. And it should be added that apart from the general interest which on this ground must attach to Mr. Morris's work, he is entitled to special gratitude for having grappled with a poem which no translator but a poet is likely to handle with sustained success. The *Aeneid* (why *Aeneids* Mr. Morris should explain) is a work so complex in its texture, so full of poetical reserve, of so exquisite a workmanship, and uniting so many elements of epic majesty, romance, pathos, eloquence, that if the air of poetry be wanting to it a translation of Virgil is apt at times to flag, or to lapse into dulness and rhetoric.

The breath of poetry informs the whole work, but this must not be held to imply that Mr. Morris has not taken a strict view of his duties as a translator. He has studied the language of Virgil in all its uncommon and original turns with the care of a scholar; the number of lines in each book is, if we mistake not, accurately reproduced; the periods are ended as Virgil ended them, and his unfinished lines never finished. Mr. Morris's metre, the long ballad verse, sets the whole poem, as it were, to a national and popular music, and thus suggests a main characteristic of the *Aeneid*—a work, by the by, which has been so mercilessly dissected for scholastic purposes and (perhaps partly in consequence) has met with so much unreasonable and piecemeal criticism that it has almost come to be forgotten how genuinely Virgil was accepted, not merely by men of letters, but by the people of Rome, as the true poetical representative of his time. And this ballad character of the *Aeneid* is not merely suggested by Mr. Morris's metre, but by his constant and most Virgilian choice (sometimes amounting to mannerism) of antiquarian language, as well as by the general liveliness and flavour of his diction. Nor does Mr. Morris ever lose sight of the incomparable grace and beauty of soul that inspired Virgil's verse—into which, indeed, as a few specimens will show immediately, he sometimes reads a new poetical feeling of his own. It may be said, indeed, that the general effect of his work is quite unique, and that, since Dryden, no Englishman has translated Virgil with such insight and sympathy. Dryden has, of course, a power and mastery of his own which enables him at times to deal with Virgil's grander efforts as perhaps no English poet but Milton (had he attempted it) could have done; and it should also be remembered that a freer play was allowed by poets in Dryden's time than in our own to the rhetorical element, which is so strong in Virgil. But in the melodious passages of meditation and enjoyment with which the *Aeneid* abounds Mr. Morris is master of the situation, as the two following specimens will show (vii. 25, viii. 86):—

> Now reddened all the sea with rays, and from the heavenly plain
> The golden-hued Aurora shone amidst her rosy wain.
> Then fell the winds, and every air sank down in utter sleep,
> And now the shaven oars must strive amid the sluggish deep;
> Therewith Aeneas sees a wood rise from the water's face,
> And there it is the Tiber's flood amidst a pleasant place,
> With many a whirling eddy swift and yellowing with sand,
> Breaks into sea; and diversely above on either hand
> The fowl that love the river bank, and haunt the river bed,
> Sweetened the air with plenteous song, and through the thicket fled.
> So there Aeneas bids his folk shoreward their bows to lay,
> And joyfully he entereth in the stream's o'ershadowed way.

[second passage omitted]

Much of the chill dread of the opening of Virgil's *Inferno* is preserved in the following beautiful passage (vi. 268):—

> All dim amid the lonely night on through the dusk they went,
> On through the empty house of Dis, the land of nought at all,
> E'en as beneath the doubtful moon, when niggard light doth fall
> Upon some way amid the woods, when God hath hidden heaven,

[quotes next 18 lines]

But it is a pity that a translator who, as a rule, cultivates the most scholarly accuracy should repeat a conventional blunder which mars so much of the beauty of the passage, and render *faucibus Orci* 'the jaws of hell.' If we are not mistaken, *fauces* means not the jaws but the throat, metaphorically (as in a house) any close passage, and here, the narrow entrance to Orcus. The idea of hell as a monster with jaws was as foreign to Virgil as to the whole of the Greek and Roman mythology, in which the imagery of the underworld is mostly drawn from houses and cities. And there is another point here to which it may be of interest to draw attention. Does *consanguineus Leti sopor*[1] mean sleep or lethargy, as has been suggested by an ingenious critic? We incline to think the latter; partly, because sleep has no proper place among the *terribiles visu formae*,[2] partly, also, because the lines under consideration contain an interesting reminiscence of Lucretius, iii. 459, seqq., where disease, sorrow, grief, fear and lethargy are mentioned together:—

> His accedit uti videamus, corpus ut ipsum
> Suscipere immanis *morbos* durumque dolorem,
> Sic animum *curas acris luctumque metumque*
>
> ★ ★ ★ ★ ★ ★
>
> Interdumque gravi lethargo fertur in altum
> Aeternumque *soporem* oculis nutuque cadenti.[3]

The argument might not be worth pressing were it not that the sixth Aeneid shows other marked traces of Virgil's study of Lucretius' third book.

Let us now try Mr. Morris in another vein, that of invective. The following is his rendering of Dido's great speech (iv. 365):—

> Traitor, no goddess brought thee forth, nor Dardanus was first
> Of thine ill race, but Caucasus on spiky crags accurst
> Begot thee, and Hyrcanian dugs of tigers suckled thee.
> Why hide it now, why hold me back, lest greater evil be?

[quotes next 18 lines]

And this of Drances' eloquence (xi., 342):—

> A matter dark to none, and which no voice of mine doth need,
> Thou counsellest on, sweet king; for all confess in very deed

---

[1] Sleep, the brother of Death.　　　　[2] Shapes terrifying to behold.
[3] Then follows this, that as the body falls victim to terrible diseases and harsh pain, so the mind falls victim to biting cares, grief and fear . . . Sometimes, in a heavy lethargy, it is carried off into a deep and eternal sleep, when the eyes and head fall nodding.

They wot whereto our fortune drives, but fear their speech doth hide;
Let him give liberty of speech, and sink his windy pride
Because of whose unhappy fate and evil life and will—
Yea, I will speak, despite his threats to smite me and to kill,
So many days of dukes are done, and all the city lies
O'erwhelmed with grief, the while his luck round camps of Troy he tries,
Trusting to flight, and scaring Heaven with clashing of his sword.
One gift, meseems, thou shouldest add, most gracious king and lord,
Unto the many gifts thou biddest bear to the Dardan folk,
Nor bow thyself to violence, nor lie beneath its yoke.

In these passages and in some others of the same character Mr.
Morris's genius is, we think, less successful in reproducing the spirit
and animation of the original; the English halts where the Latin is a
continuous stream of rapid movement. And in one or two places in
the last passage something is lost by inaccurate translation. *Unhappy
fate* is too modern and vague to be an equivalent for the distinct Roman
conception of *auspicium infaustum*, which rather means *unhappy fore-
casting* or *foresight*, and so *unhappy leadership*; and surely *lumina ducum*
does not mean *the days* or *lives of leaders*, but the light which they shed;
this, at least, would seem the more poetical idea. We mention these
small points only after some consideration, and because we have found
Mr. Morris, as a rule, as careful in his renderings as he is scrupulous
and delicate in his handling of metre and rhythm. More than once,
indeed, we have found that an expression apparently inaccurate was,
on second thoughts, justified by a consideration of the whole poetical
conditions of the passage.

We conclude these remarks by the expression of a hope that it may
be found possible to publish this book in a cheaper form. A translation
of such beauty should be accessible to the large number of people
whose circumstances have put the original Latin and Greek classics
out of their reach, and to whom works of this kind would open a new
world of ideas.

36. Chaucer a healthier influence than Morris

1875

Sidney Lanier's article 'Paul H. Hayne's Poetry' was published in the *Southern Magazine*, January 1875, xvi, 40–8. The early pages discuss Hayne, Morris and Chaucer. Text from *Sidney Lanier. Centennial Edition* (Baltimore, 1945), v, 322–5.

For Lanier and Hayne, see headnote to No. 30.

At a time when the war of secession had left the South in a condition which appeared to render an exclusively literary life a hopeless impossibility, Mr. Hayne immured himself in the woods of Georgia, and gave himself wholly to his pen. Perhaps this was the most convincing method he could have adopted of testifying by acts to his poetic *nascitur*,[1] for it was striking an audacious challenge-blow on the very shield of Fate, and probably none but a poet would have dared it. Doubtless, the struggle which succeeded was passionate, fierce, often bitter, sometimes despairing; one finds traces of all this along the music of these verses. It is pleasant now to open *Legends and Lyrics* with the knowledge that the darkest of his conflict is over, and that in the growing light of appreciation his by-past shadow will show only like a dark calyx through which the poet's rose of fame is bursting.

We wish to ease our mind in the beginning of the only material quarrel we have to pick with Mr. Hayne; and, for the double purpose of setting forth our *casus belli*, and of showing the reader what manner of work Mr. Hayne can do in the most difficult of poetic forms, we quote the sonnet addressed

TO WILLIAM MORRIS

In some fair realm unbound of time or space,
Where souls of all dead May-times, with their play

---

[1] Birth, vocation.

Of blissful winds, soft showers and bird-notes gay,
Make mystic music in the flower-bright place,
Yea, there, O poets! radiant face to face,
Keen heart to heart, beneath the enchanted day
Ye met, each hearkening to the other's lay
With rapt, sweet eyes, and thoughts of Old-World grace.
'Son,' saith the elder bard, 'when thou wert born,
So yearned toward thine my spirit's fervency,
Flamelike its warmth on thy deep soul was shed;
Hence the ripe blood of England's lustier morn
Of song burns through thee; hence alone on thee
Fall the rich bays which bloomed round Chaucer's head!'

This sonnet was written on reading the 'L'Envoy' in the third volume of Morris's *Earthly Paradise*. Now—though Mr. Hayne is by no means the only person who has likened William Morris to Geoffrey Chaucer —the enthusiastic belief that the spirit of the older poet has come to shine again in the later one, has never been more tenderly and reverently embodied than in this lovely sonnet; but, protesting that we owe some keen delights to Mr. Morris, we totally dissent from the opinion that there is at bottom any such resemblance betwixt him and Chaucer as to entitle him to any sonship or heirship of the latter. Moreover, we believe that this theory involves far more than a mere critical estimate of the likeness or unlikeness of two poets; nay, we are sure that Mr. Hayne and all modern poets would do well to drink much of Chaucer and little of Morris. For—to indicate briefly some points of contrast —how does the spire of hope spring and upbound into the infinite in Chaucer; while, on the other hand, how blank, world-bound, and wearying is the stone *façade* of hopelessness which rears itself uncompromisingly behind the gayest pictures of William Morris! Chaucer is eager, expectant. To-day is *so* beautiful, perhaps to-morrow will be more beautiful: life is young, who knows?—he seems to cry, with splendid immeasurable confidence in the reserved powers of nature and of man. But Morris does not hope: there is, there will be, nothing new under the sun. To-morrow? that may not come; if it does it will be merely to-day revamped; therefore let us amuse ourselves with the daintiest that art and culture can give: this is his essential utterance.

Again, how openly joyful is Chaucer; how secretly melancholy is Morris! Both, it is true, are full of sunshine; but Chaucer's is spring-sunshine, Morris's is autumn. Chaucer's falls upon bold mountainsides where are rocks, lithe grasses, and trees with big lusty boughs

227

and juicy leaves; where the wild motions of nature, from spring-winds to leaping fawns, are artlessly free and unspeakably blissful; and yet where all other forms, whether of monstrous, terrible or wicked, are truly revealed. Morris's, on the other hand, is a late, pleasant, golden-tinted light (with just the faintest hint of a coming chill of twilight in it), falling upon an exquisitely wrought marble which he's half-buried in the sand, and which, Greek as it is, dainty as it is, marvellous as it is, is nevertheless a fragment of a ruin. Chaucer rejoices as only those can who know the bound of good red blood through unobstructed veins, and the thrilling tingle of nerve and sinew at amity; and who can transport this healthy animalism into their unburdened minds, and spiritualize it so that the mere drawing of breath is at once a keen delight and an inwardly-felt practical act of praise to the God of a strong and beautiful world. Morris too has his sensuous element, but it is utterly unlike Chaucer's; it is *dilettante*, it is amateur sensualism; it is not strong, though sometimes excessive, and it is nervously afraid of that satiety which is at once its chief temptation and its most awful doom.

Again, Chaucer lives: Morris dreams. Chaucer, for all the old-world tales he tells, yet tells them with the mouths and manners of his living time, and so gives us a picture of it like life itself. Morris stands between his people and his readers, interpreting his characters, who all advance to the same spot on the stage, communicate *per* him in the same language, the same dialect, the same tone, then glide away with the same dreamy mechanism. The *Canterbury Tales* is simply a drama with somewhat more of stage direction than is common; but the *Earthly Paradise* is a reverie, which would hate nothing so much as to be broken by any collision with that rude actual life which Chaucer portrays.

And finally—for the limits of this paper forbid more than the merest indication of a few of the many points of contrast between these two—note the faith that shines in Chaucer and the doubt that darkens in Morris. Has there been any man since St. John so lovable as 'the Persoune'? or any sermon since that on the Mount so keenly analytical, so pathetic, so deep, so pitiful, so charitable, so brotherly, so pure, so manly, so faithful, so hopeful, so sprightly, so terrible, so childlike, so winning, so utterly loving, as *The Persoune's Tale*? But where (it is enough to ask the question in such a connection) in all that William Morris has written may one find, not indeed anything like the Persoune and his tale, for that would be too much to ask—there is no man since Shakspere who has been at all capable of *that*—but anything even indicating the conception of the possibility of such a being as the Persoune? To this height, to this depth, neither William Morris nor any other man has reached since Dan Chaucer wrote. Let us Shakspere-worshippers not forget that Chaucer lived two centuries earlier than Shakspere, and had to deal with a crude poetic language which Shakspere found a magnificent song-instrument, all in tune and ready to his hand. Let us not forget that Shakspere is first poet and Chaucer second poet, and that these two repose alone, apart, far, far above any spot where later climbers have sunk to rest. And this adjuration is here made with a particular and unequivocal solemnity, because of the conviction that we expressed in the outset of this subject, that the estimate of these two poets which would have them like enough to be father and son, involves deeper matter than mere criticism. For if it be true that William Morris is Chaucer in modern guise; if it be true that by virtue of this nineteenth-century dress, Chaucer, the glowing, actual man and lover and poet and priest and man's brother, is changed into Morris, the aimless sunset-dreamer of old beautiful dreams; if Chaucer's hope is in five hundred years darkened to Morris's thin-veiled despair, Chaucer's joy to Morris's melancholy, Chaucer's faith to Morris's blank, Chaucer's religion to Morris's love-vagueness; if, we say, it be possible that five centuries have wrought Chaucer, that is life, into Morris, that is a dream-of-the-past: then, in God's name, with all reverence, what will five more centuries do to us? A true Hindu life-weariness (to use one of Novalis' marvellous phrases) is really the atmosphere which produces the exquisite haze of Morris's pictures. Can any poet—and we respectfully beg Mr. Hayne to think upon this view of the matter, being emboldened to do so by our regard for his devotion to letters and for his achievements in that behalf—can any poet, we say, shoot his soul's arrow to its best height, when at once bow and string and muscle and nerve are slackened in this vaporous and relaxing air, that comes up out of the old dreams of fates that were false and of passions that were not pure?

SIGURD THE VOLSUNG

1876

37. Theodore Watts, unsigned review, *Athenaeum*

December 1876, no. 2563, 753–5

According to his biographers, this was the first of ten reviews of Morris's books which Watts—later Watts-Dunton—(1832–1914) contributed to the *Athenaeum* between 1876 and 1897; see T. Hake and A. Compton-Ricketts, *The Life and Letters of Theodore Watts-Dunton*, 2 vols (London, 1916), esp. Appendix to Vol. II. Watts knew Morris personally and had a high regard for Morris's writings, though he was hostile to his later Socialism.

Purely narrative sections of the review are omitted, as is the introductory account of the sources.

Mr. Morris is the very *Frunsmidr Bragar*—the Poetry-smith of the Northern Olympus. There is no affectation in such antiquarianism as we get here. The poet is quite soaked in Odinism,—soaked as completely as Charles Lamb was soaked in Elizabethanism,—as completely as Thackeray was steeped in the genteel perfumes of the eighteenth century. Mischance has thrown Mr. Morris among railways, telegraphs, newspapers, and much 'smoke.' He cannot help being surrounded by such foolish comforts as these; but how he hates them he has told us in the *Earthly Paradise*. His body is in Queen Square, but his soul is in Ultima Thule,—far away in that mysterious 'Island of Darkness,' where everything is magical, where, according to Tacitus, the very sun himself utters a cry when he gets up, and on whose shores, washed by the billows of an infinite ocean, 'many shapes of gods' stand clustering—gods who are nothing more than heroes—fraternizing

230

with heroes who are nothing less than gods. He consents to breathe the smoke with us, but it is in the atmosphere of the Golden Past that he lives. The consequence is, that the spontaneity—real, and not apparent merely—of this reproduction of the temper of a bygone age is as marvellous as the spontaneity of the form in which it is embodied; while, for purity of English, for freedom from euphuism and every kind of 'poetic diction' (so called), it is far ahead of anything of equal length that has appeared in this century.

[section omitted]

On the whole, we cannot but think this poem Mr. Morris's greatest achievement. It is more masculine than *Jason*—more vigorous and more dramatic than the best of the stories in the *Earthly Paradise*. For it is, as we have said, a more genuine expression of a genuine mood. And this mood, though not the highest, is yet high; the mood of the simple fighter, whose business it is to fight, to yield to no power whatsoever, whether of earth, or heaven, or hell—to take a buffet from the Allfather himself, and to return it; to look Destiny herself in the face, crying out for quarter neither to gods nor Norns; knowing well that the day prophesied is sure, when, breast to breast, gods and men shall stand up to fight the brood of evil, storming the very gates of Asgard; when Loki shall take and throttle the mighty Freir, and strangle him, the while the Fenrir Wolf gulps down the Father of the Gods himself, digesting in a sea of gastric juice the universe to chaos! And that quaint homeliness blent with sublimity which is the characteristic of the Northern mythology, finds a sympathizer in Mr. Morris, such as it has never had before outside the nations that are purely Teutonic.

The verse is exceedingly musical. With regard, however, to the selection of the metre, we cannot think it a happy one for a poem of such a length. Rask has pointed out the hexametrical character of Icelandic verse, but English hexameters are essentially lyrical, and therefore are unfit for the heavy business of dramatic narrative. That law of accentuated verse, the effect of which is that, when the pause falls after the third foot (as in hexameter), it is double the length of the pause falling after any earlier or later foot, becomes intensified when the line is either dactylic or anapæstic. The result of this is, that in English hexameters the back of every line is broken exactly in the middle, and produces an unpleasant monotony, unless the writer, every now and then, quite alters the character of the line,—as Mr.

Tennyson does in 'Maud,' and as Mr. Swinburne does in 'Hesperia,' *e.g.*:—

Comes back to me, stays by me, lulls me with touch of forgotten caresses,
One warm dream clad about with a fire as of life that endures;
The delight of thy face, and the sound of thy feet, and the wind of thy tresses,
And all of a man that regrets, and all of a maid that allures.

Note the splendid effect of the third line. But to get this one must, no doubt, write in quatrains.

That this is a noble poem there can be no doubt; but whether it will meet with ready appreciation and sympathy in this country is a question not so easily disposed of. Dr. Hueffer is no doubt right in saying that the story of the Niblungs is the epic of all the Teutonic peoples; but are we of these? There has of late been a great deal of talk about our 'Teutonic forefathers,' and our close kinship with the Germans of to-day. Of such a close kinship we should be quite willing to be proud, if it could be proved to exist. It does not follow that because we speak a German tongue we must be a German people. Language is not a final and absolute test of race, and almost everything else but language—almost everything that denotes the temperament of a people —seems to point to the conclusion that the basis of the population did not cease, after the arrival of the shadowy White Horse, to be Celtic, as it had been. One proof, perhaps, of this is that, although the very names of the days of the week are the names of the Northern gods, there is scarcely a tittle of folk-lore derived from Odin, or Freir, or Thor, or Loki, whose doings are not much more familiar to our non-reading classes than those of the gods of Polynesia. And a people cannot read itself into a folk-lore. A great novelist used to say that he believed no tales that were not told him by his great-grandmother. To the Scandinavian, the Edda was literally, as the word imports, a 'great-grandmother' telling her tales. And the truth is that we in this country have, properly speaking, no great-grandmother's tales older than the legends about Robin Hood. Even Arthur has no more real vitality than Jack the Giant-killer and Cormoran. Not Blackmore, nor Bulwer, nor even Mr. Tennyson, can ever galvanize him into the hero of a popular epic. What with Saxon upon Celt, and Norman upon Saxon, we have lost both 'Sigurd the Golden' and the 'Blameless King.'

38. Edmund Gosse, review, *Academy*

9 December 1876, x, 557–8

Gosse (1849–1928) was one of the most prolific reviewers and literary journalists of his time.

The opening account of the story is omitted.

So familiar is the story to our readers that we need hardly retell it. Suffice it to say that Mr. Morris has treated it in a manner fully worthy of the heroic plan. The style he has adopted is more exalted and less idyllic, more rapturous and less luxurious—in a word, more spirited and more virile than that of any of his earlier works. His first small volume was full of colour and quaint form; it reproduced with un-equalled brilliance the strange romantic beauty of minute mediaeval architecture and ornament. But there seemed more of art than of nature, more of culture than of inspiration. In *Jason* the whole field of vision was enlarged and humanized; there was less attention paid to detail but more to composition; there was manifest for the first time a power of poetic narrative unrivalled in our time. In the *Earthly Paradise* the same delightful qualities were continued and ripened, but the chord of melancholy languor was dwelt upon almost to excess. In *Love is Enough* higher places of the imagination were reached, and the mystical sadness had a nobler bearing. In the *Story of Sigurd*, however, for the first time, Mr. Morris is no longer 'the idle singer of an empty day,' but the interpreter of high desires and ancient heroic hopes as fresh as the dawn of the world and as momentous. The atmosphere of this poem is sharp and cold; a strong sense of the primal virtues, of honour, physical courage, duty to the gods and the kings, tender homage to women, interpenetrates the entire theme and gives it a solemn and archaic air. No lesser genius would have succeeded in winging a level flight through so many thousand lines without sinking to the plane of common men and common thoughts. In this poem, so steeped is the author in the records of the heroic past, so intimately are his sympathies connected with those of the mythical age of which he writes, that we walk with demigods to the close, and have no need to be told of the stature of our companions. In the presence of so much simplicity, and so much art that conceals its art, it is well to point out how supreme is the triumph of the poet in this respect. It is perhaps on this very account, and because the ordinary tone of the poem is so elevated and so heroic, that the passages which allow of pastoral and emotional treatment seem of unequalled charm and delicacy. Where so much is noble, but where all is rapidly-progressing narrative, it is not easy to select a passage for quotation which will not lose its peculiar excellence by being separated from its context. Perhaps the first meeting of Gudrun and Brynhild will bear extraction as well as any other:—

> So they make the yoke-beasts ready, and dight the wains for the way,
> And the maidens gather together, and their bodies they array,
> And gird the laps of the linen, and do on the dark blue gear,
> And bind with the leaves of summer the wandering of their hair:
> Then they drive by dale and acre, o'er heath and holt they wend,
> Till they come to the land of the waters, and the lea by the woodland's end;
> And there is the burg of Brynhild, the white-walled house and long,
> And the garth her fathers fashioned before the days of wrong.

[quotes next 24 lines]

The versification will be noted as in some respects peculiar; it depends on accents and not on syllables, each line containing as many cadences as the ordinary alexandrine, but being irregularly anapaestic instead of regularly iambic. There are always six feet in every line, but these are of very varying value, the earlier ones being generally amphimacers, that truly heroic foot which Coleridge compared to the thundering hoofs of a race-horse. Speaking less technically, the measure is a lax ballad-metre, capable of very considerable variety.

While, however, commending the style of this poem, we cannot help feeling that it will present in many places grave difficulties to the general reader. In no previous work has Mr. Morris adopted so consistent an archaism in language and phrase. The long study of Icelandic literature, too, has enamoured him of the periphrases for the gods, gold, the sea, and other objects of constant reference, which are so curious a feature of that language. To meet with the same peculiarities in a volume totally unannotated will, we are afraid, give *The Story of Sigurd* an air of pedantry from which its substance is wholly free. For instance, when we read that Volsung and his sons

> Ran swift o'er Aegir's acre,

it is not every one of us that may happen to remember that Aegir was the husband of the giantess Ran, goddess of the sea. It is quite another thing for a poet to say that his heroes rushed over the fields of Poseidon, for long custom has made an acquaintance with the elements of Greek mythology a necessity of ordinary culture; we are not as yet so well instructed about the deities of our own forefathers. So much for phrases; the language of Mr. Morris is hardly less learned. He uses 'eyen' for 'eyes,' 'fowl' for 'birds,' and 'learn' in the awkward, old-fashioned transitive sense of 'teach,' and this not once or twice, but constantly. Mr. Morris seems to maintain much the same attitude towards ancient speech that Spenser did when he was writing the *Shepherd's Calendar* and the *Faery Queen*. It is an attitude worthy of a master of language, and not for a moment to be confounded with the mock-archaism of a Chatterton or a Shenstone, but it is distinctly a position of danger.

We have no space left to dwell on the points in which Mr. Morris has seen fit to deviate slightly from the original narrative. The most important seems to be the omission of that relationship which connected Atli with his victims, the Niblungs. In the poem before us, Atli's rage is an almost purposeless greed of gold; in the Edda, on the other hand, he is represented as being a son of Budli, and therefore brother to Brynhild. In the short prose story of the 'Drap Niflunga' it is distinctly represented that dissension arose because Atli charged the Niblungs with having caused Brynhild's death. The hand of Gudrun is, according to this version, used as a means of reconciliation, and she stirs up Atli to fresh vengeance that her own wrongs may be revenged. We are inclined to think that Mr. Morris, by casting aside this account, has deprived himself of a valuable connecting link in the chain of retribution.

39. Unsigned review, *Saturday Review*

20 January 1877, xliii, 81–2

Mr. Morris's Northern Poems are not only interesting in themselves, for those qualities of dim beauty and sweetness long drawn out in which few poets since Spenser can approach him, but as recalling attention to the whole cycle of Northern mythology. Nearly half a century ago Mr. Carlyle, in his essay on the Nibelungen Lied, spoke with 'gratitude and love' of the unknown singers of that 'wondrous old tale,' with 'its true epic spirit, its meaning and charms for us'; and again, in his Lectures, he found out the perennial value of the old Odin worship which was the centre of the Northern religions. But since then, till very lately, there has been no re-creation of the stories themselves for a modern public, no attempt to reinvest the characters of the Sagas and their German counterparts with a human interest. At last, however, and in the same year, 'music and sweet poetry agree' to recall Sigurd or Siegfried, Chriemhild or Gudrun, from their sleep of ages; in Bayreuth and in London Wagner and Morris make simultaneous celebration. Perhaps this is no more than a coincidence; and no doubt with the German the dominant motive was one that is absent from the English poet—that is to say, a national motive. But Mr. Morris's own interest in this subject is a sign of the times. Let us not call it a reaction against the influence of the South, against Greek art and classical tradition; rather it is a new development of that very Renascence which brought Greek models back to Europe—it is a fresh departure in the 'search for beauty and pleasure' which the Renascence began. Science, in showing the essential unity of all mythologies, has given the hint; and now the artist asks, if Greece in gazing upon the Sun created Apollo, the North in the same way created Sigurd, and how is Sigurd less beautiful than Apollo? Change what must be changed, for the Athenian, 'ever delicately moving through most polluted air,' put the Northman, Goth or Volsung, toiling over the waste and the fell, or feasting while the storm beats upon his hall, and you have the same field for poetry, the same eternal human passions, and the same needs, 'hunger and labour, seed-time and harvest, love and death.' Human nature is wide, it is true, and the 'note' of a Northern poem must be different from the note of a Southern; the Greek is full of a sense of order, the Saga-maker of a sense of mystery; but the humanity is at bottom the same in both. It is in the admirable way in which he has wedded these two elements, the living and human element, and the special Northern element of mystery—a mystery as of the storm, a sense of dark dragon-haunted places, of unknown forces ringing in man's life—that Mr. Morris has made good his claim to be considered in the first rank of modern poets. We regard this *Story of Sigurd* as his greatest and most successful effort; of all poetical qualities strength, subtlety, vividness, mystery, melody, variety—there is hardly one that it does not exhibit in a very high degree.

A poem is not a novel, the charm of which depends on the surprises of the plot, and therefore there is no harm done if a reviewer tells intending readers the story that they must expect to find in the book. We will proceed then, without apology, to do this with the *Story of Sigurd*; especially as we shall thus be enabled in the most natural way to choose out some of the lovely passages, full of subtle imagery or noble eloquence, with which the poem abounds. There are four books, named after the dominant characters in them—Sigmund, Regin, Brynhild, and Gudrun. The first, as is generally the case with the Saga literature, reaches back some way into genealogy; it tells not of Sigurd, but of his father Sigmund, and his grandfather Volsung. It is in the dwelling of this last that the story opens, with the wooing and wedding of his daughter Signy by Siggeir, the King of the Goths. It was a wedding full of doom; for in the midst of the feast a 'mighty man' strode into the hall and planted, not an apple of discord among them, but a sword deep in the wood of the mystic Branstock, the tree that grew there, and left it, 'Odin's gift,' to the warrior that would draw it forth. All failed till Sigmund came:—

> At last by the side of the Branstock Sigmund the Volsung stood,
> And with right hand wise in battle the precious sword-hilt caught,
> Yet in a careless fashion, as he deemed it all for nought:
> When lo, from floor to rafter went up a shattering shout,
> For aloft in the hand of Sigmund the naked blade shone out
> As high o'er his head he shook it: for the sword had come away
> From the grip of the heart of the Branstock, as though all loose it lay.

Deep envy filled the heart of Siggeir at this; he tried first to buy the sword from Sigmund, and then, when that offer failed, he invited the

Volsungs treacherously to the 'house of the Gothkings,' 'that the dusky days and drear might be glorious with their presence.' The story of the visit, of the ambush, of the battle, and 'the ending of all Volsung's sons, save Sigmund only,' the birth and wild woodland life of Sinfiotli, Signy's son, the new treasons of Siggeir and his death, the murder of Sinfiotli, the second marriage of Sigmund, his last battle and 'the death of him,' and the hopes of his queen Hiordis—such is the story of this first book; and it is only in the beginning of the second that we come to the birth of Sigmund's son, Sigurd, who is to outdo the glories of his father. Like the young Achilles at the feet of Chiron, like many a hero in all mythologies, Sigurd has his first lessons from a mysterious and unearthly teacher—

> Again, in the house of the Helper there dwelt a certain man
> Beardless and low of stature, of visage pinched and wan:
> So exceeding old was Regin, that no son of man could tell
> In what year of the days passed over he came to that land to dwell:
> But the youth of King Elf had he fostered, and the Helper's youth thereto,
> Yea and his father's father's: the lore of all men he knew,
> And was deft in every cunning, save the dealings of the sword:
> So sweet was his tongue-speech fashioned, that men trowed his every word;
> His hand with the harp-strings blended was the mingler of delight
> With the latter days of sorrow; all tales he told aright;
> The Master of the Masters in the smithying craft was he;
> And he dealt with the wind and the weather and the stilling of the sea;
> Nor might any learn him leech-craft, for before that race was made,
> And that man-folk's generation, all their life-days had he weighed.

It is he who teaches Sigurd strange things, helps him to take the horse Greyfell, 'come of Sleipnir's blood, the tireless horse of Odin,' and tells him of his kindred, and 'of the gold that was accursed from ancient days.' In the winning this gold lies the 'deed' that Sigurd's heart has been pining to do since his childhood. 'Tell me,' he says, as the crafty Regin tempts and taunts him—

> 'Tell me, thou Master of Masters, what deed is the deed I shall do?
> Nor mock thou the son of Sigmund lest the day of his birth thou rue.'

> Then answered the Master of Sleight: 'The deed is the righting of wrong,
> And the quelling a bale and a sorrow that the world hath endured o'erlong,
> And the winning of a treasure untold, that shall make thee more than the kings;
> Thereof is the Helm of Aweing, the wonder of earthly things,
> And thereof is its very fellow, the War-coat all of gold,
> That has not its like in the heavens, nor has earth of its fellow told.'

The story that follows, the central story of all this Nibelungen cycle, is that of the hoard of gold which is ever a curse to its possessor, and which yet the great and the noble are fated to possess. It has of ancient time belonged to the elf Andvari, 'in the uttermost part of the world.' But Regin, who tells the tale, is one of the three sons of Reidmar, and brother to Otter, the hunter who 'wades the highways wet,' and to Fafnir, whose 'brow is of hardened iron.' To them in days long gone the gods had come wandering—Odin, the Father of the Slain, Loki, the World's Begrudger, and Hæmir, the Utter Blameless; and craftily Loki had slain Otter on his way. The vengeance of Reidmar and his sons is to lay a snare for the gods as Hephæstus did for Ares, and to hold them fast till they had sent Loki to bring with him as a ransom this treasure of gold, with the Ring of Andvari, the Sword, the Helm, and the War-coat. The curse that lurks in them has instant effect almost; death lives in the gold as it lived in the florins found by Chaucer's 'Riotours.' While Regin is absent, Fafnir slays his father Reidmar,

> that he alone may keep
> The gold of the darksome places, the candle of the deep.

Regin flies away, 'lest his blood be cast on the guilt'; and once, long after, wanders back to the land, to find the house rent and ragged, the gold heaped up, and rolling upon it a mighty serpent, who is none other than Fafnir, changed into a Worm by brooding upon the treasure, as Otter had changed into the shape of the hunting-beast by brooding upon the prey. Long, long years passed by, and Regin, 'dwelling with the short-lived folk of men,' was for ever on the watch for the destined hand that should win him back the treasure, and 'bring his heart its rest.' He sees that in Sigurd he has what he has wished for, and Sigurd answers all too readily to the fatal invitation. But Regin must forge him a sword, for no sword of the earthly makers will pierce the armour of the Serpent. At last the sword is made—it is the old Odin-given sword of Sigmund reforged—and Sigurd sets out on the quest, passing onward with Regin

> About the cold-slaked forges, o'er many a cloud-swept bent,
> Betwixt the walls of blackness, by shores of the fishless meres,

till they come to the glittering heath, and the 'deserted land' of the Worm. How Sigurd meets the Wise One; how he lies in ambush in a pit in the Serpent's path; in what weird fashion the folds of the monster enwrap him 'with the swaddling of Death'; how he smites upward and slays; how, chancing to taste the blood of the Serpent, he learns hidden mysteries and the meaning of the cries of the eagles around; how he slays Regin in time to prevent his treachery; how he finds the gold, and arms himself with the Coat and the Helm of Aweing, and takes the Ring of Andvari—all this it would be long to tell. Success that carries its curse with it is Sigurd's fate. Turning home-wards, he comes to Hindfell, and there wakes Brynhild, the 'sleeping beauty,' who lies clad in armour till the sword of the destined man shall 'rend her fallow bondage.' It is here that the human and tragic interest of the poems begins, with the mutual passion of these two, the strongest man and the wisest and most beautiful woman in the world. He has awakened her from the magic sleep into which Odin had thrown her for a season. Of Brynhild, who once was the fellow of the gods and the 'Victory Wafter,' he has made 'her that loveth,' and on her finger, with exchange of oaths, he sets Andvari's ring.

The scene now changes to the Burg of the Niblungs and the hall of King Giuki, whose children are Gunnar, 'the great and fair'; 'the wise-heart Hogni'; Guttorm, 'of the fierce and wandering glance'; and Gudrun, 'the white-armed Niblung maid.' It is with the love of Gudrun for the 'golden stranger' Sigurd and all its consequences that the rest of the story deals. She dreams that a falcon, 'whose feathers were all of gold and his eyes as the sunlit glass,' flew and nestled in her bosom—a dream which of course her wise nurse interprets of a mighty lover that is to come from other lands:—*Externum cernimus, inquit, adventare virum.*[1] By a strange freak of destiny, it is to Brynhild, in her new home in Lymdale, that the maid who is fated to be Brynhild's supplanter goes to learn the full meaning of the dream. All happens as might be feared. Sigurd comes, is welcomed in the Niblung hall, and fights the Niblung battles, and all unconsciously becomes beloved of the Niblung maiden, though he himself loves none but Brynhild. But Grimhild, 'the wise wife,' Gudrun's mother, has other ends in view for Sigurd; and, with a skill that she has learned of old, she mixes a cup for him at the banquet. This is the beginning of the curse; 'the soul was changed in him,' and Brynhild is forgotten, and nothing remem-bered but a dim sense of happiness lost. More in sympathy with her look of sorrow than for love of her, he approaches Gudrun:—

> He knows in an instant of time that she stands 'twixt death and love,
> And that no man, none of the Gods can help her, none of the days,
> If he turn his face from her sorrow and wend on his lonely ways.

[1] We perceive, he said, a stranger approaching.

So they are married, and she is happy, 'as one that hath gotten the best'; while he walks as in a dream; and far away in her fire-encircled palace Brynhild sits, 'weary-hearted,' on her dark blue throne. For a picture of sheer loveliness we know of few more perfect than the poet's account of the wedding-eve, when Sigurd and Gudrun are left alone,

> till at last, amidst her tears,
> The joy and the hope of women fell on her unawares;

and little by little the new love grows upon Sigurd; 'the tangle straighteneth before him,' though his youth is gone. But the same spell which Grimhild has wrought on him she works upon her son Gunnar, who 'bethinks him of the maiden sitting alone,' Brynhild, in her fire-ringed house. How this new wooing is accomplished by Sigurd's riding through the fire-wall, his aspect changed by the wise-wife's magic into that of Gunnar, the strange cold betrothal, the wedding, the contention between the queens, and Brynhild's wrath and shame at the bitter deceit that has been practised upon her—all this follows on rapidly, and hurries Sigurd and with him all the Niblung race to their doom. The Ring is what brings the curse to its effect. Given back by Brynhild, as she believes, to her husband, Gunnar, but really to Sigurd, and by him to Gudrun, this latter in a wild moment of triumphant rage shows it to her rival and tells the whole secret of the wooing. From this moment the story is one of blood and murder, 'of broken love and troth.' Brynhild must have the death of Sigurd; and he is killed by Gudrun's brother Guttorm, as he lies sleeping in her arms—only awaking to fling 'the Wrath' at the flying murderer and to strike him to the ground. Brynhild's own death follows soon, her one prayer being that she may be laid side by side with Sigurd on the funeral pile:—

> How then when the flames fare upward may I be left behind?
> How then may the road he wendeth be hard for my feet to find?
> How then in the gates of Valhall may the door of the gleaming ring
> Clash to on the heel of Sigurd, as I follow on my king?

The story might well end here, had the tellers of Sagas and of the *Nibelungen Lied* so chosen. But, as is well known to readers of the 'Northern cyclics,' Gudrun must marry again, not for love, but for the hope of avenging herself upon the kin that slew her lord. The fourth book, then, is the tale of her wedding with Atli, the 'king of the Eastland folk' (the historic Attila), of the trap they laid to entertain

and slay the whole host of the Niblung people, and of Gudrun's second
and final vengeance upon those who had been the instruments of her
own revenge. When all the Niblungs are slain and the victorious
earls of Atli have feasted themselves full in the Golden House, it is
Gudrun herself who, in obedience to the fierce law of kindred among
a barbarous people, sets the fire to burn the house over those who in
slaying her brethren have only fulfilled her bidding; and with her
own hand she pierces Atli to the heart. And here is the ending of
Gudrun:—

Then Gudrun girded her rainment, on the edge of the steep she stood,
She looked o'er the shoreless water, and cried out o'er the measureless flood:
'O Sea, I stand before thee; and I who was Sigurd's wife
By his brightness unforgotten I bid thee deliver my life
From the deeds and the longing of days, and the lack I have won of the earth,
And the wrong amended by wrong, and the bitter wrong of my birth!'

She hath spread out her arms as she spake it, and away from the earth she leapt
And cut off her tide of returning; for the sea-waves over her swept,
And their will is her will henceforward: and who knoweth the deeps of the sea,
And the wealth of the bed of Gudrun, and the days that yet shall be?

This is hardly the place to dwell upon that wide field of interesting
questions which a study of this fine rendering of the wonderful
Northern story, and a comparison of it with the older renderings, must
necessarily suggest. Otherwise it would be curious to remark the
points of difference as well as of contact, the seemingly accidental
shifting and transference of names, the variation in the characters that
is revealed by a parallel reading, for instance, of the *Story of Sigurd*
and of the *Nibelungen Lied*. For example, Gudrun has taken the place
of the beautiful Chriemhild, who reappears as Grimhild, the royal
witch; Regin is here the Smith himself, while in the *Heldenbuch*[1] he is
the Dragon, the Smith's brother, the Fafnir of this poem; the Sword,
'the Wrath of Sigurd,' which is only forged successfully at the third
trial, has a different object altogether from the sword Balmung. Mere
dialectical changes of name—Atli for Etzel, Gunnar for Gunther,
Hogni for Hagen, &c.—are unimportant; but the great differences of
all, those of the winning of the hoard and of the relations between
Brynhild and Sigurd, affect the whole course of the poem. There can
be no comparison between the story that Regin tells—the story of
greed in wild waste places transforming a hero into a 'wallowing'

[1] Collection of medieval heroic poems.

monster—and the clumsy incident of the *Heldenbuch*, where Sieg-fried's finding of the treasure is brought about by a string of purpose-less accidents. And in the Saga, as Mr. Morris adapts it, how high above the coarse Brunhild of the German poem towers Brynhild, endowed with the wisdom of Odin and beauty untold, but hemmed in by a fate most tragic and most human! It is a sound instinct that directs this modern teller of old tales to the northern in preference to the southern source; to the Sagas rather than to the *Nibelungen Lied*.

40. Unsigned review, *Literary World*

February 1877, vii, 136–7

A brief review of the American edition.

In *Sigurd the Volsung* we have at once the manliest and the loveliest work of Mr. Morris's genius. The atmosphere of soft and slightly enervating sadness which pervaded the *Earthly Paradise* and *Jason* is replaced by one clearer and more tonic. These Norse heroes fight under skies fraught with storm, and awesome with the shadowy foot-steps of the hastening Norns; but they fight with cheerful and steadfast valor, and they die triumphant. The last word of all, which 'ends their strange, eventful history,' is not the empty echo of 'in vain! in vain!' but a promise, a watch-word,—or rather a pass-word for admission to a brighter and securer life:—

> They are gone, the lonely, the mighty, the hope of the ancient earth:
> It shall labor and bear the burden as before the days of their birth;
> It shall groan, in its blind abiding, for the day that Sigurd hath sped;
> And the hour that Brynhild hath hastened, and the dawn that waketh the dead;
> It shall yearn and be oft-times holpen, and forget their deeds no more
> Till the new sun beams on Baldur and the happy, sealess shore.

The form of the Niebelungen story which Mr. Morris has chosen for illustration is that contained in the Icelandic saga of the Volsungs, of which the poet published a literal prose translation some five or six years since. He prefers this Icelandic form to the more familiar one adopted by Jordan for his great poems of the Niebelungen or Sigfrid's saga, and by Wagner for his trilogy. He speaks of it, in the preface to the aforesaid prose translation, as 'the most complete and dramatic form of that great epic of the North, which ought to be to all our race what the tale of Troy was to the Greeks'; and he has brought to the execution of his own long-meditated version a high and constant enthusiasm, and a tempered force and finished grace of poetical expression, which will go far toward securing for his subject the supreme place in our affections which he claims for it.

The poem is in four books or divisions. The first, 'Sigmund,' contains the story of the ancestry of the great Sigurd (Sigurd being identical with the Sigfrid of the German Niebelungen), and especially of his father, Sigmund himself, a most illustrious hero. The second, 'Regin,' records the birth of Sigurd; his fostering by Regin, the king of the dwarfs; how he slew, when scarcely arrived at manhood, the great serpent Fafuir, who guarded, upon the Glittering Heath, that immense treasure of gold, so famous in all Scandinavian story, which brought doom to all who obtained it; how he subsequently slew Regin himself, and carried his treasure to the burg of the Niblungs or Niebelungen. In the third book, 'Brynhild,' the passion of the story culminates. We hear once more, but with unexampled interest, the original of the countless fables of Sleeping Beauty and Fairy Prince: how Sigurd, riding towards the cloudy home of the Niblungs, finds Brynhild asleep upon Hindfell, and breaks the strong enchantment which had bound her; of their betrothal, and the cruel craft which parted them; of Sigurd's marriage to the daughter of the Niblungs,—Gudrun,—and of Brynhild's to the Niblung prince Gunnar or Gunther; of the anguish of both when the plot was discovered which had estranged them; of their love, their honor, their struggles, and their death. The fourth book, 'Gudrun,' tells of her subsequent marriage to Atti, and the frightful manner in which he avenged the death of Sigurd upon her Niblung brethren.

Meagre as this outline is, it may suffice to give some slight idea of the power and consistency of the story. To illustrate by the ordinary method of quotation the splendor of Mr. Morris' literary treatment is a far more difficult matter; for the strong thread of the narrative is hardly broken by a single episode, and, for so long a poem, the equality of excellence in the versification is marvellous. We open the book at random, and light on the melodious quatrain in which Gudrun is introduced:—

> And there is Gudrun his daughter, and light she stands by the board,
> And fair are her arms in the hall as the breaker's flood is poured.
> She comes, and the earls keep silence; she smiles, and men rejoice;
> She speaks, *and the harps, unsmitten, thrill faint to her queenly voice.*

And space must certainly be made for the exquisite passage which describes the bridal journey of Brynhild, when she went heartbroken, yet unflinching in her obedience to Fate, to fulfil her troth plighted to Gunnar:—

> So wear the ten days over, and the morrow morn is come,
> And the *light-foot expectation* flits through the Niblung home;
> And the girded hope is ready, and all people are astir,
> When the voice of the keen-eyed watchman from the topmost tower they hear:
> 'Look forth from the burg, O Niblungs! and the wargate of renown;
> For the wind is up in the morning, and the Mayblooms fall adown.
> And the sun on the earth is shining, and the clouds are small and high,
> And here is a goodly people, and an army drawing nigh.'

[quotes next two stanzas]

We have heard the complaint made that the versification of *Sigurd* becomes painfully monotonous after no long reading. To ourself, it is the most satisfying English measure ever yet adopted for the telling of a long story in verse. No English measure can compare with the Latin hexameter for such a purpose,—not even the blank verse of Milton or of Tennyson. But this, which is founded on the original Niebelungen measure, only infinitely refined and beautified, seems to us to approach within sight of the unattainable model. It is noble, yet changeful; supple and sustained. There is a kind of wistful sweetness, both in its hurrying anapests and its lingering iambics, which makes them cling to the memory; while the frequent use of alliteration marks its kinship with the primeval forms of Scandinavian story. Whatever its immediate reception may be, William Morris's *Sigurd* is certain eventually to take its place among the few great epics of the English tongue.

41. Unsigned review, *North American Review*

March 1877, cxxiv, 323-5

During the past few years the study of early Northern literature has received a strong impulse through the editing and translating of the more important texts, as those of the Eddas, both prose and poetic, and of the *Volsunga Saga*, itself versified by Messrs. Magnússon and Morris. These works, among others of the same class, have been made accessible to the English public since 1842; but for the further effort to popularize this literature by poetic treatment, we are mainly indebted to the abounding labors of Mr. Morris.

To make the Eddas interesting is no easy task, if it be sought to preserve the spirit of the Northern myths in accomplishing it. For us the world of Scandinavian tradition is more archaic; it is separated from us by a wider interval in development than are the remains of Grecian or Indian antiquity, though in time it is a thousand years nearer to us than they; and being thus remoter from modern sympathies, it affords less plastic material for the poet, though for the scholar it has value and interest of the first order. Like the savagery of certain low races, it represents the survival of ruder stages in man's development than are to be found in the oldest records of the more favored races; it abounds in valuable data for study, but is somewhat deficient in available poetic heroes, and for this reason the world has refused to interest itself greatly in the Northern mythologies. From the popular point of view, indeed, the Sagas and the Eddas, in their original spirit, are singularly uninteresting; for modern poetic value they are too primitive, too incoherent in form; they carry us back to a harsh and gloomy current of ideas, to characters and actions completely alien. For modern poetic treatment, therefore, those characters and actions require an elaborate rehabilitation at the hands of the artist.

This is what Mr. Morris has given us in *Sigurd the Volsung*; he has retold, in the modern temper, the story of the Fafnismál and the Prose Edda, a part of the story which is elaborated in the *Nibelungenlied*. What it is in the original we need not retell; the wranglings of those preternatural beings in battle, in lust, or in the search for the treasure of gold, recall to our mind the monstrous deities of Polynesian mythology, Pele and Lono, or that demi-porcine god Kamapuaa, whose mighty hoof scored channels for torrents in the walls of a deep valley from which, after he had devastated it, he sprang away and escaped at a single bound. With such crude material, in the increasing stringency of poetic competition, Mr. Morris found himself occupied; and how has he dealt with it, how has he rehabilitated it for English readers? His method is, in a word, the contemporary English method of treating the antique; to recast it, namely, in the forms of modern sentiment. Whether in poetry, painting, or criticism, this method is substantially the same; it is that of Mr. Tennyson in his *Idylls of the King*; it is that of the Italianizing Preraphaelite painters; it is Mr. Ruskin's method when he criticises Greek art or character. To reproduce the antique, not as the ancients felt it, but as we feel it,—to transfuse it with modern thought and emotion,—that is the method that is now 'in the air,' as the French say, among Mr. Morris's fellow-artists; and it is the main source of the interest which Mr. Morris has given to his own work, as well as the source of its weakness.

Now we need hardly remark that this method is essentially falsifying, nor shall we have to seek far in the present poem for illustrative instances. Take, for instance, this passage in the second book, an apostrophe put into Brynhild's mouth:—

All hail, ye Lords of God-home, and ye Queens of the House of Gold!
Hail thou dear Earth that bearest, and thou Wealth of field and gold!
Give us, your noble children, the glory of wisdom and speech,
And the hearts and the hands of healing, and the mouths and hands that teach.

That represents no possible sentiment of the mediæval North; nor does this, of the 'Niblung Maiden,' in the third book:—

She murmured words of loving as his kind lips cherished her breast,
And the world waxed naught but lovely and a place of infinite rest.

Nor, again, does this, taken from the same book:—

They saw their crowned children and the kindred of the kings,
And deeds in the world arising, and the day of better things;
All the earthly exaltation, till their pomp of life should be passed,
And soft on the bosom of God their love should be laid at the last.

Here we are in the full current of the nineteenth century; its self-consciousness, its love of nature, its aspirations, its affectations, its pathetic fallacies, all are in these passages; they even express the tone of its popular religious sentiment. In these passages we are clearly quite as far from the time of the Eddas as it is yet possible to be; they have nothing in common with the sentiment of the time which they aim to describe. There is abundance of passages more truly imagined than these, but the false tone is always near at hand; in general it must be said that Mr. Morris's mediævalism is unreal, that his heroines and divinities appear not in their ancient forms, but in the 'Anglo-Saxon attitudes' that are at present so dear to English art. Yet the poem, in spite of its unreality, in spite of its mannerism, abounds in beauty and vigor of expression. The imitation of the archaic style is, indeed, carried to excess, as if to cover the lack of the antique spirit; 'learn' for *teach*, 'cherishing' for *kissing*, 'burg,' 'eyen,' 'glaive,' 'tomorn,'—these are a few among hundreds of mannerisms; yet in the main the diction is effective. With the conduct of the story we have to find some fault,— a deficiency in rapidity and directness. In a narrative poem of ten thousand lines, based upon a plot that, as we have intimated, left much to be desired in respect of unity, there was need to accent strongly the linking points of the story, to mark its articulations, so to speak, with especial distinctness. In doing this Mr. Morris has not perfectly suc- ceeded, and in consequence *Sigurd*, as a story, reads a little heavily. The interest of the poem depends in considerable part upon individual passages,—in this respect illustrating again the modern English taste in poetry,—and failing somewhat in the total impression, the ἀρχιτεκτονία of which the ancients thought so much more than we think, and perhaps not erroneously. The metre that Mr. Morris has chosen is an alliterative line of six accents, with a foot generally trisyllabic; and in his hands it is flexible and musical, though it does not escape the dangers of monotony. Whether as to melody, form, or sentiment, the examples we have given must suffice. *Sigurd* abounds in beautiful and quotable lines, and in healthfulness of tone is a distinct advance upon Mr. Morris's previous poems; but much is still wanting to it in this respect. It has undeniable power, undeniable beauty; and yet it is too much the outcome of a transient *vogue* in sentiment to insure a very long remembrance.

42. Unsigned review, *Atlantic Monthly*

April 1877, xxxix, 501-4

Mr. Morris's Norse epic has come upon us quietly. While attention is clamorously invited to inferior and ephemeral works, and dissension is rife over much which is hardly worth the reading, a great poem of almost solitary beauty, profound, complete, intensely interesting and significant by virtue of its subject to all who have a trace of Scandinavia in their speech and lineage, arises upon the world of letters with all the familiar mystery of a new day. *Sigurd, the Volsung,* is the second great English epic of our generation (let us pause and reflect how rich we are), and it ranks after Tennyson's 'Arthuriad' in order of time only. It fully equals that monumental work in the force and pathos of the story told, while it surpasses it in unity and continuity of interest, and may fairly divide with the *Idyls of the King* the suffrages of the reading world on the question of poetical form.

The story of Sigurd is founded upon, and indeed closely follows, the *Völsunga saga,* the Icelandic prose form of the *Niebelungen Lied.* It is a subject which has long haunted Mr. Morris's imagination. In 1870 he published in connection with Eiríkr Magnússon, translator of the Legends of Iceland, a literal prose version of the saga, accompanied by metrical versions of some of the lays of the elder Edda on which that in its turn is supposed to have been founded some time in the prolific twelfth century. In his brief preface to this prose translation, Mr. Morris speaks of the *Völsunga saga* as 'the most complete and dramatic form of the great epic of the North . . . that story which should be to all our race what the Tale of Troy was to the Greeks,— to all our race first, and afterwards, when the change of the world has made our race nothing more than a name of what has been,—a story, too,—then should it be to those that come after us no less than the Tale of Troy has been to us.' And in the fourth volume of the *Earthly Paradise,* in his introduction to the 'Fostering of Aslaug,' the poet makes affectionate allusion to the fascination exercised over him by the whole

mighty drama of which Aslaug's story is but a doubtful episode, and
to his dream of one day giving it a fuller illustration:—

> A fair tale might I tell to you
> Of Sigurd who the dragon slew
> Upon the murder-wasted heath;
> And how Love led him unto Death
> Through strange, wild ways of joy and pain.
> Then such a story should ye gain,
> If I could tell it all aright,
> As well might win you some delight
> From out the wofullest of days.
> But now have I no heart to raise
> That mighty sorrow laid asleep,
> That love so sweet, so strong, so deep,
> That as ye hear the wonder told,
> In those few, strenuous words of old,
> The whole world seems to rend apart
> When heart is torn away from heart.
> But the world lives still, and to-day
> The green Rhine wendeth on its way
> Over the unseen golden curse
> That drew its lords from worse to worse
> Till that last dawn in Atli's hall
> When the red flame flared over all,
> Lighting the leaden, sunless sea.

Certainly, if the resolute work of genius in many departments of
art could effect the ascendancy of any body of legend over the heart
of a race, the great Niebelungen tragedy must have won largely on
our affections during the last few years; and Mr. Morris has now
accomplished more in this direction than all his predecessors. The
Icelandic saga is especially superior to the Germanic lay in its presentation of the character of Brynhild, to which it gives added splendor
and symmetry, while rendering it intensely and most movingly
human. And the Brynhild of Mr. Morris's Sigurd rises by the unearthly
grandeur of her traits and mystery of her sufferings, and by the inviolate purity of her passion, a whole heaven above the most illustrious
heroine whether of Greek story or of romance.

The poem has a singular equality of beauty; and, noble as the opening passage is, there is hardly even a transient falling away from the
level of it, until the last word of the fateful tale is told.

There was a dwelling of kings ere the world was waxen old;
Dukes were the door-wards there and the roofs were thatched with gold;
Earls were the wrights that wrought it, and silver-nailed were its doors;
Earls' wives were its weaving-women, queens' daughters strewed its floors;
And the masters of its song-craft were the mightiest men that cast
The sails of the storm of battle adown the bickering blast.
There dwelt men merry-hearted, and in hope exceeding great
Met the good days and the evil, as they went the ways of fate;
There the gods were unforgotten, yea, whiles they walked with men,
Though e'en in that world's beginning rose a murmur now and again,
Of the midward time and the fading, and the last of the latter days,
And the entering in of the terror, and the death of the Peoples' Praise.
Thus was the dwelling of Volsung, the King of the Midworld's Mark,
As a rose in the winter season, a candle in the dark. etc.

King Volsung was the grandfather of that Sigurd whom the poet
calls the Peoples' Praise. Sigmund, the father of the hero, was the last
of ten sons, the nine of whom, together with their royal old father,
were treacherously slain by Siggeir, king of the Goths, who had
married their only sister, 'the snow-white Signy.' Sigmund escaped
and took refuge in the woods, where Signy ministered to him for
a season. The story of these two is in itself exceedingly thrilling, and
we can with difficulty pass it by without quotation, but it is kept in
due subordination to the yet more sublime and memorable tale of
Sigurd, who was the posthumous child of Sigmund by a late marriage
with Hiordis, the daughter of Eylimi, the king of the Isles. The account
of the fostering of Sigurd includes the comparatively familiar tale of
the mighty smith Regin, the king of the Dwarfs, who forged for
Sigurd out of the fragments of Sigmund's glaive his immortal sword,
the Wrath:—

The Light that had lain in the Branstock, the hope of the Volsung tree,
The Sunderer, the Deliverer, the torch of days to be.

Regin gave Sigurd instruction in all manner of magic lore and told
him, in the course of that fore-ordained tuition, the mystical story of
his own ancient but now nearly accomplished life:—

Then unto this land I came, and that was long ago
As men-folk count the years; and I taught them to reap and to sow,
And a famous man I became: but that generation died,
And they said that Frey had taught them, and a god my name did hide.
Then I taught them the craft of metals, and the sailing of the sea,
And the taming of the horse-kind, and the yoke-beasts' husbandry,

251

And the building up of houses; and that race of man went by,
And they said that Thor had taught them, and a smithying carle was I.

. . . .

Then I taught them the tales of old, and fair songs fashioned and true,
And their speech grew into music of measured time and due,
And they smote the harp to my bidding, and the land grew soft and sweet;
But ere the grass of their grave-mounds rose up above my feet,
It was Bragi had made them sweet-mouthed, and I was the wandering scald;
Yet green did my cunning flourish by whatso name I was called,
And I grew the master of masters. Think thou how strange it is
That the sword in the hands of a stripling shall one day end all this!

For Sigurd, incited by Regin, slew Fafnir, the brother of Regin, who
in the guise of a serpent guarded upon the Glittering Heath the
renowned Treasure Horde, which brought doom sooner or later to
all who possessed it. And he slew Regin also, when the treachery of
the latter was manifest, and bound the fateful Horde upon his divine
steed, Greyfell, and fared forth to the land of the Niblungs, or Niebelungen. But he halted upon his way, on the height of Hindfell, and at
the crisis of the story; for there he found the armed maiden, Brynhild,
sleeping, and awoke her because the hour was come. We may live
and read long before we meet with poetry more noble in thought,
more celestially sweet and satisfying in form, than the pages which
describe the meeting and mutual recognition of these immortal lovers.
The 'wise redes' of Brynhild to Sigurd before their parting, the
counsel which she gave him, and which she deprecated while giving
with so divine a humility and courtesy as but the echo of his own
unformulated wisdom, have been done into English more than once.
We give a few random extracts:—

Be wise and cherish thine hope in the freshness of the days,
And scatter its seed from thine hand in the field of the peoples' praise.
Then fair shall it fall in the furrow, and some the earth shall speed,
And the sons of men shall marvel at the blossom of the deed;
But some the earth shall speed not; nay, rather the wind of heaven
Shall waft it away from thy longing—and a gift to the gods thou hast given,
And a tree for the roof and a wall in the house of the hope that shall be,
Though it seemeth our very sorrow, and the grief of thee and me.

. . . .

Wilt thou do the deed and repent it? Thou hadst better never been born!
Wilt thou do the deed and exalt it? Then thy fame shalt be outworn!
Thou shalt do the deed and abide it, and sit on thy throne on high,

And look on to-day and to-morrow as those who never die.

. . . .

Love thou the gods, *and withstand them*, lest thy fame should fail in the end
And thou be but their thrall and their bondsman, who wert born for their
 very friend;
For few things from the gods are hidden, *and the hearts of men they know,*
And how that man rejoiceth to quail and crouch alow.

. . . .

I have spoken the word, beloved, to thy matchless glory and worth;
But thy heart to my heart hath been speaking, though my tongue hath set it
 forth,
For I am she that loveth, and I know what thou wouldst teach
From the heart of thine unlearned wisdom, *and I needs must speak thy speech.*

They then swore vows of eternal fidelity, vows which were broken,
as we know, because the two fell victims to a cruel snare. Almost every
reader is familiar with the outline of that heart-rending story, and we
will not anticipate the interest of the few who are not so, by recounting
it here.

After all, quotation, however copious, is vain, as every worthy
reader will acknowledge when he turns the last page of the poem, and
feels for a moment as if the whole earth were made void by its ending.
We have tried to select those passages which best show how deeply
Mr. Morris has entered into that 'dark and true and tender' heart of
the North, which the world, after ages passed in the worship of Greek
ideals, is only just beginning to fathom.

It remains to say a few words about the peculiarities of Mr. Morris's
manner and the measure which he has so happily adopted for this his
greatest work. It is natural, first of all, to compare the latter with the
metre of his translation of the *Æneid,* his last long poem, and it is very
remarkable that a verse which is so nearly the quantitative equivalent
of the fourteen syllabled measure, chosen by the poet for his translation, should be as distinguished for its wayward and unwearying
melody as the latter was for a perfectly mechanical and intensely disagreeable sing-song. Our disappointment and exasperation with *Æneids*
—for we had thought Mr. Morris the one man on earth fit to make a
perfect English translation of Virgil—are yet too recent to be mentioned with due critical calmness; but in return he has now, as it seems
to us, fixed forever the most appropriate form of rhymed verse for
an English epic. A hexameter composed like this, of iambic and ana-
pestic feet with a constant variety of relative arrangement and a fluc-

tuating cæsura, has many of the qualities which render the Latin hexameter most delightful; and we would like well, in our solemn dubiety about English hexameters, to see a translation into the measure of *Sigurd* both of the *Georgics* and the *Æneid*, as scholarly as Mr. Morris's own and as musical as this might be. The foundation of the verse is of course that of the original German *Niebelungen*, of which Carlyle wrote so charmingly when the Lied first came into fashion. 'A strange charm lies in these old tones, where in gay, dancing melodies the sternest tidings are sung to us; and deep floods of sadness and strife play lightly in little curling billows, like seas in summer. It is as a meek smile, in whose still, thoughtful depths a whole infinitude of patience and love and heroic strength lie revealed.' But Mr. Morris has rounded and enriched the metre of the lay by the much more liberal employment of anapests, a foot which he had shown himself capable of managing with peculiar grace in *Love is Enough*. The nearest approach to the effect of this finished and beautified measure has been made by Mr. Swinburne in some of his choruses, and particularly in that very famous one from 'Atalanta in Calydon,'—

> Before the beginning of years
> There came to the making of man, etc.

which is indeed precisely similar, except that two lines are made of one.

Concerning Mr. Morris's unsparing rejection of Latin words and his free employment of archaic expressions, it need only be said that these peculiarities are so exactly suitable to the character of his present work as to blend with its faultless general harmony and be hardly noticeable in it.

43. Henry Hewlett, review, *Fraser's Magazine*

July 1877, xvi, 96–112

The review is entitled 'Mr. Morris's "Sigurd" and the "Nibelungenlied"'; some of the narrative comparison has been omitted.

H. G. Hewlett (1832–97) was a civil servant, historian and literary reviewer.

The great Gothic Epos has at last obtained incorporation into the literature of the only important nation of Gothic origin from which it was absent, and in a form which, in spite of many shortcomings, will doubtless be accepted as worthy of the subject and of the artist. Avowedly or otherwise, we English are apt to entertain a decided conviction that in our sub-branch of the family the finest qualities of the Germanic and Scandinavian branches are united with the smallest share of their defects, and it must flatter our national pride to find that Mr. Morris has observed a similar proportion in framing this version of a myth which may be regarded as common property. He has selected as the ground-plot of his work up to a certain point the rendering of the *Volsunga Saga*, with which the translation issued by Mr. Magnússon and himself some years ago has already familiarised many of his readers. As earlier in date than the Teutonic version, it embodies more of the purely mythical element, and is unencumbered by the quasi-historical legendary matter which has been blended with it in the *Nibelungenlied*. Some of the more repulsive and unnatural features found in the Saga have been judiciously omitted by Mr. Morris as incapable of poetic treatment, while he has heightened the dramatic effect by the introduction of certain fragments of the myth preserved in the Elder Edda. At the culminating crisis of the tragedy, however, he has suddenly deserted his Scandinavian sources; and, for the motives of action therein held adequate to bring about the catastrophe, has substituted those of the Teutonic version. These modifications, if attended with some advantages, involve corresponding sacrifices, and it may be interesting to dwell upon both a little in detail.

With the broad outlines of the myth—which, as the theme of Herr Wagner's vast operatic series, was copiously discussed in the newspaper-critiques of the Bayreuth festival—the reader may be presumed to have a general acquaintance. For the sake of comparison, however, between the Scandinavian and Teutonic versions, it will be desirable to run through the sequence of the chief incidents which Mr. Morris has comprehended in his epic.

[omitted section]

The main points in which Mr. Morris's rendering of the myth differs from the *Volsunga Saga* concern the respective characters of Brynhild and Gudrun. The former is represented in the Saga as gifted with an acute prophetic vision, and as the conscious victim of a fate which she is powerless to avert. She foretells to both Sigurd and Gudrun, at her first interviews with them, that they are destined for each other, and to effect the ruin of her own happiness; yet, in spite of this knowledge, she plights troth with her betrayer and parts in friendship from her rival. The measure of her passion for Sigurd, and of the suffering which his desertion causes her, is at the same time heightened by her being supposed to have borne him a daughter, Aslaug, whom, on her marriage to Gunnar, she leaves in the care of her foster-father. She displays her vaticination on her death-bed by distinctly warning Gunnar of the marriage which Gudrun will make with Atli, and of the vengeance it will inevitably entail. By omitting or modifying these incidents, Mr. Morris has doubtless given the story a more natural aspect to such modern readers as cannot sympathise with heroes and heroines who rush into misfortune open-eyed; but he has done so at the expense of lowering the dominant tone of fatalism which is the characteristic note of the Odinic myth, and verifies at once its antiquity and its nationality.

Gudrun, on the other hand, is represented in the Saga as more of an Amazon than Mr. Morris appears to think becoming even in a Norse heroine. Her fierceness of temper must be explained by her having eaten, soon after marriage, a portion of the serpent Fafnir's heart which Sigurd had preserved. The effect of this diet, whereby she 'becomes greater-hearted and wiser than ere before,' is signally manifest in the closing scenes of the tragedy, which the Saga-man portrays as differing widely from Mr. Morris's version of them. Atli, instead of being an 'outland' king, is the brother of Brynhild, and it is her wrongs, rather than his wife's, that he seeks to avenge when he invites the Niblungs. Gudrun, instead of inciting him to their murder, reveals to them his intended treachery, and, when they are attacked, dons her armour and fights by their side. Her revenge is taken not on her brothers for Sigurd's death, but on Atli for their death, and effected by the murder of his and her own children, whose flesh she sets before him at a Thyestean banquet. After stabbing him and firing the hall she throws herself into the sea; but does not perish there, being cast ashore and surviving to marry a third husband, to her children by whom she relates her history.

Mr. Morris's readers will not be disposed to regret his omission of the repulsive incidents of the Saga, but will probably agree with us in thinking the alterations of character and motive very doubtful improvements. There is a sensible dramatic loss of retributive justice in ignoring the relationship between Brynhild and Atli, which enters into the original design of the myth, and is in keeping with the normal tone of Odinic theology. Gudrun, again, is consistently delineated by the Saga-man as from first to last a savage both in love and hate, and dominated, after the manner of her race, by the superiority of her congenital ties to those created by marriage. Mr. Morris less truthfully depicts her as of a more modern type; gentle by nature and mastered by a noble passion, but carried away into excesses of pride and jealousy, of which she repents too late to avert the tragic consequence; stunned for awhile by the shock of the blow that fells her idol; then brooding in silence over her wrong, and eventually changed under these influences into an incarnation of treacherous and cruel vengeance, to whom neither the ties of blood nor wedlock have any sacredness.

Two or three touches of a repulsive character in the original portraits of Signy and Sigmund Mr. Morris has allowably softened. The former is represented in the Saga as testing the endurance of the two children whom she has borne to Siggeir by sewing gloves to their flesh. This test proving too severe, Sigmund varies it, when the boys are sent to him for training, by requiring them to pull out a viper which has invaded the meal-sack. On their proving unequal to the emergency, he slays them at the instance of their mother. When the turn of Sinfiotli, her incestuous offspring, arrives to undergo Signy's test, he is not only proof against it, but submits without flinching to her further experiment of pulling off gloves and skin together. This heroism commends him to Sigmund, who, on putting him to the same trial as his luckless brothers, has the satisfaction of finding that he cares so little for a viper in the meal as to knead it into bread. In Mr. Morris's rendering, Signy subjects to no preliminary proof the only one of Siggeir's sons whom she sends to Sigmund, and the latter, on the failure of the viper-test, returns him to her unharmed. Sinfiotli's superior mettle is attested from the moment of his introduction to Sigmund by the boldness with which he wades across the torrent which divides them, and the subsequent trials to which his father puts him only makes assurance doubly sure. The poet's delicate sensibility is apparent in these modifications of the myth's harsher features, but all his pains will scarcely avail to refine it to the standard of English taste.

The principal addition from Scandinavian sources with which he has enriched his epic, is the fine fragment preserved in the Elder Edda, that describes the attempts of Gudrun's friends to console her for the death of Sigurd. The wise and heroic counsels of the Earls producing no effect, their wives and daughters recount similar calamitous experiences of their own, but all fails to unseal the fountain of her tears. At last one of her maidens uncovers the dead hero's face, and procures her the desired relief. The picture illustrates with pathetic significance what was doubtless the normal condition of human suffering under a system of theology and ethics which consecrated bloodshed, and esteemed a violent death the worthiest end of life here, the surest passport to life hereafter. If, as is possible, this scene in its original form was in Mr. Tennyson's remembrance when he wrote his tender lyric, 'Home they brought her warrior dead,' we may the more appreciate the discernment with which, in addressing an English audience, he has rejected an emotional appeal that sufficed for the Scandinavian temperament in favour of a subtler motive, the potency of the maternal instinct, to which that temperament was singularly unresponsive.

The alteration which the entire myth undergoes in the *Nibelungenlied* is too extensive to be described in full detail, and it may suffice to point out the chief differences of treatment between it and the Scandinavian version.

[omitted section]

The extent to which a study of the *Nibelungenlied* has influenced Mr. Morris's presentment of the myth is almost confined, as will be seen, to the assimilations of Gudrun's motives to those of Kriemhild. Save in this instance his portraiture is obviously borrowed from that

of the *Volsunga Saga*. A far more detailed comparison might be made
between the two versions than we have had space enough to attempt;
but the reader who has followed us thus far will probably have no
difficulty in judging of their respective merits. Notwithstanding the
verdicts of F. von Schlegel, Lachmann, and other German critics in
favour of the *Nibelungenlied*, we have little doubt that Englishmen
generally will approve Mr. Morris's implied preference of the *Volsunga Saga* for the groundwork of his composition. In the qualities
which are pre-eminently requisite for the selection of an epical theme
—singleness of aim, simplicity of motive, severe dignity, and profound
pathos—the Saga version appears to us incomparably superior. The
structural defects of the Teutonic version are doubtless in a measure
due to the interweaving of later legend with the ancient mythical
fabric; but, taking the story as it stands, its fitness for artistic treatment
is fatally marred by them. The complete disappearance of Brynhild
from the stage, whereon she has played so important a part, just at
the occurrence of the crisis she has precipitated, and which determines
the fate of all her fellow-actors, would alone suffice to demonstrate
the compiler's clumsy workmanship. In the Saga, on the other hand,
the significance of her figure is held steadily in view, and the outlines
of her character are consistently in keeping from first to last. Etzel,
again, who should be conspicuous in scenes one-half of which are laid
at his Court, is delineated far less clearly than Atli, who occupies a
much smaller space in the Saga-man's narrative. As an heroic personage, Siegfried will bear no comparison with Sigurd, his character
being flawed by that propensity to bully and swagger still too common
among his North German countrymen. Kriemhild, while to the full
as savage and wily as Gudrun, is stirred by ignobler impulses, and
displays less dignity of endurance. It is some compensation that the
minor characters in the *Nibelungenlied* are more individualised than
their Scandinavian counterparts—Gunther than Gunnar, Giselher than
Guttorm, and Hagan than Hogni. Hagan's personality is especially
recognisable by the grim humour which tinges so many of the words
and acts ascribed to him. Rudeger, whose introduction is due to the
admixture of later legend already noted, is so interesting a figure in
himself as to make us indifferent to the question whether the story
would or would not have been more symmetrical without him. The
Austrian compiler deserves eternal gratitude for having selected from
the heroes of popular tradition so fine a type of Christian chivalry.*

* F. von Schlegel's Æsthetic and Miscellaneous Works: *On the Poetry of the North.*

Of the attempts which have been made by some critics to identify the leading characters of the epic with historical personages of the fifth and sixth centuries after Christ, this is not the place to speak. Readers interested in the subject will find it sufficiently enlarged upon in the excellent preface and notes which redeem Mr. Lettsom's[1] uncouth and scarcely readable translation.* Whatever importance may still be attached to speculations of this kind in Germany, we doubt if English critics will pay much more heed to them than to the obsolete efforts of Fourmont and Bryant to identify Rebecca with Juno and Tubalcain with Vulcan.

Mr. Morris has happily left his work clear from all the incrustations which have accreted round the primitive mythical nucleus. He has conceded somewhat, indeed, to the recent school of mythologists who, on the strength of certain etymological evidence, have fitted this and every other love-story of Aryan origin with a 'solar' or 'cosmical' interpretation. The concession is so contrived, however, as not to spoil his narrative for unlearned readers. The description given of the situation of the Niblung city (pp. 194–5), the references made to its inhabitants as the 'cloudy people,' the stress laid upon the ruddiness of Sigurd's rings, the brightness of his countenance, and the rectitude of his government, are intelligible enough to those acquainted with the theory, and who care to look for undermeanings, but will be accepted as merely imaginative detail by those to whom the real interest of the poem lies in the springs of psychological motive and dramatic play of character, with which none of this allegorical machinery need interfere.

Apart from the interest thus excited, the work does not offer any striking features of poetic attraction. While marked by the evidences of artistic skill already noted, its obvious shortcomings in other respects are likely to impair its chances of immediate or permanent popularity. Its inordinate length alone will deter some readers even on the threshold; and the diffuseness of style which has now, we fear, become habitual with Mr. Morris, will probably weary others before they reach the end. The diction, however appropriate, is almost pedantically close in imitation to its model, the identical similes and metaphors employed by the Saga-man being often reproduced with some rhetorical amplification. Passages of novel and pictorial description are fre-

---

[1] William Nansom Lettsom published *The Fall of the Nibelungers* in 1850, and *The Niebelungenlied* in 1874.
* Second edition. Williams & Norgate. 1874.

quent, but the prevailing tenor of the narrative seldom rises above mediocrity; and beyond an occasionally nervous or graceful phrase, and a line or two exceptionally musical, the memory finds little to carry away, and the ear still less to haunt it. The ballad metre, although relieved now and then by skilful modulation, is unavoidably monotonous in so prolonged a succession of couplets. The verbal archaisms are not, perhaps, in excess, considering the poet's proclivities and the special character of his subject, but, to our thinking, are distinctly tiresome. The few passages in *Sigurd* that we remember and enjoy are just those which have a faint *soupçon* of modernness in their tone; such, for example, as the fine prophecy of Sigmund's career, put into the mouth of Signy, which embodies a nobler ideal than any expression of Scandinavian sentiment with which we are acquainted:

Fresh shall thy memory be, and thine eyes, like mine, shall gaze
On the day unborn in the darkness, the last of all earthly days—
The last of the days of battle, when the host of the Gods is arrayed,
And there is an end for ever of all who were once afraid.
There, as thou drawest thy sword, thou shalt think of the days that were,
And the foul shall still seem foul, and the fair shall still seem fair;
But thy wit shall then be awakened, and thou shalt know indeed
Why the brave man's spear is broken, and his war-shield fails at need;
Why the loving is unbelovèd; why the just man falls from his state;
Why the liar gains in a day what the soothfast strives for late.
Yea, and thy deeds shalt thou know, and great shall thy gladness be;
As a picture all of gold thy life-days shalt thou see,
And know that thou, too, wert a God to abide through the hurry and haste;
A God in the golden hall, a God on the rain-swept waste;
A God in the battle triumphant—a God on the heap of the slain,
And thine hope shall arise and blossom, and thy love shall be quickened again.

Pp. 28–9.

But the traces here and elsewhere of any anachronism in thought or feeling are so minute as to be well-nigh indistinguishable, the whole texture of the poem being steeped to saturation in the atmosphere of Odinism. This faithfulness of archaic tone constitutes at once its strength and weakness. If so fierce and repulsive a story could be made acceptable to an English audience, it should be by the telling of such an accurate and deft narrator as Mr. Morris. No artist can possibly identify himself more closely with the spirit of the age and the temper of the actors he undertakes to depict; but the greater the truth of his representation, the less his likelihood of success. Certain characteristics of that spirit and temper are, no doubt, permanently and universally exemplary. Unrepining obedience to the inflexible, and steadfast trust in the wise ordinances of the Highest Power, endurance of pain and contempt of death, are noble and inspiriting virtues for all time. But, in some vital and essential elements, public and private morality has undergone a complete and, it may be believed, a lasting change. One need not seek far for proof of it. This story is a prolonged illustration of the predominance of revenge above every other motive of human action—of the practical working of a social system based upon the fundamental principle that wrong must be requited by wrong. Handed down from father to child, generation by generation, the memory of a mortal offence done to a Scandinavian family or tribe was tenaciously and persistently cherished until the debt of death had been exacted to the uttermost. In their thirst for blood-vengeance the women were, if possible, more keen and relentless than the men. Maidenly shame, wifely duty, motherly instinct, and sisterly affection must alike give way before the imperious necessity of expiation. The annals and literature of Norway and Iceland attest how rigorously this theory of life was carried into practice, and supply chapter and verse for many a trait of manners illustrated in the fiction before us. Whether the change which the social system of the Gothic races has undergone be due to the supersession of Odinism by a religious creed and moral code of which love and forgiveness are fundamental principles, or to some other cause, may be matter for dispute; but no one disputes that the change exists. If there be one point upon which, in this age of discordant opinion and unsettled belief, moralists of all schools—Christian, Positivist, and Agnostic—are found to agree, it is in accepting love as the noblest, and denouncing revenge as the meanest, of human motives. And, to say nothing of the prevalence of just and humane laws which are the best expression of public conscience, it is unquestionable that, in their dealings with one another, the majority of cultivated men and women, whatever be their creed, act up to a standard of self-restraint and forbearance that approximates not very remotely to the Christian ideal. A poem, therefore, which, like *Sigurd*, reflects, with hard, uncompromising realism, an obsolete code of ethics, and a barbarous condition of society, finds itself irreconcilably at discord with the key of nineteenth-century feeling. Deprived of its strongest claim to interest, a sympathetic response in the moral and religious sentiment of its readers, it can only appeal to the intellect as a work of art, or as a more or less successful attempt at antiquarian restoration. It may be admired and applauded by the lettered few; but it will not be taken to the nation's heart, nor its language incorporated in the common speech. The greatest poets of our time who have been fascinated by the attraction of similar themes, have perceived their unfitness for realistic treatment, and that the only practicable method of inspiring interest in them is by some allegorising or spiritualising process of adjustment to the modern standpoint. To preserve the external verisimilitude of the symbol while changing its inner meaning, and bringing this into harmony with a new sphere of thought, is the special function of the artist. Age after age, as our race grows, and modifications take place in its religious, moral, and social systems, the myths and legends upon which its youth has been nursed can thus be accommodated to the current order of belief, and their dry bones be made to live. The opportunity of employing a great racial, pre-historic myth as a potent engine of modern ideas is one that might have tempted a less ambitious poet than Mr. Morris. His artistic aims are, however, different from these, and he has chosen not to avail himself of the occasion.

44. Unsigned review, *International Review*

September 1877, iv, 696–9

A New York review of the American edition of *Sigurd* (1877), under the heading 'Recent American Books'.

It may be that in this century of diplomacy and over-conscious civilization the writing of a truly national epos has become an impossibility; but with this reservation it is safe to admit that Mr. Morris's *Sigurd the Volsung* possesses as much of the heroic quality as the unepic character of the age will allow. To call him a Gothic Homer would perhaps be a little hyperbolical, but we have little doubt that, had he lived a thousand years earlier, when the Odinic mythology was still a vital element in the life of the Gothic nations, he would have created a Gothic epos which would have occupied a position in the Germanic literature corresponding to that which the *Iliad* now occupies in the Greek. As it is, his poem impresses us rather as an achievement (and as such a great one), than as a strong and spontaneous outburst of primitive emotion. Its underlying, inspiring force is enthusiasm, which is a comparatively superficial quality, rather than faith, without which no epos is possible. Of course, it would be unreasonable to demand of a modern poet that he should have faith in a defunct pagan mythology, which is the same as to say that it would be unreasonable to expect of him that he could write an epic. For even Christianity is at the present day too much a matter of argument to furnish the inspiring force necessary for the creation of a Christian world-epos; and since the age of the Crusades has passed by without producing any such poem, we fear the opportunity has been irrevocably lost. The Catholic Church, which is the only surviving monument of medievalism in religion, being the only church which has not stripped itself of its mythological encumbrances, possesses indeed as yet some of the more external conditions for such an achievement, but even if a great bard should arise within its pale, he would find himself too hopelessly out of sympathy with the spirit of the century to fathom the full meaning of its struggles, and doubts, and dim aspirations. The inevitable conclusion, then, is that the epic age, if it be not irrevocably past, can only reappear in a distant future, when all the tremendous moral and intellectual forces, which now bewilder us by their chaotic magnificence, shall have crystallized into a clearer and wider system, from which the lost faith may rise again in a nobler and more enduring form.

In the development of his plot Mr. Morris has not followed entirely either the Icelandic or the medieval version of the Niblung legend, but has made a free and judicious use of both, according as his purpose required. In the two first books, relating the early history of the Volsungs, concerning which the *Nibelungen Lied* is silent, the saga tale is rendered with but slight modifications. The most wildly grotesque features are eliminated, and the characters of the heroes sufficiently humanized to reach the sympathies of modern men. And still the barbaric magnificence of that age, as the saga describes it, is in no way softened, while at the same time the joys and sorrows of King Volsung and his sons have a power to move us which in the Icelandic tale is utterly wanting. We might quote a dozen passages where Mr. Morris has evidently felt the pressure of his modern audience, and adapted his narrative to their refined ears; in the scene, for instance, where Sigmund slays the she-wolf who had eaten his nine brothers, he does not (as in the saga), anoint his mouth and face with honey and bite the wolf's tongue, pulling it out with his teeth, but he simply breaks his bonds and kills the beast with his fetters. Again, when his sister sends her and Siggeir's son to him in the forest, he sends the lad back to his mother instead of slaying him.

At the beginning of the third book, however, the spiritual atmosphere of the poem undergoes some subtle change, which is felt more easily than it is defined. The poet here begins to draw his material from the old German epic. The grim simplicity of Norse paganism which pervades the opening cantos is momentarily lost sight of, and the glitter and pomp of medieval chivalry with 'horse and hawk and hound' take its place. In this there is to our minds an implied anachronism—an anachronism of sentiment rather than of fact. The whole description of the court of the Niblungs is redolent with medieval feeling, which is indeed not to be wondered at, as it is directly borrowed from the medieval *Nibelungen Lied*, without any strong effort to tune it into accord with the more Norse elements of the poem.

But criticisms like these are after all of minor importance when compared with the really great and enduring qualities which *Sigurd the Volsung* possesses in such an eminent degree. First, the genuinely Gothic spirit which breathes from every verse, and stirs the hidden Gothic fibres in our own nature. We know no other poet, modern or ancient, who has fathomed so fully and expressed so finely the old Germanic sentiment for the sword, the fateful magic of gold, and the other distinct elements of Gothic civilization.

We have hardly space to analyze in detail the many beauties of this singularly beautiful poem. From the very first the reader's ear is captivated by the simple stateliness and purity of the verse, which flows on with a calm majestic movement, like that of a broad river reflecting the deeds of the successive generations that toil, struggle, and die on its shores. In the very vocabulary there is a Saxon muscularity and strength which accord well with the primitive grandeur of the theme. Even Homer is said occasionally to nod; but Mr. Morris never for a moment yields to drowsiness or fatigue. He retains from beginning to end the same firm grip on his subject, and the manly directness with which he describes even situations to which squeamish ears might take exception, immediately wins the reader's heart and disarms the critic. Where all is so excellent, it is difficult to choose any passage especially adapted for quotation; we select, however, at random the scene where Sigurd, after having ridden through the wall of flame, awakes Brynhild, the sleeping valkyrie:

Then he looked on his bare bright blade, and he said: 'Thou—what wilt thou
  do?'
For indeed as I came by the war-garth thy voice of desire I knew.
Bright burnt the pale blue edges, for the sunrise drew anear,
And the ruins of the Shield-burg glittered, and the east was exceeding clear;
So the eager edges he setteth to the Dwarf-wrought battle-coat,
Where the hammered ring-knit collar constraineth the woman's throat;
But the sharp Wrath biteth and rendeth, and before it fail the rings,
And, lo, the gleam of linen and the light of golden things;
Then he driveth the blue steel onward, and through the skirt and out,
Till nought but the rippling linen is wrapping her about;
Then he deems her breath comes quicker and her breast begins to heave,
So he turns about the War-Flame and rends down either sleeve,
Till her arms lie white in her raiment, and a river of sun-bright hair
Flows free o'er bosom and shoulder and floods the desert bare.
Then a flush cometh over her visage and a sigh upheaveth her breast,
And her eyelids quiver and open, and she wakeneth into rest.

Outside of Tennyson's *Idylls of the King*, we know no poem in the whole range of English literature which illustrates so strikingly the strength and beauty of Saxon speech; and in single lines we venture to think (with all due admiration for the laureate's marvelous work) that Mr. Morris has surpassed him. What can, for instance, be finer than this?—

Ah! my love shall fare as a banner in the hand of thy renown.

And the spears in the hall were tossing as the rye in a windy plain.

——and the wild hawks overhead
Soughed 'neath the naked heavens as at last he spake and said.

Again, as a substitute for the Homeric interludes, with their sonorous, polysyllabic splendor, it is hard to imagine any thing more felicitous than the plain vigorous Saxon of lines like the following:

And the morn and the noon and the even built up another day.

In single, oft-recurring epithets like 'the white-armed Gudrun,' 'the bright-eyed Brynhild,' 'the wise-heart Hagin,' Mr. Morris naturally recalls the Homeric λευχώλενος, γλαυχῶπις, and πολύμητις,[1] but the reminder is rather a pleasant one, and somehow seems to add to the epic strength and dignity of the poem.

In his characterization Mr. Morris never departs from the simple and direct methods of the sagas, leaving the action to speak for itself, and never disturbing the narrative by any attempt at analysis or personal reflections. He has indeed shown before now that he has studied the Old Norse literature to good purpose, but his former experiments with Icelandic themes always seemed to us unnecessarily fragmentary and incomplete, and hardly seemed to justify us in expecting any thing truly great from him in this direction. Viewed, however, in the light of preparatory studies, these early labors, no doubt, have their value, and we would no more think of quarreling with the poet for having published them than we would blame a Raphael or a Rubens for exhibiting the contents of his portfolio. *Sigurd the Volsung* will always remain the crowning achievement of Mr. Morris's life, and we are none the less willing to accord to him the praise which is his due, because he has taken us and all the world by surprise. He has produced a work whose grandeur and beauty will make it for all time to come monumental in the annals of English literature.

---

[1] White-armed, bright-eyed, and many-counselled.

45. Oscar Wilde on Morris and the English Renaissance

1882

Oscar Wilde (1856–1900) was poet, playwright, journalist and propagandist for Art. In January 1882 Wilde delivered a high-flown lecture on 'The English Renaissance of Art' to a curious audience in the Chickering Hall, New York. His account of nineteenth-century developments included several direct references to Morris, while his conclusion is full of overtones of Morris's social ideas. These sections are printed here.

From Robert Ross, *The First Collected Edition of the Works of Oscar Wilde*, 15 vols, *Miscellanies* (1908), 251–2; 275.

William Morris, substituting for the simpler realism of the earlier days a more exquisite spirit of choice, a more faultless devotion to beauty, a more intense seeking for perfection: a master of all exquisite design and of all spiritual vision. It is of the School of Florence rather than of Venice that he is kinsman, feeling that the close imitation of Nature is a disturbing element in imaginative art. The visible aspect of modern life disturbs him not: rather it is for him to render eternal all that is beautiful in Greek, Italian, and Celtic legend. To Morris we owe poetry whose perfect precision and closeness of word and vision has not been excelled in the literature of our country, and by the revival of the decorative arts he has given to our individualised romantic movement the social idea and the social factor too . . .

. . . hence the enormous importance given to the decorative arts in our English Renaissance; hence all that marvel of design that comes from the hand of Edward Burne-Jones, all that weaving of tapestry and staining of glass, that beautiful working in clay and metal and wood that we owe to William Morris, the greatest handicraftsman we have had in England since the fourteenth century . . .

. . . For what is decoration but the worker's expression of his joy in work? And not joy merely—that is a great thing yet not enough—but that opportunity of expressing his own individuality which, as it is the essence of all life, is the source of all art. 'I have tried', I remember William Morris saying to me once, 'I have tried to make each of my workers an artist, and when I say an artist I mean a man'.

46. Edith Simcox, review, *Fortnightly Review*

June 1882, xxxi, 771-9

Edith Simcox (1844-1901) has become well known through K. A. Mackenzie's *Edith Simcox and George Eliot* (London, 1961). In his Introduction to the volume, p. xi, Professor G. S. Haight states that her numerous critical articles 'show fine critical intelligence and amazing versatility'.

All who wish to take a hopeful view of the possibilities and future of English art will hail the publication of Mr. Morris's little volume of Lectures as in itself the most hopeful symptom which has shown itself for many years. The poet of the *Earthly Paradise* has been an employer of labour and a seller of divers articles of manufacture quite long enough for him to speak with the authority of experience, if experience had unhappily impelled him towards Carlylesque generalisations about the folly and roguery of the world beneath him. But Mr. Morris does not stand aloof, in finely descriptive indignation, from the common herd of makers and sellers. Intimacy with the manifold shortcomings of both classes has produced an uncommonly keen and circumstantial sympathy with their difficulties; but the sympathetic sense of difficulty stops short of despair, even when conjoined with the personal discouragements of the artist.

Mr. Morris speaks with generous warmth of his obligations to Mr. Ruskin, and it would therefore be ungracious to make his praises cast a reflected shadow on the elder writer. But it is allowable to suggest that the despairing tone of Mr. Ruskin, and the qualified but unextin-

guished hopefulness of Mr. Morris, are both justified by the social and
political preconceptions which determine their attitude towards the
practical problems of art and industry. Mr. Ruskin preaches and illustrates by his own 'practice the duty of paying for every article pur-
chased the equivalent of its real worth. When a collection of minerals
was offered to him for two-thirds of its value, as he did not care to
spend as much as they were worth, he bought two-thirds of the collection for the price at which the necessitous dealer offered the whole
(*Arrows of the Chase*, ii. 84). But a man of the world may be excused
for despairing of the possibility of making the mass of purchasers as
scrupulous as Mr. Ruskin. It requires more virtue to surrender voluntarily an unjust advantage than merely to put forward the claim for
a just one. Mr. Morris begins, so to speak, at the other end. In view of
'the danger that the present course of civilisation will destroy the
beauty of life,' he does not appeal to artists or connoisseurs for higher
aims or more enlightened patronage. He appeals direct to the mass of
the people, urging them to do the thing which they must naturally
most desire to be able to do, namely, take pleasure in their daily work.

He is severe upon the notion that there might be one art for the
rich and another for the poor. 'Art is not so accommodating as the
justice or religion of society, and she won't have it.' And in the Second
Lecture, called 'The Art of the People,' he propounds a definition
which supplies the reason why. '*That thing which I understand by real
art is the expression by man of his pleasure in labour.*' This is the 'art made
by the people and for the people, as a happiness to the maker and the
user' which may grow up here or in any other community which first
attains to the two virtues, love of justice and simplicity of life.

For those of us that are employers of labour, how can we bear to give any man
less money than he can live decently on, less leisure than his education and
self-respect demand? Or those of us who are workmen, how can we bear to
fail in the contract we have undertaken, or to make it necessary for a foreman
to go up and down spying out our mean tricks and evasions? Or we, the shop-
keepers—can we endure to lie about our wares that we may shuffle off our losses
on someone else's shoulders? Or we, the public—how can we bear to pay a
price for a piece of goods which will help to trouble one man, to ruin another,
and starve a third? Or still more, I think, how can we bear to use, how can we
enjoy something which has been a pain and grief for the maker to make?
I say all classes are to blame in this matter, but also I say that the remedy lies
with the handicraftsmen, who are not ignorant of these things like the public,
and who have no call to be greedy and isolated like the manufacturers or

middlemen; the duty and honour of educating the public lies with them, and they have in them the seeds of order and organisation which make that duty the easier.

No theme recurs more frequently throughout the Lectures than this: that labour is normally pleasurable; that there must be something radically wrong, either in the work itself or in the conditions under which it is done, if it is impossible for a reasonable man to take pleasure in doing it. Mr. Morris recognises three possible categories of work—mechanical work, intelligent work, and imaginative work, of which the two latter differ more in degree than kind. Those to whom his definition of real art appears paradoxical will no doubt think it Utopian to contend that all human work should be either intelligent or imaginative, or both; to them perhaps masons or bricklayers are but base mechanical churls at best. They have never seen or thought about the difference between a Roman brick wall, a piece of honest English brickwork (say like the chancel of St. Mary's, Crown Street, in St. Giles's), and the last house wall run up by a speculative builder in the last invented London suburb; and yet from the workman's point of view the difference is as marked as from the artist's. Over and above the pleasure of laying every brick exactly in its place; over and above the carnal 'lust of finishing,' as John Wesley called it, which makes every finished yard of brickwork a pleasure to its author, every perfect piece of workmanship in this or any other line brings with it something of intelligent and imaginative delight in its fitness and perfection as a part of the larger whole to which it belongs.

We remember how, when old Kester, whose spécialité was thatching ricks, found himself condemned to cease from thatching on the seventh day, his most spiritual exercise was an admiring pilgrimage round and about the ricks of his own admirable thatching. Even in the case of work which affords little or no scope for ornamentation or the production of supererogatory beauty, because the form of the thing to be made is strictly conditioned by its purpose, the workman has a rightful claim to the double pleasure of contributing to make a perfect tool and of knowing the purposes to which it will be put. The making of scientific instruments, for example, if done without understanding or good-will, may be as mechanical as the running of a plaster cornice, but it may also be as intelligent and imaginative as the chisel strokes of a working artist allowed to finish a capital his own way, if the instrument maker knows what *savant* has ordered the new tool and what problem it will be employed in solving.

Notwithstanding his lawful preference for handwork, Mr. Morris refrains from any general denunciation of machinery, and it is obvious that the general emancipation of a numerous race from the burden of overmuch mechanical toil can best be effected by the help of what weavers, picturesquely elliptical, used to call 'power.' No skilled work —and there is skill in the guidance of machinery—can be called wholly mechanical, in which the mind and senses are free to aim at excellence.

'Many a grin of pleasure,' Mr. Morris avers, 'must have gone to the invention of the quaint designs of anonymous artists in the ancient days. While they were at work, at least, these men were not unhappy, and I suppose they worked most days, and the most part of the day, as we do.' And the wholesome happiness of their daily labour had its fruit in the abundant production of works of art such as we are now glad to hoard in museums. The ideal of the British workman at the present day is to be well paid for leisurely, careful, excellent work-manship, but he is not disposed to take the leisure and give the care at the expense of his payment. The ideal of the employer or overlooker of the British workman is to get passable work done as fast as poss-ible, and if either the pay or the quality has to be sacrificed, it is his interest to sacrifice quality rather than not turn over his capital the desired number of times per annum. Unfortunately there are plenty of mechanics whose dexterity can take the form of pace instead of excel-lence, and these men have not yet taken the lofty view of their social mission suggested by Mr. Morris. They are able, maybe, owing to the vast demand for the evil thing, to earn as much by doing slovenly work fast as they could earn by doing thoroughly good work at leisure. It is true they don't *enjoy* doing the bad work, but they cannot afford to indulge a sentimental preference when out of employ. And so they supply us, their customers, with the scamped work of which we all complain, when we have bought what we asked for at its market price;—with a result to the workman not very different from that imagined by Mr. Morris: 'If I were to work ten hours a day at work I despised and hated, I should spend my leisure I hope in political agitation, but I fear—in drinking.'

Then again there are commodities, invented only that some dealer may make a profit by persuading people to buy them, though they are tiresome to make and useless to possess. All such labour is pure waste, and the gratuitous disagreeableness of this useless work, together with the mass of unnecessarily bad work, has led even reasonable and humane people to the rash conclusion that all work is naturally dis-

agreeable, a necessary evil, to be endured, as an enlightened manufacturer tells his workpeople, because men 'hope by working to earn
leisure.' In other words, it is assumed that all the work of the world
is done against the grain, whereas Mr. Morris has been lecturing us
all the time upon the opposite text—that no work which cannot be
done with pleasure in the doing is worth doing at all. To explain the
puzzle he turns to his own experience:—

For I tried to think what would happen to me if I was forbidden my ordinary
daily work; and I knew that I should die of despair and weariness unless I
could straightway take to something else which I could make my daily work;
and it was clear to me that I worked not in the least in the world for the sake
of earning leisure by it, but partly driven by the fear of starvation or disgrace,
and partly, and even a very great deal, because I love the work itself; and as
for my leisure, well I had to confess that part of it I do indeed spend as a dog
does—in contemplation, let us say—and like it well enough; but part of it also
I spend in work: which work gives me just as much pleasure as my bread-
earning work—neither more nor less—and therefore could be no bribe or hope
for my work-a-day hours.

Then next I turned my thoughts to my friends: mere artists, and therefore,
you know, lazy people by prescriptive right. I found that the one thing they
enjoyed was their work, and that their only idea of happy leisure was other
work, just as valuable to the world as their work-a-day work; they only
differed from me in liking the dog-like leisure less and the man-like labour
more than I do.

I got no further when I turned from mere artists to important men—public
men. I could see no signs of their working merely to earn leisure. They all
worked for the work and the deed's sake. Do rich gentlemen sit up all night in
the House of Commons for the sake of earning leisure? if so, 'tis a sad waste
of labour. Or Mr. Gladstone? he doesn't succeed in winning much leisure by
tolerably strenuous work; what he does get he might have got on much easier
terms, I am sure.

It must not be supposed that because Mr. Morris recognises the
close connection between morals, politics, and art, these lectures are
taken up exclusively with the burning problems of social economy.
The little volume, it is true, has a rare and admirable breadth of view
and firmness of grasp. Every artist and artisan, every liberal politician
or social reformer, will be the better for reading it. Dealing ostensibly
with a comparatively narrow subject, it shirks, as we have seen, no
point of contact between this subject and the many others naturally
connected with it; but all these subsidiary subjects are treated in the
selfsame spirit as the main theme. Art is to be popular, imaginative,

and delightful as well as, or rather in consequence of, its being serviceable, intelligent, and moral. What more than this can Utilitarians
demand from science, industry, and politics? But to the Utilitarians
who think science, industry, and politics enough without any imaginative delight in beauty for its own sake, and who would see with indifference 'the faculty of design itself gradually fade from the race of
man,' Mr. Morris may suggest a doubt: 'Sirs, shall we approach nearer
to perfection by casting away so large a part of that intelligence which
makes us *men*?'

It is a shame to take a book so delightfully free from all kinds of
arrogant self-righteousness as a text for preaching; but the reflection
cannot but suggest itself to a disinterested reader: If all advocacy of the
special claims of science, politics, and industry were as careful of the
claims of the rest, and all as careful of the claims of art as Mr. Morris
is to give due place and weight to other than artistic considerations,
with how much less waste and friction than at present all the good
intentions of the world would work together. Similar appeals, pointing to the same goal of simplicity and justice, might be made on
exactly parallel lines, from the social point of view: the right of the
workman to ease and leisure (available both for canine 'contemplation'
and a refreshing change of labour), and that of the public at large to
a chance of buying good work;—from the political point of view: that
all classes must have a share in government to secure justice for themselves, and that all who have a share in governing must have reached
a high level of intelligence and morality, so that they may render
justice also to each other;—and from the industrial point of view:
that labour may not be wasted through the miscalculations which
allow a larger reward to enterprise wasted in exploitation than to
enterprise expended on production.

We cannot help hoping that, as a consequence of his digressions
into adjacent fields of thought, Mr. Morris's words will have weight
with some of the many worthy people at home therein, who, as he
admits, think of art as trifling, and renounce contentedly whatever
pleasures it might give. 'Art for art's sake,' art as a refined and subtle
pleasure for the favoured few, art as a fashion for the rich, or a cheap
charity for the poor, are the objects of his confirmed distrust and dis-
belief. Mr. Morris is as sure that such art is impossible as that it would
be worthless if it were possible. He rejoices in knowing that it is
impossible; that art must either be popular, a source of genuine pleasure
to the men employed in handicrafts, or it must cease to exist. He dis-

trusts—and surely no one has a better right—the sincerity and earnest-ness of the so-called 'artistic movement' mainly associated with his name, because of the share which fashion has had in its success as well as in its falling short of success. A social clique may bring blue plates and grey papers into vogue, just as an inconspicuous youth may be quizzed into celebrity by a comic paper, but the vogue will be as short-lived in the one case as in the other, unless the mass of householders attain to a sincere and spontaneous preference for harmony, beauty, and—we might add—elbow-room. Mr. Morris frankly informs the rich buyers of pictures and patrons of the arts in general that if they really knew or cared anything about art, they would refuse to live in ugly ill-built dwellings, crowded up with superfluous upholstery; if they really enjoyed the beauty, they would really suffer from and rebel against the ugliness, and tradesmen would have to defer to an authorita-tive demand for wares few and good instead of many, cheap and nasty.

Even in the minor matter of house furnishing it is by no means clear that the reformation of the national taste may not have to origi-nate with the class of artisans. Here is Mr. Morris's list of the fittings necessary to the sitting-room of a healthy person; a room, he explains, which the owner 'would not have to cook in much, or sleep in gener-ally, or in which he would not have to do any very litter-making manual work.' These necessaries are—'First, a bookcase with a great many books in it; next, a table that will keep steady when you write or work at it; then several chairs that you can move, and a bench that you can sit or lie upon; next, a cupboard with drawers; a vase or two to put flowers in,' and unless bookcase or cupboard be very beautiful with painting or carving, there should be added some real works of art on the walls. Now, as the majority of Britons cannot expect to live in houses that are fit to be seen until the expiry, let us say, of all the building leases granted in the last half-century, rich and poor start at an equal disadvantage in the pursuit of beautiful simplicity indoors. In fact, with things as they are now, good work being so artificially scarce as to command almost more than its considerable real value, the advantage is really in the hands of any one *who can make these necessaries for himself.*

Every one knows the pathetic idiom of modern townsfolk, accord-ing to which the 'home' does not mean the house or dwelling-place, but the bits of sticks and 'things' which accompany the family in its wanderings from one rack-rented chamber to another. It would be a happy fruit of Mr. Morris's teaching if workmen, who are paid to spend unhappy days in making tables that *won't* keep steady on their legs, chose to solace themselves in leisure hours by making for their future 'home' tables and the rest that would fulfil this modest condition. The cost of plain seasoned wood to a workman in the trade might be a little more than the price of such ready-made furniture as a thriving mechanic can afford. But the seven years' apprenticeship which there is room for between school and marriage will leave leisure enough to finish most of the necessaries of a 'home' in a style that will outlast many generations, and maybe tempt collectors in dark ages yet to come. If this plan were to be tried, middle-class drawing-rooms would soon learn to be ashamed of faring worse than workmen's parlours, and the men who had cultivated their craft for love of it for themselves, would find their own example create a class of customers for such work as they might do with pride and pleasure.

Mr. Morris's belief that 'the general education that makes men think, will one day make them think rightly about art,' suffers some shock (as we gather from a note to the Third Lecture) from the indifference shown at such educational centres as Westminster School and the University of Oxford to the threatened destruction of Ashburnham House and Magdalen Bridge. But it would be at least as fair to quote such cases of artistic vandalism in high places to prove the incompleteness even of our highest forms of education. The builder who cuts down a cedar rather than make one villa in a row a shade less hideous than its neighbours, and the academic authorities who defer helplessly to the dicta of those 'whose business it is to know' about such mysterious things as bridges, show exactly the same intellectual defect; a defect only to be remedied by education, enabling them to form an independent judgment as to the proportionate force of considerations belonging to different genera. Any education must be incomplete that does not include some exercise of practical intercourse with things and a glimpse at least of 'that kindly struggle with nature, to which all true craftsmen are born.' This kind of knowledge, if it came to be rated at its true value, might be taught in school to those whose destiny lies away from workshops as easily as book learning is taught to tiny imps with a wide experience in the traffic of City streets and markets.

Of course Mr. Morris would have every craftsman taught to draw and to draw from the human figure; but when it is a question of applying such elementary knowledge of drawing as is to be gained under the auspices of South Kensington, we are compelled to ask, as in the cognate problem of technical instruction, 'Who is to instruct our instructors, so that they may not, like blind leaders of the blind, land their scholars in a ditch, or *impasse* of laborious bad taste?' As yet, no doubt, South Kensington has done no appreciable harm in England, whatever abominations its spirit may have been accessory to in India. But it is evident that art teaching cannot be evolved for ever from the inner consciousness of a Government department; unless schools of art-workmanship grow up from which such a department can learn, it will soon be able to teach nothing, except middling drawing-masters like itself. The danger signalised by Mr. Morris, of imagining that trees can grow from the top downwards, is very real and present here. Probably, if we wished to know the best way of giving technical instruction to the men in a given trade, our safest course would be to ask a score of the most intelligent workmen employed in it to tell us everything that they had at any time wished to know in relation to their work. But technical instruction, excogitated *de haut en bas*, is at worst useless, and will be neglected. Until the custom of using *some* kind of decorations for buildings, clothes, and furniture is absolutely extinct, the workman is compelled to use such decoration as he can— in other words, which he has been taught to use; and bad teaching is consequently much worse than useless, for it cannot remain inoperative. To take a small instance of the dangers which beset an official system: hundreds of thousands of children and young people 'pass' annually in free-hand drawing at the examinations of the Science and Art Department. The copies set them consist mostly of some vase, conventionalized leaf, or scroll work, in outline, the two sides of which most often are alike. Now of course the precedent of Giotto's O may be cited to prove that a true artist can draw freely with mechanical accuracy, but according to the legend, Giotto began with sheep, not with circles, and it is almost self-evident that the last thing a young draughtsman will be able to accomplish with a really free stroke is to make two sides of a leaf 'balance,' as it is called in the jargon of the schools, *i.e.* correspond exactly as nothing in nature and few things in real art do. When freedom of stroke has been acquired there is no harm in adding this superfluous dexterity, but it would clearly be disastrous to train the rising generation of artificers in the belief that ornamentation can display no higher merit than that of having two sides alike.

For the present, at any rate, we need wish for no better antidote to weak or faulty teaching in these matters than the spirited, picturesque, and magnanimous discourse of Mr. Morris. We must pass by un-noticed many fine or pleasant passages and phrases which it would have been a pleasure to quote, but there is one reference to 'an ugly word for a dreadful fact,' which we must just mention to show that it is not, so to speak, a mere lowering of the artistic franchise that Mr. Morris aims at, a mere extension to the class of skilled artisans of the sweetness and light supposed to flourish within the range of middle-class æstheticism. 'Ancient civilisation was chained to slavery and exclusiveness, and it fell.' Modern civilisation will fall likewise, instead of growing into fresh artistic life, unless it can deal with what we call 'the residuum.' And to what quarter can we look hopefully for help in this task, except to that which Mr. Morris has appealed to already? Let the manufacturer and the mechanic moralise each other (and settle amongst themselves which shall have the honour of begin-ning), but it is the mechanic alone that can moralise his labourer. The upper hundred thousand must set the fashion—of decent living—to the millions below them.

This vast, and, as some might think, hopelessly remote aim—as well as the abolition of 'carpet gardening' and the regeneration of decorative art—is included in the cause in which Mr. Morris seeks to enlist his hearers and readers, and, to conclude in his own words: 'That cause is the democracy of art, the ennobling of daily and common work, which will one day put hope and pleasure in the place of fear and pain, as the forces which move men to labour and keep the world a-going.'

47. Unsigned review, *Century Magazine*

July 1882, xxiv, 464–5

It is always a fresh surprise to find reflected in such books and art-works as appear the most removed from public life and politics the spirit of the great world of government and commerce. For this world busies itself with matters that seem quite alien to the thoughts of many authors and artists. Often one detects in them a distinct note of protest or contempt for it, and therefore naturally supposes that it would be the last to have an influence on them. But struggle as men will, and persuade themselves as they may that they can rise superior to their environment, the facts are that the environment is sure to exert its good or bad effect sooner or later. Mr. William Morris, who is not only a ready and pointed lecturer on the decorative arts, but a highly popular writer of modern epics—not only an artist in decoration, but a successful business man, reflects, in spite of himself, the prevalent tone which his masters and associates assume toward that patient, if somewhat dull, monster, the public. It is true enough that he declares, in the lecture on 'The Lesser Arts,' with which the collection begins, that 'I, neither, when I think of what history has been, am inclined to lament the past, to despise the present, or despair of the future; that I believe all the change and stir about us is a sign of the world's life, and that it will lead—by ways, indeed, of which we have no guess—to the bettering of all mankind.' This is a sort of *Credo* which is all very well to make, but which is not borne out by the tone of the lectures. A low-spirited-ness, not to say a hopelessness, pervades all his remarks, and the very fervor with which he chants his creed at the outset makes one guess the hollowness of his belief. Against it set this statement in 'The Beauty of Life': 'The danger that the present course of civilization will destroy the beauty of life. These are hard words, and I wish I could mend them, but I cannot while I speak what I believe to be the truth.' And when he has done with outlining a somewhat formless and shadowy 'philosophy of the decorative arts,' and reaches practical matters, when he gives valuable suggestions in decoration of interiors in the fourth lecture, what does he call his address? 'Making the Best of It.' This, by all odds the most fruitful and encouraging lecture of the five, bears in its title the feeling of profound discouragement that exhales from every part of the book. It is merely, one may say, the Morris phase of the glorious British privilege of grumbling. But where there is chronic discontent, there is likely to be a persistent cause for discontent. Now, Mr. William Morris has, for himself, very little to complain of. There was doubt-less a time when he had not yet sold many editions of *The Earthly Paradise* in America and England, nor yet of *The Story of Sigurd the Volsung*, his translation of the *Æneid*, and other volumes of verse. And, at one day, Morris wall-papers had not invaded Anglo-Saxondom to such an extent that the classic bar-rooms of Leadville exhibited their peculiar designs above Eastlake dados. But what makes Mr. Morris now such a Jeremiah about architecture and decorative art? Is it that there are still many, many lords in Great Britain who need kicking? Or do the enormously rich bankers, manufacturers, and mine-owners excite his wrath? For, to tell the truth, the general impression got from his lectures is that obtained from the face of the Englishman whom Thackeray loved to pursue, note-book in hand—the impression that he could not be happy unless he were kicking some one, or being by some one kicked. But Mr. Morris ought to have not only the calm satisfaction of worldly success, but a conscience which tells him that in some respects at least, he has been an honor to his country—if not from the excellence of his wall-paper patterns, yet surely from the fact that he has not truckled with artistic snobbery, but has followed his natural bent and striven to be a highly educated First Artisan rather than a fifth-rate Royal Academician.

Others of the famous band to which Mr. Morris belongs have done more bragging and far less effective work. The preraphaelites had no more useful members than he—perhaps for the reason that in artistic matters his aim was not too high. The late Dante Gabriel Rossetti, for instance, although in many respects the leader in art and literature, is not likely to exercise in the long run an influence so wide-spread as Mr. Morris, because his audience is very restricted in comparison. As a painter, Rossetti must be slow in impressing workmen of other coun-tries, owing to the scarcity of his pictures, supposing them to have so much of the impressive quality as certainly belonged to his poems. John Addington Symonds is more comparable with Mr. Morris. His many-volumed and many-paged *Renaissance in Italy* shows, like these lectures, the impress of John Ruskin *minus* the irritating extravagance of the latter, but also *minus* the exciting quality. Now, both Rossetti and Ruskin appear to have had more power in swaying Mr. Morris's ideas of art than is healthful; they have encouraged him in the national malady of discontent, which itself undoubtedly arises from the national malady of misgovernment. We are told continually, and more here than in England, be it remarked, that Great Britain has the finest government on earth—in view of which it is singular that her art and literature are infected with a tone that can proceed from nothing else but a malady latent in the social fabric. Why these contemptuous letters, vilifications, outpourings of scorn from Mr. Ruskin? Why this grimace of seclusion on the part of Tennyson? Why the unfrank position held by the late Mr. Rossetti before the British public? And why all these whimperings from Mr. Morris, whom, as much as, if not more than, all these men, the publics have encouraged, supported, and enriched? It may be the prejudice of a foreigner that attributes these remarkable results to the unhealthy and anomalous state of affairs in the Mother Country, which still permits a dull and often immoral upper class to distribute fashions in politics, literature, and art, and to keep alienated and deprived of their rightful weight in public affairs and private society the strongest, healthiest, and cleverest portions of the population in the British Empire. It is this note that Mr. Oscar Wilde almost struck in the only poem strong enough to float a recent volume of verse,—'Ave Imperatrix',—and it is to the fact of his approaching it at all that must be attributed the arousing of that small measure of applause which he has recently forfeited by his ridiculous performance in the United States.

48. Unsigned review, *Athenaeum*

16 September 1882, no. 2864, 374–5

These lectures, by the author of *The Earthly Paradise*,—himself a practised decorator and artist, or rather, as he prefers to call himself, a 'craftsman,'—were delivered in Birmingham, London, and Nottingham. It would be difficult to give a general account of them, because they traverse very large and not very clearly defined fields of opinion; but it is easy to indicate what is their tendency, to praise their energy and common sense, and even to illustrate the occasional bits of whim, the genial dogmatism, and the poetic fancy which add not a little to their charm and secure for Mr. Morris the sympathy of his hearers. Excellent lectures have been delivered with earnestness equal to his, and yet have moved no one; and men as learned as our author have failed to make themselves heard; but even the truisms of Mr. Morris catch the ears of his audiences, and fix themselves in the memory of most of those who read his books.

The secret of Mr. Morris's success lies in the fact that the last thing he is thinking of is Mr. Morris. One of the first things he mentions—and he delights to repeat the declaration again and again—is his indebtedness to Mr. Ruskin. Speaking about 'The Lesser Arts' to a body of craftsmen, he justly calls attention to his text, which is taken from the writings of the first Oxford Slade Professor, and truly it is one the British workman has not by any means taken to heart, *i.e.*, the chapter in the second volume of *The Stones of Venice*, 'On the Nature of Gothic and the Office of the Workman therein.' The main subjects of these discourses are the honourableness, and above all the delight to the worker, of work honourably done. The intelligent exercise of the lesser arts will 'beautify our labour,' and the workman will take a pride in his work. 'No man,' adds Mr. Morris,

will any longer have an excuse for talking about the curse of labour; no man will any longer have an excuse for evading the blessing of labour. I believe there is nothing that will aid the world's progress so much as the attainment of this. I protest there is nothing in the world that I desire so much as this, wrapped up, as I am sure it is, with changes, political and social, that in one way or another we all desire.

Such optimism is in itself refreshing, even to those who refuse to believe with Mr. Morris that, in the ordinary sense of the words, Westminster Abbey, or even the church of St. Sophia, a much more probable example, was built, *i.e.*, designed or invented, by 'men like you and me, handicraftsmen, who have left no names behind them, nothing but their work.' This notion of the powers of the handicraftsman is put forward so often in these pages, that it is incumbent on a critic to challenge its truth, and even, in a practical way, its value. Briefly, then, let us say there is no proof that such craftsmen as those Mr. Morris addressed are, or ever were, or ever will be, capable of the feat attributed to them. That, if prepared by the practice of generations, a considerable number of the members of such an audience might, each man according to his powers, have borne a part in such a work is, of course, a truism. But that the splendid artistic motives of St. Sophia, or, still more, the perfect grace and dignity of the Abbey, were due, in the ordinary sense of the term, to what we call a handicraftsman, or any number of handicraftsmen, is little else than a charming delusion of an enthusiastic lover of his art and his kind. No proof of the lecturer's theory can be produced, and the analogies of history and recent experience directly contradict it.

Perhaps, however, Mr. Morris merely means that a modern professor of the artistic crafts or lesser arts may, if he follows the 'Lamp of Truth,' hope to have a share in the production of triumphs of design. Something to this effect appears, if we read it rightly, on pp. 55–7 of this book. Qualified as is the statement referred to—which we regret not to be able to quote—it is difficult to accept it in its entirety without large reserves. Still, much as we may demur to Mr. Morris's views of the sphere of the handicraftsman, it is impossible not to turn with pleasure to the wholesome passage which follows, and which describes eloquently the bearings of the lesser arts on many grand facts in human history:—

Now as these arts call people's attention and interest to the matters of everyday life in the present, so also, and that I think is no little matter, they call our attention at every step to that history, of which, I said before, they are so great a part; for no nation, no state or society, however rude, has been wholly without them; nay, there are peoples not a few, of whom we know scarcely anything, save that they thought such and such forms beautiful. So strong is the bond between history and decoration, that in the practice of the latter we cannot, if we would, wholly shake off the influence of past times over what we do at present.

[two sentences omitted]

When I think of this, and the usefulness of all this knowledge, at a time when history has become so earnest a study amongst us as to have given us, as it were, a new sense; at a time when we so long to know the reality of all that has happened, and are to be put off no longer with the dull records of the battles and intrigues of kings and scoundrels;—I say when I think of all this, I hardly know how to say that this interweaving of the Decorative Arts with the history of the past is of less importance than their dealings with the life of the present, for should not these memories also be a part of our daily life?

It may be that not one of the carvers whose exquisite work enriched the regal architecture of Westminster, not one of the mosaicists who spread glorious tints on the walls of St. Sophia—nay, not one of the designers to whom we owe these buildings, these immortal thoughts in stone—knew anything of the history of that which was past to them. This consideration, however, does not affect the justice of the demand made by Mr. Morris on the intelligence of the craftsman. If the views Mr. Morris enunciates can be impressed on the mind of the craftsman, they will undoubtedly ennoble his work. And the histories of the battles that marked the 'death days of empires,' and swept the workmen and their works into oblivion, may ultimately prove worthy of the attention of the typical craftsman in the intervals of his labour.

Having affirmed the value of the lesser arts, Mr. Morris proceeds to ask of his audience whether they will have these good things or whether they will cast them from them. He remarks—and it is impossible not to agree with him—that it is time such an audience answered these questions; and if they reply in the affirmative, that they should set about carrying their wishes into effect. The Decorative Arts are, our author says, in a state of anarchy which makes a sweeping change necessary and certain. He fears that the world 'will be clean rid in her impatience of the whole matter, with all its tangle and trouble.' To such a pass have matters come, through the neglect, falsities, and perfunctory performances of the handicraftsmen of this and recent generations. What is to be done? what shall those do who long for a reform in the arts? and in whom shall they seek to kindle an eager desire for beauty, and, better still, for the development of the faculty that creates beauty? Help is not to be had by making art 'the fashion,' as some have suggested. The only real help, says Mr. Morris, for the Decorative Arts must come from those who work in them; 'nor must they be led, they must lead.' Craftsmen must all be artists, and good artists, too, before the public at large can take real interest in what they produce. Commerce, 'which should be called the greed of money,' cannot and will not help. The handicraftsman must again join the artist, from whom he has been divorced, or rather with whom he has failed to keep up in the work of the world. How is he to do this and regain the place Mr. Morris believes the craftsman once occupied? He must, we are told, study nature and the history of art. What he has to learn of the former is so obvious to our author that he does not dwell upon it. We are not quite so sure of this, and indeed Mr. Morris qualifies the declaration with a 'now,' which would seem to indicate that he hopes to return to the matter by-and-by. The workman must study, and, above all, learn to understand, ancient art, lest the feebleness of the art about us should enfeeble him. The museums of London will help the seeker after beauty, and they ought to be open, we are told, seven days in the week, best of all on the seventh. Perhaps he had better study nature in the open air on one day at least. Preliminary instruction is needed to enable the visitor to use the national collections at their best. The 'ghost of the great church at Westminster' and the neighbouring hall will, smirched and falsified as they are, help the learner. English art, though not the biggest or the best of its kind, is, though limited, good and above all sincere. This advice is followed by a fine outburst against the Renaissance commonly so called, which 'over-seas'

had extinguished all nature and freedom, and art was become, in France especially, the mere expression of that successful and excellent rascality which in the flesh no long time afterwards went down into the pit for ever.

How the learner is to avail himself of the light of art may be gathered from the following:—

You will see by all that I have said on this study of ancient art that I mean by education therein something much wider than the teaching of a definite art in schools of design, and that it must be something that we must do more or less for ourselves: I mean by it a systematic concentration of our thoughts on the matter, a studying of it in all ways, careful and laborious practice of it, and a determination to do nothing but what is known to be good in workmanship and design.

The art of drawing should be taught to all, but 'designing cannot be taught in any school.' Drawing the figure is essential, at least it is the best mode of study. Such is the sum of the practical part of the counsel Mr. Morris has to give to working men desirous of bettering their condition, technically, morally, and artistically. It is advice offered by one who has done his utmost to carry his convictions into effect, and in several respects has not wasted his labour or spent himself in vain.

The remaining lectures are: 1, 'The Art of the People,' which has so close a relationship to the preceding lecture that it demands no separate criticism, although it is in no respect inferior; 2, 'The Beauty of Life'; 3, 'Making the Best of It'; 4, 'The Prospects of Architecture in Civilization,' which is not encouraging, although it is not hopeless. As to the style of these discourses, Mr. Morris would do well to rid himself of his taste for false archaisms and affected roughness of expression, which at the best are but whims unworthy of his powers.

49. Cloud-Cuckoo-Land in Hammersmith

1885

Unsigned article, *Saturday Review*, January 1885, lix, 43–4.

This lively article, entitled 'Nephelococcygia—*chez*—Hammersmith' (Cloud-Cuckoo-Land in Hammersmith) is an attack on Morris as a Socialist.

The evil communications of the *Pall Mall Gazette* having corrupted the good manners of the *Daily News*, the readers of the morning paper have nearly as good a chance as those of the evening one of an 'interview.' On Thursday last the *Daily News* interviewed Mr. William Morris—Mr. Morris, the poet, as he is sometimes called for distinction's sake. Here Mr. Dullman interrupts and says, 'Oh yes, you disapprove of interviewing, and you are going to write an article on an interview.' Precisely, Mr. Dullman, we disapprove of interviewing, and we are going to write an article on an interview. For, in the first place, the principle of hating the traitor, but making proper use of the results of his treason, is, if judiciously applied, a most proper as well as a most useful and ancient principle. And, secondly, though the interview is a silly, a vulgar, and a very inconvenient way of eliciting on one side or uttering on the other the views of any person on any subject, yet when those views are once put forth in print they become as much *publica materies* as the report of a trial or of a speech in Parliament or on the platform. If this argument is not good enough for Mr. Dullman, he shall have no better; indeed it is possibly disobedience to an invaluable precept of the Scriptures to give him any argument at all.

The *Daily News'* interviewer went to talk to Mr. William Morris about Socialism, and, with that strict equity which is natural to us, we shall admit that he reported the talking without any sauce of remarks about Mr. Morris's hair or his boots or the colour of his shirts, or anything of that kind. He, the reporter, confesses ingenuously that he has not given the 'fire and eloquence' of Mr. Morris's words, and we are happy to bear testimony to the strict truth of this statement. For so excellent an artist in English as Mr. Morris used to be, his utterances here recorded are curiously ineffective, though by no means less so than his written words in Socialist periodicals, since he left off poetry, which he understood, and took to politics, of which he knows nothing. Nor is the matter much better than the form. People who remember a certain correspondence in the *Standard* not many months ago may have faintly hoped that Mr. Morris would give the *Daily News'* interviewer some new lights on that very difficult point of conscience and conduct, the fact of a capitalist and 'profit-monger' denouncing capitalists and profit-mongers without, as far as is known, making the least attempt to pour his capital into the lap of the treasurer of the Socialist Church, or to divide his profits weekly with the sons of toil who make them. These things, apparently, it was not lawful to mention; at least Mr. Morris seems to have denounced profit-mongers quite easy and free, and the polite interviewer was as careful to abstain from any reference to wall papers as well-bred men in Mr. Chamberlain's company are said to be to avoid talking of a screw-steamer or a corkscrew, nay even of an election scrutiny, or a newspaper letter signed 'Scrutator.' This reticence does the highest credit to Mr. Morris's conscious innocence and to the fine feelings of the interviewer; but it perhaps deprives the interview of something of its piquancy. However, we must take interviews as we find them. In the first place, Mr. Morris wants 'an educated revolution.' We should say that the effect of education in any sense in which Mr. Morris can be supposed to use the word would infallibly be that nobody would revolute. But perhaps as a poet Mr. Morris has a finer insight into the connexion of cause and effect than we can boast. An interesting work just published informs us that Mrs. Annie Besant was led to discover the non-existence of God by meditations on the existence of whooping-cough, and after this singular version of tar-water and the Trinity, according to the kirk of the other complexion, all things become possible. Mr. Morris believes that 'the old order can only be overcome by force,' which is, by the way, so broad a hint that the old order should prevent itself from being overthrown by promptly 'scragging' the new, that, if we or any other wicked aristocrat cynics had given it, *Justice* would have shrieked at us. In order to compass this system of intelligent destruction on the banks of the Thames, Mr. Morris wants 'a body of able, high-minded, competent men.' When Mr. Heady and Mr. Highmind and Mr. Competent have assembled to the number (as it is stated in the orderly mathematical fashion which frequently distinguishes crazes of this kind) of two thousand, they are to preach a change involving 'a life in which every human being should find unrestricted scope for his best powers and faculties.' 'Je demande, Messieurs, je demande l'arresta-tion des coquins et des lâches'[1] was surely a small order compared with this. When Mr. Morris was young—and, if we may venture to say so, when he was not foolish—he wrote a delightful story about a person who painted God's judgments in purple and crimson. In what colours do you paint a life in which every human being, &c.? The colours of the lunar rainbow?

It is, however, consoling for the upper classes (and, the whole scheme being quite definite, it may be well for everybody to know that, according to the interviewer, but whether on Mr. Morris's authority or not is not quite clear, he is an upper class if he has more than 300*l.* a year, and in the millennium will be taxed accordingly) to feel that Mr. Morris would like to convert them too. He feels that they will take it fighting (we heartily hope he is right), but he would like them to be convinced beforehand that they have no business to fight. This, by the way, argues a very decent conception of strategy on Mr. Morris's part, for when you have got *Pallor* and *Pavor*,[2] and *Mens non conscia recti*[3] among your foes, then you can go in and win. But how the wicked 300*l.* a year upper classes are to be convinced of sin Mr.

---

[1] I demand the arrest of the rascals and the cowards.
[2] Two names of the God of Fear.
[3] A mind not conscious of right.

Morris did not inform the interviewer. Only he strenuously protested that it was quite a mistake to think that Socialism would be 'bovine toil in a drab universe.' That particular form of God's judgments will not, Mr. Morris says apparently, be painted in drab. The poet then cursed Free-trade and competition, and people who care for nothing but profits (here the temptation above referred to must have been awfully strong on the interviewer), and so forth. And he blessed Mr. Ruskin and the students' Socialist society in the University of Edinburgh. Radicals, we learn, 'must give up their Radicalism before they become Socialists,' which accounts for the sadly insufficient character of Mr. Chamberlain's Socialist orthodoxy. Another saying, which the interviewer found 'pithy,' was that in Germany Socialism was organized, powerful, and consistent, because 'the Reichstag is the only platform where German Socialism can assert itself; in England anybody can say anything anywhere.' This is by far the most telling tribute to freedom of speech that we ever remember to have seen. Then Mr. Morris comminated war and Colonial Federation (a device to keep up profit-mongering), and avowed that the working classes are not Jingoes. And he confessed that the Social Democratic Federation had unluckily had a little split, which is melancholy, but by no means contrary to precedent. And he summed up to the effect that 'the abolition of classes would tend to the general elevation of all society'; and that, 'when the change comes, there will be no discontented class left to form the elements of a new revolution.' In this last remarkable proviso timid persons may see an awful threat to which Marat's request for so many hundred thousand heads was mild, while others may chuckle over the guarantee which Mr. Morris thus gives that his revolution will arrive exactly at the same time as MM. les Coquecigrues.[1]

A Society for the Utter Abolition and Total Suppression of Discontent! Can it be possible that in any of the other seventy-four comedies *dont l'Eternal s'amuse*[2] a more amusing scene has recently been put on than the solemn formulation of such a project? Nobody has ever been able very clearly to understand the Socialist programme for doing away with classes or with property or with profits or with anything else except heads and the prosperity of a country. But even the lucubrations of that remarkable Socialist who not very long ago devoted much time and pains to the task of showing that the probable

---

[1] Non-existent birds; therefore, never.
[2] Which entertain the Eternal.

presence of more salmon than sprats or more sprats than salmon on the fishmongers' slabs in the co-operative communities of the future could be adjusted so as not to offend the principle of equality might turn pale if he were asked to organize the suppression of discontent. How is it going to be done? By the simple recipe of Mr. Lewis Carroll's queen, 'Off with his head'? Your poets are often terribly bloodthirsty fellows when they take to practical politics; but, if Mr. Morris is going to cut off the head of everybody who is discontented, he will suddenly be confronted with an appalling complication of the problem in the shape of discontent on the part of the executioners. No doubt the abolition of discontent follows on the discovery of a life in which every human being should find unrestricted scope for his best powers and faculties; or perhaps the discovery of a life, &c., follows on the abolition of discontent. To a choice of which pair of propositions or to both of them Mr. William Morris is heartily welcome.

'N'est-ce pas complet, ce désastre? N'est-ce pas artistiquement complet?'[1] asked Théophile Gautier pathetically enough in reference to his country's downfall and the misery and disarray of Paris and the destruction of his own chances of a quiet old age. Of another kind, no doubt, but not less artistically complete and rounded off, is this spectacle of the intellectual disaster of the intelligence of a man who could once write *The Earthly Paradise* and can now formulate these two propositions about the disappearance of all discontented classes and the change involving a life in which every human being finds unrestricted scope for his best powers and faculties. Mr. Morris cannot look out of his window, or into his looking-glass, or back over his life without seeing how flatly contrary to the whole course of nature and experience—a course with which the arrangements of society have nothing to do—is this cloud castle of his. His very arguments, or what he apparently gives for arguments, trip him up. One of his pithy remarks, according to the interviewer, was 'Competition develops its opposite—Socialism.' And would not Socialism develop its opposite—competition? All things are double, one against another is an uncommonly true saying, no doubt; but it is as true for one end of the pair as for the other. But, Socialism once gained, nothing apparently that has happened is going to happen any further; discontent having ceased, milk and honey having begun to flow, and everybody having been set down to the equal banquet (for ourselves, we do not like either milk or honey much, and are rather glad to think that

[1] Isn't it complete, the disaster? Isn't it artistically complete?

Mr. Morris's 'cultured' propagandists will probably have finished us by that time), the course of nature will be changed. 'The little hawks,' as Mr. F. W. Newman once rapturously put it in an argument against flesh-eating, will no more display their 'divine dexterity' in spitting the little larks; the mice will have one eternal game in the prolonged absence of the cat; the result of the taxation of all incomes over three hundred a year will enable the three-hooped pot to have ten hoops, and an Earthly Paradise (quite different from that which Mr. Morris used to sing so sweetly) will come into existence and never be disturbed by supply and demand, or human greed, or nature's grudging, or the laws of mechanics and chemistry. Now there are, doubtless, as an authority which Mr. Morris knows very well has it, 'Help-runes, Love-runes, and great Power-runes, for whomsoever will, till the world falls in ruin.' But we do not think that the counsel to send divers —that is to say, two thousand—young men, high-minded and well-educated to preach the abolition of discontent, and the importance of discovering a life in which every human being shall find unrestricted scope in the actual conditions of nature and human nature, is one of them.

THE ODYSSEY OF HOMER

1887-8

---

50. E. D. A. Morshead, two reviews, *Academy*

April 1887, xxxi, 299 and March 1888, xxxiii, 143-4

Morshead (1850-1912) was a classical scholar and translator who taught at Winchester. Each review is of one volume of the translation.

When, more than ten years ago, we were all of us reading the 'Lovers of Gudrun', and were dazzled by the strange new brilliancy of the unsetting sun of the North, many must have said that it would be a good day for English literature if the 'double might of hand' that had drawn Jason and Medea as unerringly as it had drawn Kiartan and Gudrun would turn to the one complete epic of Greece, and tell us, once for all, of the wanderings of Odysseus. It was something of disappointment, or at least of hope deferred, when Mr. Morris gave us the more elaborated, yet far less perfect, *Aeneid. Sigurd*, it is true, quenched all regrets for a time. If stronger or nobler poetry than its final portion has been written during the present century, I admit myself unable to name it. And now an instalment, at all events, of the long-desired *Odyssey* is in our hands; it is not to be thought of that it should remain an instalment. If the charm of writing it be, as it must be, even greater than the charm of reading it, Mr. Morris can surely not pause, still less desist; to do so would argue him more, or less, than human.

There is not, to my mind, any true criticism in mincing matters, in qualifying the good as abstractedly imperfect, or the bad as containing the potentiality of goodness. If to be reminded in every line of the Homeric method and fluency of narration; if to have the figures of

293

Odysseus, and Nausicaa, and Alcinous, acting and speaking with the same straightforward simplicity as they use in the original; if to find on every page lines that recall Homer at his best, and Mr. Morris's best work elsewhere; if to feel everywhere the sunlight 'of that old-world morn'—if, I repeat, the presence of these merits makes a good translation of Homer, then I think this is not only the best verse translation of any part of Homer that I have ever seen, but one of the best literary efforts, in this kind, that we possess. I do not say that it is faultless—there are tricks or mannerisms in it which recur somewhat artificially, not leaving on the mind quite the same effect as the recurrent phrases of Homer. And the question of the true metre for translating Homer, like the question of free will, 'finds no end, in wandering mazes lost.' But here is half the *Odyssey*, translated line for line, without serious omission or expansion, in the metre, and by the poet, of *Sigurd*.

But in opinions about poetry 'the mind of a man,' as Homer would say, 'fleets hither and thither, and ponders in divers ways.' It is high time to desist from giving judgments, and to show Mr. Morris's work, so far as may be possible, by extracts—with this proviso, that one of the special charms of his work inevitably evaporates in such a process—the charm of its consecutiveness. Everyone knows that of Homer, and especially of the *Odyssey*, this is the unique merit—that we pass from book to book, from the narrative about Odysseus to the narrative of Odysseus, with 'a free onward impulse.' Alone, perhaps, among epics, the *Odyssey* leaves us wishing there was more of it. Unless I am much mistaken, readers of this translation, apart from any knowledge of the original will feel the same.

Let us see Telemachus set forth upon his voyage (bk. ii., ll. 420–8) 'mid the sounds of 'wind, wave, and bark.'

> But Grey-eyed Athene sped them a happy wind and fair,
> The north-west piping keenly across the wine-dark sea.
> But Telemachus bade his fellows, and egged them busily,
> To gear their tackling duly, and they hearkened and so did;
> For into the mid-thwart's hollow the pine-tree mast they slid
> When up aloft they had raised it; then with forestays it they stayed,
> And hauled the white sails upward with ox-hide ropes well laid.
> With the wind the mid-sail bellied and the purple wave began
> To roar out aloud round the keel, as forth the good ship ran.

This has the very breath of the sea—the second line is pure Homer; the little thing one would wish altered is a word of which Mr. Morris is extremely fond—'egged'—which rather suggests surreptitious encouragement. Any one can see—or, rather, hear—how Mr. Morris varies the cadence of a metre which in less skilful hands is apt to have a certain un-Homeric monotony.

Let us match, against this departure, the landing of Odysseus upon Phaeacia (bk. v., ll. 391–405).

All dead the gale was fallen, and all was calm and clear,
And no breath of air was about; then he saw the land anear,
As he looked forth very sharply upraised on a swelling sea:
And as dear as the life of a father to his children seemeth to be,
Who in sickness hath been lying and wasting away for long,
And suffering grievous torment, and worn by the God of wrong;
But now the Gods release him, and his life is dear and good—
E'en so dear unto Odysseus was the sight of land and wood;
And he swam on stoutly, striving to tread the earth once more
But when at last he was gotten within shouting space of the shore,
Then indeed he heard the thundering of the surf on the reefs of the sea,
For flung forth on the rocks of the mainland the swell roared dreadfully,
And all things there were weltering in the salt-sea wave and the foam,
And therein was no haven for ships and no wind-free harbouring home,
But crags and jutting nesses and reefs by the sea washed o'er.

Has 'the surge and thunder of the *Odyssey*' ever sounded in finer English than this?

There is a more sombre land than sunny Phaeacia, and Circe shall point the way thither (bk. x., ll. 506–18).

Step the mast, and the white sails spread ye, and sit ye there beside,
And the breath of the wind of the Northward shall waft thee on thy way.
But when through the stream of Ocean thy ship hath passed on a day,
There, then, is Persephone's Grove in the long deserted land
Where the tall black poplars flourish and the fruitless willows stand.
There by deep-eddying Ocean haul up upon the bank,
And go thy ways unto Hades and his dwelling dark and dank,
Where the stream of Flaming Fire into Grief-River goes,
And the Water of the Wailing, a rill that from Hate-flood flows.
And thereby is a rock and the meeting of two roaring rivers wide;
Draw up thereto, O hero, and e'en as I bid thee abide.
There, then, a pit shalt thou dig of a cubit endlong and o'er,
And thereby the due drink-offerings to all the dead shalt thou pour.

It is impossible to make adequate extracts from the following book, the νέκυια,[1] where Odysseus does the bidding of Circe, and the images

[1] The book of the dead.

of the bodiless dead come thronging around him. It is perhaps the most powerful and pathetic scene in the whole of Homer, and it shows Mr. Morris at his best, if, as I think, his sympathy is deepest with the early wistful gaze of man into the spirit-world. If selection were to be made, perhaps the prophecy of Tiresias's spirit (xi., ll. 100–137), and the subsequent converse of Odysseus with Anticleia, would bear off the palm. But it must suffice to say so, and leave readers of the *Academy* to verify or disprove.

There is no table of errata appended. It may therefore be worth while to note some little flaws. In iii., ll. 148 and 190; in iv., l. 42; in xii., l. 59—there are slips, either of pen or press. In iii., l. 324, there is a misleading disorder of the words; in iv., l. 187, there is an awkward, though perhaps inevitable, attraction of 'him' for 'he'; in l. 841 αἰπύν[1] is rendered 'baleful,' which loses the force of the phrase; in vi., l. 24, the verb is assuredly ill-chosen; in x., l. 132, the grammar or punctuation is confusing; in xii., l. 82, φαίδιμε[2] is not exactly = 'lief and dear.'

A purist would perhaps find fault with the rhymes in i. 383–4; ii. 297–8; x. 171–2. The recurring use of the word 'flit' in the transitive sense of *making* fly, strikes one, writing apart from books of reference, as unusual; so does 'flockmeal' (x., l. 119), and 'dorsars' (vii., l. 96). Aegisth*us* is always Aegisth*eus*, one hardly sees why; 'the whale-great sea' for μεγακήτεα πόντον (iii., l. 158) is courageous, but suggests rather 'great as a whale' than 'full of great whales,' which is surely the meaning. Perhaps others besides myself will be ignorantly puzzled at 'heap up his howe' for σῆμα χεύω[3] (ii., l. 222, &c.), till the memory of the Maes-howe by the Stones of Stennis, in Orkney, comes to their rescue.

But let us end, as we began, by gratitude. There are many translations of the *Odyssey*, and several good ones; but time has brought us the best, from Mr. Morris.

In April, 1887, the present writer had the opportunity of expressing, in the *Academy*, the hope that Mr. Morris would not long 'leave half-told' the story of Odysseus. That hope has found fulfilment far sooner than, in such cases, is usual. There are few things, perhaps, on which people differ more widely than on the merits of a translation—and the reason is not far to seek. A masterpiece like the *Odyssey* possesses nearly every poetical merit that could be named; but it by no means follows that it presents each of those merits to each of its readers in an equal degree. We have instinctively a favourite literary quality, and we carry

---

[1] Steep, hard. [2] Brilliant. [3] To raise a mound.

into our reading of a translation an unconscious desire to find in it, above all things, that quality of the original which we prefer. We do not, perhaps, adequately examine ourselves whether what we like best in the *Odyssey*, or any such poem, is its highest quality—so hard is it, even with the aid of Homer, to cry 'Sursum mentes!' and rise above our lower to our higher appreciation. I recognise this so fully that I am half-ashamed that I cannot express any other opinion on Mr. Morris's second volume than that which I formed about his first. Of all verse translations of Homer that I have seen this seems to me to be the best, to have most of the matter and the manner of the original. But I am fully aware that a defective appreciation of the original, in matter and manner, will vitiate one's judgment of a translation. I know that good judges find Mr. Morris's version faulty, particularly in mannerism and the coinage of compound words in English. There is nothing for it but to plead one's plea, illustrate it as far as one may by extracts from the translation, state the qualities which it seems to share most fully with the original, and leave the verdict to the jury that is always sitting—the lovers of Homer.

The *Odyssey*, perfect as an epic, is, if possible, more perfect as a romance or fairy-tale. It bears, I think, a much stronger mark of individual genius than the *Iliad*. I never have felt any intrinsic difficulty in believing that certain parts of the *Iliad* are by a different hand or hands, while the *Odyssey* seems to me so intensely one as to make the idea that it is a compilation almost visionary; the art of collaboration would have reached the miraculous stage. And this individual genius in the *Odyssey* seems to me pre-eminent in the art of story-telling, of romantic narrative. We may prefer the *Iliad*, we may challenge the *Odyssey*, or any other poem, to match its best passages, its most memorable lines; but few will say, I think, that tale for tale, it is told with the perfect, simple, unconscious art of the *Odyssey*. It is finer in episodes; not so fine or complete as a whole. If this be so, the presence of this same skill in a translator would, in my own view, cover a multitude of minor sins. It is a *sine qua non*, though not the only one.

Secondly, for a verse translation, some approximation to the dignity and rapidity of the Homeric measure is essential. The couplets of Pope, the Spenserian stanzas of Worsley and Conington, form the high-water mark of what can be done in those directions; but the antitheses, the forced pauses, of the one, and the festooning of the separate stanzas, by the other, cancel a quality of the original which, as probably the translators themselves felt, even more keenly than their readers must feel can very ill be spared. Of the first of these two qualities—that of poetic power in romantic narrative pure and simple—Mr. Morris is completely master. I hazard the opinion that no English poet, since Chaucer, has possessed exactly this gift in so eminent a degree. There may be higher gifts, but this is a peculiar one that all can recognise and enjoy. It is the common quality in poems otherwise so widely different as 'The Lovers of Gudrun,' 'The Hill of Venus', 'Bellerophon in Lycia,' and this version of the *Odyssey*. Anyone to whom this gift conveys a special pleasure will find it hard to make much ado about the mannerisms which undoubtedly appear in Mr. Morris's style—defects on which a surely superfluous stress has been elsewhere laid. I do not myself admire, *e.g.* the rendering (book xiv., l. 73) of 'ὅθι ἔθνεα ἔρχατο χοίρων'[1] by 'where penned were the piglings' crew'; on the other hand, the much-criticised version of book xiii., l. 388— 'Τροίης λύομεν λιπαρὰ κρήδεμνα'[2] 'We loosed aforetime the shining coif of Troy,' seems to me exactly what Homer says, exactly the metaphor in which Euripides followed him, exactly a case in which Mr. Morris is both bolder and wiser than his critics. Let anyone read for himself the passages (pp. 294, 245) where these expressions occur, and judge if mannerism can be charged upon them as a whole. My strong impression is that half these 'mannerisms'—I do not say all of them—are more careful approximations to Homer's manner than some critics have discerned. As to the 'Phaeacians oar-fain' (p. 232, l. 36) for Φαιήκεσσι ἐιλήρετμοισι[3] what is the objection? We speak of a person as 'heart-sick,' of Carlyle as 'world-weary,' without scruple or blame; why may not the Phaeacians be 'oar-fain'? Homer calls them so by a compound, not a periphrasis. Suppose 'oar-fain' is not elsewhere used in English literature—well, somebody once used 'heart-sick,' or 'world-weary,' for the first time.

On the second point—the suitability of the metre of *Sigurd* as a representation of Homer—most people have made up their opinion one way or other. I cannot deny that, for translating Homer, rhyme is a fetter as well as a grace; that all rhyming couplets, in whatever metre, do break up 'the pure line's gracious flow,' the Homeric music, in some degree. The couplet, in fact, diverts our thoughts somewhat from the line or the paragraph—even Mr. Morris cannot overcome this

---

[1] Where a group of young pigs came.
[2] We loosed the shining head-dress of Troy.
[3] Oar-loving Phaeacians.

result, though at times (to repeat an illustration from vol. i.) he touches the actual harp of Homer.

> ἀκραῆ Ζέφυρον, κελάδοντ᾽ ἐπὶ οἴνοπα πόντον.[1]
> 'The north-west piping keenly across the wine-dark sea.'

The difficulty lies in the fact that rhyme inevitably balances two lines in some degree; and Homer never balances his lines.

But it is time to fulfil the pledge made above, and to be silent while Mr. Morris shows us, in English, his idea of Homer. Let the scene be the slumber of Odysseus, in the magical bark of the Phaeacians, while she speeds him over the sea for the last time (book xiii., ll. 19–32, p. 234)

> E'en then upon his eyelids did sleep and slumber speed,
> Sweetest, and most unbroken, most like to death indeed;
> But she, as over the plain the stallions' fourfold yoke
> Rush, driven on together by the whiplash and the stroke,
> And rear aloft and speed them, and easy way they make,
> So rose her stern on the sea waves, and following on her wake
> Rolled on the dark blue billow of the tumble of the sea:
> So all unscathed and steady she sped, nor swift as she
> Might fly the stark gerfalcon, the swiftest of all fowl,
> As swiftly running onward she cleft the sea-flood's roll,
> Bearing a man most like to the gods for his wisdom and guile,
> Who many a sorrow had suffered, and was soul-tossed on a while
> As he went through the warfare of men and the terrible deeds of the deep;
> But slept there now unfearful, and forgat all woes in sleep.

As poetry and translation, this must speak for itself; but one may say, in passing, what a scene is here for an artist! The slumbering chieftain and the men of Scheria in their mystic bark, not to see Scheria again! And the voyagings and toils of Odysseus, like that other weird of which Shakspeare wrote, are thus 'rounded with a sleep.'

The warning of Odysseus to Amphinomus, to escape from the imminent doom of the Wooers (book xviii., ll. 130–50, p. 333), seems to me at once one of the gentlest and one of the most impressive things in the *Odyssey*; nor does it suffer in Mr. Morris's hands:

> There is nought more mightless than man of all that earth doth breed,
> Of all that on earth breatheth and that creepeth over it.
> For while God giveth him valour and his limbs are lithe and fit,
> He saith that never hereafter the vale shall he abide;

---

[1] The fresh-blowing north-west wind murmuring (roaring) across the wine-dark sea.

But when the gods all-happy fashion his evil tide,
Perforce that load of sorrow his stout heart beareth then;
For in such wise still is fashioned the mood of earthly men,
As the Father of Gods and of menfolk hath brought about their day.
Yea, e'en I amongst men was happy in times now passed away,
And wrought full many a folly, and gave way to my heart's desire.
. . . Therefore indeed let no man in unrighteous fashion live,
But hold in peace and quiet such things as God may give.
But O me! how I see of the Wooers what fearful folly they plan,
Whereas the goods they are wasting, and shaming the wife of the man,
Who not for long I tell thee from his well-loved fatherland
Will yet be aloof; nay, rather e'en now he is hard at hand.
But thou—God lead thee hence, that this man thou may'st not meet
When he hath gotten him homeward to his land the dear and sweet;
For when under his roof he cometh, and they deal betwixt and between,
The Wooers and he, nought bloodless shall be the work I ween.

It is hard to read this without a touch of sorrow that not even so could
the courteous and kindly Amphinomus escape his doom and the
'mighty edge' of Telemachus' spear.

Every reader of *Sigurd*, with the 'Day of the Niblung's Need' in his
memory, will turn instinctively to book xxii, the Μνηστηροφονία.[1]
It is beautifully translated; yet I think that the physical horrors of the
slaughter—which Homer, in his direct simplicity, will not spare us—
do not altogether suit Mr. Morris's mood. He is better when his hand is
more at liberty, when he can show us the tossing strife in the hall of
Atli, with Gudrun looking upon it in the silence of many memories and
one great resolve. To the final scene, however, he gives all the Homeric
directness (book xxii., ll. 380–90, p. 411):

But about his house peered Odysseus, if yet a man there were
Who, shunning the black doom-day, was left a-lurking there;
But adown in the dust and the blood he beheld them all lying about,
Yea, as many as the fishes which the fishers have drawn out
With a net of many meshes from out the hoary sea
Up on to the hollow sea-beach; there heaped up all they be
Cast up upon the sea-sand, desiring the waves of the brine;
But the sun their life is taking with the glory of his shine.
Thus, then, in heaps the Wooers on one another lay.

Of minor criticisms I have not many to make. In vol. i. Mr. Morris
always wrote Aegisth*eus* for Aegisth*us*, in vol. ii. he insists (see book

[1] The killing of the suitors.

xxiv., *passim*) on calling them the Cephellenians, one sees not why. In book xiii., l. 166, the epithet δολιχήρετμοι[1] looks odd in the form 'long-oar-wont'; the word *ingates* = 'entrances' (p. 235) is certainly unfamiliar so, I think, is 'twi-car' (p. 268), and 'wrap,' in the sense of 'snatch' (p. 275); 'godless' hardly conveys, in English, the idea of 'unprompted by a god,' 'conveying no heavenly omen,' which is certainly the meaning of book xv., l. 531; in book xvi., l. 401, γένος βασιλήϊον κτείνειν[2] is something more than 'in a kingly house to kill'; there is a tendency to throw an apparently superfluous 'then' into the emphatic place at the end of the line (see book xvi., ll. 2, 421, &c.). The press seems to have made slips in book xvii., ll. 8, 207; there is something uncomfortable in the rhythm of ll. 69, 284, of book xiv., l. 87 of book xviii.; some awkwardness in the order of l. 62 of book xvi. But these are small matters. I can but conclude with repeating an opinion that this version of the *Odyssey*, now happily completed, is, not perfect but, worthy of the pen that wrote *Sigurd* and the *Earthly Paradise*. Few would desire higher praise.

---

[1] Using long-oars.
[2] To kill a descendant of a kingly race.

51. Oscar Wilde, unsigned reviews, *Pall Mall Magazine*

26 April 1887, xlv, 5 and 24 November 1888, xlvi, 3

The attribution of these unsigned reviews is given in the bibliography to Robert Ross's edition of Wilde, *Miscellanies* (1908), by Stuart Mason. The reviews are entitled 'William Morris's Odyssey' and 'Mr Morris's Completion of the Odyssey'.

I

Of all our modern poets, Mr. William Morris is the one best qualified by nature and by art to translate for us the marvellous epic of the wanderings of Odysseus. For he is our only true story-singer since Chaucer; if he is a Socialist, he is also a Saga-man; and there was a time when he was never wearied of telling us strange legends of gods and men, wonderful tales of chivalry and romance. Master as he is of decorative and descriptive verse, he has all the Greek's joy in the visible aspect of things, all the Greek's sense of delicate and delightful detail, all the Greek's pleasure in beautiful textures and exquisite materials and imaginative designs; nor can any one have a keener sympathy with the Homeric admiration for the workers and the craftsmen in the various arts, from the stainers in white ivory and the embroiderers in purple and gold, to the weaver sitting by the loom and the dyer dipping in the vat, the chaser of shield and helmet, the carver of wood or stone. And to all this is added the true temper of high romance, the power to make the past as real to us as the present, the subtle instinct to discern passion, the swift impulse to portray life.

It is no wonder then the lovers of Greek literature have so eagerly looked forward to Mr. Morris's version of the Odyssean epic, and now that the first volume has appeared, it is not extravagant to say that of all our English translations this is the most perfect and the most satisfying. In spite of Coleridge's well-known views on the subject, we have always held that Chapman's *Odyssey* is immeasurably inferior to his *Iliad*, the mere difference of metre alone being sufficient to set the former in a secondary place; Pope's *Odyssey*, with its glittering rhetoric and smart antithesis, has nothing of the grand manner of the original; Cowper is dull, and Bryant dreadful, and Worsley too full of Spenserian prettinesses; while excellent though Messrs. Butcher and Lang's version undoubtedly is in many respects, still, on the whole, it gives us merely the facts of the *Odyssey* without providing anything of its artistic effect. Avia's translation even, though better than almost all its predecessors in the same field, is not worthy of taking rank beside Mr. Morris's, for here we have a true work of art, a rendering not merely of language into language, but of poetry into poetry, and though the new spirit added in the transfusion may seem to many rather Norse than Greek, and perhaps at times, more boisterous than beautiful, there is yet a vigour of life in every line, a splendid ardour through each canto, that stirs the blood while one reads like the sound of a trumpet, and that, producing a physical as well as a spiritual delight, exults the senses no less than it exalts the soul. It may be admitted at once that, here and there, Mr. Morris has missed something of the marvellous dignity of the Homeric verse, and that, in his desire for rushing and ringing metre, he has occasionally sacrificed majesty to movement, and made stateliness give place to speed; but it is really only in such blank verse as Milton's that this effect of calm and lofty music can be attained, and in all other respects blank verse is the most inadequate medium for reproducing the full flow and fervour of the Greek hexameter. One merit, at any rate, Mr. Morris's version entirely and absolutely possesses. It is, in no sense of the word, literary; it seems to deal immediately with life itself, and to take from the reality of things its own form and colour; it is always direct and simple, and at its best has something of the 'large utterance of the early gods.'

As for individual passages of beauty, nothing could be better than the wonderful description of the house of the Phæacian king, or the whole telling of the lovely legend of Circe, or the manner in which the pageant of the pale phantoms in Hades is brought before our eyes. Perhaps the huge epic humour of the escape from the Cyclops is hardly realised, but there is always a linguistic difficulty about rendering this fascinating story into English, and where we are given so much poetry we should not complain about losing a pun; and the exquisite idyll of the meeting and parting with the daughter of Alcinous is really delightfully told. How good, for instance, is this passage taken at random from the Sixth Book:

But therewith unto the handmaids goodly Odysseus spake:

'Stand off I bid you, damsels, while the work in hand I take,
And wash the brine from my shoulders, and sleek them all around.
Since verily now this long while sweet oil they have not found.
But before you nought will I wash me, for shame I have indeed,
Amidst of fair-tressed damsels to be all bare of weed.'
So he spake and aloof they gat them, and thereof they told the may,
But Odysseus with the river from his body washed away
The brine from his back and his shoulders wrought broad and mightily,
And from his head was he wiping the foam of the untilled sea;
But when he had throughly washed him, and the oil about him had shed
He did upon the raiment the gift of the maid unwed.
But Athene, Zeus-begotten, dealt with him in such wise
That bigger yet was his seeming, and mightier to all eyes,
With the hair on his head crisp curling as the bloom of the daffodil.
And as when the silver with gold is o'erlaid by a man of skill,
Yea, a craftsman whom Hephæstus and Pallas Athene have taught
To be master over masters, and lovely work he hath wrought;
So she round his head and his shoulders shed grace abundantly.

It may be objected by some that the line

With the hair on his head crisp curling as the bloom of the daffodil,

is a rather fanciful version of

οὐλας ἧκε κόμας, ὑακινθίνῳ ἄνθει ὁμοίας,[1]

and it certainly seems probable that the allusion is to the dark colour of the hero's hair; still, the point is not one of much importance, though it may be worth noting that a similar expression occurs in Ogilby's superbly illustrated translation of the *Odyssey*, published in 1665, where Charles II's Master of the Revels in Ireland gives the passage thus:

> Minerva renders him more tall and fair,
> Curling in rings like daffadills his hair.

No anthology, however, can show the true merit of Mr. Morris's translation, whose real merit does not depend on stray beauties, nor is revealed by chance selections, but lies in the absolute rightness and coherence of the whole, in its purity and justice of touch, its freedom from affectation and commonplace, its harmony of form and matter. It is sufficient to say that this is a poet's version of a poet, and for such surely we should be thankful. In these latter days of coarse and vulgar literature, it is something to have made the great sea-epic of the South

[1] His hair flowed down like the hyacinthine flower.

native and natural to our northern isle, something to have shown that our English speech may be a pipe through which Greek lips can blow, something to have taught Nausicaa to speak the same language as Perdita.

II

Mr. Morris's second volume brings the great romantic epic of Greek literature to its perfect conclusion, and although there can never be an ultimate translation of either *Iliad* or *Odyssey*, as each successive age is sure to find pleasure in rendering the two poems in its own manner and according to its own canons of taste, still it is not too much to say that Mr. Morris's version will always be a true classic amongst our classical translations. It is not, of course, flawless. In our notice of the first volume we ventured to say that Mr. Morris was sometimes far more Norse than Greek, nor does the volume that now lies before us make us alter that opinion. The particular metre, also, selected by Mr. Morris, although admirably adapted to express 'the strong-winged music of Homer,' as far as its flow and freedom are concerned, misses something of its dignity and calm. Here, it must be admitted, we feel a distinct loss, for there is in Homer not a little of Milton's lofty manner, and if swiftness be an essential of the Greek hexameter, stateliness is one of its distinguishing qualities in Homer's hands. This defect, however, if we must call it a defect, seems almost unavoidable, as for certain metrical reasons a majestic movement in English verse is necessarily a slow movement; and, after all that can be said is said, how really admirable is this whole translation! If we set aside its noble qualities as a poem and look on it purely from the scholar's point of view, how straightforward it is, how honest and direct! Its fidelity to the original is far beyond that of any other verse-translation in our literature, and and yet it is not the fidelity of a pedant to his text but rather the fine loyalty of poet to poet.

When Mr. Morris's first volume appeared many of the critics complained that his occasional use of archaic words and unusual expressions robbed his version of the true Homeric simplicity. This, however, is not a very felicitous criticism, for while Homer is undoubtedly simple in his clearness and largeness of vision, his wonderful power of direct narration, his wholesome sanity, and the purity and precision of his method, simple in language he undoubtedly is not. What he was to his contemporaries we have, of course, no means of judging, but we know that the Athenian of the fifth century B.C. found him in many places difficult to understand, and when the creative age was succeeded by the age of criticism and Alexandria began to take the place of Athens as the centre of culture for the Hellenistic world, Homeric dictionaries and glossaries seem to have been constantly published. Indeed, Athenæus tells us of a wonderful Byzantine blue-stocking, a *précieuse* from the Propontis, who wrote a long hexameter poem, called *Mnemosyne*, full of ingenious commentaries on difficulties in Homer, and in fact, it is evident that, as far as the language is concerned, such a phrase as 'Homeric simplicity' would have rather amazed an ancient Greek. As for Mr. Morris's tendency to emphasise the etymological meaning of words, a point commented on with somewhat flippant severity in a recent number of *Macmillan's Magazine*, here Mr. Morris seems to us to be in complete accord, not merely with the spirit of Homer, but with the spirit of all early poetry. It is quite true that language is apt to degenerate into a system of almost algebraic symbols, and the modern city-man who takes a ticket for Blackfriars Bridge, naturally never thinks of the Dominican monks who once had their monastery by Thames-side, and after whom the spot is named. But in earlier times it was not so. Men were then keenly conscious of the real meaning of words, and early poetry, especially, is full of this feeling, and, indeed, may be said to owe to it no small portion of its poetic power and charm. These old words, then, and this old use of words which we find in Mr. Morris's *Odyssey* can be amply justified upon historical grounds, and as for their artistic effect, it is quite excellent. Pope tried to put Homer into the ordinary language of his day, with what result we know only too well; but Mr. Morris, who uses his archaisms with the tact of a true artist, and to whom indeed they seem to come absolutely naturally, has succeeded in giving to his version by their aid that touch, not of 'quaintness,' for Homer is never quaint, but of old-world romance and old-world beauty, which we moderns find so pleasurable, and to which the Greeks themselves were so keenly sensitive.

As for individual passages of special merit, Mr. Morris's translation is no robe of rags sewn with purple patches for critics to sample. Its real value lies in the absolute rightness and coherence of the whole, in the grand architecture of the swift, strong verse, and in the fact that the standard is not merely high but everywhere sustained. It is impossible, however, to resist the temptation of quoting Mr. Morris's rendering of that famous passage in the twenty-third book of the epic, in which Odysseus eludes the trap laid for him by Penelope, whose very faith in the certainty of her husband's return makes her sceptical of his identity when he stands before her; an instance, by the way, of Homer's wonderful psychological knowledge of human nature, as it is always the dreamer himself who is most surprised when his dream comes true.

Thus she spake to prove her husband; but Odysseus, grieved at heart,
Spake thus unto his bed-mate well-skilled in gainful art:
'O woman, thou sayest a word exceeding grievous to me!
Who hath otherwhere shifted my bedstead? full hard for him should it be
For as deft as he were, unless soothly a very God come here,
Who easily, if he willed it, might shift it otherwhere.
But no mortal man is living, how strong soe'er in his youth,
Who shall lightly hale it elsewhere, since a mighty wonder forsooth
Is wrought in that fashioned bedstead, and I wrought it, and I alone.
In the close grew a thicket of olive, a long-leaved tree full-grown,
That flourished and grew goodly as big as a pillar about,
So round it I built my bride-room, till I did the work right out
With ashlar stone close-fitting; and I roofed it overhead,
And thereto joined doors I made me, well-fitting in their stead.
Then I lopped away the boughs of the long-leafed olive-tree,
And, shearing the bole from the root up full well and cunningly,
I planed it about with the brass, and set the rule thereto,
And shaping thereof a bed-post, with the wimble I bored it through.
So beginning, I wrought out the bedstead, and finished it utterly,
And with gold enwrought it about, and with silver and ivory,
And stretched on it a thong of oxhide with the purple dye made bright.
Thus then the sign I have shown thee; nor, woman, know I aright
If my bed yet bideth steadfast, or if to another place
Some man hath moved it, and smitten the olive-bole from its base.'

These last twelve books of the *Odyssey* have not the same marvel of romance, adventure and colour that we find in the earlier part of the epic. There is nothing in them that we can compare to the exquisite idyll of Nausicaa or to the Titanic humour of the episode in the Cyclops' cave. Penelope has not the glamour of Circe, and the song of the Sirens may sound sweeter than the whizz of the arrows of Odysseus as he stands on the threshold of his hall. Yet, for sheer intensity of passionate power, for concentration of intellectual interest and for masterly dramatic construction, these latter books are quite unequalled. Indeed, they show very clearly how it was that, as Greek art developed, the epos passed into the drama. The whole scheme of the argument, the return of the hero in disguise, his disclosure of himself to his son, his terrible vengeance on his enemies and his final recognition by his wife, reminds us of the plot of more than one Greek play, and shows us what the great Athenian poet meant when he said that his own dramas were merely scraps from Homer's table. In rendering this splendid poem into English verse, Mr. Morris has done our literature a service that can hardly be over-estimated, and it is pleasant to think that, even should the classics be entirely excluded from our educational systems, the English boy will still be able to know something of Homer's delightful tales, to catch an echo of his grand music and to wander with the wise Odysseus round 'the shores of old romance.'

52. Mowbray Morris, unsigned article, *Quarterly Review*

October 1888, clxvii, 407–8

In the course of an article on Matthew Arnold, the critic took the chance to condemn Morris's *Odyssey* in Arnoldian terms.

Mowbray Morris (1847–1911) was a man of letters and editor of *Macmillan's Magazine*.

It is impossible to read these passages without one's thought straying for a moment to one who has violated these first principles, as they may be called, of Homeric translation more persistently and notoriously than did any of the translators from Chapman downwards who are reviewed in these Lectures. By this clumsy travesty of an archaic diction, Mr. William Morris, in his translation of the *Odyssey*, has overlaid Homer with all the grotesqueness, the conceits, the irrationality of the Middle Ages, as Mr. Arnold justly says that Chapman overlaid him; but with this difference, that this grotesque manner was natural and common to the Elizabethan writers, and to Chapman in particular; with Mr. Morris it is but an extreme form of that affectation which plumes itself on despising the thoughts, manners, and needs of its own time, and is, in effect, the most odious shape that false culture can assume. And thus, in spite of his own genuine poetical faculty,—and in what measure this is, or at least was, his, every one knows who has read his beautiful and noble Epic of *Jason*—and in spite of some really fine and vigorous passages, where his sense of poetry and his own good sense have triumphed for a time over the ignoble fetters imposed on them, Mr. Morris has only succeeded in producing the most signal monument of the eccentricities and caprice of an age so fruitful in both.

53. Edward Dowden : 'Mr. Morris has found a faith'

1888

Dowden (1843–1913) was Professor of English Literature at Trinity College, Dublin. He contributed frequently to the *Academy*. In *Transcript and Studies* (1888) he included an article 'Victorian Literature' in which he expressed relief that Morris had escaped from his 'unheroic melancholy' into faith—even if in Socialism.

Rossetti escaped from reality to romance, yet at a serious cost; and the life which should have been so full and joyous to the end was saddened and turned awry. He escaped through his imagination from a world of turmoil and dust, of strife and greed, of commerce and manufacture, of vulgar art and conquering science; he escaped for there was little in him of the passion of the reformer to overcome his repugnance, and bid him stand fast and do battle with the world. Mr. William Morris, as seen in his earliest volume of poems—a volume full of beauty and strangeness—might appear to have much in common with Rossetti.

Romantic beauty and chivalrous passion and tragic-picturesque situations attract him, and where can he find these in our work-a-day world? Miles and Giles and Isabeau, Constance fille de fay, and fair Ellayne le Violet, are infinitely more pleasing company than Thomson and Johnson and Jones. The blue closet, the little tower, the ancient walled garden 'in the happy popular land,' are far more delectable places for a lover of romance than the fields and streets of our nineteenth century. In the *Earthly Paradise*, though he may claim to be more than the idle singer of an empty day, and to lay ghosts, in truth the author lays no ghosts that haunt the hearts and brains of modern men. Nor is he in any but a superficial sense a disciple of Chaucer. The ride to Canterbury on breezy April mornings to the sound of jingling bells or the miller's bagpipe, under the conduct of jovial Harry Bailly, and in company with a parson who wrought and taught Christ's doctrine, and a ploughman inspired with the hearty benevolence of a Hercules, is all unlike the foiled search of an earthly paradise by weary wanderers. In what soft western land to which they have come without purpose or design, the disappointed questers, now grown old, exchange their northern stories with the old men of the city for stories of Greece. And month blooms and fades into month, and season into season, and at last death comes and makes an end alike of joy and sorrow. An unheroic melancholy, a barren autumnal sadness, broods over the whole poem. The flame of passion and endeavour rises up and sinks down again into coldness and ashes, and our eyes follow the brightness and dwell upon the gloom with a strange, enervating, æsthetic satisfaction. We come to hate death, not knowing what it means, and to love life, though of it we know even less; and the earth and heaven are but as a curtain hung around a narrow room in which play and laughter and weeping are heard; and last of all there is silence. Such poetry (and all the more because it comes from a spirit robust and vigorous in its sympathy with human passion) is in truth the poetry of despair.

But since *The Earthly Paradise* was first imagined Mr. Morris has found a faith. His heartiness of nature would not permit the passion of the reformer to remain dormant within him; his quarrel with the present time is acute; he still dreams indeed of an earthly paradise, but now he sees it afar off in the Socialist millennium. Though we get from Mr. Morris no original verse comparable with that of his earlier volumes, and though we may doubt of his millennium, we cannot but rejoice that he has quitted that strange dreamy western land, and stands a singer of hope in the streets of London. At least as a protest against the greeds and cruelties and unloveliness of the present there is a worth in lines which tell his dream of the future:—

> Then all *mine* and all *thine* shall be *ours*, and no more shall any man crave
> For riches that serve for nothing but to fetter a friend for a slave.
> And what wealth then shall be left us when none shall gather gold
> To buy his friend in the market, and pinch and pine the sold?
> Nay, what save the lovely city, and the little house on the hill,
> And the wastes and the woodland beauty, and the happy fields we till;
> And the homes of ancient stories, the tombs of the mighty dead;
> And the wise men seeking out marvels, and the poet's teeming head;
> And the painter's hand of wonder; and the marvellous fiddle-bow,
> And the banded choirs of music: all those that do and know.[1]

Better, far better, *Chants for Socialists* with faith, however inadequate for the wants of the soul, and hope and charity, than the *Earthly Paradise* with all of life a melancholy dream.

[1] From 'The Day is Coming', the first of Morris's *Chants for Socialists*.

SIGNS OF CHANGE

1888

54. Unsigned review, *Saturday Review*

19 May 1888, lxvi, 607–8

Entitled 'The Earthly Inferno', this review is thoroughly hostile to
Morris's new political commitment.

We wish we could introduce Mr. William Morris, the poet, to Mr.
William Morris, the political revolutionist, between whom there has
long been alienation. The one might learn a great deal from the other.
The author of the lectures printed under the title of the *Signs of Change*
would find his dreams—half idyllic, half bloodthirsty—rebuked in
advance by the more truly inspired wisdom of the poem the title of
which, by a happy irony, he appends to his name at the front of this
work. Mr. Morris, like the wanderers whose illusions and sufferings
and failure he told in noble verse, has himself set out in search of an
earthly paradise. Like them, having passed through much affliction, he
would find, if he had his way, that he had arrived at a place very
different from that of his dreams. He might find himself in an earthly
inferno. 'So,' as a poet he knows sings, 'with the failing of our hoped
delight, we grew to be like devils.' Mr. Morris, in the volume before
us, describes a state of things which does not exist, and proposes, as a
cure for it, a state of things which could not possibly exist. With a
certain artistic sense, in which he is not likely to be wanting, he darkens
his picture of the present in order to heighten the charms of the dream
of the future which he displays before his own duped vision. He writes
as if the disclosures which have been made before the Lords' Committee
on the sweating system gave a true picture of our industrial organisation, though they really apply only to four trades subject to very special
conditions.

Society, according to Mr. Morris, is divided into two classes; robbers and the persons whom they plunder, masters and slaves. These two classes are commonly called employers and labourers, or capitalists and workmen, but their moral relation is, in Mr. Morris's view, best expressed by the terms which he uses. Labour produces everything, and is, therefore, entitled to everything. But as labour cannot be set to work without capital—which supplies it with the means of livelihood while the products on which it must subsist are in the process of creation, and with the instruments, such as tools, machinery, buildings, in and by which it works—it is absolutely under the control of capital, and must submit to the terms which the capitalist imposes. As the capitalist, too, must live, and as he cannot eat spinning-jennies nor clothe himself with steam-engines, it might occur to Mr. Morris that he is as much in the power of the labourer as the labourer is in his power, and that the terms master and slave, plunderer and plundered, might be converted. The number of the labourers, and their competition with each other for work, compels them, in Mr. Morris's view, to accept such wages as are compatible with bare and comfortless existence. But competition is not entirely on one side. If the competition of labourers tends to lower wages, the competition of manufacturers tends to lower prices, and the labourer, who is the maker of one thing and the purchaser of many, finds the good and evil at least balanced. It further tends to equalize wages in different employments, which, as Mr. Mill points out, is a result of competition in harmony with the Socialist ideal. Further, there is a competition of employers for labourers, of which the result is to raise wages. That competition leads to adulteration and the production of articles cheap and nasty is true; but there is a competition also in excellence of quality as well as in vileness, and the action taken by the State through armies of inspectors in the protection of the purchaser in derogation of the maxim *caveat emptor* enforces this better competition.

These are truisms, but it is necessary to re-state them when they are questioned by sciolists or denied by demagogues. The grave fact, however, remains. Are the English labouring classes in the position of starved, ill-clad, miserably housed, over-worked, and mentally impoverished destitution which is alleged? There is some incongruity in bringing Mr. Giffen's facts and researches into juxtaposition with Mr. Morris's dreams. Mr. Morris speaks of over-production for the sake of profit to the employer leading to exhausting over-work on the part of the labourers. Mr. Giffen has pointed out that a relative decline in the material productions of English industry is due in some degree to the success with which the labouring classes have enforced shorter hours of labour, and their disposition, to use his phrase, 'to take things easy,' a state of mind which is in some degree in harmony with Mr. Morris's socialistic ideal. So far are things from going from bad to worse that of late years an increase of population has been accompanied by a decrease of pauperism; the deposits in savings banks and the number of depositors—chiefly working men and the tradesmen depending upon working men—have greatly increased. As these savings represent a surplusage of earnings over spending Mr. Morris's theory of starvation wages, or wages little above starvation point, is scarcely in harmony with the facts. Mr. Morris advocates his socialistic reconstruction of society, which is mostly borrowed from Fourier, for this reason, among others, that the organization of labour would leave leisure for the innocent recreations and elevating pursuits of life. Mr. Giffen has pointed out that there is a steady increase among the self-supporting population of the country of the classes devoting themselves to art, science, literature, amusements, and education. This fact exhibits a tendency in the direction of Mr. Morris's desires.

The fact is that, under the system of competition, the evils which Mr. Morris would abolish by Socialism are gradually curing themselves. To this fact Mr. Morris carefully shuts his eyes, or, when he cannot shut his eyes, he closes his mind. He denounces gradual reforms as leading men away from his own remedy of violent revolution. He looks forward, as possibly 'the best we can hope to see,' to a time when 'the struggle, getting sharper and bitterer day by day'—it is becoming less sharp and less bitter day by day—'will break out openly into a slaughter of men by actual warfare instead of the slower and crueller methods of peaceful commerce. If we live to see that, we shall live to see much; for it will mean the rich classes grown conscious of their own wrong and robbery, and consciously defending them by open violence; and then the end will be drawing near.'

Like some of his predecessors of the French revolutionary period, Mr. Morris mingles with his bloodthirsty aspirations dreams of a land flowing, not so much with milk and honey as with milk and water, of a society in which fellowship shall supersede mastership, in which men shall play at work and work at play, and society shall be dissolved in a sickly, spoony, and languid sentimentality which would probably issue in a hate like that of the soliloquist in the Spanish cloister. This, of course, is not his statement; it is our rude but faithful translation. For ourselves we believe that he entirely mistakes human nature. Sir William Grove's speculations are not necessary in order to show that antagonism is the law of the world, that conflict and competition are essential to the development of an energetic manliness of character, that the relations of men to each other are naturally and necessarily those of leaders and followers, masters and servants, of rivals and not of fellows in Mr. Morris's lackadaisical sense of the term—a sense incompatible with real comradeship and hearty goodwill.

In conclusion, may we commend to Mr. Morris his own earlier wisdom:—

> Dreamer of dreams, born out of my due time,
> Why should I strive to set the crooked straight?

He has endeavoured to build 'a shadowy isle of bliss amidst the beatings of a steely sea,' unconscious of what he once knew, that 'its ravening monsters mighty men must slay,' if they are to be slain, 'not the poor singer of an empty day.'

55. Unsigned review, *Today*

November 1888, x, 153–4

Today was the journal of the Fabian Society, which was hostile to the Marxism of the Socialist League and of Morris.

Mr. William Morris is about the only Socialist who can write with the pleasing certainty that his literary productions will be read; and, therefore, there lies upon him a weight of responsibility from which all we ordinary scribblers are delightfully free. Unfortunately the burden sits but airily on his brawny shoulders, and his utterances on the platform are apt to smack too much of the 'hare-brained chatter of irresponsible frivolity.' When such deliverances are made to a Socialist audience, who knows him and who overlooks the eccentricities of the lecturer in its liking for the man, or to a roomful of 'cultured' and curious persons who having seen the picturesque figure of the author of *The Earthly Paradise* go away satisfied, and forgetting all that they have heard, the amount of harm done is a minus quantity. But when he takes to publishing his views it is a different matter; for many of them are such as, if taken to represent the opinions of Socialists generally, would go far to render Socialism a subject of mockery to sane men and women. For instance we gather from the little volume before us (*a*) that the author *desires* to bring about a civil war (p. 46), and to create suffering for the purpose of intensifying discontent (p. 48), and rejoices in the fact that the Socialists are still only a sect and not yet a party (p. 52). Now we have no hesitation in saying that if once the hard-headed English workmen, on whose action the future of their class depends, came to believe that these ideas of Mr. Morris' were in any degree representative, the present by no means un-brilliant prospects of Socialism in England would vanish like a dream, and all the good work of the last few years would be worse than undone. Happily no such mistake is likely to be made, so far at any rate as the workmen are concerned; for the rapid conversion of so many of our writers and lecturers to political methods has left Mr. Morris almost alone in the possession of his peculiar views. The effect of this change has been immensely to raise his value to us. Just in proportion as the importance of the active propagandist declines so does the value of the poet and artist appreciate. Some of Mr. Morris' best services to Socialism may be seen in the Arts and Crafts Exhibition in Regent Street, some of his worst in the volume before us.

On the historic and art critical essays in it we do not care to say very much. Providence not having endowed us with those gifts of infallibility and universal knowledge which it has conferred on most other reviewers we have a, doubtless foolish, diffidence in criticising the works of specialists. But we would venture humbly to protest that things artistic are hardly in quite so parlous a state as Mr. Morris appears to think. If we have lost the mediæval cathedral we at least have the nineteenth century oratorio and opera. The art of the architect and builder has been replaced by that of the composer and executant. Whether the world has lost or gained by the change is of course a matter of taste. The fact is that when our Socialist artists and critics set about wailing over the 'Decline of Art' they use the term in much too restricted a sense. To mention no other branch of art it seems to us that the age which has produced Dickens and George Eliot, Balzac, Thackeray, Zola and George Meredith, has little to fear from comparison with any of its predecessors. Of course the fact that we have good music and good landscapes, good novels and good portraits, is no reason why we should have hideous public buildings and drawing-room decorations which set the teeth on edge; but it is a reason why we should not be perpetually whining, however tunefully, about the 'Decline of Art.' To sum up, Socialists will do well to buy Mr. Morris' latest book for they will derive thereupon much pleasure and some profit, but they had better keep it to themselves and not lend it to their, as yet unconverted, acquaintances.

A DREAM OF JOHN BALL

1888

56. Unsigned review, *Pall Mall Gazette*

16 March 1888, xlvi, 3

Dreams are apt to be capricious and disappointing. They turn from summer to winter, from comedy to tragedy, from exultation to despair, in the twinkling of a bedpost. We cannot complain, then, when Mr. Morris's *Dream of John Ball* suddenly changes from a romance into a lecture; yet we cannot but deplore the transformation. For the romance is charming, the lecture commonplace. A statement of economic history from a Socialist point of view is not rendered more luminous or more impressive by being couched in the form of a prophecy, and punctuated with exclamations of surprise. To those who are already familiar with this interpretation of events, Mr. Morris's *Short History of the English People* is simply dull. Those, on the other hand, to whom the doctrine is new, will scarcely find it clear or convincing. A plain and ordered statement would serve their purposes better. But the romance—ah, that is a different affair! So far as it goes, it is full of the vision and the faculty divine. Nothing can be simpler than its matter. The dreamer dreams himself in a Kentish village on a summer afternoon, five hundred years ago. Standing at the market cross, he hears the hedge-priest John Ball, newly freed from the Archbishop's prison at Canterbury, address the insurgent peasantry, attributing the ills of the time to 'cruel men fearing not, and kind men daring not, and wise men caring not, and the saints in heaven forbearing.' The speech is interrupted by the approach of a body of arbalestiers and men-at-arms, headed by the sheriff and certain knights. The peasants, among whom are many doughty longbowmen, prepare to receive them warmly, and, after a sharp tussle, come off victorious. The dead are carried to the village church, while the living prepare for their march towards London on the morrow; and throughout the summer night, John Ball and the dreamer keep watch in the chancel beside the bodies of friend and foe. It is now that the dream turns into a prophetic lecture accepted by John Ball as a message from 'the King's Son of Heaven.' The moon sets and the sun rises, and thus the dreamer ends his prophecy:—

Then shall those things, which to thee seem follies, and to the men between me and thee mere wisdom and the bond of stability, seem follies once again: yet, whereas men have so long lived by them, they shall cling to them yet from blindness and from fear; and those that see, and that have thus much conquered fear that they are furthering the real time that cometh and not the dream that faileth, these man shall the blind and the fearful mock and missay, and torment and murder; and great and grievous shall be the strife in these days, and many the failures of the wise, and too oft sore shall be the despair of the valiant; and backsliding, and doubt, and contest between friends and fellows lacking time in the hubbub to understand each other, shall grieve many hearts and hinder the Host of the Fellowship: yet shall all bring about the end, till thy deeming of folly and ours shall be one, and thy hope and our hope: and then—the Day will have come.

Nothing can be more delightful than Mr. Morris's picture of the Kentish hamlet, nor anything more vivid, in the midst of its dreamlikeness, than his description of the battle. In prose, no less than in poetry, Mr. Morris has a genius for suggesting beautiful things. His prose, if not quite regular according to composition-book rules, is a strong and supple literary instrument. He treats language as a plastic material, to be kneaded, not chiselled or cast. We can plainly trace the influence, every here and there, of the sagamen whom Mr. Morris has studied so lovingly. The book, too, is not without a touch of his poetic quality, in the shape of a spirited song sung by the Kentish yeomen, with the refrain:

> Bent is the bow on the lily lea,
> Betwixt the thorn and the oaken tree.

'As they sang,' writes the dreamer, 'a picture of the wild woods passed by me, as they were indeed, no park like dainty glades and lawns, but rough and tangled thicket and bare waste and heath, solemn under the morning sun, and dreary with the rising of the evening wind and the drift of the night-long rain.'

Mr. Burne-Jones's frontispiece illustrates the distich:

> When Adam delved and Eve span
> Who was then the gentleman?

Graceful though it be, the design suggests a new reading.

Who was then the husbandman?

Anything more amateurish than the grand old gardener's manner of digging it would be hard to conceive. Yet his spade is primitive only in the sense of being ineffectual.

THE HOUSE OF THE WOLFINGS

1889

57. Unsigned review, *Saturday Review*

26 January 1889, lxviii, 101–2

The review takes the form of a parody of the more obvious characteristics of the prose style (and typography) used in the
romances.

The tale tells that in times, whether long past or near at hand it skilleth
not, there was found in the land of the Beefings, which is compassed
by water, and in the town called of Lud, a wondrous Lamp which
lightened the nations. And the light of it was renewed every seven
days on the last day of the week, and for that the Lamp itself was
called the Day of Saturn. But some there be that give other rede of
that name, for they say it was called the 'Day' because it lightened the
nations, and 'of Saturn' because oftentimes the light seemed hard and
harsh to them of little worth and skill, and that the god Saturn is
fabled to have been no easy god of temper. But the Lamp was served
by a chieftain whom they called Out-giver (for in this tongue everything is called something else), and it was his to watch it and to order
its light and to do the services that befell. And of these services not
the least, God wot, was to sally forth against certain wights which sent
Books in numbers from what men called the press. And to deal therewith Out-giver had with him a stout following of champions, and
they were girt each with two swords. And the name of the one was
Fool-queller, and the name of the other was Praise-giver. And whatsoever man Fool-queller bit, that man went anguishing for many days;
but on whose shoulder soever they laid Praise-giver, proud man was
he for the rest of his life. And for the light that the Lamp shed on

321

evil men's ways and the sharp bitings of Fool-queller there were that loved not the Day of Saturn; howsoever, the more folk and the wiser did set great store by it.

Now it fortuned that one day Out-giver sat by the pulleys and gear of the Lamp, and his champions with him, and the good mead-horns did their good office. Then said Out-giver:—'Men of mine, there is a new book which cometh from one William Morris, and well ye know the man. Verily of a time all good men loved him; for he made runes and rhymes that bewitched men's hearts, and, as he sat in the Square of the Queen, he fashioned high seats for the hall, and crocks of cunning ware, and hangings for the daïs, and mighty windows of many colours for the Minster. A great man he was and a great tale was told of him. But, when he had left the Square of the Queen and had betaken himself to the Street that goeth toward Oxenford, and thereafter, behold wealth or wayward wit, or the will of the Godfolk that feast otherwhere in their merriment, did sore things with this William, so that he became, yea almost as the other William, whose name is to menfolk and Godfolk accursed. And he sought out evil-fellowship and he spake foolish words, and he herded with the Hind-ings and the Cunnings of Ham, and the wight that is named Burns (but not the Sagaman) and other losels. Yet still in the making of books the man is no mean man; and what shall we do with this?'

So there spake unto him one of the mightiest of his champions, who could drive Fool-queller into the hardest skull and wield Praise-giver so deftly that the touch thereof was as honey to the tongue and as the down of swans to the skin. And he said, 'I will meddle not nor make with these runes of William. For behold he has fashioned strange letters for this his book, and the reading of it maketh the eyes to burn and rankle, and withal I loved him once and I fear to love him less now. So, therefore, this adventure is not for me.'

And Outgiver turned to another; and he said, 'And what sayest thou?' Now this man was of less fame than the first, and his skill of fence was less cunning, and there were who loved him not. Yet it was said of him that never had he feared the face of book, save it were the book of a friend that he could not praise, or the book of a foe that he needs must blame. And he said 'Give it me,' and they gave it, and he saw that of Fool-queller there would be no need that day, yet not wholly would the matter be the wielding of Praise-giver. And the rest of his dealings with the book of William Morris, the weaver of webs for the wealthy and the singer of songs for the wise and the foolish, ye shall read in another tongue. For of a truth it is well that each should speak in his own tongue, and not in that which is not his own, if haply it ever were the tongue of any man.

Some of the characteristics of *The House of the Wolfings* may be gathered from the foregoing preamble, and if the weapon which our plagiarist or mimic has called 'Fool-queller' had to be used at all, it is towards these characteristics that it would be directed. It has pleased Mr. Morris to employ types which we can best describe as a kind of modified blackletter, and of which our printers shall give such specimens as they can:—

𝕿he tale tells that in times long past there was a dwelling of men beside a great wood. Before it lay a plain, not very great, but which was, as it were, an isle in the sea of woodland, since even when you stood on the flat ground, you could see trees everywhere in the offing, though as for hills, you could scarce say that there were any; only swellings-up of the earth here and there, like the upheavings of the water that one sees at whiles going on amidst the eddies of a swift but deep stream.

Thus does Mr. Morris make his e's and his o's and his great T's. Now, as a matter of archaism, this is very pretty; but as a matter of actual eye-pasture for persons whose eyesight is not quite that of the gay goshawk, it is extremely tormenting. We can only say that, after reading *The House of the Wolfings*, which is by no means long (scarcely two hundred small quarto pages), our own eyes smarted and dazzled in the most uncomfortable fashion, and that everybody to whom we have submitted the book experienced the same sensation. Secondly, the specimen will have shown also that Mr. Morris has got, if possible, almost more archaic in style than ever, even in prose (of which and of verse the volume is almost indifferently made up). Personally we do not mind this much; though there are some persons of excellence who do. But we own that Mr. Morris's angular e's and o's have made us nearer to taking their point of view than we ever were before.

That there are condolences and vails, however, to those who can taste Mr. Morris at all is a mere matter of course, whenever the author of 'Rapunzel' and 'The Watching of the Falcon' leaves the politics, in which he is so singularly to seek, alone, and betakes himself, in whatever queer guise, to the art of poetry, which he knows so well. The *Seizain* (if there were no such word, we should hereby invent it; but it has good authority) on the title-page has so much of that dreamy melody which penetrated the *Earthly Paradise* itself, and especially its introductory verses, that we must quote it whole:—

> Whiles in the early Winter eve
> We pass amid the gathering night
> Some homestead that we had to leave
> Years past; and see its candles bright
> Shine in the room beside the door
> Where we were merry years agone
> But now must never enter more,
> As still the dark road drives us on.
> E'en so the world of men may turn
> At even of some hurried day
> And see the ancient glimmer burn
> Across the waste that hath no way;
> Then with that faint light in its eyes
> A while I bid it linger near
> And nurse in wavering memories
> The bitter-sweet of days that were.

This is the only piece of modern speech in the book, and it happens also to be printed in good legible capitals, instead of in the eye-torturing Gothic letter of the text. That text itself tells, to put the argument very briefly, of the strife of the Markmen with the Romans, and their victory, at the cost of the life of their own chiefs. Extremely exact or cautious scholars may say, perhaps, that Mr. Morris, in meddling with the dangerous words 'mark,' 'mote,' &c., has taken hypothesis occasionally for evangel; but there is no very great harm in this. The descriptions of the dwelling and House of Wolfings, and of their prophetess maiden, the 'Hall-Sun' or guardian of the great Lamp, and of the loves of Thiodolf, the War Duke, and a strange lady of the wood, and of the wiles of 'Fox' the scout, of the 'Hall-Sun's' meeting with her mother, and, lastly, of many excellent fights between the Markmen and the children of the She-Wolf, their namesakes of another blood, are all good reading for those who can attune their ears. Here, for instance, is a passage where the matter and form are alike good, when the cæsura is duly marked and the proper swing of the verse given. It is not so good as the last fight of Sinfiötli in the opening of *Sigurd the Volsung*, but may please some tastes better:—

In many a stead Doom dwelleth, nor sleepeth day nor night:
The rim of the bowl she kisseth, and beareth the chambering light
When the kings of men wend happy to the bride-bed from the board.

It is little to say that she wendeth the edge of the grinded sword,
When about the house half builded she hangeth many a day;
The ship from the strand she shoveth, and on his wonted way
By the mountain-hunter fareth where his foot ne'er failed before:
She is where the high bank crumbles at last on the river's shore:
The mower's scythe she whetteth; and lulleth the shepherd to sleep
Where the deadly ling-worm wakeneth in the desert of the sheep.
Now we that come of the God-kin of her redes for ourselves we wot,
But her will with the lives of men-folk and their ending know we not.

As we pass on we come to a piece of conduct on Thiodolf's part
which it were well if certain Englishmen minded at Souakim and
elsewhere:—

But it must be said that when the foemen turned their backs, and the chase
began, then Thiodolf would nowise withhold his might as in the early battle,
but ever led the chase, and smote on the right hand and on the left, sparing none,
and crying out to the men of the kindred not to weary in their work, but to
fulfil all the hours of their day.

For thuswise would he say and this was a word of his:
Let us rest to-morrow, fellows, since to-day we have fought amain!
Let not these men we have smitten come aback on our hands again,
And say 'Ye Wolfing warriors, ye have done your work but ill,
Fall to now and do it again, like the craftsman who learneth his skill.'

One more extract, and we can commend the book to those for whom
it is fitted. It is from the last interview of Thiodolf and the 'Wood-
Sun,' his divine or half-divine love in the past. She comes to him on
the eve of the fatal battle in black raiment, barefooted and ringless, the
'thrall of sorrow':—

Thou sayest it: I am outcast; for a God that lacketh mirth
Hath no more place in God-home and never a place on earth.
A man grieves, and he gladdens, or he dies and his grief is gone;
But what of the grief of the Gods, and the sorrow never undone?
Yea verily I am the outcast. When first in thine arms I lay
On the blossoms of the woodland my godhead passed away;
Thenceforth unto thee was I looking for the light and the glory of life
And the Gods' doors shut behind me till the day of the uttermost strife.
And now thou hast taken my soul, thou wilt cast it into the night,
And cover thine head with the darkness, and turn thine eyes from the light.
Thou wouldst go to the empty country where never a seed is sown
And never a deed is fashioned, and the place where each is alone;
But I thy thrall shall follow, I shall come where thou seemest to lie,

I shall sit on the howe that hides thee, and thou so dear and nigh!
A few bones white in their war-gear that have no help or thought,
Shall be Thiodolf the Mighty, so nigh, so dear—and nought.

These are good rhymes, as old Mr. Pope used to say.

58. Henry Hewlett, review, *Nineteenth Century*

August 1889, xxvi, 337–41

A particularly appreciative response to the romance, by the
critical reviewer of *Sigurd* (No. 43).

Your invitation, my dear Editor, gives me a welcome opportunity of
recognising the special claims to notice of Mr. William Morris's *House
of the Wolfings.* None of his recent writings will be generally read, I
think, with more unqualified pleasure. His genius has always seemed
to breathe most freely in the atmosphere of prehistoric or semi-historic
mythology, whether Gothic or Greek, and the subject of his present
choice happily affords scope for illustrating certain characteristic conceptions which the Gothic and the Greek minds held in common. For
the material framework of his epic he has resorted to Northern Europe
at the time of the earliest Roman invasion, when the Gothic communities upon the banks of the Elbe kept their primitive institutions of
Mark, Thing and Folk-mote unchanged; when totemism and exogamy
were still inviolate customs, and the grim religion of Odinism maintained its hold upon the affections and satisfied the aspirations of its
believers. The spiritual motives and human interest of the story are
independent of time and place, and turn upon the eternal conflict
between Love, Fate and Conscience, the doubtful issue of which is
finally determined by the 'stern lawgiver' Duty. The level of the prose

narrative is broken at frequent intervals by waves of ballad-verse, appropriate to the utterances of the chief speakers, and occasionally varied by lyrical outbursts of more impassioned feeling.

The tale opens with a graphic picture of the idyllic life led in time of peace by the Wolfings, a great family of the Mark Kindreds, amid the forest-clearing beside the Mirkwood water, where it had fixed its seat. Prominent in this picture is the homestead or Roof of the clan, externally 'framed of the goodliest trees of the wildwood ... and clay wattled with reeds;' internally fashioned church-wise, with a central nave or hall, separated by two rows of pillars from its aisles, and having a daïs at the further end, above which hangs the Hall-sun, a holy lamp ever kept burning by its appointed guardian, the fairest maiden of the house. On a summer evening, when the foremost warriors are grouped on the daïs round their mighty chief Thiodolf, with his supposed foster-daughter, the guardian of the Hall-sun, beside him, the quiet scene is disturbed by the sudden arrival of a swift runner, bearing a 'ragged, burnt, and bloody arrow,' the symbol that summons the Marksmen for united defence against a common danger. The invaders, described as a 'Welsh,' or foreign, race of fierce marauders from the Southlands, prove to be an army of the Romans, hitherto known only by report as a formidable foe. The tidings of its approach at once rouses the watchful and warlike Goths, and Thiodolf, mustering them to arms, announces that on the morrow he will march at their head to the assembling-place of the Kindreds.

While the rest spend the eve of departure in preparing their battle-gear, in feasting, or sleep, he enters the forest to keep a moonlight tryst with his love, 'the Wood-sun,' one of the Valkyrie, or Choosers of the Slain. An immortal 'daughter of the Gods,' but passionate and tender as a mortal woman, she had given her heart to his youthful beauty and hardihood, twenty years before, when at the victorious close of a single-handed combat with three champions of the Huns, he was found by her sinking from exhaustion, and restored to life and love. Their union, of which the Hall-sun's guardian was the offspring, yet remained secret. At this interview she tells him of her forebodings that the coming contest is pregnant with the doom of his death and her own desolation, unless he consents to avert it by wearing a charmed hauberk she has brought for his protection. Disdainful of danger, he strives to dispel her fears, but without avail. His chivalrous scruples to enjoy an immunity his fellows-in-arms cannot share, and his avowed mistrust that the finely-wrought mail (wherein he recognises the handiwork of the man-hating dwarfs) carries some unkindly spell, are quieted by her assurances that, though chief of the Wolfings, he is not of their kin, but sprung from the Gods, like herself, and that no evil glamour lurks in her gift; and he agrees reluctantly to accept it.

At the folk-mote of the Marksmen he is chosen by general acclaim first war-duke of the host; but, impressed by the warning of an ancient seer who discovers an ill omen in the hauberk, he doffs it before encountering the enemy. Tidings that the Marksmen have triumphed in their first engagement, and that Thiodolf, though unmailed, has escaped without a wound, is brought to the women at the Wolfing-stead, where the Hall-sun's guardian, who inherits her mother's gift of partial prescience, has been impelled to utter troubled visions of alternate victory and disaster. Among the listening women is the disguised Wood-sun, who, in renewed alarm for Thiodolf's safety, proceeds to recover the hauberk from the place where he had left it, and seeks another meeting with him in the forest. Redoubling her fond entreaties that he will not court the fate which menaces their love by refusing to wear the hauberk, and spurning by an indignant protest his doubt lest care for his own life should involve unknown peril to the Wolfings, she exacts his promise to consent. In the ensuing conflict the Marksmen, despite their stout defence and skilful tactics, are worsted and baffled, and the invaders, taking a circuitous route through the forest, reach the Wolfingstead, which (the women having fled at their approach) they strongly entrench. Thither the Marksmen quickly return to attack them, and the armies encounter beside the river. At the moment of onset Thiodolf suddenly drops his great sword, 'Throng-plough,' and falls swooning, though unsmitten, to the ground. Borne off the field by his comrades, he recovers from the swoon, but remains dazed in mind, without a clear sense of his obligations as war-duke, or his habitual eagerness for victory, but dreamily conscious of his longing for the Wood-sun, whom he imagines near him. The Goths, bewildered by his unwonted mien, fight with heavy hearts. When, rousing himself by a desperate effort, he plunges into the fray and again falls swooning, they are driven back, and only escape destruction owing to the indecision of the Roman captain.

During the breathing-space that follows this battle the guardian of the Hall-sun, who has fathomed the secret of her birth, and the mysterious curse her mother has invoked, interposes to save her father from dishonour and the Wolfings from ruin. Bringing about a last interview between her parents, she insists with affectionate frankness upon the alternatives before them, adjuring her mother to think what it will profit,

> That after the fashion of Godhead thou hast gotten thee a thrall
> To be thine and never another's whatso in the world may befall;

and bidding her

> mighty father make choice of death in life,
> Or life in death victorious and the crownèd end of strife.

Rising under the stress of this appeal to her spiritual height, the Wood-sun confesses the deception born of her love, whereby she had sought to ward off the stroke of doom, and laments the miserable failure of her scheme:

> If my hand might have held for a moment, yea, even against his will,
> The life of my beloved! But Weird is the master still!

Knowing that the hauberk (which one of her sisterhood, enamoured of a mortal, had once obtained by fraud from a malignant dwarf) would confer protection upon the wearer at the cost of his forfeiting power as a leader, she had blindly sacrificed all other interests to the desire of saving Thiodolf's life. But the helpless man, whom she has so spell-bound that he owns his willingness to abandon duty and ambition for her sole sake, is not the hardy warrior of her ideal. The sight fills her with self-reproach, and she bids him doff the hauberk. He obeys, and in a moment regains his true manhood. Putting away as a shameful dream the illusion of an unheroic and disloyal life which her glamour had wrought, but pardoning her fond deceit as venial in one 'of the God-kin, because they know not the hearts of men,' he bids her take comfort in the proud memory of his 'scorn of death,' and the conviction that, though awhile sundered, 'our love hath no end.' With this tender farewell, unshaken by her 'bitter wailing,' he passes to the field. Reinspirited by his presence, the Marksmen rally their forces, surround the Romans in their entrenchment, and carry the four gates by storm. After a fierce struggle round the Wolfingstead, which the besieged in their desperation set on fire, the besiegers burst into the hall in time to quench the flames, slaughter or capture the garrison, and rescue their prisoners. Thiodolf, meeting the Roman captain on the threshold, spurns him with an unarmed hand, but receives his sword-stroke in the heart and dies at the climax of victory.

Owing perhaps to familiarity with them in the legendary literature of Greece and Judæa, stories of immortal lovers of mankind, of rare minds gifted with prophetic insight, and the enchantments of evil spirits, appear the least unreal of all forms of mythus. In Mr. Morris's epic these elements are blended so skilfully with historic and pictorial realism that the *vraisemblance* is almost perfect. Some intermixture of ancient and modern thought was of course inevitable in dealing with moral motives, but for the most part the keeping of the Gothic ideal is admirably sustained, and the features wherein its mental type resembled the Greek, its abiding sense of the mastery of Fate, and bold yet not irreverent handling of religious beliefs, are brought out with great force. Many delicate vignettes of landscape, stirring scenes of action, and vivid portraits brighten the sombreness and relieve the pathos of the main design. The prose is a pure draught from 'the well of English undefiled,' and its prevailing archaism stops far short of pedantry. The verse is simple and strong, unblemished by the faulty accentuation and diffuseness of diction which too often mar one's enjoyment of *The Earthly Paradise*. Single lines occur of striking vigour, such as that which describes the hauberk:

This grey wall of the hammer in the tempest of the spear.

Alike in its healthiness of moral tone, imaginative truth, and artistic skill, *The House of the Wolfings* seems to me to mark a distinct advance in the quality of Mr. Morris's work.

59. Unsigned review, *Atlantic Monthly*

June 1890, lxv, 851–4

An appreciative review of the American edition of 1890.

Mr. Morris is a long-practiced story-teller, and in the present tale he employs a very perfect art. It is a narrative of the summer campaign between a gathering of Gothic Marksmen and some Roman legionaries who were making a foray into their country. It begins with a pastoral scene, disclosing the clearing along the river, in which the House of the Wolfings stood, above the meadows and pasture, and hemmed upon the other side by the Wild Wood. Thither comes the tidings of the threatened invasion, borne by the runner with the war-arrow; and immediately the action of the piece commences with the arming of the people, the setting forth of the host, joined by the contingents from other villages, each under its own banner, and the grand folk-mote of all the kindreds at the chief meeting-place of the entire clan. There leaders are chosen, and, the reports of scouts and stragglers having given warning that this new enemy, the Romans, is near at hand, part of the host goes out to meet them. The first ambuscade and the first battle are won by the Goths; but the main body of the Romans has meanwhile taken the country on the flank, and, passing the open ways by guides, has fallen on the House of the Wolfings itself. The Goths follow, upon these tidings, and by two lines of march come up with the Romans, after which there is much various fighting, ending in the overthrow and destruction of the entire Roman force in the Wolfing stronghold. This is the material part of the narrative, and the opportunities it affords for scene-painting, landscape, and battle, under conditions strange to us, are fully availed of.

With all this, however, mingles another poetical element. Thiodulf, the war-duke of the host, is loved by a goddess, the Wood-Sun, and by her has had a child, now grown to womanhood, who is the priestess of the people, and called the Hall-Sun, because she cares for the lamp that is kept burning continually under the roof of the House of the

Wolfings. The Wood-Sun knows that her lover, Thiodulf, will be slain in these wars, and she has gained by stratagem a hauberk which, wrought by the Dwarfs, will preserve his life if he will wear it; but a curse goes with it, and the warrior will be saved only by the loss of his cause and people. The Wood-Sun does not tell of this, but Thiodulf is fearful of some such charm, and leaves the hauberk with the Daylings, and succeeds against the Romans, until the Wood-Sun again intervenes, and, obtaining the hauberk by disguise, tells Thiodulf there is no harm in it, and persuades him to wear it. The consequence is that in the thick of the battle and at its crisis the chief is overcome with faintness, and loses his opportunity and the day. The Goths, defeated, retire into the Wild Wood. Thiodulf's daughter, the Hall-Sun, who has the second-sight, has now discovered the cause of the trouble, and by her intervention the Wood-Sun confesses to Thiodulf her lie, bids him take off the magic armor, and though seeing the end of their love in his approaching death, yet consents to it. Next morning the storm of attack begins under Thiodulf, now restored to his full faculties, and in the moment of victory he dies. In this portion of the plot lies the ethical element of the narrative, and out of it grows the supernatural element, of which much is made in the characters of the Wood-Sun and the Hall-Sun, through whom the life of the people is brought into relation with destiny and the gods.

We have chosen to give the outlines of the story as the best way of exhibiting to the reader the varied character of the saga; and if he is familiar with Mr. Morris's handling, he will perceive at once that this is a story after the poet's own heart, and that in it wide scope is given for the special traits of his genius. Something must be added, to make the matter clear, concerning the literary style and mould into which the poetry is run. The larger portion is prose, but the speeches are usually given in verse. The prose itself, however, is not ordinary prose, but is written in a peculiar and artificial style, well sustained, but having the effect to remove the work out of the domain of prose. Though measured, it is not rhythmical to any such degree as to arouse a particular metrical expectation in the reader, and it thus escapes the principal defect of so-called poetical prose. On the other hand, it brings about an illusion akin to that worked by ordinary verse form. It is very beautiful in its general movement and color, and very noble in phrase; its affectation, even, sympathizes with the Gothic element in the work itself. It is such prose as only a poet could write, and it does effect what the poet intended. Those who hold that prose is not the best medium for poetical thought will easily find objections to the poet's method; independently of all that, he succeeds in his aim. The test of his experiment lies rather in the question whether, having chosen this form, he should not have kept to it, whereas, as has been said, he has put the speeches, as a rule, into rhymed verse. The answer seems to us to depend on whether or not the change is natural in its place, and maintains the illusion already obtained by the prose. For ourselves, we must acknowledge that this change appears in each instance arbitrary, and also that at the moment of the transition the illusion is destroyed, and recurs only after an interval, and then in the different form of poetical expression. The poems, so to speak, are as much a change as it would be in an English book to find extracts in French. Not only is continuity broken, but consistency is lost. This, however, is an individual impression, and is apposite rather to the question, which has been raised, whether Mr. Morris may not have illustrated in this work a new literary form of mingled prose and verse, with a future development before it, analogous to the old and now well-worn forms of the epic and the drama. It does not appear to us that this is any other than a hybrid product of art, or that it contains in itself any principle by which the repugnance and incongruity of prose and poetry as modes of expression can be harmonized. Prose has been written in a poetical spirit before now, and has produced the illusion here sought for. This is of a lower intensity and less reality than the illusion of the epic or the drama; and in this work it does not show more power.

Within the limits which Mr. Morris has set for himself by his choice, the work itself is one of extraordinary beauty in detail, and rich both in minute and broad effects. The author's characteristics shine through his words, as must be the case in creative literature; and, most prominent of all, the artistic nature is clear. Each of his chapters becomes, sooner or later, a picture, admirably grouped, lovely or grand in its unity, but with that care for light and shade and posture, even for costume and framework, which discloses the artist: sometimes there is but one figure, sometimes there is a throng; now the scene is under the sunshine of the clearings, often in the shadow of moonlight or the thicket; here a stormy dawn, there a midsummer afternoon; but throughout there is the pencil of the artist. This quality in his work is especially felt in the heightening of the external beauty of the home surroundings of the Goths, in the carving of the woodwork of the House of the Wolfings, in the contents of their chests of precious stuffs and jewels, and generally in the manual decoration of the properties which he has chosen to use. Out of all this comes, in part, the singleness of impression and the poetical illusion which are implicit in the narrative, and in part, also, the sense of artificiality and tenuousness of fact, which will be felt even by those who lend themselves most willingly to the poet's magic. A second trait is the strong expression of the social union of the Marksmen as one people, generally most powerfully brought out in the speeches of Thiodulf as their leader, and of the Hall-Sun as their 'soul' (so she calls herself); their tribal self-consciousness, as an evolutionist would say. The delight of Thiodulf in the thought that his life, through his deeds, will live on and become immortal in their destiny as a folk among men springs certainly from a modern feeling, or gains by it; so that the doctrine of the brotherhood of men in races and kindred, and their duty to society as a part of a larger life, has seldom been so nobly and almost triumphantly expressed. The source of this in Mr. Morris is not far to seek. The great shadow of the English race is also cast backward to make this little body of a few thousand warriors loom larger on the confines of our history. So one may detect separately many of the strains that the poet has woven into a tale which is an expression of emotions and beliefs and tastes that are more vital now than they were in the days of the Roman border wars. In one point Mr. Morris has been extraordinarily successful. We have been told in books of the position and character of the women of the Goths, and from these hints he has worked. The Hall-Sun is the idealized type of this womanhood; in the story she does not stand alone, but is surrounded by a throng of companions, unlike other women in poetry, with a kind of heroism, dignity, and serviceableness, which lends a main element of attraction to the narrative.

Criticism, however, does but half its work in making such a volume known, and discriminating between the several elements of which it is compounded. It is a harder task to give any appreciative account of the charm of the story; of its inventive power; its northern sense of life and strength and the delight of action; its simple handling of many adventures; its broad, clear sketches of the borderland of the forest, and of existence in its quiet glades and by the river; the picturesqueness of its trophies and emblems; the aloofness of its gods; the naturalness of its superstitions, and, more particularly, of the phrase and measure in which all this is set forth in color, and landscape and the murmur of a people's life. For these we refer the reader at once to the volume, in which he will find, after all criticism, one of the few contributions of our present time to imaginative literature.

THE ROOTS OF THE MOUNTAINS

1890

60. Unsigned review, *Spectator*

8 February 1890, lxv, 208–9

A vigorous attack on Morris's archaic language.

This is a good thing spoilt. Had Mr. Morris been content to tell us about the men of Burgdale, 'their friends, their neighbours, their foemen, and their fellows-in-arms,' in a style which would be easily comprehended of the ordinary plain person, the freshness and novelty of this attempt to reconstruct the Pagan ideal of rural life would have pleased where it now only exasperates. From beginning to end, the story is written in what a critic has happily called 'Wardour Street English.' Mr. Morris disdains to use a good English phrase, no matter how old, that is still current. It is his constant endeavour to unearth the archaic, or to coin some quasi-archaic phrase. Thus, he disdains to use the expression 'great with child,' and must needs talk of women 'big with babes;' and reaches the *reductio ad absurdum* of his method by his avoidance of the homely but expressive figure, 'as the crow flies,' in order to substitute for it some laborious periphrasis. He will not talk of shooting with, but *in* the bow. People are not buried, they are 'borne to mound.' This studied research of the antique sometimes leads Mr. Morris into positive error. His disinclination to use the term 'track' induces him to talk of the 'slot of men.' Now, unless we are greatly mistaken, the term 'slot' not only never is, but never was, correctly used of men. It is surely the object of a writer of a simple tale of primitive life to appeal to a wide circle of hearers. But Mr. Morris curtails his circle very considerably by using a lingo which to many people would prove unintelligible. Take one passage: 'Within these

335

houses had but a hall and solar, with shut-beds out from the hall on one side or two, with whatso of kitchen and buttery and out-bower men deemed handy.' Ordinary persons who are not skilled in the Wardour Street dialect will be fairly stumped. This may be vulgar, but Mr. Morris drives us into Philistinism by such words as 'eme,' 'mazer,' 'carline,' 'flockmeal,' 'heft-sax,' 'sackless,' 'flatlings,' and the like. 'Come hither,' says one of the characters on p. 37, 'and handsel him self-doom for thy fool's onset.' It is a sort of travesty of that laboriously simple and artfully artless work, Professor Freeman's *Old English History for Children*. This, then, is the first great blot on the work, that it is not written in dialect, and yet requires a glossary. What would an ordinary novel-reader know about 'handselling' a person 'self-doom'?

Another drawback is a lack of clearness in the descriptive passages. The opening chapter which tells of the geography of Burgdale is so bewildering that one longs for a good map. The book ought certainly to have been illustrated. Then it must be admitted that the names are a trifle irritating,—*e.g.*, Penny-thumb, Face-of-God, Bristler, Wood-wicked, Woodwont, Bowmay, Spearfist, God-swain, Wolf-stone, and the like. As to the story itself, into which we found it necessary to read ourselves with a good deal of effort, it is infected with the same spirit of miscellaneous archaism as the style. Burgdale is a strange composite of Scandinavian and Homeric elements. Its inhabitants lived in a pre-Christian age, but they dwelt in much plenty and ease of life, and were exceedingly strong in their arts and crafts. We do not gather that they had umbrellas, but the 'foul-weather weed,' worn by Face-of-God is evidently nothing more nor less than an overcoat,—to use an un-Wardour-Street-worthy neologism. Moreover, they were not alto-gether unacquainted with the usages of the operatic stage, and at appropriate moments would declaim and sing in preference to adopt-ing a prose narrative style. They also possessed fiddles, evidently of the most orthodox pattern, and—except for the absence of such vulgar products of civilisation as railways, steamers, and telegraphs—were as refined and cultivated as the people of to-day, only that their womankind were more athletic, and capable of fighting like veritable Amazons. In fine, we are almost drawn to believe that *The Roots of the Mountains*, so far from being an attempt to reconstruct a Saturnian age, is nothing else than a poetical sketch of the Morrisian Millennium. It falls in, curiously enough, with what Mr. Morris said the other day in a lecture as to the ideal sort of life that people ought to live when Socialism carries the day. Still, this may be a mere coincidence, and

Mr. Morris may have had no end in view save that expressed in the graceful lines on his title-page,—lines greatly superior to any of the other poetry in the book. He says:—

> Whiles carried o'er the iron road
> We hurry by some fair abode:
> The garden bright amidst the hay,
> The yellow wain upon the way,
> The dining men, the wind that sweeps
> Light locks from off the sun-sweet heaps—
> The gable grey, the hoary roof,
> Here now—and now so far aloof.
> How sorely then we long to stay
> And midst its sweetness wear the day,
> And 'neath its changing shadows sit,
> And feel ourselves a part of it.
> Such rest, such stay, I strove to win
> With these same leaves that lie herein.

That is a real picture, and all of us have experienced the longing, and can sympathise with an author in his attempt to people a landscape with the creatures of his imagination. The result has been, in our opinion, only partially satisfactory, owing to the causes we have mentioned above; but there are still many happy descriptive touches, and the characterisation in two or three instances is simple and effective. We may quote one passage in which the hero, who is rather a blunderer in his love-affairs, is informed by his betrothed, on her learning that he is in love with another woman, that she will take it upon her to announce the severance of their troth:—

Then she held her peace a long while, nor did he speak one word: and they were so still, that a robin came hopping about them, close to the hem of her kirtle, and a starling pitched in the apple-tree hard by and whistled and chuckled turning about and about, heeding them nought. Then at last she lifted up her face from looking on the grass, and said: 'These are idle words and avail nothing: one thing only I know, that we are sundered. And now it repenteth me that I have shown thee my tears and my grief, and my sickness of the earth and those that dwell thereon. I am ashamed of it, as if thou hadst smitten me and I had come and shown thee the stripes, and said: See what thou hast done! hast thou no pity? Yea, thou pitiest me, and wilt try to forget thy pity. Belike matters will arise that will call me back to life, and I shall once more take heed of the joy and sorrow of my people. Nay, it is most like that this I shall feign to do, even now. But if tomorrow be a new day, it is to-day now and not to-morrow and so shall it be for long. Hereof belike we shall talk no more, thou and I. For as the days wear, the dealings between us shall be that thou shalt but get thee away from my life, and I shall be nought to thee but the name of a kinswoman. Thus should it be even wert thou to strive to make it otherwise; and thou shalt *not* strive. So let all this be; for this is not the word I had to say to thee. But hearken! now we are sundered, and it irketh me beyond measure that folk know it not, and are kind, and rejoice in our love, and deem it a happy thing for the folk: and this burden I may bear no longer. So I shall declare unto men that I will not wed thee.'

The attitude of the speaker is unlike that of Dido, and yet there is a certain reminiscence of the fourth *Æneid* throughout the passage. Another resemblance, most probably entirely accidental, is curiously close:—'Thy voice,' says Iron-face to Sunbeam, 'is as sweet as the voice of the songbirds singing in the dawn of early summer soundeth to him who hath been sick unto death.'

NEWS FROM NOWHERE

1891

---

61. Lionel Johnson, review, *Academy*

23 May 1891, xxxix, 483–4

Lionel Johnson (1867–1902), one of the poets contemporary with Yeats and associated with the nineties, produced a good deal of literary journalism.

Not long past, there was published a book, of an ugliness so gross and a vulgarity so pestilent, that it deserved the bonfire and the hangman, the fate of no worse books in a bygone age. The book has been bought by tens of thousands, and by hundreds of thousands, in England and America; clubs and societies have been called after its author's name. That book is *Looking Backward*. It purported to give us an insight into the perfected society of the future; and what we saw was a nightmare spectacle of machinery dominating the world. Yet, despite the ugly and the vulgar features of Mr. Bellamy's dream, it was easy to sympathise with his intention: that modern society is far from perfect, that competition can be most cruel, that our conditions of life are restless and mean, few will deny. Whether the preaching of Socialism or of Communism be a happier solution of our difficulties, than a strong faith in the virtues of patience, of courage, and of time, is another question. We are all agreed, that the existing state of the world is not over pleasant.

But among all the Utopian or ideal pictures of a reformed world, drawn for our contemplation by enthusiasts, this book by Mr. William Morris has a singular charm. It cannot, indeed, rank with the great schemes of Plato, More, and Bacon: it has far less perfection of workmanship, less completeness of design, less dignity of tone. But these

'Chapters from a Utopian Romance' do not pretend to completeness; they aim at one thing only, the description of an 'Epoch of Rest.' Life to-day is restless, busy, and troubled; full of sordid cares, and wasted by laborious trifles: we hurry and scramble round the world, pushing and hindering one another, losing all the peace and joy of life. Mr. Morris here shows us, what sort of life he would like to live, what is his conception of the *mens sana in corpore sano*.[1] And from that point of view we will dwell upon the book, with only one remark about the preliminary politics, or the historical origin, of the happy state which it depicts. Mr. Morris draws a vivid, and upon the whole, a convincing sketch of the social revolution in its last stages of open conflict, and a no less vivid sketch of its ultimate outcome; he does not tell us the details, nor even sketch outlines, of the most important period, the period of transition. He gives us a dim notion, just a vague glimpse; but so far as his book be meant for more than a beautiful dream, it is here that he is weak. No man, however inclined to fight side by side with Mr. Morris, could risk the terrors and the horrors of civil war, unless he had a greater certainty than this book could give him, that all the misery and the blood-shed would end in peace and happiness; not in some English version of the French Republic, or even of the American Commonwealth.

But we are not bound to take *News from Nowhere* as a socialist guide book: let us consider it as a vision of the Promised Land. The two chief tenets of this new faith are these: pleasure in work is the secret of art and of content; delight in physical life upon earth is the natural state of man. Whatever interferes with that pleasure, and with that delight, is wrong; work that cannot be done with pleasure, ideas that fill men with despair and gloom, stand self-condemned. We must have no grinding and tyrannous machines of labour; no poisonous and blighting influences of thought. If your factory life makes of you a sickly shadow, or a sullen brute; if your subtil introspection turns you into a barren dreamer, or a moping pessimist: then, says Mr. Morris, and surely we all say so too, then away with those manufactures and with those metaphysics! Life has become endlessly complicated by all sorts of interests and of wants, that do not make life happier; we must simplify ourselves, and return to 'the primal sanities' of nature. That fine phrase of Mr. Whitman describes the spirit of this book: we are sophisticated, let us go home to the early 'primal' sources of simplicity and joy; we are perplexed, let us go back to the sources of 'sanity' and

[1] Healthy mind in healthy body.

strength. Upon the relations of art and work, no one is any longer doubtful, where the truth lies. Although little advance be made towards the perfect conditions of beautiful workmanship, in theory we are all agreed. But the second point is less firmly recognised. What Browning called 'the mere joy of the living' becomes less valued every day. Nowadays people seem to pride themselves upon having headaches of body and soul; to relish the sensitiveness of their nerves, thier delicate and diseased condition. Effeminate persons give us sonnets upon nature, full of fantastic sentiments, and of refined phrases; but a twenty miles' walk or a sleep under the stars would be to them a painfully athletic pleasure. Nor have they that loving and personal regard for the very earth itself, which Mr. Morris so rightly prizes: that sense for the motherhood of the earth, which makes a man love the smell of the fields after rain, or the look of running water. These things, to the modern poet, are so much material for rhyme and metaphor: 'rain' and 'pain,' 'stream' and 'dream.' We have fallen in love with a way of torturing nature into complicity with our vague emotions: we should do well to gain the Homeric simplicity and grandeur of mind, the Lucretian sense of majesty and power, the Virgilian sense of rapture and of glory, in the presence of the natural earth. Mr. Morris, from his earliest poems up to this book, has always shown this rightness of mind, this healthy delight in physical existence, because the world is so exhilarating and so lovely. Man has been distinguished from the other animals in many ways; not the least distinction is this: that man alone takes a double pleasure in his life upon earth, a pleasure of the mind and of the senses.

Mr. Morris, in his account of the reformed world, reminds us of many various authors. Much of his homely affection for the seasonable works of agriculture recalls those 'homespun Georgics,' as Southey called them, of Tusser,[1] redolent of the farm and field, full of honest country mirth and manners. Then, again, many phrases in the old man's description of this new Arcady remind us of Athenian writers and ideas: 'We live amongst beauty without any fear of becoming effeminate, we have plenty to do, and on the whole enjoy doing it. What more can we ask of life?' It is like Pericles' great speech: Athens, he said, is very admirable, φιλοκαλοῦμεν γὰρ μετ' εὐτελείας καὶ φιλοσοφοῦμεν ἄνευ μαλακίας.[2] Only we cannot help having a general

---

[1] Thomas Tusser (1524-80) wrote on farming topics.
[2] 'Our love of what is beautiful does not lead to extravagance; our love of things of the

impression that Mr. Morris's Utopia or Arcadia, for all its beauty and its energy, would be a little stupid. Perhaps, in his laudable dislike of everything affected or merely academic, Mr. Morris represents his ideal folk as underrating slightly the very joy and pleasure of books and learning. Upon the whole, his conception of man, as he should be, has much in common with Aristotle's: not, of course, in the practical ideas of citizenship and of politics, but in the moral ideas of man's character and business. 'A long life of virtuous activity, according to your own nature, and as developed by exercise.' Mr. Morris would accept that definition of a good life. But it includes the full development of all the faculties; one faculty cannot do duty for another. One man is good at harvest, and another over painting, and a third in literature; now Mr. Morris at times is inclined to say, that if you are serviceable in the fields, it will do instead of improving your mind with books. It is merely an excess of zeal, in defence of despised and neglected employments, that so makes Mr. Morris unjust to those which have been exalted with exaggeration. There are too many books in the world; we judge too much by a literary standard; we ignore the culture of mind and body in other ways; but good books remain the best things in the world, after the hills and the fields.

The picture of London, embowered in orchards and set with gardens, is very inviting; but there is one thing which in conscience we cannot pass by. Mr. Morris classes together as 'silly old buildings' and as 'poorish buildings' St. Paul's and the British Museum; and he speaks of St. Martin's-in-the-Fields and of the National Gallery in one breath as 'an ugly church' and a 'nondescript ugly cupolaed building.' That any man, and far more that Mr. Morris, should couple together the splendid works of Wren and of Gibbs with the absurd productions of such as Wilkins, is deplorable. There are many men—and I am not ashamed to be one—who, while enjoying and reverencing to the full the medieval masterpieces, would give up a dozen other cathedral churches, could that save St. Paul's from destruction. It is bad enough to have Wren's design spoiled by such an abomination as the present reredos; but that is removeable. The attack of Mr. Morris will remain. Is it that Vitruvian design in architecture is to him very much what 'frigid classicality' is in literature? Let me quote the wise words of Mr. Selwyn Image:[1]

---

mind does not make us soft.' From Pericles' funeral speech in Thucydides Book 2, ch. 4. Rex Warner's translation (London, 1954).
[1] Selwyn Image (1849–1930) was an artist, poet and essayist.

Do not go demanding everywhere your own idols. In many shrines learn to worship the Divinity, which is revealed entirely at none. For sensitiveness, for flexibility, for an inexhaustible capacity of appreciation, send up your perpetual prayers.

But there is so much beauty, so much strength, so much sanity in this short book, that our chief thoughts of it must be thoughts of gratitude. Its readers will turn, again and again, to these virile and pleasant pages, and especially to those which tell of England's natural beauty, of the sylvan Thames, and of the Oxfordshire meadows. Like that other Oxford poet, who loved 'the shy Thames shore,' Mr. Morris consoles and heartens us. We see, our eyes clear of city smoke,

> Bathed in the sacred dews of morn,
> The wide aerial landscape spread—
> The world which was ere I was born,
> The world which lasts when I am dead;
> Which never was the friend of *one*,
> Nor promised love it could not give,
> But lit for all its generous sun,
> And lived itself, and made us live.[1]

62. Maurice Hewlett, review, *National Review*

August 1891, xvii, 818–27

This thorough discussion, entitled 'A Materialist's Paradise', is by the novelist and essayist M. H. Hewlett (1861–1923).

Once upon a time a philosopher, using Pope as a spring-board, uttered the uncompromising paradox that 'an honest God's the noblest work of man.' It is a proposition which will go far too far, for present occasions. It points, however, to a corollary which no one can reasonably refuse: namely, that the interest of paper paradises is mainly

[1] Matthew Arnold, 'A Wish', stanzas 9 and 10.

biographical. Nobody cares to discuss the potentialities of the *Republic* or the *Utopia* from the present, or any past, point of view; but both have a high interest historically as gauges of contemporary polity. Personally, of course, they are priceless documents. If you would discover of what a man is essentially capable, get him in a rapture; and it is because St. Augustine went into two—the very alpha and omega of human aspiration—that the *De Civitate Dei* and the *Confessions* visit us so nearly. Paradises on paper are, it would seem, products of subjectivity and the *Zeitgeist*. Of the two forces, the first is always worth our study, and the second may be.

And so it is that, when we have read *News from Nowhere*, we lay it slowly down (it is a pretty poem) with mingled feelings containing this little substratum of comfort, that now at least we know Mr. Morris. This various person, this dazzling creature who has at times irritated and bewitched a large part of London, composed of equal parts of antiquary, artist, poet, upholsterer, scolder of dons, and sympathetic retailer of old-time stories, has revealed himself, and, behold, he is one of us. He might be in the City, familiar with its banquets; he might be in the Record Office, loving its parchments and faded caligraphy; he might be (and is he not?), like any mother's son of us, reliant, warm-blooded, fond of beauty and not inclined to analyse or dig far down for it, proud of his broad chest and clean limbs and pardonably inclined to think they count for something, impatient of restraint and fond of short cuts. That seems to be the 'real Mr. Morris,' and we may assuredly not quarrel with so engaging a specimen of our *genus*. But, if I may say so, 'il a les défauts de ses qualités.' If he is more generous, he lacks the comprehensiveness of Plato (Plato would never have abolished slavery by freeing the slaves or killing their owners); if he is more in earnest, he wants the urbanity of Sir Thomas (Sir Thomas would not have used the word 'damn' twice in as many lines [p. 176]). The difference seems to be that he writes as a man of affairs, while they wrote as men of ideas; he is angry, they were philosophic. Now, it is to be confessed, after reading this last of the apocalypses, that philosophy is the wear for a convincing paradise-maker. Mr. Morris, with his fine human impatience, has been tempted into being superficial, at cutting off leaves, instead of striking at roots; and again, with his artistic appreciation of blue distances and hazy retrospects, he has been ravished away into constructing a future which shall consist mainly in rejuvenated relics. Is that scientific; is it history? We may doubt it. Relics shorn of their feretories are apt to look inadequate. The fourteenth century was well as an epitome of the thirteenth and a forcing-bed for the fifteenth. How will it logically follow the twenty-third or sufficiently prepare the twenty-fifth?

But does Mr. Morris (who may have a sense of humour somewhere) wish to be taken seriously? I pay him the doubtful compliment of believing that he does, and venture to indicate the two fallacies which betray his structure. He has, I conceive, exaggerated the dependence of human nature upon its environment: he is convinced that the conditions of human welfare are physical. Grounding on the first, he would violently overthrow institutions and *compel* freedom; enraptured with the second, he has allowed his perception to govern his reason. The result is not an earthly, but an earthy, Paradise; and the change of adjective makes all the difference between an honest recognition of rank and a state of blank complacency which in a savage or one of the lower animals we should call grovelling. Let me hasten to justify.

When Mr. William Morris went to sleep one night and thereupon began his vision, he found himself in a leisurely country, geographically familiar, but socially incredible. It seemed the difference of winter and summer. He had left behind him a time of repression and mechanical observance, and had leapt into a region of ample growth and a fruity abundance of physical delight. The sun shone daily (although it was but June); all the women were fair; the men were strapping; the buildings, shops, halls, and houses, were intelligently and lovingly built; the trees, the flowers, the birds, the very sky spoke more frankly and enthusiastically to his grateful senses. Everything he had ever loved (and here his speech frequently betrays him) ,was before his eye—frescoed walls, pictured mythology, bold design in glass and 'pot-ware', costly damasks and embroidered webbings, drapery rather than dresses, mediæval bridges instead of iron ones; a teeming, expansive growth instead of a concentrated, introspective, fevered struggle. Buxom girls in fresh cotton gowns kissed him for morning greeting; they held his hand as they talked; they leaned on his shoulder as they served him at table. Broad-shouldered youths, in doublet and hose, and metal girdles curiously wrought, acted as his guides and grooms, and opened to him, as they toiled, their light young hearts and enthusiasms.

Humanity at large was an extension of these types: the units of the world kissed freely, and mankind was really akin. So deep-seated, so far-reaching, was this sense of brotherhood that all the watch-dogs of society hitherto known to experience—parliaments, police, soldiers and sailors, priests and newspapers—had vanished or been relegated as curious relics (duly labelled) to museums and national galleries. There were no organizations for national defence: the Continent appears to have shared the lack of things defendable. There were none for mutual defence: every man was coheir of his neighbours. Community of goods, free exchange of husbands or wives, exemption from authority external or internal, of conscience or of police, complete fairly enough the attributes of the new State.

Yet, with all this and more which was strangely new, Mr. Morris found a great deal was old, much which his trained eye detected to be 'fourteenth-century work.' Furniture, the patterns of chintzes and friezes and cornices, dress, architecture, speech and language, loco-motion, were fresh from the times of Chaucer and the Painted Chamber; so, largely, were manners. The folk-moot, to be sure, was somewhat more antique; but it might easily have stood for a County Council in its dotage, and we have no details as to the extent of its jurisdiction. In matters of faith and ethics there was the same curious mixture of revival and departure. There was an appreciation of Nature and her simpler manifestations reminiscent of Chaucer; there was a keenness of sensuous pleasure never attained by our English poet and, plainly, nourished on Boccaccio. By the side of this there was a delight in laborious work, in physical toil, and a corresponding distrust of books and learning which must be confessed a strikingly new feature, not warranted by experience of History or of Nature, but springing from causes whose ultimate roots Mr. Morris was at no pains to probe deep. The population had not increased for a hundred and fifty years, and yet was wholly altered in physique as well as in temper. The *English* nation had disappeared. The race was now *Italian*: artistic, not serious; sensuous, not speculative; emotional and yet superficial; energetic and yet self-indulgent.

The spirit of the new days, of our days, was to be delight in the life of the world, intense and overweening love of the very skin and surface of the earth on which man dwells, such as a lover has in the fair flesh of the woman he loves; this, I say, was to be the new spirit of the time. (p. 147.)

The spirit of the new time loses nothing in the emphasis of its ex-position.

Mr. Morris's inquiries into this bizarre state of things elicited the explanation that it had been forwarded by a Trafalgar Square massacre, a universal strike, and a capitulation of employers so wholesale that there were thereafter no 'employed' in the modern sense. With hired labour ceased 'forced labour'; and 'commercialism' ceased. And, 'commercialism' once gone, the conditions of the præ-commercial life and that life itself veritably revived. Love was præ-commercial, and love, it seems, was sexual instinct. Beauty præ-commercial, and Beauty was a physical attribute and connoted health. Religion, præ-commercial or not, had utterly vanished from the State and the individual. Man could now conceive of nothing higher than he saw or felt; he asked nothing more than to grow with the plants and birds. Positivism, even, as a curious passage shows, was not practised, because it was so obvious.

In times past, indeed, men were told to love their kind, to believe in the religion of humanity, and so forth. . . . But now, where is the difficulty in accepting the religion of humanity, when the men and women who go to make up humanity are free, happy, and energetic, and most commonly beautiful of body also, and surrounded by beautiful things of their own fashioning, and a nature bettered and not worsened by contact with mankind? (p. 148.)

Faith, therefore, is a condition of religion; and, since there is nothing behind appearance, there is nothing to believe. The consolations of this life without faith are, it will be noticed, 'freedom,' happiness, energy, 'beauty of body,' and artistic environment, all subsisting vividly in consciousness; and, of these, freedom, it is manifest, has a physical basis and may be licence, happiness consists in material comfort and sensuous satisfaction, the other three explain themselves. And then there is another passage which contains the ideal of these splendid creatures. Ellen is contrasting her times with the past. In the old days, says she,—

You, grandfather, would have had to work hard after you were old; and would have been always afraid of having to be shut up in a kind of prison along with other old men, half-starved, *and without amusement*. And as for me, I am twenty years old. In those days my middle age would be beginning now, and in a few years I should be pinched, thin and haggard, beset with troubles and miseries, *so that no one could have guessed that I was once a beautiful girl*. (p. 177.)

There is something ludicrously artless in this deliverance, something of a complacency too naïve, in fleshly perfection, frankly finite and not a little pitiful. It is as if a pheasant were endowed with sensibility and lamented the moulting season.

A great Nature-worship has set in; everything points to a deep joy in mere sensation, and to a deeper, vaster ignorance of what underlies it. Flesh is not grass; it is God. Why seek farther? Why find types, emblems, figures in this good life? 'Why indeed?' thrills Ellen. Hear her:—

She led me up close to the house, and laid her shapely sun-browned hand and arm on the lichened wall as if to embrace it, and cried out, 'O me! O me! How I love the earth and the seasons and weather, and all things that deal with it, and all that grows out of it,—as this has done! .... The earth and the growth of it and the life of it! If I could but say or show how I love it!' (pp. 227–8.)

This is fine rhythm and a fine apostrophe. It is a strong utterance, only too sincere. To some of us its power shrivels with the discovery that this growth is adequately represented by luxuriant development of matter, this life by the quivering of the atmosphere under a summer heat, this rapture by the purposeless flutter of a butterfly recking neither of its chrysalis not of its bourne. Then comes, naturally, the thought of Death. Now, the thought of Death is kept away as much as possible. We have to gather the new views from scattered hints and ejaculations. Here is the opinion of old Hammond, the Sage and Choragus of the little comedy. 'My friend, you must know that we are too happy, both individually and collectively, to trouble ourselves about what is to come hereafter' (p. 114). Elementary for a Sage! Next, here is Ellen's view. Ellen is the *Zeitgeist* embodied and a poetical figure. She has been talking of the contrast of her cottage life, working hard when she chooses and because it makes her 'prettier to look at and healthier and happier,' and the cottage life of the nineteenth century, hard work willy-nilly, old age, wrinkles and scanty locks. 'I love life better than death,' she concludes; and it is not hard to discover what life implies to her. Now take the Oxford Student (new style). 'What is to come after this?' asks Mr. Morris, musing over some art-work of the period. 'I don't know, we will meet it when it comes,' is the answer. *Quien Sabe?*

> . . . . . What of hereafter?
> Credat Judæus! Who knows, till we try,
> What humours a Heaven may not furnish for laughter,
> What sorrows a Hell, when to-morrow we die?

Last, take Dick the hero, the young Adonis of this enchanted garden. Autumn saddens him: he won't think of it. 'It is then, in the autumn, *when one almost believes in death.*' (p. 232). Here, then, is the new creed concerning the Last Things: a creed in the main obstructive, timid, agnostic. And then one thinks of Socrates. 'I cannot persuade Crito, my friends, that I am that Socrates who methodizes each part of the discourse; but he thinks that I am he whom he will shortly behold dead, and asks how he should bury me. But what I some time since argued at length, that when I have drunk the poison I shall no longer remain with you, but shall depart to some happy state of the blessed,—this I seem to have urged to him in vain, though I meant to console both you and myself. . . . You must have a good courage, then, and say that you bury my body.' And then, 'Crito, I owe a cock to Asclepius; will you remember to pay the debt?' There is more significance than humour in such a last speech. It is a creed in little. And one thinks, again, of Francis of Assisi with his 'Welcome, Sister Death!' and his 'educ de custodiâ animam meam' as his swan-song of aspiration and release. This is poetry; more, it is philosophy itself. Now, since Death is a fact and the nature of Life an open question, it is still a choice between a transcendentalism which gazes through the veil and sees a dim vista behind it and a hedonism which stiffens it with embroidery that it may be the harder to rend. But to the ostrich in his native sand Death proves himself still a potent fact.

The Greeks worshiped spiritual beauty, and embodied it in physically beautiful forms, because Greek humanism coalesced with Greek idealism, and made such forms true abstractions, true figures of ideas. Hence Greek philosophy went abreast of Greek art: one defined, the other expressed; one manifested what the other saw. Nature was impressed with the God-like, and Greece confessed a fine Pantheism. The Franks found Christianity with Hellenism behind it. In a blend of both with their own passionate realism, they gave us Christian art and ethics. Man to them—as to the Greeks—was a kernel in a husk, a horned snail straining forward, hampered by a shell. Abstraction took the form of emblem rather than of symbol, a loveliness of acts rather than of types. The God-like—God—was seen through nature, and the Christian world bowed before Pan-en-theism. For Greece, Nature was God; for Italy, God was Nature. Narrow as is the thread of reasoning which separates the two, it shows itself real in Phidias and in Botticelli, in Spenser and in Plato. Love is the instinctive longing of the soul for Beauty. Beauty? It is the transfiguration of Truth. Truth? It is the identification of subject and object. And where may that be found? With God. These are not Mr. Morris's approximations. With him Beauty receives the definition of the *hareem*, Truth is a *façon de parler*, and God disappears. 'La question de Dieu,' said a Parisian editor once,* 'manque d'actualité.' It may be so, of course; but it is at least consistent with Pantheism or with transcendentalism; and either of these hypotheses is

---

* The story is Emerson's; in his address on 'Worship.'

tenable, and can satisfy reason or hope. That of Mr. Morris and his school, one may take leave to say, will satisfy neither. A race of fleshly perfection, worshipping phenomena, relying on appearance, arguing from sensation; a nation of strong men and fair women, conscious of their own growth and of their country's, owning an art which springs from and is directed to Nature, Simplicity, Truth, which yet sees no significance, no shadow behind these comely forms, dreams no future, owns no standard, accepts no explanation, needs no justifying. This is a strange race, impossible and to most of us unsavoury. Moreover, these wild results are to spring from the slaughter of 'commercialism,' and the extinction of class-slavery.

But it is as ungracious as idle to quarrel with a poet. We must be thankful for what is best in him and give him his full meed of rope. To argue or to exhort is as little beseeming as to complain that Fra Angelico's Beatific Visions would ultimately pall. Only, we may remember that the Frate offers us a convention of various concepts, and that Mr. Morris invites us to realise *his* beatitudes. Giovanni is singing *Te Deum* with his face to the altar; Mr. Morris is preaching in the vernacular with his face to the people. And when a preacher tells you of his ideals, suggests that you should make them your own, urges you (finally) to assist in their accomplishment, it is lawful to inquire how far they meet your case. To many, I presume to say, they will fall absurdly short of a dignified or even reasonable existence. 'Grant her in health and wealth long to live' is, it must be owned, a somewhat gross petition. But it is Mr. Morris's ideal. Longevity, sprouting health, ample satisfaction of appetite, meet you at every turn. It is true he abolishes money and private property; but that is not abolishing wealth. The goal of the wealth-seekers is the satisfaction of appetite, and it is a finite view to take of existence that it has no aims more extended than that.

In sober truth, the very pith of the scheme is materialistic, the humanism of a sensuous temperament which sees the beauty of appearance and is too indolent or too indifferent to look deeper. 'This world and the growth of it and the life of it!' It is all very real to Mr. Morris, and hence his poem smacks of the soil, 'has a kind of taste.' This body, glowing with the flush of health or the sun-given graduations of rose-pink, carnation and red-brown,—this body of ample bosom curving and heaving like the waves of a morning sea, supple throat, well-set head, glossy hair inviting homage and caress,—this radiant body he will clothe in silken tissue and cloth of finest web. Its round arms shall be girt with barbaric bracelets of bold design; he will hang quaint chains round its brave throat and circle its waist with a zone of damascened steel. This lovely animal shall be frank and winsome; her mouth shall smile to yours in kisses, her fingers thrill you with their touch. She shall be yours if you will, dwell with you and bear you children as lovely as herself. The prospect would be pleasant, would be well-nigh perfect, if one could so gaily assume a be-all and end-all here. But if the pretty clay which Mr. Morris handles so tenderly and, withal, wistfully, should haply prove no more than mere seeming and the veil of another principle? Other pleasures there assuredly are than the glow of sunshine on the cheek, the light of desire in the eyes. Work, hard work, is good, but not so good as its end, and it may vary in degree. The earth and the growth and life of it, again, signify somewhat other than man and the growth and life of *him*. If thought and consciousness are not the reality of man and the index of his possibilities and origin; if it is more momentous what he feels than what he thinks and (therefore) what he *is*, then Mr. Morris's anxiety to have done with commercialism and caste and class-slavery are natural enough. But he will not abolish slavery by abolishing capitalists and employers (even assuming that every master is a villain and every man a martyr) and the fact that there is another and a worse slavery inherent in every one of us and eradicable only from within, points out that Mr. Morris's cherished remedies are but skin-deep, and no permanent remedies at all. Animal love and animal beauty, 'the lust of the flesh, and the lust of the eyes, and the pride of life,' are very volcanoes, breeding eruption and riot; burning fiercely, they scorch, and may not always be quenched by being let loose.

And *this* is the kind of slavery which to escape is life indeed. And Mr. Morris knows no way, or hints of none. He will sing of battles and victories of labour over capital; he will prate of the extinction of money and the advent of days when Steinberg Cabinet and Latakia shall be had for the asking; but, had he condescended to history further, he would have known that in times a few decades removed from his fourteenth-century a remedy was offered, a way opened to secure at once enjoyment and freedom, emancipation and dignity. Remove the sting of slavery and slavery itself is of small account. See to what a man essentially *is*, or may be; and it matters nothing what he has or has not. 'Sanctissima Paupertas,' the thirteenth-century substitute for 'Pretiosissima Voluptas' of the good time coming, was not the cold bride of a rapt ascetic, but the virgin (radiant through her tatters) who proclaimed the doctrine of serene destitution—happiness independent of mere possession—and the spouse of a man who looked on Nature with the tender eyes of the Nazarene, and saw behind the phenomena of life the great shadow of God. The teaching of the Sermon on the Mount may be extravagant, may be fanatical; but it was lived by thousands of 'slaves' in the thirteenth-century. It may be Oriental; but it was realised in Italy and in England. Much of it may be the Platonism of Alexandria, the mysticism of Philo; but an unlettered poet of Provençal blood lived its life and incarnated its substance. The Sermon on the Mount was spoken again in the *Cantico Degli Creature*—the Song of Created Things—and means and obstacle to man's independence, Sacrament and Carnality its antitype, sank before self-respect, the joy of real existence, and the spontaneous worship of a simplified being imaging the primal Simplicity,—the One, the Great, and the All.

Hence Mr. Morris's plan of 'Simplicity made easy' pales before the old achievement of 'Simplicity shown difficult.' In the one case mechanism is exhibited in the very absence of apparent mechanism; in in the other case triumph follows as the fruit of strenuous endeavour. Hence we may gather the futility of this 'Vision;' hence, too, we may see, if we will, the real remedy and goal of our groaning efforts. It lies, as all that is of value has ever lain, in education and renunciation. Pare off what is clay and clogs aspiration; foster what is ether and strains towards its fount. Now, this will not be accomplished in A.D. 2050, and may be not in A.D. 3050. For this reason alone, perhaps, it will not please Mr. Morris. He is impatient of attainment; effort irritates him. His house at Hammersmith, he tells us, is dingy and irksome. His vision tells him of a sylvan Thames, a spacious architecture and splendid trappings for glorified carcases; he is in a hurry to begin. But Mr. Morris—poet, artist, seer, though he be—must face facts: he must (he really must) read history. And if History tell him that the spirit of the time (not the spirit of a clique or two) is for Socialism and against Individualism; if she tell him that humanity can be transformed by transforming the institutions which are of its own making; if she tell him that free love by the light of Nature and the pampered lives of intelligent animals will stimulate innocence, fine art, and the higher existence; if she tell him that it is possible to revive the accidents of the fourteenth-century without a vestige of the religion which (good or bad, Catholic or Lollard) was its very breath; if, lastly, she assure him that the good of the race has best been served by indulging the appetites of its grosser parts and leaving the soul to find its level in a slough of sensuality and drowsy oblivion—if History tell him this, there's an end of the matter. History cannot lie though Historians can. But history will tell him nothing of the kind. The course of the world tends otherwise. Antinomianism (ephemeral convenience!) will spring indeed in a transcendental atmosphere, and flourish under Pantheism. Human nature needs no encouragement to begin to make excuses. But nowhere does it crop up with so chaotic a rankness as in this latter-day Neo-Epicureanism of artists who ignore their souls and of poets who despise philosophy. And History is probably saying to herself, 'Here is a man of parts whose eyes are open and his mind firm. If, notwithstanding, he must needs propose that Instinct should govern Reason, I can *teach* him nothing. But at least I can laugh at Instinct flouting Plato and Dante, Shakespeare, Spinosa, and Fichte.' For History has a sense of humour.

63. Nordau on Morris's degeneracy

1892

Max Nordau (1849–1923) was a Jewish-Hungarian writer on moral and social questions. He denounced the decadence of late nineteenth-century culture in *Entartung* in 1892, including a section on the Pre-Raphaelites; the book provoked Bernard Shaw's reply in *The Sanity of Art*.

From *Degeneration* (London, 1896), the second edition of the English translation, 98–9.

William Morris is intellectually far more healthy than Rossetti and Swinburne. His deviations from mental equilibrium betray themselves, not through mysticism, but through a want of individuality, and an overweening tendency to imitation. His affectation consists in mediævalism. He calls himself a pupil of Chaucer. He artlessly copies whole stanzas also from Dante, *e.g.*, the well-known Francesca and Paolo episode from Canto V. of the *Inferno*, when he writes in his 'Guenevere':

> In that garden fair
> Came Lancelot walking; this is true, the kiss
> Wherewith we kissed in meeting that spring day,
> I scarce dare talk of the remembered bliss.

Morris persuades himself that he is a wandering minstrel of the thirteenth or fourteenth century, and takes much trouble to look at things in such a way, and express them in such language, as would have befitted a real contemporary of Chaucer. Beyond this poetical ventriloquism, so to speak, with which he seeks so to alter the sound of his voice that it may appear to come from far away to our ear, there are not many features of degeneracy in him to notice. But he sometimes falls into outspoken echolalia, *e.g.*, in a stanza of the *Earthly Paradise*:

> Of Margaret sitting glorious there,
> In glory of gold and glory of hair,
> And glory of glorious face most fair—

where 'glory' and 'glorious' are repeated five times in three lines. His emotional activity in recent years has made him an adherent of a vague socialism, consisting chiefly of love and pity for his fellow-men, and which has an odd effect when expressed artistically in the language of the old ballads.

POEMS BY THE WAY

1892

64. Richard Garnett, review, *Illustrated London News*

9 January 1892, c, 50

Garnett had reviewed *The Defence of Guenevere* in 1858; see No. 2.

Thirty-three years ago *The Defence of Guenevere and other Poems*, by William Morris, aroused profound interest and lofty hopes in such lovers of poetry as valued song for itself rather than as the exponent of ideas equally or better adapted for the medium of prose. Mr. Morris had no ideas in those days; he was a poet or he was nothing. The same cannot be said now, nor would it be well that it could be said. The experience of life has not failed, nor ought it to have failed, to furnish Mr. Morris with a creed by which his later verse is in great measure leavened, and contributes much to its enrichment so long as it is the leaven and not the loaf. We can allow but little poetic worth to Mr. Morris's purely socialistic poetry, so far as we are acquainted with it, in this volume or elsewhere. But the general spirit of humanity imported into his verse animates it with new beauty and significance, and vindicates the poet from the imputation, to which he once pronounced himself obnoxious, of being the mere 'idle singer of an empty day'. Mr. Morris's verse is no more idle than the nineteenth century is frivolous. 'The still, sad music of humanity' is audible throughout his more fanciful compositions, almost, we might even venture to deem, in proportion to their fancifulness. He is far more pathetic, far nearer the heart of mankind, in singing of the imaginary burghers of 'The Burghers' Battle' than of the Cockney victim of an actual scuffle in Trafalgar Square.

This pervading intensity of human feeling marks Mr. Morris's last volume as in one respect a great advance upon his first. As regards more strictly poetical qualities, the fact is otherwise, but this must not be interpreted as indicating any abatement of the author's poetical power. He has simply, since his venture of 1858, given his power a new application; he has forsaken lyric for epic, and produced work immensely transcending in scope and importance not merely his early ballads but the promise of them. It would take many such volumes as that of 1858 to rival *The Earthly Paradise*, that cyclopaedia of poetical romance which, without disparagement to the almost equally beautiful *Jason* and *Sigurd*, chiefly guarantees Mr. Morris's renown with the latest ages of our literature. *Poems by the Way*, as the title imports, are casual visitations of the Muse, a mere backwater in the majestic river of sonorous song. This promised, it may be frankly admitted that, while always dramatic and picturesque, the new pieces are in the former point of view less concentrated, in the latter less vivid, than the poems of 1858. The poet is everywhere; the master is seen in only two pieces, to which we should assign a first-class rank, not only among Mr. Morris's productions, but among all productions of contemporary poetry. One is the above-mentioned 'Burghers' Battle', a poem peculiar and almost unique in its pathos as the pathos of anticipation, the sorrow of strong men whom calamity has not yet reached, but who mark its inevitable approach, and realise it as if it were actually upon them; fore-boding blended with resignation, lamentation without complaint. It is marvellous, too, how the pathos is helped by the burden continually recurrent throughout the poem, and giving it a key-note. The other is 'The Message of the March Wind', where the wind brings to the poet and his love in their country village the murmurs and the moans of the great far-off city—

> Hark the wind in the elm-boughs! from London it bloweth
> And telleth of gold, and of hope and unrest;
> Of power that helps not; of wisdom that knoweth
> But teacheth not aught of the worst and the best.

[quotes next five stanzas]

It will be seen that Mr. Morris can give forcible expression to his ideas so long as he is permitted to resort to the concrete. Imagery is essential to him; he is the craftsman who carves his sermon on the pulpit rather than the preacher who enforces it by word of mouth. The success of his pieces is generally almost in the ratio of the opportunity afforded for pictorial illustration and for his other great distinguishing faculty of poetical narrative. He is distinctly the story-teller among modern poets, the antitype not of the medieval troubadour, but of the medieval romantic minstrel. Brevity is not a note of his order of singer, and for a sufficient reason: lords and ladies wanted to be amused through winter evenings, and winter evenings were long. Their modern representative loves to expatiate over a story, and has nothing of the tremendous energy of Rossetti's ballads. Flowers spring up in his way and he stops to gather them; he unrolls a panorama as with a wand; Rossetti reveals a landscape as with a flash. Both methods have their advantages; one disadvantage of Mr. Morris's, of which we are at this moment acutely conscious, is the impediment it imposes to quotation. No justice is possible within our limits, and we can only declare that the varied contents of this volume comprise admirable specimens of narrative ballad. 'Goldilocks and Goldilocks', in particular, is a lovely picture of the innocence of the young world, when all the iniquity was concentrated among witches and dragons. We do not find 'Winter Weather', which we had hoped to have seen reprinted from the *Oxford and Cambridge Magazine*.

Typographically, this volume is an apotheosis—the poet's fame certified, and his spirit externalised, in the superb type designed by himself, characters and paper respectively black, red and white as the three perfections of Little Snowflake, and with initial letters intricate as the artificial foliage at Lamia's marriage feast. It is a goodly sight. We only venture to suggest that the lines are somewhat too closely set, especially in the first page of the text. Where there is no printing in red but the ever-present marginal reference to the title of the poem, the massiveness of the type and blackness of the ink—excellent things in themselves—give a heavy aspect to the page. The ancient scribes and printers whom Mr. Morris has followed had sound reasons for economy of space in the dearness of paper and vellum. These have ceased to operate, and Mr. Morris could afford to make us 'windows in heaven'.

65. Oliver Elton, review, *Academy*

February 1892, xli, 197

Oliver Elton (1861–1945) was a private tutor and reviewer, and then lectured at Owens College, Manchester. He was later to become Professor of English at Liverpool.

Those who feared that Mr. William Morris would be made less of a poet by his Socialism have had ample reason to be disappointed; it was a false alarm. If by Socialism he meant, not the articles of a programme, but a passion for equal justice, a sympathy with outcast classes, and a vision of coming redress, then Socialism has done its part towards giving Mr. Morris's work a strength and substance which in the days of the *Earthly Paradise* it could not always claim. The song once too languorous vibrates oftener; the faint voices of those pale shadows, who moved, 'strengthless heads of the dead,' breathing eternal regrets as they vanished into their luminous mist, have begun to speak in more human tones. We are not, indeed, told the dates of the various pieces now given us for the first time; but some of them appear recent, and it is not impertinent to say that they are written under a different inspiration to any with which readers of Mr. Morris's previous verses are familiar.

The songs, nevertheless, which are written expressly in honour of the 'Cause' are not always the happiest or strongest in the book. Lacking in the accent which perpetuates the great popular lyrics on the lips of men, they have something in common, both in spirit and manner, with the hymns like the 'Song in Time of Order' and the 'Pilgrims' (to take two very different instances), which Mr. Swinburne made in his most generous moments; and, like these, they are really rather for the recluse enthusiast and dreamer than for the people, despite their intention.

> Come, shoulder to shoulder ere the world grows older,
> The Cause spreads over land and sea;
> Now the world shaketh, and fear awaketh,
> And joy at last for me and thee.

or again

> Come hither, lads, and hearken,
> For a tale there is to tell
> Of the wonderful days a-coming,
> When all shall be better than well.

Sincere as these lines are, can anyone say that they are the true, spontaneous, successful utterances of the singer at his best? For that we must look elsewhere.

Another influence strongly colouring this volume is that of the old Norse life and literature, the poet's love for which is well known. Traces of this influence appeared long since in his work, and he has of late been more industrious than ever, not only in writing Sagas of his own, but in translating the Norse prose classics. The union of such an enthusiasm with the Socialistic impulse is not, it is fair to conjecture, a mere coincidence to Mr. Morris. The simple, fighting, and manly life of the Sagas, with its bloodshed and crudity deducted, contains elements which he would like well to see embodied in his new society, destined to supplant our sophisticated and corrupt one. At least, whether this be his feeling or not, the 'Lines to the Muse of the North' express better than any comment the abiding attraction which the Norse life and poetry has had for the student of Homer and Chaucer.

> O Muse that swayest the sad Northern song,
> Thy right hand full of smiting and of wrong,
> Thy left hand holding pity; and thy breast
> Heaving with hope of that so certain rest!

Perhaps in the two latter lines the poet may read something into the breast of the Muse of the North that never was there. But, whether he is right or wrong, the effect of the belief upon his work is manifest; and we can well understand why so large a portion of the book is given up to ballads from the Danish and Icelandic, and ballads made more or less on the model of them.

Now, the Norse influence, just like that of Socialism, is certainly one that has given additional vigour and glory to the poet's verse; yet, here again, it is no contradiction to say that the actual ballads he has written expressly on Norse subjects are by no means his best and most characteristic work. There is, after all, something hopeless about the attempt to revive a literary form nearly as it flowered in a set of circumstances now extinct. The experience that gave that form breath and power can-

not really be lived over again by the most searching and tender imagination, or by any process of 'steeping the mind' in books; and the
result is something like that which attends the efforts, all meritorious
and all failures, to write Greek plays. The failure is due, not to lack, but
to misapplication, of poetic gift. Therefore, with whatever zeal and
grace these revivals are conducted, we cannot help coming back from
them and asking what the poet has to tell us concerning his more
personal and direct message. The originality of this volume is that it
contains several poems telling us something which Mr. Morris has
hardly told us in print before. I do not refer to verse like the following:

> Upon an eve I sat me down and wept,
> Because the world to me seemed nowise good,
> Still autumn was it, and the meadows slept,
> The misty hills dreamed, and the silent wood
> Seemed listening to the sorrow of my mood;
> I knew not if the earth with me did grieve,
> Or if it mocked my grief that bitter eve.

Are not the scene and the mood familiar? It would not be hard to find
thousands of lines of this melodious, equal-tinted, subdued quality in
the *Earthly Paradise*. The writer has the gift of turning out any number
of them without sinking or failing, and young Oxford has imitated
him to its heart's content. But now different is this, with its concrete
images, its touches of music and colour:

> There is wind in the twilight, in the white road before us
>   The straw from the ox-yard is blowing about;
> The moon's rim is rising, a star glitters o'er us,
>   And the vane on the spire-top is swinging in doubt. . . .
> Come back to the inn, love, and the lights and the fire.
>   And the fiddler's old tune and the shuffling of feet;
> For there in a while shall be rest and desire,
>   And there shall the morrow's uprising be sweet.

Better still, from the 'Meeting in Winter':

> They shall open, and we shall see
> The long street litten scantily
> By the long stream of light before
> The guest-hall's half-open door;
> And our horses' bells shall cease
> As we reach the place of peace;
> Thou shalt tremble, as at last

The worn threshold is o'erpast,
And the firelight blindeth thee:
Trembling shalt thou cling to me
As the sleepy merchants stare
At thy cold hands slim and fair,
Thy soft eyes and happy lips
Worth all lading of their ships.

There is no space to quote from poems like 'Hope Dieth: Love Liveth,' or like 'Love Fulfilled,' or from that lyric of antique grace, 'Spring's Bedfellow,' or from the piece that is perhaps the strongest Mr. Morris has written, 'Mother and Son.' In this last there are strokes with a fearless ring that reminds us strongly of Rossetti's 'Jenny'; and the whole volume, indeed, not only betokens a splendid vitality of gift with surprises yet in store, but recalls at every turn that its author is one of a famous fraternity, of whom one other still survives, and who have been animated, despite all their differences, by a certain common spirit, and endowed with similar cunning in the craft of song.

SOCIALISM: ITS GROWTH
AND OUTCOME

1893

---

66. Unsigned review, *Athenaeum*

18 November 1893, no. 3447, 965

This review contrasts *Socialism*, the joint work of Morris and
Belfort Bax, with Dr Schäffle's *Theory and Policy of Labour
Relations*. Its bland criticism is very effective.

Another work on similar subjects is *Socialism: its Growth and Outcome*,
by Messrs. William Morris and Belfort Bax, also published by Messrs.
Sonnenschein & Co. This book is very different in appearance from that
which we have just noticed, which is produced in the plain fashion
common to the books in the 'Social Sciences Series'. The book of which
Mr. William Morris is the principal author is produced in a style as
consistent with his poetic and artistic surroundings as is to be expected,
and its margins, its paper, its type and binding make it a pleasure to
behold. When we come, however, to the contents where, of course, we
find a cultivated and a pleasant style, we discover, indeed, a history of
what has frequently been described—the growth of Socialistic opinion
from the days of the ancients to those of Saint-Simon, Fourier, Owen,
Karl Marx, and the Paris Commune; but, while there is much therefore
about the 'growth', the 'outcome' is dealt with only in the last two or
twentieth and twenty-first chapters, and in a somewhat perfunctory
fashion. We should hardly like to use language which would not be
that of politeness about writers so civilized and so civil; but we fail to
find the slightest guidance, and we fail even to discover anything that
is new in these two chapters. They might be sermons upon Socialism
preached from a pulpit by one of the fashionable clergymen of the day

in whom Socialism assumes its pleasant 'society' forms, and who does not wish to drive away from his church the capitalists who support its institutions. The book will be read because it is so pretty and so pleasant, but we fear that it will not increase the sum of human knowledge.

67. Unsigned review, *Critic*

February 1894, xxi, 107

The *Critic* was a New York cultural journal.

Last year an Italian scientist, Attilio Brunialti, in his monograph on 'Lo Stato Moderno,' traced, side by side, the growth of the state in theory and history. The authors before us have performed a similar service for socialism, whose triumph in the near future they endeavor to prove inevitable by a succinct examination of universal history. It is always difficult to criticise a book whose literary qualities fascinate us, while at the same time we clearly recognize the error of the authors' main views. This is the case with the volume in hand—a volume written in Mr. Morris's most exquisite style, and sincerely urging the most untenable of socialism's tenets. The historian cannot fail to see at first glance that Messrs. Morris and Bax have read extensively, in historical literature, both those works dealing with primitive institutions, and those describing more recent epochs. This is evidenced by the complete rejection of Sir Henry Summer Maine's patriarchal theory, as well as by the adoption of the best results of Ihering, Bachofen, Sohm, Stubbs, McLennan and Gross. As is usual with amateur historians, we find a certain boldness in accepting offhand solutions of some of the most vexed problems of history, such as the origin of the mediæval manor and city. Their critical views also are not trustworthy, since their sole standpoint for judging an epoch is their estimate of the workman's happiness during that period. Lack of space prevents us from refuting some of the main propositions, which, often erroneous, as often stimulate the mind to active thought by their suggestive originality. Like Carlyle in *Past and Present*, Messrs. Morris and Bax surround the Middle Ages with a halo of glory; and, in addition, they contend that the 'bourgeois' historians, Hallam, Green, Freeman and Stubbs, have purposely exaggerated the gloom of that period, in order to cause modern civilization to appear the more brilliant by the contrast. It is needless to say that this view is absurd, and that, in our opinion, the differences in favor of our century are more than even those writers would admit. One of the contentions in favor of this view is that 'the whole of our unskilled laboring classes are in a far worse position as to food, housing and clothing than any but the extreme fringe of the corresponding class in the Middle Ages.' The falsity of this statement will appear when we consider what awful ravages such plagues as the Black Death created. Towards the middle of the fourteenth century four great plagues swept over England, and of these the most severe was that of 1349. England was then sparsely inhabited, having only four millions of inhabitants, of which over half were carried off, while in London the proportion of living to dead was two to three. The Rev. Dr. Jessopp describes a marital quarrel, illustrating in a most gruesome manner the terrific mortality. Reginald Goscelin had a dispute with his wife Emma about her dower. The question was never settled. 'Before the day of hearing came on, *every one* of Emma Goscelin's witnesses was dead, and her husband was dead too.' A year ago cholera visited Europe, and killed but a few thousand people, absolutely and relatively a surprisingly small number. Even in the most crowded towns the mortality was not great, while in New York a few deaths nearly caused a panic. In view of such facts, does not our authors' assertion bear the stamp of absurdity on its face? The history of mediæval plagues proves in a negative way that modern hygiene has immeasurably improved the housing of all people. Need we call into witness the filthy rushes of Shakespeare's contemporaries?

Some misprints and inaccuracies of fact may be pointed out. Prof. Gross's name appears with a superfluous 'e' suffixed. Then, as lately Channing and Higginson, our authors adopt Roger's hypothetical explanation of Tyler's rebellion. Later, Messrs. Morris and Bax seem to think that Charles V. was first elected German Emperor, and that by marriage he subsequently acquired Spain. The truth is so well known that it is needless to explain the error. Besides, few will admit the statement that the most constitutional act of the Roundheads was the trial of Charles I.; so eminent an authority as Hallam certainly does not. Adam Smith's *Wealth of Nations* was not published in 1771, but in 1776, the year of the Declaration of Independence.

After the purely historical part, a brief résumé is given of the theories of such men as Fourier, St. Simon, Lamennais, Babœuf, Blanc, Marx, Lassalle and Proudhon. As a climax the authors demonstrate 'how the inevitable transformation of civilization into socialism is most likely to happen,' and how society will appear when thus organized. This picture is one in many respects ennobling to cherish as an ideal. The question is, whether it is realizable, man's nature being as it is. The skeptical reader will gain by the perusal of this essay, for the views are nothing if not original. As in Rousseau's *Discours sur l'Origine de l'Inégalité chez les Hommes*,[1] throughout this book all the sins of modern society are laid at the door of private property. The volume, however, is welcome as an attractive exposition of the main ideas of a most altruistic and sincere socialist, Mr. William Morris, who—paradoxically enough—is a maker of wall papers and printer of books that only the rich can aspire to possess.

[1] *Discourse on the Origin of Inequality among Men.*

68. Unsigned article, *London Quarterly Review*

April 1894, xxii, 84–8

The article, entitled 'Four English Socialists', also discusses the *Minutes of Evidence taken before the Labour Commission* by Tom Mann and Sidney Webb, as representative of a more practical form of Socialism.

The new book on Socialism by Mr. William Morris and Mr. Bax is a very good example of the comparative ease with which the undisturbed reformer can make taking and attractive his golden schemes. Here are no awkward questions to be answered, no difficult problems constantly recurring and the destructive criticism passes uncriticised, the constructive narrative flows evenly along. The book follows the historical method, and contains a review of the whole history of European society in a very brief compass, for though there are many pages there is little print. 'A neat rivulet of text meanders through a meadow of margin,' as on Sir Benjamin Backbite's beautiful quarto page. This historical review has been done so many times that we confess we think it was scarce worth while to perform the task again. The only new matter is in the brief Introduction and in the last chapter, which is called 'Socialism Triumphant,' and as these open a window into the Socialist mind they are worth attention. The Introduction in eighteen pages convicts modern life of hypocrisy and sham 'in its family relations, morality, religion, politics, and art.' It reads more like the diatribe of a dyspeptic than the writing of a poet and a metaphysician, and though it ends on a note of hope (in the prospect of Socialism), the final consolation is hardly more convincing than the dyspeptic's trust that to-morrow his indigestion will be gone. Out of very bad things are to come forth very good. The special characteristic of modern society, it appears, is universal hypocrisy. This is evident in 'our present family of blood relationship,' where the brotherhood of blood almost extinguishes the sense of duty in friendship, and where, if a strange child be adopted, 'the proceeding is cloaked by change of name, assumption of mystery, and abundance of unconscious ceremonial.' This last is one of the freshest and most ingenious grievances we have encountered! The ties of kinship must give way before the 'reason' of mature life, and it were hypocrisy for the maturely reasonable man to allow them to restrain any personal desire or taste. Yet these stern writers would make some allowance; they would allow us to wear 'a light and easy yoke of sentiment,' since even maturity admits that 'it is not unreasonable' to wish to 'pay back with some little kindness' those who have cherished us before reason and maturity came, and 'not unreasonable, too, to look with some special sentiment on brothers and sisters,' because we lived familiarly with them 'when they and we were innocent and undeveloped'! The conclusion of the whole matter is:

> The family professes to exist as affording us a haven of calm and restful affection and the humanising influences of mutual help and consideration, but it ignores quietly its real reason for existence, its real aim—namely, protection for individualist property by means of inheritance, and a nucleus for resistance to the outside world, whether that take the form of other families or the public weal, such as it may be (p. 7).

We presume the Socialists desire that affection arising from kinship should be no stronger than the affection felt for the race, except for the 'light and easy yoke of sentiment,' which itself will disappear when the municipal nursery receives the infant, and boys and girls live familiarly with those of other parents in innocent undevelopment. Yet all art, which is the true record of humanity, attests that the love of child for parent and of parent for child is elemental, and the grave and beautiful piety which the Latins built upon the claims of kinship still restrains and humanises men not undeveloped and not innocent. Human nature may be affected by changes in the conditions of life, but the elemental emotions are to-day what they were when Homer wrote, and we very much doubt whether even the abolition of pocket-money, and the teaching of the solidarity of mankind by a representative of the State, will make a boy forget that his mother bore him. But for fear of seeming irreverent we should accuse the Socialists of a joke when they talk so glibly of changing human nature, brutalised and degraded as it is, in their eyes, by the influence of commercialism; but we presume this miracle of change is a serious article of their optimistic faith.

It is hardly necessary to follow these Jeremiahs in their view of religion or morality, which 'is simply commercial necessity mas-

querading in the forms of the Christian ethics,' a fact 'illustrated by the predominance amongst the commercial classes of a debased Calvinistic theology, termed Evangelicalism'; nor do we learn from them with any surprise that politics and art share the prevailing unreality to the full. That there is considerable ground for this vigorous philippic no man would deny, but that the impression they convey is a fair one very few men would care to assert. We turn to the picture they draw of society as it will be, with the hope that their description of the future will be drawn with some more show of discernment of the caricature of the present. They are careful to state that they give merely their own view, and that their sketch has received the approval of no great Socialistic council, endowed with prophetic power. We start well, with the dis-appearance of civil law, 'an institution based essentially on private property,' and a tendency on the part of criminal law to become ob-solete, as it would 'concern itself only with the protection of the person.' Burglary, for example, of the community's food and drink would be wholly unknown. The great organisation that would direct production and distribution would be a system of federal councils, and 'it would be the necessary duty of the central body to safeguard the then recognised principles of society,' to stereotype perfection, in fact. We have next a description of the new conscience, which will render criminal law un-necessary:

As regards the future form of the moral consciousness, we may safely predict that it will be, in a sense, a return on a higher level to the ethics of the older world, with the difference that the limitation of scope to the kinship group in its narrower sense, which was one of the causes of the dissolution of ancient society, will disappear, and the identification of individual with social interests will be so complete that any divorce between the two will be inconceivable to the average man. . . . . The religion of Socialism will be but the ordinary ethics carried into a higher atmosphere, and will only differ from them in degree of conscious responsibility to one's fellows. Socialistic ethics would be the guide of our daily habit of life; socialistic religion would be that higher form of conscience that would impel us to actions on behalf of a future of the race such as no man could command in his ordinary moods (pp. 298, 299).

This is a very tempting passage, but we will only make one remark. Even supposing that this new morality took the place of the old one, and the conscience of the race had a lodging in every man's nature, what reason is there to suppose that the new morality would be more universally *acted upon* than the old? *L'homme moyen sensuel* of to-day has a conscience which he very frequently disobeys; why should the average man of to-morrow be always obedient to the conscience of to-morrow? The answer, we presume, is, that he would be obedient because of the 'identification of individual with social interests.' But the passions and desires of men to-day often make them act in a manner very adverse to their interests, and it is entirely inconceivable that the social interest would always accord with each man's temporary interest. One point where the Socialistic scheme fails is this: they neglect to provide that power which the world has always desired, the power that will make men do the right when they know it, even under the stress of temptation. Unless they can banish temptation from their world, we fancy the average man will hardly be so automatically obedient to the social voice as they hope. A society has not been redeemed when it has been made comfortable. We have not space to follow this Utopia through all its streets, which will be very beautiful—it is enough to say that the chapter details the arrangement which will convert the country into a picture by Burne-Jones. Marriages would be associations that might be dissolved at will by either husband or wife, and no disgrace would attach to either party, in cases of dissolution of the voluntary tie, since we presume neither would have committed any act contrary to the social interest. Labour would be made pleasurable for all. And, finally, so peaceful and happy would mankind be that fiction would die for want of material. That material is to be found apparently, not in the nature and passions of man, but only in the 'futilities of a society of inequality wielded by a conventional false sense of duty.' No suspicion of Satan is allowed within the precincts of this paradise. It is a beautiful dream, though as a reality we fancy it would be rather tiresome to face always 'the eternal calm,' and we only regret that the writers should so consistently 'reckon without Dame Nature, their hostess.' The one serious aspect of the matter is that many uncritical readers of this and such-like books are led to call themselves Socialists, and to take political action in various ways on the ground that such action tends to Socialism. From the reverie of these two Communists we turn to the practical proposals of more hard-headed men.

69. F. W. H. Myers on Morris's *Weltanschauung*

1893

Myers (1843–1901) was poet, critic and student of psychic phenomena. His article 'Modern Poets and the Meaning of Life' discussed Tennyson and 'our two great poets who survive,' Swinburne and Morris, in relation to the problems raised by the impersonality of the universe.

From *Nineteenth Century*, January 1893, xxxiii, 93–111 (100–4 on Morris); reprinted in *Science and a Future Life with Other Essays* (London, 1893).

When we turn from Swinburne to William Morris we pass into a very different emotional clime. Similar as the two poets are in thoroughness of artistic culture and in width of learning, the personal temperaments which their poems reveal are in some sense complementary. In Swinburne we have seen the vivid but detached intelligence rendering in turn with equal eloquence, and apparently with equal satisfaction, every attitude of mind which the known cosmic laws, construed strictly as against man's hopes, can be shown to justify. In Morris we have a man equally hopeless indeed, but not equally indifferent to hope—steeped, rather, in all the delicate joys, the soft emotions, which make the charm of life, and feeling at every turn with sad discouragement the shadow and imminence of the End. He is above all things the poet of Love; but in his poems love is never without the note of yearning, the sense of an unseizable and fugitive joy:—

> Love is enough: while ye deemed him a-sleeping,
> > There were signs of his coming and sounds of his feet;
> His touch it was that would bring you to weeping,
> > When the summer was deepest and music most sweet:
> > In his footsteps ye followed the day to its dying,
> Ye went forth by his gown-skirts the morning to meet:
> > In his place on the beaten-down orchard-grass lying
> > Of the sweet ways ye pondered yet left for life's trying.

We asked ourselves but now whether Liberty, which Swinburne sang, could still be said to offer a permanent motive and object in life for the mass of mankind. To this question Morris has an unexpectedly definite answer. He desires, indeed, a reconstruction of society far more radical than the mere republican demands. He embarks with light heart on a task which one might have thought difficult enough to supply the world with unrealised ideals for a thousand years. Yet he believes that this socialistic reconstruction will be effected so rapidly that the problem as to the subsequent aims and occupations of mankind confronts us almost at once. And, as the stanza above quoted suggests, it is in Love that he finds the main, though not the only, interest of the happy and equalised race to be.

Now we may certainly say that just as Liberty represents the next stage of human progress after Peace and Plenty, so does Love represent the next stage beyond Liberty. When men have got their communities arranged to their mind, they will find time—as a number of leisured persons find time already—to devote their main attention to such happiness as the relation between the sexes can bring. But here, almost for the first time, the question of the unknown future begins to have a practical bearing on life. If love is at once brought thus into prominence and also deprived of all beyond its earthly fruition, is there not a fear lest it should either sink into mere animal passion or lose its tranquillity in yearning pain? Morris has treated this question in two ways; answering it generally in the sadder tone, and as though from actual experience; but once with resolute cheerfulness, in a polemical composition. Let us take this latter first.

It is sometimes urged as an advantage attending the loss of belief in a future life that those who count this life as all are more eager to make their fellow-men happy in it. Without further assenting to this view, we may admit that Morris's belief in earth as the only possible Paradise has helped to drive him, by the most generous road, into a socialism where we may watch him tossing between various Scyllæ and Charybdes with which we are not here concerned. What now interests us is the delightful romance in which he has described earthly life led happily, with no thought of life beyond. What to retain, what to relinquish, has here been carefully thought out. Religion and philosophy disappear altogether; science and poetry are in the background; but we are left with the decorative arts, open-air exercise, and an abundance of beautiful and innocent girls. The future of the human race, in short, is to be a kind of affectionate picnic.

I know not, indeed, how the given problem could have been more attractively solved. But how long will life last thus, à la Rousseau? Will the haymaking lovers go on haymaking for countless generations and still keep their emotions at precisely the right temperature? Dangers of one kind need no insistence; and as for troubles in a higher air, it may be noted that nothing in *News from Nowhere* strikes a truer note than the author's yearning regret at severance from his bewitching heroine—the daughter of a world to be. He feels that in order to live her life he must himself be changed; and although he speaks of the needed change as if it were but a forgetting of pain and sorrow, a re-entry into Eden,—yet when we compare his picture of that ideal life with his or any active man's life here and now, we feel that there will be more loss than gain; and that the fuller pleasure cannot compensate for the absence of moral evolution.

That old and just gravamen against almost all theological paradises— that they provide for joy but not for progress—holds good of Morris's many imagined paradises as well. They are abodes of unchanging bliss, dimly felt to be in themselves unsatisfactory, though attractive in comparison with the briefer pleasures which man's common life affords. If they are to be enjoyed without satiety, there must, as in 'Ogier the Dane,' be a transformation of personality, a forgetfulness of the heroic deeds and strenuous joys of earth. Yet, on the other hand, these strenuous joys are never felt to have any clear advantage over the amorous paradises, on account of their hazardous shortness. Orpheus gains no victory in argument over the Sirens; whose invitations would be irresistible if there were not so much reason to suspect their good faith. And in the 'Hill of Venus,' that most terrible of all pictures of remorseful satiety, a Christian hope has to be invoked in order that there may seem to be any other alternative than endless loathing or endless death.

Perhaps, indeed, the fact may be that man is not constructed for flawless happiness, but for moral evolution. Few passages in Morris are more affecting than those in which the Wanderers, who have failed to find the Acre of the Undying, express at once their half-shame at having undertaken that quest, and their regret that it has been all in vain. In the lines in which their poet pleads their excuse, he manages to remind the reader of many valid reasons which impel to that bootless desire:—

> Ah, doubt and fear they well might have indeed.
> Cry out upon them, ye who have no need
> Of life, to right the blindness and the wrong!
> Think scorn of these, ye who are made so strong

That with no good-night ye can loose the hand
That led you erst thro' Love's sweet flowery land!
Laugh, ye whose eyes are piercing to behold
What makes the silver seas and skies of gold!
Pass by in haste, ye folk, who day by day
Win all desires that lie upon your way!

It is from no lack of sympathy with heroism that Morris has tarried in this world of soft regrets. Seldom has heroic passion, god-like endeavour, been so painted as in that scene between Sigurd and Brynhild on the summit of Hind-fell:—

And where on the wings of his hope is the spirit of Sigurd borne?

But all that triumphant adventure rests in the last resort on the existence of Odin and his halls of gold; Odin, seen sometimes in visible form, and encouraging the younger heroes with memory of their sires, whose valour reaps now its high reward:—

For on earth they thought of my threshold, and the gifts I have to give,
Nor prayed for a little longer, and a little longer to live.

It is the privilege of poetry thus 'simple, sensuous, and passionate' that the singer can reveal himself without self-consciousness, and utter without loss of dignity the inward softness of the strong. Who has dwelt longer than this robust and manly worker in that sunlit mist of yearning which hangs suspended above the watershed of joy and pain? Who has breathed more intimately the last forlornness, and such an inward cry as oftenest is only guessed in a tear?

Come down, O love, may not our hands still meet,
Since still we live to-day, forgetting June,
Forgetting May, deeming October sweet—
—O hearken, hearken! through the afternoon,
The grey tower sings a strange old tinkling tune!
Sweet, sweet, and sad, the failing year's last breath,
Too satiate of life to strive with death.

And we too—will it not be soft and kind,
That rest from life, from patience and from pain,
That rest from bliss we know not when we find,
That rest from Love which ne'er the end can gain?—
—Hark, how the tune swells, that erewhile did wane!
Look up, love! ah, cling close and never move!
How can I have enough of life and love?

If in these October stanzas we have the last fruitless attempt at resignation, in the poem which preludes to November we have a mood more dreadful still. We have the recognition that the Cosmos has no true place for man; we have that underlying aspect of Nature which, once seized, is no less than appalling; when the familiar garden seems alien and terrible as a gulf in the Milky Way; and, nakedly confronted with the everlasting universe, man that must die feels more than the bitterness of death:—

> Look out upon the real world, where the moon,
> Half-way 'twixt root and crown of these high trees,
> Turns the dead midnight into dreamy noon,
> Silent and full of wonders, for the breeze
> Died at the sunset, and no images,
> No hopes of day, are left in sky or heart;—
> Is it not fair, and of most wondrous worth?
>
> Yea, I have looked and seen November there;
> The changeless seal of change it seemed to be,
> Fair death of things that, living once, were fair,
> Bright sign of loneliness too great for me,
> Strange image of the dread eternity,
> In whose void patience how can these have part,
> These outstretched feverish hands, this restless heart?

We have traced in the work of these two poets almost every mood of feeling possible to high-minded men under the shadow of an inevitable doom. There has been courage, and there has been calm; there has been the solemn sadness of impossible resignation, and that imperious cry for Life! more Life! which is the very voice of the human heart. Is this then all? and must poets in every age be content to renew the old desiring, and to fall back baffled from the same impalpable wall of gloom?

THE WOOD BEYOND THE WORLD

1895

70. Theodore Watts, unsigned review, *Athenaeum*

2 March 1895, no. 3514, 273-4

This review pleased Morris, who wrote to thank Watts for his discriminating sympathy; see Introduction, pp. 3-4.

It is an extremely interesting fact that Mr. Morris in exercising his rare poetical gift has so often of late turned from metrical to unmetrical forms. Though his romances must needs be taken as being in some measure the outcome of his studies in Saga literature, they hold, in conception no less than in execution, a place of their own. If the name 'metreless poem' can properly be given to any form of imaginative literature, these romances are more fully entitled to that name than anything that has gone before. In all poetry an indispensable requisite must be form of some kind, and what form can there be without metre? The measured prose used by Leconte de Lisle and others is as far removed from poetic art as from prose art, and consequently has perhaps no right of existence at all. In English we have between rhyme-measures and measured prose a magnificent rhymeless movement, our decasyllabic blank verse. The tone of this, however, is so elevated that not even Tennyson has been able to reconcile the English ear to 'familiar blank verse.' Hence the want of another medium is often deeply felt.

In the unmeasured 'prose poetry' of De Quincey and Mr. Ruskin the movement is rhetorical, and has, therefore, as little to do with poetry as have the rhetorical movements of 'The Lily and the Bee' of Samuel Warren, or the 'Leaves of Grass' of Walt Whitman. But when, as in Mr. Morris's romances, the form of imaginative literature is imbued

376

throughout with poetical colour rendered in a perfectly concrete diction—when the sentences (built on the simple method of poetry and not on the complex method of prose) have a cadence in which *recognized* metrical law has been abandoned, a cadence whose movement is born of the emotions which the words embody—may not such a form of literature be properly called poetry?

This is the question which presents itself to the reader who tries to examine critically the lovely story before him. To enter here upon the question whether a poem without metre can really exist is impossible. Moreover, it has already been discussed in these columns. Yet we may remind the reader that although modern criticism takes form and not matter to be the essence of poetry, it was not so with the old criticism; it was not so with Aristotle, upon whose principles the old criticism was professedly built.

When some years ago we had occasion to compare, or rather to contrast with each other, the two great renderings of the Niblung story, the *Völsunga Saga* and the *Nibelungenlied*, we came to the conclusion that, owing to its extraordinary unity in the development of *motif*, the old unmetrical version of the story was more completely covered by Aristotle's definition of an epic than was the metrical and more modern one of the Germans. And assuredly, if Aristotle would have given the name of poem to the *Völsunga Saga*, he would never have hesitated to bestow that name on *The House of the Wolfings* or *The Roots of the Mountains*. Intensely poetic and intensely dramatic, moreover, as are the Icelandic Sagas, they are lacking in one of the most delightful qualities of the unmetrical poems of Mr. Morris just mentioned—that delicate sense of beauty in which the author of *The Earthly Paradise* has had no superior even in the epoch which has inaugurated the neo-romantic movement; and this last exquisite story of his must be held to surpass the best of its predecessors in poetical feeling and poetical colour, and to equal them in poetical substance. Here more abundantly than ever we get that marvellously youthful way of confronting the universe which is the special feature of Mr. Morris's genius. It is not easy to realize that it is other than a poet in the heyday of a glorious youth who tells with such gusto this wonderful story, how once upon a time, in the Land of Somewhere, young Golden Walter, on the eve of taking ship for foreign lands, saw a sight which at one moment seemed real and at another a dream—a royal lady of surpassing beauty accompanied by a woman thrall whose loveliness was still more bewitching, and a dwarf whose hideousness was more fascinating still; how he saw them go on

377

board a strange ship and sail away; how he believed the ship and those who went in her to be real until shortly afterwards he saw the same three in the streets of his native town; how subsequently having taken sail himself, he again saw the same royal lady, the same woman thrall, and the same dwarf; how on landing on a still more remote coast, connected by a mysterious pass with a land of magic, he threaded that pass alone and discovered who the mysterious three really were, and met with adventures among them more wonderful than any of these recorded in the 'Arabian Nights.'

[two long quotations omitted]

With regard to the diction of the above extracts, there are those for whom it will possess great charm, and there are those whom it will repel. Is it legitimate and is it wise for an artist to return up the stream of the literature in which he works in order to preserve some of the best of the old beauties of his language from being swept away by modern innovations? We think the question must be answered in the affirmative. Such recurrences to elder styles are common in all the arts. Sometimes, indeed, they are of great value. It is the commonplace and vulgar mind that clings to the stucco horrors of Pimlico architecture, simply because they are more modern than the architecture of Elizabeth or the architecture of Queen Anne. And so in literature. As time goes on it is inevitable that a language should suffer mutilation, it is inevitable also that good writers should be found who look back to beauties of the language that have been left behind. Spenser did this; so did Shakspeare; so did certain great prose writers of the early years of the nineteenth century. Had it been otherwise, how should we ever have had the prose of Southey, Lamb, Landor, De Quincey, after the degraded state into which the English language sank in the time of L'Estrange? And then, over and above the verbal texture of the book, what about the poetical spirit vitalizing it? Here, indeed, we touch upon a vast question.

For something like three hundred years have Euphuism, the love of being didactic, and prose rhetoric been eating into English poetry. The greatest poets of the sixteenth and seventeenth centuries suffered grievously from Euphuism; even Shakspeare was, at one time of his life, in danger of being ruined by it.

As to the didactic element, the idea that the primary function of poetry was the enunciation of thoughts was at the bottom of the aridity of the eighteenth century; and even the great Romantic revival did not fully cure English poetry of this tendency. The love of preaching ate into the wings of Shelley. It threatened even Keats at the outset of his career. It made of Wordsworth a writer of quintessential prose who could occasionally take a glorious spring into poetry. It could not, of course, ruin Coleridge, but its effect upon him was so disastrous that his truly precious work is confined to about half a dozen poems. And as to Euphuism and rhetoric, without discussing their destructive effect upon the poets of our own time, we may say that Euphuism is the one fault of Tennyson, and that whenever Rossetti and Mr. Swinburne pass out of the region of pure poetry, the one passes into the region of Euphuism, the other into that of rhetoric. It was left to our own time to produce the one poet of the nineteenth century upon whom Euphuism, the didactic spirit, and rhetoric have exercised no influence whatever; that is to say, the one poet whose work is poetry and nothing else. Of all our writers Mr. Morris is, save in his unfortunate polemical chants, the most purely romantic. His genius is in very truth that

> Lady of the Mere,
> Sole-sitting by the shores of old Romance,

who is the real owner of the fountain of youth. At the age of sixty or thereabouts, he is still pouring out his lovely things, more full of the glory of youth, more full of romantic adventure and romantic love, than any of the beautiful poems in his first volume. By the side of this exhaustless creator of youthful and lovely things, the youngest of the poets who have just appeared above the horizon seems faded and jaded.

What then is his position among the poets of our time? Within a dozen years the poetical firmament of Europe has suffered a great change. The deaths of Rossetti, Hugo, Matthew Arnold, Browning, Tennyson, and finally Leconte de Lisle have left a gap in the world of letters as vast as that which followed the deaths of Keats, Shelley, Byron, Scott, Goethe, and Coleridge between 1821 and 1834. If poetry is to hold the place it has hitherto held in pure literature, what are now the greatest names in the world of letters, not only of England and America, but of Europe? With regard to certain prominent European writers, such as Tolstoi, Mr. Ruskin, Ibsen, Zola, Mr. Meredith, these, having come to the front as *prosateurs* (though the last mentioned is also a poet, and a very original one), are not perhaps to be ranked alongside the poets. For whatever may come to pass in another century or two, the poet in our own time is still, as he has always hitherto been, the protagonist in the arena of pure literature.

With regard to France, admirable as are some (indeed many) of the contemporary French writers, there is no one, not even M. de Hérédia, who can be placed in the front rank. In France as in England, and in England as in old Greece, it is not the number of lines, but the accent of those lines, which makes a poet a major or minor. Still, quantity of good work is of course a most important part of the question, and if so admirable an artist as M. de Hérédia should live to write three or four times the number of lines that he has at present written, there will be a Frenchman in the foremost ranks of contemporary poetry.

In intellectual grip of a subject, and in certain other equipments common both to the poet and the prose writer, M. de Hérédia is in his own way equal to the late Leconte de Lisle in another way. Indeed, while Leconte de Lisle's style is undeniably hard and cold, notwithstanding the spacious form he adopts, the style of M. de Hérédia has as much of the warmth and flexibility of life as can perhaps be got into the sonnet of octave and sestet. And if France has no living writer to be set in the front rank, the same must certainly be said in regard to Italy. That the two leading poets of the world are Englishmen—Mr. Swinburne and Mr. Morris—is recognized by all criticism that is worthy of the name. But were there ever two great poets so unlike each other?

71. Unsigned review, *Spectator*

July 1895, lxxv, 52–3

Morris wrote to the editor to deny the suggestion of allegorical intention; see Introduction, p.3.

Many truths have been lighted up and shown to the world by the torch-light of allegory. Macaulay says that the *Pilgrim's Progress* is the only work of its kind which possesses a strong human interest, and that other allegories only amuse the fancy, and that even in Spenser's *Faery Queen* the allegory is pursued beyond the bounds of tediousness. 'We become sick of cardinal virtues and deadly sins, and long for the society of plain men and women.' It was the shadowy author of the *Visions Concerning Piers Plowman*, who saw the world as it were 'a fair field full of folk,' wherein some were working and wandering, setting, sowing, and ploughing 'full hard,' while others wasted in gluttony and vice the goods that the workers had stored together. In those old visions, as two centuries later in *The Faery Queen*, we find virtues and vices personified in human forms, and labelled 'Fals-semblant' and 'Lady Meed,' so that we may have no doubt of their true characters. The writers of allegories in modern days are more reticent; we are not even given a key whereby to unlock the painted doors, we are merely invited to enter, and we must find out for ourselves the parentage and lineage of the heroes and heroines. There are probably many people who read an allegory as they read a fairy-tale, without seeking for hidden meanings, and, read in such simple fashion, *The Wood Beyond the World* is a delightful tale of adventure set in a mediæval setting, wherein a youth called Golden Walter leaves his home and sallies forth to strange lands, trusting to his good sword and ready wit to win his way through whatsoever may befall him. At the outset of his voyage he sees a vision:—

So Walter stood idly watching the said ship, and as he looked, lo! folk passing him toward the gangway. These were three; first came a dwarf, dark-brown of hue and hideous, with long arms and ears exceeding great, and dog-teeth that stuck out like the fangs of a wild beast. He was clad in a rich coat of yellow silk, and bore in his hand a crooked bow, and was girt with a broad sax. After him came a maiden, young by seeming of scarce twenty summers; fair of face as a flower; grey-eyed, brown-haired, with lips full and red, slim and gentle of body. Simple was her array, of a short and strait green gown so that on her right ankle was clear to see an iron ring. Last of the three was a lady, tall and stately, so radiant of visage and glorious of raiment, that it were hard to say what like she was; for scarce might the eye gaze steadily upon her exceeding beauty; yet must every son of Adam who found himself anigh her, lift up his eyes again after he had dropped them and look again on her, and yet again, and yet again.

The three disappear in a ship which displays a green banner with the device of a 'grim wolf ramping up against a maiden,' and Walter determines to seek for them. He and his comrades sail on in their good ship until they come to an unknown shore—happily not so inhospitable a shore as the seekers for the Earthly Paradise fared upon—and here Walter espies a cleft in the rocky boundary, and, leaving his friends, pursues his way in search of the creatures of his vision. He at last encounters the hideous Dwarf; then the Maid with the iron anklet, with whom he enters into a compact of friendship; and lastly, the fascinating Lady, who welcomes him to the Golden House. There is a beautiful description of the house:—

So an hour before sunset he saw something white and gay gleaming through the boles of the oak-trees, and presently there was clear before him a most goodly house builded of white marble, carved all about with knots and imagery and the carven folk were all painted of their lively colours, whether it were their raiment or their flesh, and the housings wherein they stood all done with gold and fair hues. Gay were the windows of the house; and there was a pillared porch before the great door, with images betwixt the pillars both of men and beasts: and when Walter looked up to the roof of the house, he saw that it gleamed and shone; for all the tiles were of yellow metal, which he deemed to be of very gold.

How Walter kills a lion, and is beguiled by the beautiful Lady, frees the Maid, and escapes with her, and the tragic end of the King's Son, the Lady, and the Dwarf, is told in a delightfully poetical fashion. The description of the Lady in the magic wood and bower of pleasance, reminds us of Vivien:[1]

> A robe
> Of samite without price, that more exprest
> Than hid her, clung about her lissome limbs,
> In colour like the satin shining palm
> Or sallows in the windy gleams of March.

Perhaps the scene in the folk-mote of the Bear-people when the Maid claims succession to their queenship, and gives a sign of her power by the revival of her faded flower-chaplets, is the best in the book. 'Lo, then! as she spake, the faded flowers that hung about her gathered life and grew fresh again; the woodbine round her neck and her sleek shoulders knit itself together and embraced her freshly, and cast its scent about her face. The lilies that girded her loins lifted up their heads, and the gold of their tassels fell upon her; the eye-bright grew clean blue again upon her smock; the eglantine found its bloom again, and then began to shed the leaves thereof upon her feet; the meadow-sweet wreathed amongst it made clear the sweetness of her legs, and the mouse-ear studded her raiment as with gems. There she stood amidst of the blossoms, like a great orient pearl against the fret-work of the goldsmiths, and the breeze that came up the valley from behind bore the sweetness of her

[1] The wily and malignant character in Tennyson's 1859 Idyll 'Merlin and Vivien'.

fragrance all over the man-mote.' The whole scene in the Doom-ring, with its circle of rough men, its ancient centre figure, and its tribunal of hewn stone, suggests pagan rites, but the language in which the Maid accuses the Bear-folk of want of faith, is distinctly scriptural. Almost we hear her declaiming 'Ye hypocrites; ye can discern the face of the sky; but can ye not discern the signs of the times?' We read the fairy-tale with a grateful consciousness that Imagination is still alive, and passing us by clad in quaint garments of a bygone fashion, when we spy the serpent in this Eden; and then we are once more haunted by the shadow of the story with a purpose. It is borne in upon us that the Lady who raises false lions in the path, and allures the King's Son and the Merchant's Son with her honied words and false kisses, is a worse sorceress than Medea or Circe; she is the Lady Meed of Langland's vision; she personifies Capital itself, just as the Maid whom she holds captive personifies Labour. Mr. Morris preaches his Socialism in the most seductive and poetical form, and he ends his story in a Utopia where Labour and the Merchant's Son, whom we imagine to be the ideal Englishman, are the sovereign powers, after Aristocracy, in the person of the King's Son, has been made to assume the likeness of the Merchant's Son and then scotched, and Capital with her creature, the bloated aristocrat, has also come to a bad end. Capital spreads her nets in vain before the Merchant's Son; she tempts him with pleasure and luxury; she speaks fairly to Labour before him, but in secret she plots her downfall and ruin, and allows her creature the Dwarf to torment her. The Maid tells Walter of the wisdom she learned of 'the old woman [by whom we conclude is meant Nature] perfected betwixt the stripes of her mistress;' and Mr. Morris would have us remember, in the fable of the faded flowers, how it is Labour's doing that the deserts blossom like the rose, the fields are tilled, and the rivers are compelled to water the land, though he fails to tell us how Labour accomplishes all this without the help of Capital, unless we are led to infer that Labour, in claiming the succession to the queenship, claims also to appropriate the accumulations that constitute Capital. It is, of course, unfair to drive an allegory too far home; but we confess to being a little puzzled by the suggestions of Mr. Morris's Socialism. It is evident that he wishes to portray the downfall of some great power that cannot endure a new state of things, and as she will not accept the emancipation of Labour, or her thrall's alliance with the dominant power, thereby gives herself the death-blow. To our mind, there is a little obscurity about the Dwarf and his place in the fable; he says himself that he is what the Lady has made him, and we conclude that he personifies the evil result of the ill-used power of Capital, and that he is slain with his own weapon, his power being taken from him by the new popular form of government and placed in the hands of Labour.

The old theory of equality is one to which we gladly subscribe, but we cannot forget the everyday fact that in each pan of milk the cream rises to the top, and that intellect and health, and what Mr. William Watson would call the 'poorer virtues,' such as thrift and foresight and prudence, are not distributed equally among men, and that always there will be spendthrifts and accumulators, those who sow and those who reap, those who are born to rule and those who are born to serve. The story of *The Wood beyond the World*, taken as a fairy-tale, is poetical and highly imaginative, but if we are compelled to look into its teaching we are reminded of the mirror in which we now see life darkly, and of an ancient mirror in which the faces look somewhat distorted, though the frame is quaintly set and enriched with jewels; we are delighted when the poet forgets his philosophy, and at no time is his idealism wearisome, nor are we deluged with 'cardinal virtues and deadly sins.'

BEOWULF

1895

---

72. Theodore Watts, unsigned review, *Athenaeum*

10 August 1895, no. 3537, 181-2

We can well imagine that this translation of *Beowulf* into rhymeless alliterative lines will seem uncouth to the general reader whose ear is familiar only with the quantitative scansion of classic movements and the accentual prosody of modern rhyme and blank verse. But if the business of the translator of an ancient poem is to pour the old wine into the new bottles with as little loss as possible of its original aroma, Mr. Morris's efforts have been crowned with entire success.

The archaic atmosphere of an old poem is, of course, the result of its verbal texture no less than of its informing temper, and the antiquated English and antiquated movements of Mr. Morris bring his readers far nearer to the original than any later form could have done. With regard to the metre, the most poetically minded of the commentators on the poem, Mr. Stopford A. Brooke, has some excellent words upon the extreme difficulty of translating *Beowulf*:

Translations of poetry are never much good, but at least they should always endeavour to have the musical movement of poetry, and to obey the laws of the verse they translate. A translation made in any one of our existing rhyming metres seemed to me as much out of the question as a prose translation. None of these metres resemble those of Anglo-Saxon poetry; and, moreover, their associations would modernize the old English thought. An Anglo-Saxon king in modern Court dress would not look more odd and miserable than an Anglo-Saxon poem in a modern rhyming metre.

We have frequently said that the only modern poet who could translate *Beowulf* was the author of *Sigurd*, the one great epic of the nineteenth century, whose sympathy with the Old English temper is nothing less than marvellous. Yet even for a genius so rare as his, and a knowledge of the subject so exhaustive, the task must have been one of immense difficulty. So powerful is the vision at work in this glorious poem, that it seems the product not of a poetical artificer, but of Nature herself. And in some measure this effect is due to the peculiar happiness of the metrical form in which it is embodied. The last crowning excellence in all poetry is that it shall seem to be inspired, and one of the greatest aids to this is that the struggle between matter and form shall be so little apparent that the movement seems the inevitable outcome of the emotion of him who tells the tale or sings the song.

Every language has, of course, an instinctive leaning towards the rhythmic movement that is natural to its genius. The great qualities of eagerness and dignity which characterize the Homeric poems arise in large measure from the fact that the quantitative hexametrical movement is so natural an expression of the genius of the Greek language that in the Homeric lines it seems to be as inevitable a rhythm of Nature's as the rhythm of breathing. And so, again, in that language whose fecundity of rhymes is so enormous that every man who speaks it is a born rhymer. Even work so artistic as that of Dante seems inevitable in its form, and on that account inspired.

With regard to modern English verse, no student of poetry can have failed to indulge in speculations as to what would have been the course of English metres had not the struggle between the scansion of the native forms and the Romance measures been decided by the advent of the genius of Chaucer, who thus sneers at alliteration: 'I cannot geste, rom, ram, ruff, by my letter.' Notwithstanding that English passed from an inflected to an uninflected tongue, the bias of the English ear remained as strongly towards alliterative bars as is the bias of the Italian ear towards rhyme. Apart from the paucity of English rhymes, the power of the ancestral strain is so great that English poets may, as we have before remarked, be divided into those who are born rhymers and those whose every couplet shows that rhyme is to them not a spur, but a curb. The greatest masters of free rhyming are no doubt Coleridge and Shelley in their best work, but the reason why so few English poets have succeeded in producing much rhymed work that seems free from artifice is connected very deeply and very subtly with the fact that our ancestors found the perfect music in the alliterative movements of *Beowulf*, and afterwards of *Piers Plowman*. Whatever may be said for or against this generalization, however, it is certain that in all languages not only passion, but all strong emotion, is naturally and instinctively alliterative, and no scansion seems so absolutely the scansion of Nature as that which governs the verses of *Beowulf* and other Old English poems.

Sometimes Mr. Morris does, no doubt, load the second division of the line with too many syllables, forgetting that in this respect there is a great difference between an inflected and uninflected language. Whether the Old English versifier used the short line with only one or two slurred syllables, or the long Cædmonian line where the unaccentuated syllables are many and variable, the music of his lines depended as much on the unaccentuated syllables as on the accentuated ones, and the overloading of a bar seems to have been instinctively neutralized by a free use of liquids. No doubt, as Wright pointed out in his introduction to *Piers Plowman*, the quicker pronunciation of Middle English required a greater number of syllables to fill up the same space of time as that occupied by a line of the same length in what it was once the fashion to call Anglo-Saxon, owing to the more slow and impressive pronunciation of the older language; but Langland always took care of his consonants and liquids, so that there should be no pebbly movement.

With regard to the poem itself, the temper and the execution of *Beowulf* afford another proof how little the growth of civilization and all its accomplishments can do in the way of enriching the vision and the faculty divine.

[concluding narrative section omitted]

OLD FRENCH ROMANCES

1896

73. Unsigned review, *Nation*

June 1896, lxiii, 88–9

Under the title *Old French Romances* (Scribners), Mr. William Morris has reissued for the general public his versions of four mediæval French tales, already printed for the æsthetic few at the Kelmscott Press. The new edition contains also a brief but valuable introduction by Mr. Joseph Jacobs,[1]—of which we need say only that it displays its author's customary erudition in matters of this kind, not to mention his gay and at times even jovial manner. The stories chosen by Mr. Morris are four of the five in the little volume 'Nouvelles françaises en prose du 13ième siècle,' published as long ago as 1856 by MM. Moland and d'Héricault (the fifth tale in that collection being the delightful *chante-fable* of 'Aucassin et Nicolete,' which Mr. Andrew Lang has done into English, as everybody knows). The present volume contains, then, the stories of 'L'Empereur Constant,' 'Ami et Amile,' 'Le Roi Flore et la belle Jehane,' and 'La Comtesse de Ponthieu' (or, as Mr. Morris prefers, 'Istore d'Outre-Mer'). In the case of the first two of these, readers of Old French will regret that the translations should be based upon the decidedly inferior prose forms of the tales rather than on the earlier and more poetical narratives in verse which are preserved to us. The last two exist in French only in prose, and we must perforce be satisfied with them as they are. All four stories are, however, in any form engaging and delightful. The first, 'L'Empereur Constant,' Mr. Morris has already retold (with some variations derived from other forms of the legend) in the *Earthly Paradise*, as 'The Man Born to be King.' The second, 'Ami et Amile,' is the most famous mediæval representative of stories about perfect friendship, like that of David and Jonathan or of

---

[1] Joseph Jacobs (1854–1916) was a folklorist, literary editor and Jewish historian.

Orestes and Pylades. The third, 'Le Roi Flore et la belle Jehane,' gives us one of the mediæval forms of the Cymbeline story of a wager about a wife's virtue. The last, 'La Comtesse de Ponthieu,' describes a strange and pathetic adventure extrinsically connected with the Crusades. It is probable that all the tales were originally Byzantine or Oriental.

It is perhaps not a matter of consequence whether Mr. Morris's version is philologically sound or not (it really is not very bad from this point of view), for he does not profess to be a philologist. The question of the character of the English style he has adopted has, on the other hand, some interest. A German has already written a dissertation on the sources of the *Earthly Paradise*; perhaps we may later get one on the sources of Mr. Morris's Romantic grammar. We should like to know, for example, how he came to be so fond of the ugly word 'much' used as an intensive ('a *much* valiant man,' 'a *much* good dame,' p. 119). His conjugation strikes us at times as having a curious similarity to that of the American negro ('And the Emperor Constans ... did do christen his wife,' p. 23; 'The Emperor did do slit the belly of him with a knife from the breast down to the navel,' p. 6). We are somewhat at a loss to translate into the vernacular such locutions as 'much long aloof thence' (p. 13); and though the statement that the young Constans 'entered into the garden all a horseback' (p. 14) seems to reproduce the French *si entra ou gardin tout à cheval*, it can hardly be called a current English equivalent of it. But no doubt the style adopted by Mr. Morris, both here and in his translations of the Northern Saga, is intended to be caviare to the general. One thing is sure, that the style of the Old French narrators stood in no such relation to the common speech of mediæval France as Mr. Morris's to our tongue. And if translation be reproducing as nearly as possible the manner and tone, as well as the matter, of the original, this is not translation at all.

74. A Radical tribute to Morris

1896

Robert Blatchford, article in *Clarion*, October 1896, no. 253, 324–5.

Blatchford (1851–1943) founded the *Clarion* in 1891 as a radical weekly: some of his articles were reprinted in 1893 as *Merrie England*. He was a successful popular journalist, who derived inspiration from Morris's ideas.

I cannot help thinking that it does not matter what goes into the *Clarion* this week, because William Morris is dead. And what Socialist will care for any other news this week, beyond that one sad fact? He was our best man, and he is dead. How can we think of the movement to-day but as a thing struck motionless? How can we remember our own poor feeble trials, aspirations, desires, as we stand by the brink of that mysterious silence into which our brightest spirit has disappeared? Who cares to read, who to write in such an hour?

When the news reached me first, I thought of asking some friend who had known William Morris more intimately, or longer than I had, to write his obituary for the *Clarion*. I did not do that because, though I felt very ill-fitted for the task, I yet felt a strong desire to attempt it. Or perhaps it would be more correct to say that I could not persuade myself in this case to relinquish the post of honour to another.

I have long held William Morris in great esteem, and I feel his loss too nearly to be able to write much or well about him or his work at this present time. 'William Morris was a noble artist and a noble man. We loved him, and honoured him, and we deplore his death.' That is what every socialist will say—for Morris had not an enemy in the world—and when that is said, who feels like saying more—as yet!

I have just been reading the obituary notices in some of the London papers, and I feel sick and sorry. The fine phrases, the elaborate compliments, the ostentatious parade of their own erudition, and the little covert sneers at the Socialism Morris loved; all the tawdry upholsteries of these journalistic undertakers seem like desecration. Under any

circumstances it would anger a man to hear a professional orator uttering rounded periods over the body of a dear dead friend, but in this
case it revolts one, for William Morris was the soul of sincerity, and the
Press is notoriously insincere.

William Morris was our best man; and he is dead. It is true that much
of his work still lives, and will live. But we have lost him, and, great
as was his work, he himself was greater. Many a man of genius is
dwarfed by his own creations. We could all name men whose personalities seem unworthy of their own words and actions; men who
resemble mean jars filled with honey, or foul lamps emitting brilliant
beams. Morris was of a nobler kind. He was better than his best.
Though his words fell like sword strokes, one always felt that the
warrior was stronger than his sword. For Morris was not only a genius,
he was a *man*. Strike at him where you would, he rang true. Look him
straight in the eyes, and it was like looking up at the heavens—there
was nothing but purity between you and the stars. Grip him by the
hand, and you would feel like thanking God that you had met a man.
His face was as honest as a lion's and you accepted his word as you
accept the date from an almanac. This is a censorious world, and as a
rule, let a man be chaste as ice, pure as snow, he shall not escape
calumny. Yet have I never heard one single word of detraction or
dislike spoken of William Morris. Nor is there a Socialist to-day in
England but will feel that he has lost a friend.

He was our best man. We cannot spare him; we cannot replace him.
In all England there lives no braver, kinder, honester, cleverer, heartier
man than William Morris. He is dead, and we cannot help feeling for a
while that nothing else matters.

> You may give over the plough, boys,
>   You may take the gear to the stead,
> All the sweat o' your brow, boys,
>   Will never get beer and bread.
> The seed's waste, I know, boys,
> There's not a blade will grow, boys,
> 'Tis cropped out, I trow, boys,
>   And, Willie's dead.

That is how we Socialists feel to-day.

William Morris was the only 'celebrity' I ever sought. I am glad
to think I sought him before it was too late. It is about a year since I
went over to his house one Sunday, and sat with him for a few hours.

He told me to come again as often as I pleased. But I was loth to trouble him: it was a pity to waste him in talk. But it was a red-letter day. It was grand to find my one hero *better* than his work. It was grand to find him frank, manly, modest, as ready to listen as to speak. It was grand to see him in his loose clothes and flannel shirt, looking like some jolly sea captain fresh from the brine. For there was something strangely and wonderfully nautical about this man. He was of Viking breed. He had the eyes of a Norseman, the colour of an old salt—the bluff ways of a sailor also. You could not be in his company for five minutes without thinking of the English admirals. He smelt of the sea; and the cadence of the tides sounds in his poetry. When he lectured on Socialism or art, the platform suggested a quarter-deck, and you felt that he ought to have worn a sword and carried a large telescope under his arm. He had often been mistaken by strangers for a mariner, and was proud of it. Had he been a post-captain in Nelson's time, I should like to have been his master gunner. How we would have enjoyed ourselves.

He was verily, as he said of himself in his beautiful fore-words to the *Earthly Paradise*, 'born out of his due time.' He would have been more at home under Elizabeth, with Raleigh and Sidney and Drake. He was as true a gentleman as Sir Philip or Sir Walter, as good a poet, and would have been as great a fighter. Read his great battle in *The Roots of the Mountains*, and you will recognise the mind of a general and the heart of a soldier there. Read the battle at the township's end in *John Ball*, and you'll realise at once how happy William Morris would have been at Agincourt among the bowmen, or with Sir Richard Grenville amongst the Spaniards at the mobbing of the Revenge. One of the papers I have been reading hardly mentions the work done by Morris for Socialism, but lays great stress upon the quality and value of his decorative designs. Indeed, from reading that article one would gather that our lost teacher would be remembered chiefly on account of his improvements in wall-papers. But did Morris ever design a wall-paper as handsome as himself? Or did any decorative artist ever produce work as noble and as valuable as the personality of William Morris?

For my part, I can say but little of his art—his craftsmanship, as he called it. I have seen few of his designs; little of his printing. What I have seen seemed to me very beautiful and strong. But indeed all his work is beautiful and true, because the soul was true and beautiful from whence it came.

Of his literary work I know more, and can speak with greater confidence. It is all good. All that he wrote, poetry or prose, bears the impress of genius of the master craftsman's hand. All his work is careful, conscientious, and sincere. He never scamped. He never presumed upon his reputation. He never hurried, nor trifled, nor showed off. Beautiful as much of his poetry is, I am inclined to think his prose still better. *The Dream of John Ball* is a classic. *News From Nowhere* is the best work of its kind since *Utopia*. I know of no ideal world so pure, so noble, so *possible* as that to which William Morris leads us. The authorship of either of these two books or of *The Roots of the Mountains*, would have made the reputation of any ordinary man. But Morris was not an ordinary man, and left his fame to take care of itself.

Morris's value to Socialism was incalculable. He did honour to the cause. Its bitterest opponent could not deny the genius, nor question the integrity of William Morris. Nor could the fervour and thoroughness of his Socialism be gainsaid or discounted. Nor could the purity of his motives be so much as questioned. Here was a man of courage, probity, genius, culture, character, who believed in Socialism with the whole power of his great heart and virile intellect. He was too great to be ignored, too high to be slandered, too thorough to be misrepresented or misunderstood. He stood there an unimpeachable witness whose testimony gained tenfold force from his character. He could not be depreciated, nor silenced, nor explained away. He had to be acknowledged, and heard with deference. Now death has taken him from us, and though we have many brave, steadfast, and pure men and women left in our ranks, we have none so distinguished as he, none of like genius, none so highly placed, so fortunately circumstanced.

Morris proves for us the truth of Goethe's saying that no man can render the world a greater service than by making good the faculties of himself. Versatile as was his genius, he never made a mistake as to the nature of his real work; nor did he ever falter in its execution. To produce and to pay honour to beautiful things was his vocation, and all his experience and knowledge of social questions, added to his fervid indignation against wrong, and his melting sympathy for the unfortunate, never betrayed him into the quagmire of politics. Had he been less single-minded, less tenacious of purpose, he might have wasted his talents on uncongenial work, might have squandered golden years in useless drudgery, might have soiled his reputation and spoiled his powers by deteriorating into leadership and 'practical' affairs. We have to be grateful to him for preserving his true vocation, and for standing firm to it. The value to Socialism of a name and a fame, a personality and a life like William Morris's can hardly be estimated. He was of greater advantage to the cause than a dozen clever politicians all rolled into one.

When a man like William Morris dies I always feel tempted to rebel against the course of nature. Why should not the brave, the good, the clever, the handsome—all the useful and lovable men and women, live on until the world is peopled with the best, and we have a race of immortals worthy immortality? It seems such a wicked waste to let our Shakespeares, Nelsons, Sidneys, Carlyles, Turners, Gordons die, and give place to feebler and less worthy men. There are millions of us who might have been spared, who are of little use and less ornament to the world, who have had enough of it—but we are left here, and Morris dies. This is not pleasing. All our bravest knights, fairest ladies, sweetest singers, cleverest sailors; all our sweetest, gentlest, wisest, truest, best, ride away into the darkness, and leave the world to the follies and the greedinesses of crowds of money-grubbers, pot-hunters, fops, bores, cowards, inanities, imbecilities, and persons with a stake in the country.

There is no sense in such a system—unless our best may go to better worlds. Perhaps they do. Let us hope so. Meanwhile, one of our very best has just left us, and has left us far too soon. Some of his books are beside me as I write. They are beautiful books, true books, human books, and we wanted more of them; but we have heard the last word from William Morris. A strenuous worker, an undaunted fighter, he has worn out his lusty life, and laid down his trenchant blade, and gone to sleep with Raleigh and Spenser, and the wistful, wise Omar of the East.

> Yet ah, that Spring should vanish with the rose!
> That youth's sweet-scented manuscript should close!
> The nightingale that in the branches sang,
> Ah whence, and whither flown again, who knows?

The voice that sang of the Earthly Paradise was a sweet voice; the hand that wrought the *Dream of John Ball* was a strong hand. We shall not see such good work again for many a weary day. William Morris is dead.

75. An 'inverted apologia'

1896

A. T. Quiller-Couch, article in *Speaker*, 10 October 1896, vi, 391–2.

Quiller-Couch (1863–1944) published *Troy Town* in 1888 and was a regular contributor to the *Speaker* in the nineties. He became King Edward VII Professor of English at Cambridge in 1912.

The article is entitled 'A Literary Causerie. Mr. William Morris.'

You have been reading this week so much concerning the true poet who died last Saturday—so much in the way of reminiscence and appreciation by those who were fortunate enough to know him or to fall under his influence—that you will likely enough care very little indeed for a small tribute offered in the not very graceful form of an inverted *apologia* on behalf of those who admired the man and his work, but never underwent the spell. And yet this was the plight of a considerable number of those who happened on his writings amid the ardours of youth. They were quite honest, I really believe, in their various degrees of interest and indifference: they were not conspicuously more foolish than the young men of earlier and later generations: they were strenuous in other causes. Of course, it is easy to see now that they would have gained a great deal by giving more of their heart to Morris, but it may not be useless to try to discover why, in point of fact, they gave so little.

To be sure, fashion, or the exhaustion of fashion, will account for much. In the early 'eighties 'mediævalism,' as a popular fashion, had already outworn much of its always rather artificial vitality. Oxford men of that period may remember a certain society of 'Passionate Pilgrims' and how it ceased beautifully with the discovery that only the Honorary Secretary was passionate, and he only when upbraided for having neglected to give notice of meetings. A new 'movement' was wanted, and came in the form of Philanthropy. Believe me, I am not speaking flippantly. The teaching and death of Arnold Toynbee, the

395

outcry for the better housing of the poor, moved these young men quite seriously, and directed their attention upon another side of the facts of life; and that attention and the enthusiasm it awoke were admirable in spite of some rather absurd *sequelæ*.[1]

But could this new 'movement' take over the effects of its predecessor? Could we be at once mediæval and intensely interested in the East End of London? The prediction seems so easy now, after the event: but few people, I suppose, then foresaw that a study which kept the attention upon so much that was merely squalid—squalid to all appearance, at least—must necessarily incline on its literary side towards that realism which had for some while captivated the affections of foreigners. But the answer yet stood in doubt when Mr. William Morris announced that he would deliver an address in the hall of University College. At the conclusion of his address I should say that little doubt remained. We were babes, and he gave us the strongest meat. We came for help over rudimentary difficulties, and he stormed at us and threatened. We were choked by alternate doses of mediævalism and crude Socialism. In the end the Master of University stood up and explained that he, as chairman, felt himself out of sympathy with Mr. Morris's opinions. The disclaimer was made, I suppose, to satisfy the reporters. It was a curious meeting altogether. For some weeks after a few enthusiasts tried to persuade their comrades that the social problem could be solved by importing another Black Death and enrolling the survivors in Guilds. But the majority of young men stuck to the belief that the future of the Anglo-Saxon race might be saved by some less expensive method than decimation.

Nor did Mr. Morris's poetry provide help for us. There was no earthly reason why it should. But the mass of modern poetry and of modern fiction and history dealt with questions rather than with pageants, and we somehow felt that his poetry was empty because it dealt with pageants and not with questions. Empty, of course it was not: but full of beauty, of beauty beloved for its own sake, and therefore a hundred times more instructive to the prepared understanding than the squalid novels in which we found reading to our mind. It was all very well for him to ask us to 'forget the snorting steam and piston stroke, forget the spreading of the hideous town'; but these were just the things we could not forget, the very things we wished to hear about. We took—how blandly presumptuous it seems now!—we took his own word that he was an idle singer; we packed up *The Life and Death*

[1] Sequels, consequences.

of Jason, or a volume or two of *The Earthly Paradise,* in our portman-
teaux as the very best books for a hot idle day in the Long Vacation (so
far we were right); and, having read, we laid aside—not as prigs
consciously, I hope, but still we laid aside—because we found no
instruction in it, the poetry of a man who knew at least fifty times as
much as we concerning the questions in which we supposed ourselves
to be deep.

On the one hand we were all wrong: for poetry, as the best of
manuals might have taught us, is sufficiently justified if it please, and
please by any genuine beauty. On the other hand we had, perhaps, a
rude inkling of a real defect. For, when everything is said, *The Earthly
Paradise* remains essentially artificial. It is all very well to compare
Morris with Chaucer, and absolutely just to say that since Chaucer there
has been no such *trouvère* as Morris. But Chaucer told his stories in
terms natural and proper to his own age. Morris told his stories in
terms deliberately appropriated to an age which was not his own, and
(on his own vehement profession) vastly unlike his own. To enjoy them,
you had (mentally) to dress up and pretend you were someone else,
and listening to a singer who also pretended to be someone else.
Now, in the case of true *poetry,* which somehow keeps even its most
archaic language eternally furbished and available for special occasions,
this remove from reality is not acutely felt. But when Mr. Morris
began to write fiction in prose, the whole mediæval vocabulary and
apparatus began to look like an old and played-out bag of tricks. For
my part, I begin to have a very uneasy suspicion of the permanence of
even the sincerest prose fiction. I begin to doubt if even the very best
of it will last two hundred years and keep its true flavour. It seems to me
that I could rattle off the names of twenty novelists of this century, each
one—as a master of his own mind and of his own instrument—head
and shoulders above such a middling poet, say, as William Browne of
Tavistock, and each one already on the high-road to oblivion, and
quite certain of missing the quiet immortality which third-rate William
Browne enjoys and will continue to enjoy. Browne is at least twice as
artificial as Morris; and one may say with fair safety that he was an
inferior poet; so here is happy augury for the permanence of *The
Earthly Paradise.* But what of the Elizabethan prose romances? Who
now reads 'The Arcadian Princess' or 'Menaphon,' or even (for pleasure)
'Euphues,' or the once prodigiously popular 'Mirror of Knight-
hood'?

These were popular once; but Morris's archaic romances were never even popular. I open the last of them at haphazard, and begin a chapter with this:—

Two days thereafter the chapmen having done with their matters in Cheaping Knowe, wheras they must needs keep some of their wares for other places, and especially for Goldburg, they dight them to be gone and rode out a gates of a mid-morning with banners displayed.

I say (and am prepared to defend the assertion) that affectation of this kind may creep under the wide shield of poetry, but that in prose it is only preserved from general derision by the author's evident and pathetic conviction that he is doing the right thing, odd as it may appear.

The lack of humour which alone could make such writing possible is only apparent in his poetry, I think, when we begin to compare him with Chaucer. As we read the poems for their own sake, humour is not missed; though if anyone should ask for it, we are at once aware of and must acknowledge its absence. He has Chaucer's decorative skill in arraying his figures and incidents along a frieze of story, and more than Chaucer's skill in painting a landscape, though less than Chaucer's skill in suggesting one. And since in story-telling an ounce of suggestion is worth a pound of description, the old poet has the advantage in this respect also. On Chaucer's frieze the figures stand out in high relief, the old man seems somehow to see round them. Morris paints his with figures on the flat; with figures rather than with characters. But for colour, at any rate, the author of 'The Haystack in the Floods,' 'The Man born to be King,' and 'The Ring given to Venus,' will not yield the palm to Chaucer. He has built a spacious house, and the walls of it are beautiful walls.

76. An Anarchist tribute to Morris

1896

Peter Kropotkine, article in *Freedom*, November 1896, x, 109–10. The November number of this 'Journal of Anarchist Communism' contained several obituary tributes, including a poem by Lothrop Withington. Prose contributors were Walter Crane, Kropotkine and John Kenworthy.

Kropotkin—as it is usually spelt now—(1842–1921) was a Russian prince who became an anarchist-communist; he escaped from Russia, and was well known in London in the nineties.

William Morris was such a grand figure in the Socialist movement, and he occupied in it such a unique position, that I am afraid not to be able to do full justice to his memory in the few lines which I can write now, in my present state of health.

As a poet, he stood quite alone in modern poetry. Amidst the whining and morbid poets of our own time, who are plunged into self-analysis and self-complaint, and are utterly devoid of energy for struggle, he was almost the only poet of the joys of life—the joys which man finds in the conquest of freedom, in the full exercise of all his powers, in work—the work of his hands and his brain. No modern poet has been known to inspire men with a like love of liberty, and labour with the like vigour, like hope and trust in human nature, like confidence in the happiness that men can find in conquering full freedom and freely associating with their equals. A true poet of the Norse Vikings, of the free labourers, of free men.

These same elements he brought into the Socialist movement.

When he joined it, he, like all really powerful men, did not seek in it the position of a wire-puller or a leader. Not even that of a teacher. He simply undertook to express what the masses think and what they vaguely aspire to. He joined the ranks, and brought with him his hatred of oppression in all possible forms, and his love of equality and freedom—which he understood in its broadest sense.

This is why, when he undertook to write his own romance of the future—*News from Nowhere*—he produced perhaps the most thoroughly and deeply Anarchistic conception of future society that has ever been written. As he combined in himself the broad view of the thinker with a wonderful personification of the good practical sense of *collective* thought (the mood of thought of the masses when they occasionally, in revolutionary times, set free to work)—his ideal society is undoubtedly the one which is most free of all our State and monastic traditions; the most imbued with the feelings of equality and humanitarian love; the most spontaneously growing out of a spirit of free understanding.

Two tendencies struggle in present society. On the one side, the tradition of the centralised State of Imperial Rome and of the Church, built up on the same plan—the tradition of slavery, submission, oppression, military and canonic discipline; and, on the other side, the tradition of *the masses* who endeavoured to build up their society outside the State—the tradition of the customary law, as opposed to Roman law; of the free guilds and fraternities; of the free cities revolted against the bishop and the king; of the artisans and peasants revolted against Church and Empire. Morris entirely and unreservedly belonged to this second tradition. He was the bearer of that Scandinavian, Celtic, Teutonic, Slavonic spirit which for the last ten years has struggled against the Roman tradition. And this is why he was so little understood by all the unconscious followers of the Church-and-State tradition.

For the last few years of his life, Morris had abandoned the Socialist movement, and he frankly explained his reasons in a lecture which he delivered for the Anarchists at Grafton Hall in 1893. If the movement had gone on developing and bringing England to a Social Revolution, Morris undoubtedly would have gone under the red flag as far as the masses would have carried it. But the endurability of the workers, who patiently support any amount of capitalist oppression, deeply affected him.

Moreover, Morris, who would have gone any way with the *masses*, could not go with *parties*; and when the Socialist movement in England became a party warfare, with all its wire-pulling and petty ambitions, which he hated so deeply, he did as Garibaldi did after he felt wounded in the fight between his Italian volunteers and the Italian royal troops. He retired to his Caprera.

But the love of the masses has followed him in his retreat; and the deep traces of his activity remain with us. If the Socialist movement in England did not take that authoritarian and functionarist character which it took in Germany, Morris's influence was immense to prevent that disaster; and this influence will be felt more and more in proportion as his Socialist writings and his writings altogether are read more and more by the masses of Socialist workers.

77. Morris's 'great inspiring hatred'

1896

Edward Carpenter, article in *Freedom*, December 1896, x, 118.

Carpenter (1844–1929) was a disciple of Whitman. He lived on a smallholding at Millthorpe in Derbyshire from 1883 to 1912, and wrote poetry and social criticism.

I think that future times will look back upon William Morris as one of the finest figures of this century. In the midst of an era of finesse, sleekness, commercial dodgery, their eyes will rest with relief upon this brusque, hearty, bold and manly form.

It is not so much perhaps in the special immortality of any of his works that his greatness will lie, as (what is more) in the man himself. For, after all, Life is greater than Art; and the greatest of all artworks is the genuine expression of his own true heart which a man finds and forges for himself out of the materials of the time into which he is born. Morris stood up from the first against the current of ugly, dirty commercialism in which his lot was cast—like a man in the midst of a stream fighting against the stream, like a captain in the rout of his men withstanding the torrent of their flight and turning them back to the battle.

He hated with a good loyal hatred all insincerity; but most he hated, and with his very soul, the ugliness and meanness of modern life. I believe that was the great inspiring hatred of his life.

Everyone has remarked the contrast between the man himself—

energetic, stormy, a veritable Viking and sea-captain—and his poetry, so languid, so dreamy, so dainty of expression. Perhaps as he himself seems to have said, he was several personalities rolled into one; but it is not difficult, I think, to see how the peculiar note of his literary work was given by the fact that it was written largely as a *relief* from his surroundings. After spending his days in organising a large business, with all its irritating commercial details; after enduring polite imprisonment in the mansion of some lordling who required his aesthetic advice; after shouting himself hoarse at a street-corner; after battling with the police in Trafalgar Square; or after suffering the slings and arrows of outrageous vulgarity in all the sights and sounds of daily life; it was an intense relief, a real holiday, to him to sit down at night and dream himself back perhaps into the fourteenth century, or forward into the reflective image of it in years to come. I believe that the main part of Morris's literary work—such books as *News from Nowhere*, *The Roots of the Mountains*, *A Dream of John Ball*, *The Earthly Paradise*—came in this way, were written simply for his own recreation, and as an escape from actual conditions; and perhaps it is this which gives them their almost sluggish sense of quietude and beauty, as of a stream which, having fretted itself in its fierce descent among the rocks, meanders at length and at large among the iris-fringed meadows. His speeches, indeed, were a trump of battle, but his imaginative writings moved in the calm of dreamland.

And it is very characteristic of Morris that his chief recreation was only another kind of work. He could not understand that form of pleasure which consists in loafing your days away at a watering-place. A touch of gout in his constitution is the key to much of his character —his irritable, restless energy, his immense power of work, his sudden blazes of temper, his downrightness, sincerity, and hatred of all meanness. When ill, he was a difficult patient to keep in bed. At meals even it would happen that he could not sit still, but, jumping up from the table and talking vehemently, would quarterdeck the room.

One of the last times that I heard him speak in public was in 1889, at the Paris Socialist Congress. After the glib oratorical periods of Jules Guesde and others, what a contrast to see Morris—in navy-blue pilot suit—fighting furiously there on the platform with his own words (he was not feeling well that day), hacking and hewing the stubborn English phrases out—his tangled grey mane tossing, his features reddening with the effort! But the effect was remarkable. Something in the solid English way of looking at things, the common-sense and practical outlook on the world, the earnestness and tenacity, as of a skipper beating up against wind and wave on the great deep, made that speech one of the most effective in the session.

There is no doubt that, in the early days of the Socialist League, Morris had a hope, and a strong hope, that the little branches of the League, spreading and growing over the land, would before long reach hands to each other and form a network of free communal life over the whole country. That dream was not realised; but the impulse of growth which he gave has nevertheless been one of the most potent, most generous and humanly beautiful, of all the many impulses which have gone to make up that very complex and far-reaching movement which we call by the name of modern Socialism.

Now to think that he has gone from among us brings a strange tightening and pressure of the affections. To hundreds and thousands of unknown toilers and workers by land and sea, and all over the earth, he was and is the object of a real love; and it is at least some poor consolation that, if in the old form we miss him, still in the hearts of men and women thus multiplied his image moves and lives, and will live.

78. Walter Crane on William Morris

1896

Walter Crane (1845–1915) was an associate of Morris in the Arts and Crafts Movement; his obituary article was entitled 'William Morris: Poet, Artist and Craftsman, and Social Reconstructor.'

From *Progressive Review*, November 1896, i, 148–52.

The death of William Morris marks an epoch both in art, and in social and economic thought. The press notices and appreciations that have appeared, for the most part, have dwelt upon his work as a poet and an artist and craftsman, and have but lightly passed over his connection with Socialism and advanced thought.

But, even apart from prejudice, a hundred will note the beauty and splendour of the flower to one who will notice the leaf and the stem, or the roots and the soil, from which the tree springs.

Yet the greatness of a man must be measured by the number of spheres in which he is distinguished—the width of his range and appeal to his fellows.

In the different branches of his work William Morris commanded the admiration—or, what is equally a tribute to his force, excited the opposition—of as many different sections of specialists.

As a poet he appealed to poets by reason of many distinct qualities. He united pre-Raphaelite vividness (as in 'The Haystack in the Floods') with a dream-like wistful sweetness and flowing narrative, woven in a kind of rich mediæval tapestry of verse, and steeped with the very essence of legendary romance (as in *The Earthly Paradise*), or the heroic spirit of earlier time (as in *Sigurd, the Volsung*)—while all these qualities are united in his later prose romances.

His architectural and archæological knowledge again was complete enough for the architect and the antiquary. His classical and historical lore won him the respect of scholars. His equipment as a designer and craftsman, based upon his architectural knowledge and training, enabled him to exercise an extraordinary influence over all the arts of design, and gave him his place as leader of our latter-day English revival of handicraft—a position, perhaps, in which he is widest known.

In all these capacities the strength and beauty of William Morris's work has been freely acknowledged by his brother craftsmen, as well as by a very large public.

There is, however, still another direction, in which his vigour and personal weight were shown, with all the ardour of an exceptionally ardent nature, wherein the importance and significance of his work are as yet but partially apprehended. I mean his work in the cause of Socialism; in which he might severally be regarded as an economist, a public lecturer, a propagandist, and a controversialist.

No doubt many even of the most emphatic admirers of William Morris's work as an artist, a poet, and a decorator, have been unable to follow him in this direction, while others have deplored or even denounced his self-sacrificing enthusiasm. There seems to have been insuperable difficulty to some minds in realising that the man who wrote *The Earthly Paradise* should have lent a hand to try and bring it about, when once the new hope had dawned upon him.

There is no greater mistake than to think of William Morris as a sentimentalist, who, having built himself a dream-house of art and poetry, sighs over the turmoil of the world, and calls himself a Socialist because factory chimneys obtrude themselves upon his view.

It seems to have escaped those who have inclined to such an opinion that a man, in Emerson's phrase, 'can only obey his own polarity.' His life must gravitate necessarily towards its centre. The accident that he should have reached economics and politics through poetry and art, so far from disqualifying a man to be heard, only establishes his claim to bring a cultivated mind and imaginative force to bear upon the hard facts of Nature and Science.

The practice of his art, his position as an employer of labour, his intensely practical knowledge of certain handicrafts—all these things brought him face to face with the great Labour question; and the fact that he was an artist and a poet, a man of imagination and feeling, as well as intellect, gave him exceptional advantages in solving it—at least theoretically. His practical nature and sincerity moved him to join hands with men who offered a practicable programme, or at least who opened up possibilities of action towards bringing about a new social system.

His own personal view of a society based upon an entire change of economic system is most attractively and picturesquely described in *News from Nowhere, some chapters of a Utopian Romance*. He called it *Utopian*; but in his view, and granting the conditions, it was a perfectly practicable Utopia. He even gave an account (through the mouth of a survivor of the old order) of the probable course of events which might lead up to such a change. The book was written as a sort of counterblast to Edward Bellamy's *Looking Backwards* which on its appearance was very widely read on both sides of the water, and there seemed at one time some danger of the picture there given of a socialised state being accepted as the only possible one. It may be partly answerable for an impression in some quarters that a socialist system must necessarily be mechanical. But the society described in *Looking Backwards* is, after all, only a little more developed along the present lines of American social life—a sublimation of the universal supply of average citizen wants by mechanical means, with the main spring of the machine altered from individual profit to collective interest. The book did its work, no doubt, and appealed with remarkable force to minds of a certain construction and bias, and it is only just to Bellamy to say that he claimed no finality for it.

But *News from Nowhere* may be considered, apart from the underlying principle common to both—of the collective interest as the determining constructive factor of the social system—as its complete antithesis.

According to Bellamy it is apparently the *city* life that is the only one likely to be worth anything, and it is to the organisation of production and distribution of things contributing to the supposed necessities and comforts of inhabitants of cities that the reader's thoughts are directed.

With Morris the country life is obviously the most imposing, the ideal life. Groups of houses, not too large to be neighbourly, each with a common guest-hall, with large proportions of garden and woodland, take the place of crowded towns. Thus London, as we know it, disappears.

What is this but building upon the ascertained scientific facts of our day that the inhabitants of large cities tend to deteriorate in physique, and would die out were it not for the constant infusion of new blood from the country districts?

Work is still a hard necessity in *Looking Backwards*, a thing to be got rid of as soon as possible, so citizens, after serving the community as clerks, waiters, or what not, until the age of forty-five, are exempt. With Morris work gives the zest to life, and all labour has its own touch of art—even the dustman can indulge in it in the form of rich embroidery upon his coat. The bogey of labour is thus routed by its own pleasurable exercise, with ample leisure, and delight in external beauty in both art and nature.

As regards woman's question, it never, in his *Utopia*, appears to be asked. He evidently himself thought that with the disappearance of the commercial competitive struggle for existence and what he termed 'artificial famine', caused by monopoly of the means of existence, the claim of women to compete with men in the scramble for a living would not exist. There would be no necessity for either men or women to sell themselves, since in a truly co-operative commonwealth each one would find some congenial sphere of work. In fact, as Morris once said, 'settle the economic question and you settle all other questions. It is the Aaron's rod which swallows up the rest.'

I gather that he thought both men and women should be free, but by no means wished to ignore or obliterate sex, and all those subtle and fine feelings which arise from it, which really form the warp and weft of the courtesies and relationships of life.

Now, whatever criticisms might be offered, or whatever objections might be raised, such a conception of a possible social order, such a view of life upon a new economic basis as is painted in this delightful book, is surely before all things, remarkably wholesome, human and sane and pleasurable. If wholesome, human, sane, and pleasurable lives are not possible to the greater part of humanity under existing institutions, so much the worse for those institutions. Humanity has generally proved itself better than its institutions, and man is chiefly distinguished over other animals by his power to modify his conditions. Life at least means growth and change, and human evolution shows us a gradual progression—a gradual triumph of higher organisation and intelligence over lower, checked by the inexorable action of natural laws which demand reparation for breaches of moral and social law, and continually probe the foundations of society. Man has become what he is through his capacity for co-operative social action. The particular forms of social organisation are the crystallization of this capacity. They are but shells to be cast away when they retard growth or progress, and it is then that the living organism, collective or individual, seeks out or slowly forms a new home.

As to the construction and colour of such a new house for reorganised society and regenerated life, William Morris has left us in no doubt as to his own ideas and ideals. It may seem strange that a man who might be said to have been steeped in mediæval lore,* and whose delight seemed to be in a beautifully imagined world of romance peopled with heroic figures, should yet be able to turn from that dream-world with a clear and penetrating gaze upon the movements of his own time, and to have thrown himself with all the strength of his nature into the seething social and industrial battle of modern England; that the 'idle singer of an empty day' should voice the claims and hopes of labour, stand up for the rights of free speech in Trafalgar Square, and speak from a wagon in Hyde Park, may have surprised those who only knew him upon one side; but to those who fully apprehended the reality, ardour, and sincerity of his nature, such action was but its logical outcome and complement, and assuredly it redounds to the honour of the artist, the scholar, and the poet whose loss we mourn to-day, that he was also a man.

* At the same time it must be remembered that his knowledge of mediæval life—the craft guilds and the condition of the labourer in England in the 15th century—helped him in his economic studies and his Socialist propaganda.

THE WELL AT THE WORLD'S END

1896

---

79. H. G. Wells, review, *Saturday Review*

17 October 1896, lxxxii, 413–15

Wells (1866–1946) was at the beginning of his career as a novelist
and ideologue; he clearly saw himself as scientific in his social outlook, unlike the Utopian Morris.

The present reviewer last saw William Morris nearly ten years ago.
He drifted, as most students in London in those days drifted sooner or
later, to that little conventicle in the outhouse beside Kelmscott House,
at Hammersmith, and enlisted with something of the emotion of a
volunteer. In those days economic reform was in the air, and Socialism
was a possible force in politics. And this present reviewer, impecunious
and adolescent, imagined that here he was to meet the resolute nucleus,
the little leaven of clear-headed men, that was presently to domin-
ate the country—such as himself shouting and shoving in the yeasty
tumult. And assuredly had the huge mass of feeling that social stresses
had then evolved, and Henry George and Bellamy contributed to shape,
found for itself a directing mind, a great Socialist party might to-day
have sat in Westminster with Radicalism under its wing. But happily
for the permanence of the existing social order, it found no directing
mind. Intelligent and emotional adolescence sitting shy but earnest in
the back seats slowly forgot its idea of a council of war, and by the end
of the meeting was being vastly entertained by a comedy of picturesque
personalities. The more prominent seats were full indeed of personalities
signifying the same to the most casual eye, even in their dress. And the
discussion was earnest and quaint and original, and for the most part,
as it seemed, irrelevant. Art was for ever straying into the talk and

409

denunciations of the *bourgeois*. The Chicago Anarchists, too, were inextricably interwoven with the business. There was also a disposition to restore the Thirteenth Century well in evidence. But as to a sane enterprise towards expropriating landlords . . .! And earnest adolescence, being above all things impatient, presently gave up attending these meetings.

Most of the personalities of these gatherings have somehow got more or less entirely effaced from the present reviewer's memory. He recalls fragments: a blue serge jacket, for instance, a flannel collar, an inordinate orange tie, and a lank neck with vast Adam's apple passing upward into mist. The head, the voice of that personality have left no trace whatever. And another faceless figure of black and gold, like a banker. And a wonderful girl, designed, it seems, by Mr. Walter Crane. And a miscellany of hair ends, and ties, and voices. There was ever a cheerful cackle among these intimates before the meeting began. But above the confusion of these memories two figures remain distinct. Mr. Bernard Shaw, physically individualized with extraordinary decision, a frequent speaker, and always explicit and careful to make himself misunderstood; and the grand head, the rough voice, the sturdy figure, sedulously plain speech, and lovable bearing of William Morris.

This present volume comes to remind one of those absurd younger days, when one seriously imagined we were to be led anywhere but backward by this fine old scholar. As soon might one have taken a Herrick as a leader! His dreamland was no futurity, but an illuminated past. For him the appointed task was to restore the fragments that Rabelais and Cervantes scattered long ago, and show how beautiful that old romantic land had been. And never did he do it so sweetly and well as in this present story. *Ci-devant* adolescence, robbed of many of its downy illusions and most of its impatience, may now follow him cheerfully enough, with something of the relief of bathing after a hot and dusty road, into that land of the ancient glamour.

It is Malory, enriched and chastened by the thought and learning of six centuries, this story of Ralph and his Quest of the Well at the World's End. It is Malory, with the glow of the dawn of the Twentieth Century warming his tapestries and beaten metal. It is Malory, but instead of the mystic Grail, the search for long life and the beauty of strength. And women as well as men go a questing. Tennyson, too, gave us Malory, but with the Grail—as remote and attenuated indeed as the creed of a Broad Churchman, but the Grail still, and for the simple souls of the future and the past, all the involved gentilities of the middle Victorian years. Morris is altogether more ancient and more modern.

Save that its spirit is living, the story does not seem to be coherently symbolical. Such analysis as a transient reviewer may give discovers no clue to a coherent construction. Life is too short for many admirable things—for chess, and the unravelling of the *Faerie Queen* and of such riddles as this. Ever and again the tale is certainly shot and enriched with allegory. But as we try to follow these glittering strands, they spread, twist, vanish, one after the other, in the texture of some purely decorative incident. In the tale of the upbringing of the girl, for instance, in the little house of the Crofts, there are the strangest parallelisms with some of the deepest facts of life; and then, hither, thither leap the threads, and we are among sturdy knights, and splintering spears under the greenwood tree. 'I cannot tell,' said the lady, 'where I was born, nor of what lineage, nor of who ... were my father and mother; for this I have known not of myself, nor has any told me. But when I first remember anything, I was playing about a garden, wherein was a little house ... There was a woman at the door of the house, and she spinning, yet clad in glittering raiment, and with jewels on her neck and fingers. ... Now the woman, who as I came to know was neither old nor young in those days, but of middle age, I called mother; but now I know that she was not my mother. She was hard and stern with me, but never beat me in those days, save to make me do what I would not have done unbeaten; and as to meat, I ate and drank what I could get, as she did, and indeed was well fed with simple meats, as thou mayest suppose from the aspect of me to-day. ... She was never tender, or ever kissed or caressed me, for as little as I was. And I loved her naught, nor did it ever come into my mind that I should love her, though I loved a white goat of ours, and deemed it dear and lovely. ...

'Further, as I grew up, the woman set me to do such work as I had strength for as needs was. ... At last, one day of late summer, when I, now of some fifteen summers, was pasturing the goats not far from the house, the sky darkened, and there came up so great a storm of thunder and lightning and huge drift of rain that I was afraid; and, being so near to the house, I hastened thither, driving the goats, and when I had tethered them in the shed of the croft, I crept trembling up to the house, and when I was at the door, heard the clack of the loom in the weaving chamber, and deemed that the woman was weaving there, but when I looked, behold there was no one on the bench, though the shuttle was flying from side to side, and the shed opening and changing, and the sley coming home in due order. Therewithal I heard a sound as of one singing a song in a low voice, but the words I could not understand; then terror seized on my heart, but I stepped over the threshold, and as the door of the chamber was open, I looked aside and saw therein the woman sitting stark naked with a great open book before her, and it was from her mouth that the sound was coming: grim she looked, and awful. . . . I ran back into the storm, though it was now wilder than ever, and ran and hid myself in the wood, half-dead with fear, and wondering what would become of me. But finding that no one followed after me, I grew calmer . . . and when dusk came, stole back again to the house, though my legs would scarce bear me over the threshold into the chamber. . . . Images of dreadful things, and miseries that I may not tell thee of, mingled in my sleep for long.'

The next morning the woman bids her 'go fetch the white goat and come back to me therewith,' and leads her 'through the wood into a lawn. . . . round which was a wall, as it were, of great yew trees, and amidst, a table of stone, made of four uprights and a great stone plank on the top of them; and this was the only thing in all the wood . . . which was of man's handiwork, save and except our house and the sheds and fences about it. . . .

'I durst do naught but obey her, and I held the poor beast, that licked my hands and bleated for love of me; and now since my terror and the fear of death was lessened at her words, I wept for my dear friend.

'But the woman drew a strong sharp knife from her girdle and cut the beast's throat, and dipped her fingers in the blood, and reddened both herself and me on the breast, and the hands, and the feet; and then she turned to the altar and smote blood upon the uprights, and the face of the stone plank. Then she bade me help her, and we laid the seven faggots on the altar, and laid the carcase of the goat upon them: and she made fire, but I saw not how, and set it to the wood, and when it began to blaze she stood before it with her arms outspread, and sang loud and hoarse to a strange tune; and though I knew not the words of her song, it filled me with dread, so that I cast myself down on the ground and hid my face in the grass.'

Symbolical, too, seems the Dry Tree and the Thirsty Desert across which the two seekers ride to the Well. And between the men of the Burgh and the Wheat Wearers is something dimly like our present discontents. But this that follows is apparently pure incident; at any rate, its weird effectiveness is its sufficient and only seeming justification.

'Now on the second day of their riding this ugly waste, as they came up over the brow of one of these stony ridges, Ralph, the far-sighted, cried out suddenly: "Hold! for I see a man weaponed."

' "Where is he?" quoth Ursula, "and what is he about?" Said Ralph: "He is up yonder on the swell of the next ridge, and by seeming is asleep leaning against a rock."

'Then he bent the Turk bow and set an arrow on the string, and they went on warily. When they were down at the foot of the ridge Ralph hailed the man with a lusty-cry, but gat no answer of him; so they went on up the bent, till Ralph said: "Now I can see his face under his helm, and it is dark, and the eyes are hollow: I will off horse and go up to him afoot, but do thou, beloved, sit still in thy saddle."

'But when he had come nigher, he turned and cried out to her: "The man is dead, come anigh." So she went up to him and dismounted, and they both together stood over the man, who was lying up against a big stone, like one at rest. How long he had lain there none knows but God; for in the saltness of the dry desert the flesh had dried on his bones without corrupting, and was as hardened leather. He was in full armour of a strange and ancient fashion, and his sword was girt to his side, neither was there any sign of a wound about him. Under a crag anigh him they found his horse, dead and dry like to himself.'

And free of all symbolic trammels is the naked beauty of the last three chapters in Book III.; chapters whose very headings are a cry of delight. 'They came to the Ocean Sea,' 'Now they Drink of the Well at the World's End,' and 'Now have they Drunk and are Glad.'

The book is to be read, not simply for pleasure. To those who write its pages will be a purification, it is full of clean strong sentences and sweet old words. 'Quean' and 'carle,' 'eme,' 'good sooth,' 'yeasay' and 'naysay,' we may never return to, nor ever again 'seek to' a man, but 'fain' and 'lief' and 'loth' and 'sunder,' and the like good honest words, will come all the readier after this reading.

And all the workmanship of the book is stout oaken stuff that must needs endure and preserve the memory of one of the stoutest, cleanest lives that has been lived in these latter days.

80. A. C. Swinburne, review, *Nineteenth Century*

November 1896, xl, 759–60

The creative gift of Mr. Morris, his distinctive power of imagination, cannot be defined or appreciated by any such test of critical comparison as is applicable to the work of any other man. He is himself alone, and so absolutely that his work can no more be likened to any mediæval than to any contemporary kinsman's. In his love of a story for a story's sake he is akin to Chaucer and the French precursors of Chaucer: but if he has not much of Chaucer's realistic humour and artistic power of condensation and composition, he has a gift of invention as far beyond Chaucer's as the scope of a story like *The Well at the World's End* is beyond the range of such brief romances as 'Amis and Amile' or 'Aucassin and Nicolette.' Readers and lovers (the terms should here be synonymous) of his former tales or poems in prose will expect to find in this masterpiece—for a perfect and unique masterpiece it is—something that will remind them less of 'Child Christopher' than of *The Wood Beyond the World*: the mere likeness in the titles would suggest so much: and this I think they will not fail to find: but I am yet more certain that the quality of this work is even finer and stronger than that of either. The interest, for those who bring with them to the reading of a work of imagination any auxiliary or sympathetic imagination of their own, is deeper and more vivid as well as more various: but the crowning test and triumph of the author's genius will be recognised in the all but unique power of touching with natural pathos the alien element of magical or supernatural fiction. Coleridge could do this: who else till now has done it? And when we venture to bring in the unapproachable name of Coleridge, we are venturing to cite the example of the most imaginative, the most essentially poetic, among all poets of all nations and all time.

It should be remembered that when an allegorical intention was detected in the beautiful story of adventure and suffering and love which enchanted all readers in *The Wood beyond the World*, Mr. Morris for once condescended to disclaim the misinterpretation of his meaning, and to point out the difference between allegorical and simple narrative in words of perfect and conclusive accuracy. No commentator, I should hope, will ever waste his time on the childish task of inventing an occult significance for the incidents and adventures, the lurid and the lovely landscapes, set before him and impressed upon his memory in this later and yet more magically beautiful tale. The perfect simplicity and the supreme nobility of the spirit which informs and pervades and quickens and exalts it must needs make any but an inept and incapable reader feel yet once more a sense of wonder at the stupidity of the generations which could imagine a difference and a contrast between simple and noble. The simplest English writer of our time is also the noblest: and the noblest by reason and by virtue of his sublime simplicity of spirit and of speech. If the English of the future are not utterly unworthy and irredeemably unmindful of the past, they will need no memorial to remind them that his name was William Morris.

81. W. B. Yeats, review, *Bookman*

November 1896, x, 37–8

William Butler Yeats (1865–1939), the great Irish poet, produced a good deal of literary journalism in his early years.

That Mr. William Morris was the greatest poet of his time one may doubt, remembering more impassioned numbers than his, but one need not doubt at all that he was the poet of his time who was most perfectly a poet. Certain men impress themselves on the imagination of the world as types, and Shelley, with his wayward desires, his unavailing protest, has become the type of the poet to most men and to all women, and perhaps because he seemed to illustrate that English dream, which holds the poet and the artist unfitted for practical life: laughable and lovable children whose stories and angers one may listen to when the day's work is done. If, however, a time come when the world recognises that the day's work, that practical life, become noble just in so far as they are subordinated to the sense of beauty, the sense of the perfect, just in so far as they approach the dream of the poet and the artist, then Mr. William Morris may become, instead of Shelley, the type of the poet: for he more than any man of modern days tried to change the life of his time into the life of his dream. To others beauty was a solitary vision, a gift coming from God they knew not how; but to him it was always some golden fleece or happy island, some well at the world's end, found after many perils and many labours in the world, and in all his later books, at any rate, found for the world's sake. Almost alone among the dreamers of our time, he accepted life and called it good; and because almost alone among them he saw, amid its incompleteness and triviality, the Earthly Paradise that shall blossom at the end of the ages.

When Ralph, the pilgrim to the well at the world's end, is setting out upon his journey, he meets with a monk who bids him renounce the world. ' "Now, lord, I can see by thy face that thou art set on beholding the fashion of this world, and most like it will give thee the rue."

'Then came a word into Ralph's mouth, and he said: "Wilt thou tell me, father, whose work was the world's fashion?"

'The monk reddened, but answered nought, and Ralph spake again: "Forsooth, did the craftsman of it fumble over his work?"

'Then the monk scowled, but presently he enforced himself to speak blithely, and said, "Such matters are over high for my speech or thine, lord; but I tell thee, who knoweth, that there are men in this House who have tried the world and found it wanting."

'Ralph smiled and said, stammering: "Father, did the world try them, and find them wanting perchance?" '

And later on it is said to the seekers of the well, 'If you love not the earth and the world with all your souls, and will not strive all ye may to be frank and happy therein, your toil and peril aforesaid shall win you no blessing, but a curse.'

In the literal sense of the word, and in the only high sense, he was a prophet; and it was his vision of that perfect life, which the world is always trying, as Jacob Behmen taught, to bring forth, that awakened every activity of his laborious life—his revival of mediæval tapestry and stained glass, his archaic printing, his dreams of Sigurd and of Gudrun and of Guinevere, his essays upon the unloveliness of our life

and art, his preaching in parks and at the corners of streets, his praise
of revolutions, his marchings at the head of crowds, and his fierce
anger against most things that we delight to honour. We sometimes
call him 'melancholy,' and speak of the 'melancholy' of his poems, and
I know not well why, unless it be that we mistake the pensiveness of
his early verse, a pensiveness for noble things once had and lost, or for
noble things too great not to be nearly beyond hope, for his permanent
mood, which was one of delight in the beauty of noon peace, of rest
after labour, of orchards in blossom, of the desire of the body and of
the desire of the spirit. Like Blake, he held nothing that gave joy
unworthy, and might have said with Ruysbroeck, 'I must rejoice
without ceasing, even though the world shudder at my joy,' except
that he would have had the world share his joy. There is no picture
of him more permanent in my mind than that of him sitting at one
of those suppers at Hammersmith to which he gathered so singular a
company of artists and workmen, and crying out on those who held
it unworthy to be inspired by a cup of wine: for had not wine come
out of the sap and out of the leaves and out of the heat of the sunlight?
It was this vision of happiness that made him hate rhetoric, for rhetoric
is the triumph of the desire to convince over the desire to reveal. His
definition of good writing would have been writing full of pictures of
beautiful things and beautiful moments. 'My masters,' he said once,
'are Keats and Chaucer, because Keats and Chaucer make pictures.'
Dante he held for a like reason to be more a poet than Milton, who,
despite his 'great, earnest mind, expressed himself as a rhetorician.'
These pictures were not, I imagine, to be so much in great masses as
in minute detail. 'The beauty of Dante,' he said to me once, 'is in his
detail'; and in all his art one notices nothing more constant than the
way in which it heaps up, and often in the midst of tragedy, little
details of happiness. This book is full of them, and there is scarcely a
chapter in which there is not some moment for which one might
almost give one's soul.

THE WATER
OF THE WONDROUS ISLES

1897

82. Theodore Watts, unsigned review, *Athenaeum*

December 1897, no. 3658, 777–9

F. S. Ellis congratulated Watts on this review in a letter of
7 December 1897: 'Although, as you remark, Morris was regardless of criticism, he was by no means regardless of intelligent and
masterly appreciation such as that contained in your splendidly
written article of last Saturday, and that he should not have lived
to see it adds another deep regret to the many that we feel at his
loss.' Hake and Compton-Ricketts, *Theodore Watts-Dunton*, I,
100–1.

Hitherto, in reviewing Morris's prose poems, we have essayed to give
our readers a brief outline of the story of each; but in none of these
cases have we ever been able to satisfy ourselves that we were doing
justice to what even those who do not like them must call the most
original compositions in the imaginative literature of our time. It is not
merely that to endeavour to reproduce in colourless language any
notion of the beauty of the story was to confront a task as hopeless as
that of the gipsy girl whose first effort on being taught to write was
to represent by phonetic signs, cut on the bark of a tree, the nightingale's song; but there is between the incidents of all these stories a
certain kinship which the exquisite but quaint verbal texture of the
narrative partly conceals. Behind this texture the loveliness of each
incident seems at once familiar and unfamiliar, like the face of the

418

Persian maiden which, from behind the shifting hues of her 'Peri-woven veil,' outshone each new loveliness of each new rival face in the harem. Stripped of this verbal texture, the kinship we are speaking of becomes so apparent that the reader is apt to think the riches of the most inventive of all nineteenth century poets had, like other riches, their limits.

For this reason we do not propose to furnish an outline of the story before us. Moreover, there is another reason for adopting this course: we shall by this abstention secure more space in which to consider the series as a whole. Yet we will confess that, should we succeed in finding a proper place in literary art for a kind of work which is absolutely unique, we shall be more fortunate than we dare hope to be. The time for making such a retrospect seems to have come, for it has been hinted of late that when Morris produced the first of these saga-like narratives, in which material of the most essentially poetical kind is presented in a form which is not that of metre, nor even that of measured prose, his poetical impulse—at least, his metrical impulse—was moving towards a premature death. That this was not so none knows better than the writer of these lines. Two things, however, *had* come to an end—first, Morris's belief that the producer of artistic poetry can any longer (for the present, at least) look for recognition in this country, and, secondly, his belief that long narratives could be written in metre any more. Not that Morris had even the ordinary share of that sensitiveness to criticism from which poets are apt to suffer. No other poet of our time, and perhaps no poet of any other time, ever took up as he did the purely Olympian attitude towards the literary arena. Of late years he refused to read criticisms of his work at all until he had learnt who was the critic that wrote about him, or rather, by what authority the writer spoke.

Perhaps, however, our use of the words 'artistic poetry' requires a little explanation. The two forces that move in the production of all poetry are (as we said once when comparing, or rather when contrasting, the methods of the troubadours with the methods of the trouvères) poetic energy and poetic art. In poets of a great cycle like that of Athens in the time of the dramatists and that of England in the time of Shakespeare, these two forces are seen in something like equipoise. But great cycles are rare. Morris's early work, however, was produced in a most remarkable period in the history of English poetry. Although he was nearly of the same age as Rossetti, he was, at the beginning at least of his poetical career, as much under the influence of that powerful personality as were any of Rossetti's younger friends. And even after Morris had himself achieved a position equal to Rossetti's own, to see these two together (down at Kelmscott, for instance) was to see a sight indeed. For though Nature moulded Rossetti for a dominant personality, she moulded Morris on the same lines. If among the many classifications into which writers may be grouped there is one which divides them into those whose personalities seem greater than their work, and those whose work seems greater than their personalities, Morris belonged to the former group as surely as did Rossetti himself.

Fine as his works are, they do not seem to represent him to the full, as the works of certain other English writers, both in prose and verse, seem to represent them. Rich, for instance, as was the personality of Charles Dickens, it did not seem to be quite so rich as *Martin Chuzzlewit*. Rich as was the personality of Browning, it did not seem to be quite so rich as *The Ring and the Book*. But notwithstanding all its marvellous variety and power, Morris's work seemed less powerful and less various than Morris himself. Moreover, if Rossetti was wilful, so was Morris. The true realities of life were to him his own delightful, genial, and noble whims, literary, artistic, and social. Those who deny to him sagacity, however—great sagacity—assuredly never knew him. To the impact of only one other personality was his own in the slightest degree plastic: that of Rossetti, and at the beginning of his career this plasticity must have been marked indeed.

Now Rossetti, even in his earliest days, when he was most entirely captivated by the artless movements of Blake's poetry, was deeply impressed with the idea that imaginative literature, so soon as it passes into metrical form, becomes a fine art, and therefore subject to law. And once when a friend quoted to him the fine saying of the Arabian writer Ibn el Wardi, that 'true art lies in the abandonment of artifice,' his impromptu remarks upon the difference between artifice and art would have made the fortune of any writer on poetics. The older he got the more importance he attached to metrical form. Of this, let us quote one instance out of many. When Rossetti at Kelmscott wrote 'The Cloud Confines,' Morris (who was not in the habit of criticizing the work of his friends) made, on hearing it read, a remark upon the lines:—

> War that shatters her slain,
> And peace that grinds them as grain,

And eyes fixed ever in vain
On the pitiless eyes of Fate.

There was, Morris thought, a certain lack of rightness in speaking of
War 'shattering' victims already 'slain.' Also he suggested that the word
'them' in the second line above quoted was ambiguous. 'I suppose,'
said Rossetti, 'that you would have me say

Peace that grinds *men* as grain.

That, of course, would have prose accuracy. But when the struggle is
between prose accuracy and metrical music, prose accuracy must give
way; otherwise why write in verse at all?'

The effect of Rossetti's teaching was at that time very great; and
although it cannot be said that in his own work he bestowed more
than adequate attention upon the artistic side of poetry, his influence
may very likely have caused other writers to do so, though Morris
was not of these, to be sure. Yet this must be said of Morris's work—
that though he, the most rapid of writers, never gave to his lines the
limæ labor which Tennyson and Rossetti gave to theirs, he was, when
he wrote *The Earthly Paradise*, fully impressed with the Rossettian
theory that poetry is a fine art and subject to law, though born, like
all the other fine arts, of inspiration.

We are speaking of a time which, owing to fluctuations in criticism
and in public taste, seems far away, though as a matter of fact it is
removed from us only a few years—a time when not only Morris's
Earthly Paradise was being written, read, and applauded, but when
some of Tennyson's *Idylls of the King*, Mr. Swinburne's *Songs before
Sunrise*, and Rossetti's sonnets and ballads were filling the air with
such music as can never be heard again, for music is no longer, we are
told, to be the English poet's quest.

If, as we have said, this idea of paying great attention to the artistic
side of poetry did not run to excess in the methods of William Morris,
can the same be said of certain other poets—those called in those
antediluvian days the 'Pre-Raphaelite' group? Is the poetry, for instance, of O'Shaughnessy anything but an artistic exercise based on a
study of Edgar Poe and Mr. Swinburne? The swing of the pendulum
in the opposite direction was perhaps necessary—at all events, it came.
For a time, however, it moved very slowly; but there are those who
think it has of late years moved rapidly enough and far enough.

It would be unseemly here to criticize contemporary criticism, but it
may, without intending offence, be said that while the appreciation of

poetry as an energy is as strong as ever in the criticism of the present day, the appreciation of poetry as an art is non-existent, except in one or two quarters which we need not indicate. Compare, for instance, the remarks on accent and quantity in English verse in Crowe's forgotten treatise on versification with the laudatory remarks that we nowadays see lavished upon some line in which both quantity and accent are ignored. But to go no further back than the time when Rossetti's poems were published, compare the critical canons then in vogue with the critical canons of the present day. On account of a single cockney rhyme, the critics of that period would damn a set of verses in which perhaps a measure of poetic energy was not wanting. The critics of to-day fall for the most part into two classes: those who do not know what is meant by a cockney rhyme, and those who love a cockney rhyme.

Imperfect versification, unscannable lines, are now the hall-mark of original genius. If ever we see quoted with approval a line by Mr. William Watson—by far the best metricist among recent poets—it is certain to be one of his few unmetrical lines, certain to be a line where the main stress falls on *the* or *a* or *of.* The one serious fault that the critics could find with Mr. Swinburne's last poem, 'The Story of Balen,' was that the difficulties of the metre were with triumphant ease mastered, that the metre was so fully sustained, the rhyme so faultless, the workmanship so good. Even in Rossetti's time the swing of the pendulum seems to have begun, for at the time when his *Ballads and Sonnets* was being reviewed, he said the Catnach element of English poetry was all that criticism demanded. And this was before the time when Tennyson was disparaged because so fine a master of poetic art must needs be jejune, and when Browning is set far above him, not on account of the richness of Browning's work (and rich, indeed, it is), but because a good number of Browning's lines are only verses from the typographical point of view. To Dante Rossetti Walt Whitman was, as appears by the Allingham letters, a mere mouthing 'Orson.' The *Leaves of Grass* were a subject of 'loathing' to him, as they were to Morris. To the critics of the present time Whitman is a sort of amalgam of Shakspeare, Wordsworth, and Shelley; the musical movements of Wagner are referred to as explaining the metrical movements of 'the master.'

Though we state thus pointedly the case, we are not saying which school of criticism deserves the more respect. We merely record an interesting and suggestive fact of literary history. If in poetical criticism the wisdom of one generation is the folly of the next, it is the same in everything man says and in everything he does, so whimsical a creature has the arch-humorist Nature set at the top of the animal kingdom. As to what has brought about all these changes, we have no time to inquire into that. The causes are many, no doubt, and among them must be mentioned the passion for prose fiction. Novels bring the reader much nearer to real life than poetry, or at least they seem to do this, and they can achieve what is called 'modernity.' To achieve the same kind of closeness of touch which is within the compass of prose fiction is apparently the aim of the kind of poets who take for their motto this same word 'modernity.'

The great master of modernity in all poetic art is, of course, Villon, and priceless are his pictures of life in old France. And in a certain sense Rossetti is answerable for the new poetry of 'modernity,' inasmuch as he introduced Villon. But unluckily Villon thought that 'modernity,' to be true, has to be ugly. Had Villon given us the beautiful, the pictorial side of the France of his period—its courage, for instance, its chivalry, its pageantry—he would have lost his touch of modernity, for it is the beauty of this world which is perennial and immortal, the ugliness which is accidental and modern. And, after all, the modernity of Villon is in some degree retrieved by the beauty of his poetic art.

But neither at Villon's Helicon, the thieves' kitchen, nor in the cockney music-hall, whence poor 'Arry and 'Arriet have been driven by the invasion of the contemporary bard, can be found an atmosphere which the true poet can breathe. And as to the great poets, such a word as 'modernity' to them is meaningless. To them when at work one epoch is as modern as another. It is with the elemental in man's life that they deal, and not with the accidental. Priam's prayer to Achilles is more true, and therefore more modern as well as more truly ancient, than anything that 'Dan Leno' or even 'Little Tich' can teach the poet's soul. To Shakspeare, Cleopatra was as modern a woman as Mrs. Ford, and he could have delineated a woman of the palæolithic period, had he known that there ever had been such women, as truly as he painted Mrs. Ford and Cleopatra.

Once, many years ago, Morris was inveigled into seeing and hearing the great poet-singer Stead, whose rhythms have had such a great effect upon the 'art poetic,' the author of 'The Perfect Cure' and 'It's Daddy This and Daddy That,' and other brilliant lyrics. A friend with whom Morris had been spending the evening, and who had been talking about poetic energy and poetic art in relation to the chilly reception accorded to *Sigurd*, persuaded him—much against his will—to turn in for a few seconds to see Mr. Stead, whose performance consisted in singing a song, the burden of which was 'I'm a perfect cure,' while he leaped up into the air without bending his legs and twirled round like a dervish. 'What made you bring me to see this d—d tomfoolery?' Morris grumbled; and on being told that it was to give him an example of poetic energy at its tensest without poetic art, he grumbled still more and shouldered his way out. If Morris were now alive—and all England will sigh, 'Ah, would he were!'—he would confess, with his customary emphasis, that the poet had nothing of the slightest importance to learn even from the rhythms of Mr. Stead, marked as they were by terpsichorean pauses that were beyond the powers of the 'Great Vance,' and even of Mr. Chevalier himself.

But apart altogether from the operation of the influences we have been glancing at, Morris, after the publication of *Sigurd*, came to the conclusion that, even should the pendulum take another turn in favour of poetic art, the time for writing long narratives in verse was gone by for ever. He was far too good a critic not to know that all the qualities of a great epic are to be found in *Sigurd*. It has the eagerness of the *Iliad*, it has the romance and the picturesqueness of the *Odyssey*; while the noble rhythmic movement in which it is written is handled with the skill of a master of metre. But the critics did not appreciate it. It made no impression on the public. He was far too good a critic also not to know that, as regards narrative poetry, the modern poet works under very different conditions from those which governed him in past times. If an epic as grand as the *Iliad* and as picturesque as the *Odyssey* were written now, it would find but few readers. In the same way that the richness of stage trappings has in England destroyed the drama as a flexible form, so the flexibility of narrative poetry has been destroyed by the detailed realism of prose fiction. In a word, epics and long metrical narratives are no longer possible. Tennyson shared this view of Morris's, for once when a friend, in talking of *The Idylls of the King*, called the group an epic, he said, 'It is not an epic; the day is past for epics.'

There was a deal of acute insight shown in Poe's remark that there are, properly speaking, no such things as long poems—poems that cannot be read through at a single sitting—and that what we call epics are simply a succession of short poems. This being so, 'brevity,' which was always 'the soul of wit,' has now become the soul of poetry too.

If it is not true to say that in order to arrest the reader's attention nowadays the story has to be developed from the inside, in the Browning way, it is true that the story has now to be flashed upon the reader's mind in scenes, much in the same way that Kean used to make his audience 'read Shakspeare by flashes of lightning.'

Morris was put into this predicament: he was a narrative poet pure and simple, and poetical narratives on the old lines had become impossible. Some new form must be found; but where to find one? A friend suggested a plan which he had himself adopted—a plan in some way akin to that of the old *cantefable*, that of telling the story by sudden and short dramatic pictures enlinked by brief prose statements of the situation after the manner of stage directions. Morris saw the convenience of this method, but it was quite foreign to his genius. Moreover, he saw, as most of those who have thought over the matter see, that these poetic forms of ours, whose vitality has lasted ever since the rhymed romance measures conquered and killed off the scansion by alliterative bars natural to the English genius, must come to an end at last—must certainly be worn out some day. And as to decasyllabic blank verse, although in his first volume Morris showed that he had a true ear for it, he got at last to dislike it so intensely that he used to say with an angry laugh, 'I wish that an Act of Parliament could be passed prohibiting the use of blank verse for the next fifty years.' But, then, what other form is there left in which to embody *motifs* of a remote and an exceedingly poetical kind—those which alone Morris loved? Walt Whitman's hybrid medium he detested even more than Rossetti did; and as regards the prose of our time, this also he considered as absolutely unsuitable for the embodiment of poetic *motifs*. If ever there was a born storyteller, it was Morris. In metrical language or in language without metre, in tapestries, in book illuminations, and even, as Rossetti used to say, in 'samplers,' he must be telling stories. One poet friend of his, on account of those additions to 'Peter Harpdon's End' which still remain unpublished, advised him for years to write poetical plays, another advised him to write novels. But to write plays he must work in that very blank-verse medium that he now detested. To write novels he must engage himself with the hideous Victorian framework in which the modern dramatic picture has to be set; he must contemplate the 'sorrow and shame' of wall-papers without a dash of sage green in them, chairs and tables smelling of french polish and Tottenham Court Road, mirrors tricked out in Brixton millinery. For he knew full well that although as poet he could deal with the elemental only in human life, as a writer of prose fiction he would have to deal with the accidental and the temporary too, and hideous indeed to him were the accidental and the temporary of the present time. Was it not inevitable, therefore, that he should turn to his beloved Icelandic sagas for models? No doubt his passion for archaisms was apt to run away with him; but to say, as many are saying now, that it was in a mere spirit of whim that Morris essayed to write stories of a purely poetical *motif* in a diction that is at once concrete and archaic is to talk nonsense, and unjust nonsense. To try them by the critical canons by which we should try prose fiction of the most romantic type—of even so romantic a type as 'Undine'*—would be a great mistake and a great injustice. Although written without metre they have all the qualities of poems save those of metre alone. The atmosphere is entirely poetic; so is every incident, so is the diction—concrete, picturesque beyond that of most poets.

---

* The German romance by La Motte Fouqué.

THE SUNDERING FLOOD

1897

83. Unsigned review, *Academy*

19 March 1898, liii, 304–5

When William Morris wrote this story he seems to have had in his mind the England of Arthur and Lancelot—a dim, half-known country with here and there a walled town or a knight's castle, and the ground still uncultivated, the woods masterless 'and abounding in antres vast' and goblin-haunted hollows. He offers a curiously romantic map of this fanciful territory as it might have been conceived by the monk dwelling in the House of the Black Canons at Abingdon 'who gathered this tale.' It is the picture of such a vision as could well be entertained by a man of the experience of William Morris, who might easily dream his favourite Cotswolds into 'the Great Mountains' of the story, and add thereto torrents and steadings, and eke it out from that other chamber of remembrance where lay his early days in Essex and Epping Forest, and his knowledge of the broad lower Thames. The family likeness in his ideal landscapes excuses, if it does not justify, this theory of their origin.

Most charitable would it be, also, to assume that he had dreamed his local colour, for the circumstances are jumbled together from many centuries. In the country are abbeys, grey village churches, and friars, and as the last did not arrive in England till the reign of Henry III., they seem to indicate the date very exactly. But instead of being under a Norman king and a feudal system, the country is broken up into a number of independent communities very much as if Ithaca had intruded itself into mediæval England. Here are dales governed by their motes, towns which seem to be republics, one district at least ruled by a baron, and that Game Laws or Foresters' Rights exist there is no word to signify. On the whole, therefore, it will be sufficient to warn off those who seek for historical accuracy in their novels. We may fairly assume that as Mr. Morris deliberately jumbled his knowledge of English landscape into this wild territory of dream, so also of set purpose he confounded epochs and times, and out of his knowledge constructed this ideal period wherein he sets succeeding systems of Government side by side. Though generally treating of the prehistoric, or at any rate vague and traditionary time of the Round Table, he adds institutions as late as the fourteenth century. To do anything else than assume the confusion to be planned would be to accuse him of the grossest carelessness—the fault unpardonable in an artist.

Next we come to the manner of speech adopted by this Abingdon clerk, who must have lived very late indeed, inasmuch as though a writer may confuse the past, he cannot mingle it with the future. He writes a prose closely akin to that of Chaucer in his 'Tale of Melibœus,' except that Chaucer is less archaic and puzzling than his imitator. But, in sooth, William Morris was neither kith nor kin of Chaucer. The early poet's strength lies in the sane and clear representation of what he saw with his own eyes and believed in his own heart. Our clerk of Abingdon, supposed to represent his time, runs over with superstition: dwarfs, landwights, sorcerers absolutely throng his pages. What a very slight part witchcraft plays with the Canterbury Pilgrims! As little almost as it does in the *Decameron*. Well, Chaucer in verse, Boccaccio in prose, were in their day masters of fiction. But all the magic they deal in is the sorcery by which genius sets before us characters more living than life itself, compressing as they do the essence of many into one. Knowledge of life, that is the artist's true material, and all else but wrappage and framework. But before dealing with that prime essential of art, a word has to be said about another minor point. In this volume, as in its predecessors, the prose narrative is broken and relieved by verse, and here again Mr. Morris has chosen to give only a rough and distant imitation of his original, for his bard deigns not to alliterate, as his contemporaries did. It is not without interest to compare the effusions of this Anglo-Saxon Scald with such an admirable version as, for instance, the late Laureate's 'Battle of Brunanburgh.' We select what in our estimation seems to be the best stanza in the book, and is also complete in itself as a description of Spring:

> Now the grass groweth free
> And the lily's on lea,
> And the April-tide green
> Is full goodly beseen;

And far behind
Lies the Winter blind,
And the Lord of the Gale
Is shadowy pale;
And thou linden be-blossomed with bed of the worm
Cometh forth from the dark house as Spring from the storm.

It is pretty, but much too smooth and Morrisian. Compare it with a verse of 'Brunanburgh':

Then with their nail'd prows
Parted the Norsemen, a
Blood-reddened relic of
Javelins over
The jarring breaker, the deep-sea billow
Shaping their way toward Dyflen again,
Shamed in their souls.

There is a something of languor in the poetry of the *Sundering Flood* and no verse that will compare with that fine couplet in its predecessor,

Bitter winter, burning summer, never more shall waste and wear,
Blossom of the rose undying makes undying springtide there.

The thought is one of those felicities that continue to haunt the mind long after they have found expression, and it echoes in what is perhaps the most exquisite prose passage in the volume:

She would, as it were, tell stories of how it would betide that at last they should meet—both grown old—and kiss once, and so walk hand in hand into the Paradise of the Blessed, there to grow young again amidst the undying Spring in the land where uneasiness is come to nought; and then would she sit and weep as if there were no ending to the well of her tears.

There are in the *Water of the Wondrous Isles* many such passages, where the poet's broad and tender humanity, his deep sympathy with the low music of parting and valediction, of wistful dreams and hopes, flash out in nobly simple and pathetic words, and there are also rugged and repugnant inversions and obscurities couched in language to be abhorred. Here he neither rises so high nor sinks so low; he is nothing worse than humdrum at his dullest, and at his best seems dwelling again on some eloquent passage of the earlier book. If the *Sundering Flood* had been written before the other, our impression would have been that the ideas were dawning upon him, but had not yet ripened into full and adequate expression. At the same time this is the more

429

artistic book of the two, in so far as it shows greater evidence of plan and selection. But it is not inspired either as to its incidents or the language in which they are told.

The real gift of Mr. Morris as a romancer lay in his ability to picture some of the sweetest and most engaging figures to be found in fiction. But he saw them only with the sure, but momentary, glimpse of a poet. We may fancy him to have beheld some fair Cotswold lass and lad and to have transported them in his fancy back to the Dark Ages, to have called one Elfhild and one Osberne, and then, from his reading, to have imagined adventures appropriate to their day. But the worst of it is that the lines are so well-travelled. Like 'Roland brave and Olivier, and every paladin and peer,' Osberne must obtain his enchanted sword and, like Excalibar and Durindante, it is delivered by the hands of a supernatural visitant. It is hight 'Board-cleaver,' and the giver is Steelhead, one who might be mate to Birdalone's friend the Wood-wife. He also bestows a bow and magical arrows, and is the good fairy of the tale. To Elfhild a dwarf presents a pipe of sorcery, whose virtue may be apprehended from the pretty extract we make:

And she drew forth a pipe from her bosom and fell to playing it, and a ravishing sweet melody came thence, and so merry that the lad himself began to shift his feet as one moving to measure, and straightway he heard a sound of bleating, and sheep came running towards the maiden from all about. Then she arose and ran to them, lest they should shove each other into the water: and she danced before them, lifting up her scanty blue skirt, and twinkling her bare feet and legs, while her hair danced about her: and the sheep they, too, capered and danced about as if she had bidden them, and the boy looked on and laughed without stint, and he deemed it the best of games to behold.

The story of the love of these two forms the artless plot. If worked out in plain and simple language it would have been a pleasing essay in the *genre* of fairy tales for children, even though with all his magic and spells Mr. Morris produces no effect comparable to that, for instance, which results from the wandering of Sir Palomedes and the 'Questynge Beste' through the pages of *Mort d'Arthur*. For anything beyond that it is naught. The author had a quick and sure eye for any fair vision of men and women, but never did he master that essential of all great novels, the effect produced on character by the shocks and blows of circumstance. Barring that his lovers add a few feet to their stature and a few pounds to their weight, they are at the end what they were at the beginning, as wise and not a whit less virtuous. And where this is so it is obvious that the wildest adventure has no more literary value than an exciting paragraph in a daily paper. Nor can we believe that it is at all true to represent a boy of twelve as matchless alike in courage and wisdom. Rather are folly, and even a certain cowardice, the characteristics of that period when boys are like puppy-dogs that, though destined to be staunch and true as steel, will in their callow days fly from a kitten or a rat. But if the author's interest had lain in the growth and development of mental qualities, the Cotswold Hills of the nineteenth century would have afforded a better stage than the dim and little understood time when chivalry was dawning. For you do not make literature great by blazoning it with the picturesque elements of history. Gil Blas of Santillane, sallying forth on his old mule, his head crammed with folly and nonsense, is as enduring, yes, and as interesting a figure as the bravest and most renowned knight of Christendie.

84. Morris's 'wonderful versatility of talents'

1897

Unsigned review by H. H. Statham, *Edinburgh Review*, January 1897, clxxxv, 63–83.

The article is concerned with the *Poetical Works* (1896), the lecture 'Gothic Architecture' (1893), and *Hopes and Fears for Art* (1882). It tries to bring together the various elements in Morris's career and achievement.

Statham (1839–1924) wrote mainly on art, architecture and music.

The author of *The Earthly Paradise*—the production with which his name is most widely and popularly associated—has left behind him a reputation of very unusual quality. A poet of no mean order, he made his own poetic style in a series of works as remarkable for their general excellence of literary execution as for their voluminous character and the comparative rapidity with which they were produced. In regard to the style of furniture design and house decoration he has exercised an influence on the taste of his generation such as no single man has exercised since Chippendale. He took a keen interest in social questions, especially in those affecting the prosperity and happiness of the poorer classes, and in the whole subject of the relation of art to daily life and the means whereby modern life might be rendered more beautiful and more enjoyable. A Socialist to the core, he taught, and seriously believed with all his heart, that there was no true and living art except such as was produced by the people and for the people. He invited us to look back with admiration and sympathy to a period, the historical place of which was never very accurately defined, when the artisan made all things beautiful by mere natural instinct, and when there were no rich men and no patrons of art to spoil the simplicity of artistic aims. He renounced the Renaissance and all its works, and was one of the last to cling to the tenets of the Gothic revival, and to assert that mediæval architecture was the only true model and ideal of architecture, long after all, even of his own immediate coterie of friends and allies, had forsaken this faith. Quite late in his career he took up the subject of the reform of printing and the make-up of books, going into it with the thoroughness with which he went into everything that he took up, so that when he gave an illustrated lecture on the subject in the New Gallery some little time since, those who did not 'know the man and his communication' might have imagined that he was an expert in printing and book-production who had never devoted his thoughts to anything else. Clearly this was a man not only of remarkable versatility of talents but of wonderful energy and vitality of nature, who, though in no one branch of intellectual work did he evince genius of the highest order, yet made a strong and unmistakeable impression upon the feelings and tastes of his generation, not more by the force of his talent than by the absolute sincerity of his convictions, expressed in the speech of a man who believed every word he said.

In the new edition of Morris's poems, the volume which takes its name from the first poem, *The Defence of Guenevere*, is reprinted without alteration from the edition of 1858. Considered in connection with the later poems it holds a curiously isolated position, representing a phase of feeling and of literary style which the poet in his next production seems to have suddenly outgrown or put aside. The volume was dedicated to a prominent member of the 'P.R.B.,' and is itself essentially a representation in poetry of what used to be termed the pre-Raphaelite spirit in painting. It is a study of episodes of mediæval life, seen in all its strong colour, its profusion of detail, its mingling of savage cruelty with courage and mysticism. It is characterised by a crude realism which is sometimes very effective, sometimes grotesque, and occasionally even coarse. In one respect this early volume is typical of the main defect both of its author's literary work and of his whole character and career, viz. the total absence of the sense of humour. In another respect it differs materially from his later poetic work; it gives little promise of the facility—the dangerous facility—which the author subsequently attained in versification; it is full of angular and halting lines; *e.g.*:—

> (This in their teeth) they looked as if they deemed
> That I was spying what thoughts might be hid.

> He fought
> A good fight, may be, ere he was slain quite:

which is sheer prose and not metre at all; and at the best there is generally little finish in the workmanship, little of that perfection of expression which shows the last touch of the artist in verse. In such matters Morris seems, at this time at least, to have been careless enough; he did not want to make good literature; he wanted to tell a story effectively, to throw a new light on a situation (as he certainly does in the 'Defence of Guenevere'), to realise some of the actuality of mediæval life, and to present a vivid picture to the eye, by descriptive epithets in regard to colour and detail which are brought in so naturally that they seem not so much inventions as descriptions of what the writer had actually seen, as when the 'Good Knight in Prison' sees through his window, through 'the stanchions, half worn out with rust':—

> Close at hand
> Four spikes of sad sick sunflowers stand,
> The Castellan with a long wand
> Cuts down their leaves as he goes by,
> Ponderingly, with screwed-up eye,
> And fingers twisted in his beard.—

or in the ride through the rain to 'The Little Tower'—

> Though our arms are wet with the slanting rain,
> This is joy to ride to my love again:
> .   .   .   .   .   .

Which way through the floods, good carle, I pray?
'The left side yet! The left side yet!
Till your hand strikes on the bridge parapet.'

. . . . . .

Shake the wet off on the upland road,
My tabard has grown a heavy load.

. . . . .

They are ringing the bells, and the torches glare,
Therefore the roofs of wet slate stare.

There she stands, and her yellow hair slantingly
Drifts the same way the rain goes by.

This Homeric gift of visualising a scene, and seizing on its details, is obvious through all Morris's poetry. We come on instances of it again and again in *Jason* and *The Earthly Paradise*:—

There shall the quick-eyed Centaurs be thy friends:

And therewith kissed the boy,
Who with his black beard played, and laughed for joy
To see the war-horse in the red torch-light.

The thunder growled about the high brown hills;

For o'er the oily smooth mill head
There hung the apples growing red,
And many an ancient apple-tree
Within the orchard could he see,
While the smooth mill walls white and black
Shook to the great wheel's measured clack
And grumble of the gear within;
While o'er the roof that dulled that din
The doves sat crooning half the day.

To return for the moment to the *Guenevere* volume, one recognises in it that Morris had read his Froissart to good purpose; 'Sir Peter Harpdon's End' and 'The Haystack in the Floods' are vivid realisations of the kind of mediæval savagery which the old chronicler relates as if such deeds were a matter of course; the 'Haystack' is one of the most powerful things in the volume, and one of the best written. Others of the poems are steeped in an atmosphere of dreamy old-world romance framed in 'local colour'; the effect is enhanced by the very look and sound of the mediæval-French names:—

> Who walked in that garden fair?
> Miles and Giles and Isabeau,
> Tall Jehane du Castel beau,
> Alice of the golden hair;

> Big Sir Gervaise, the good knight,
> Fair Ellayne de Violet,
> Mary, Constance fille de fay,
> Many dames with footfall light.

The feeling for decorative effect in this poem ('Golden Wings'), for the colour in the objects named, is characteristic of a decorator poet.

> Deep green water filled the moat,
> Each side had a red brick lip
> Green and mossy with the drip
> Of dew and rain;

That 'red brick lip' is a sign of the times; it might have come out of a 'P.R.B.' picture, and indicates too the turn in architectural taste which was to lead in a brick-building generation; earlier in the century it would have been a 'marble lip.'

> The painted drawbridge over it
> Went up and down with gilded chains;
> 'Twas pleasant in the summer rains
> Within the bridge-house there to sit.

So all the details of the scene are gone through with touch after touch, till we seem to be drawn into it, and forget the modern world entirely; it was a new charm at the time, though others have waved the same wand since. But perhaps the finest of the poems that paint mediæval life and incident is that spirited lyric, less known and quoted than most things in the volume, 'The Gilliflower of Gold,' the song of the winner at a tournament, who bore the gilliflower as his lady's cognisance. The splendid lilt of this, with the touch of tenderness mingled with it, seems to express the very heart of mediæval chivalry:—

> Our tough spears crackled up like straw;
> He was the first to turn and draw
> His sword, that had nor speck nor flaw—
> *Hah! Hah! la belle jaune giroflée.*

[quotes next three stanzas]

> Once more the great swords met again,
> '*La belle! la belle!*' but who fell then?

Le Sieur Guillaume, who struck down ten;—
Hah! Hah! la belle jaune giroflée.

The third line of the last-quoted stanza is weak; but on the whole this is a Tyrtæan strain, the tune of which it is difficult to get out of one's head again. The unexpected use of the word 'giroflée' to express the clash of the swords is a fine point. As an example of the contents of this early volume, in a totally different key from the last, one may cite these exquisitely tender lines from the short poem entitled 'Summer Dawn:'—

> Far out in the meadows, above the young corn,
>   The heavy elms wait, and restless and cold
> The uneasy wind rises; the roses are dun;
> Through the long twilight they pray for the dawn
> Round the lone house in the midst of the corn.
>   Speak but one word to me over the corn,
>   Over the tender, bow'd locks of the corn.

A first volume of poems, containing so much that was both original and various, was indeed one of rare promise, in spite of obvious literary defects. It gave the idea that its author was one who could sound various pipes at will. He had the power, as exemplified in the last quotation, of expressing tender sentiment in exquisitely musical verse; he evinced keen perception of picturesque detail and colour, and the faculty of conveying the impression of them to his readers, as of something which had been under his own observation; and he showed the power of describing actions of human personages with dramatic force and spirit, although his gifts did not include either humour or the power of delineating personal character. Though the action in 'Sir Peter Harpdon' and 'The Haystack in the Floods' is vividly told, the personages have no individual character by which we could recognise them again; they are names only; we do not seem to get more of them than the costume and the scenic accessories, and the fact that one is cruel and another oppressed or unhappy. But even with this drawback the *Guenevere* volume is, in its picturesque force and variety, and, in regard to many of the poems, we may add its concentration, a strange contrast to the five volumes which represent the main bulk of Morris's poetic work, and the titles of which are best known to general readers. We may regard the *Jason* volume and the four volumes of the *Earthly Paradise* as practically one work; for *Jason* is the same order of story in precisely the same style as the *Earthly Paradise* stories, only at greater length; but for this it might just as well have formed, and probably would have formed, one of the same collection, instead of being published under a separate title. It is a curious phenomenon that a poet who, in his first published volume, showed so much variety and such picturesque quality, should have settled down in his five succeeding volumes, forming the bulk of his contribution to our poetic literature, into such an unvarying monotony of style and form as characterises these latter works; so much so that in taking up any volume of the *Earthly Paradise* one has to look at the head-line to see what story we have opened at, for there is nothing in the style or character of any one of them to distinguish it from the others; and it would be the same with *Jason* if the volume itself had not the special title. And one is tempted to ask, What influence led the poet into this rather sleepy labyrinth of dream-fancies, and what is its real value as an addition to our literature?

Something of the influence under which Morris wrote we learn from the 'L'Envoi' poem at the close of the *Earthly Paradise*. A reference to 'my master Geoffrey Chaucer' and to the 'House of Fame' indicates that he professed to be following in the steps of Chaucer, as the old poet shows himself in that class of subjective poems of which the 'House of Fame' is one, and in the revived treatment of ancient legends which he has given us in the 'Legend of Good Women.' The latter poem seems, in fact, to have been the main suggestion of the *Earthly Paradise*; it has a merit of concentration which Morris certainly did not emulate, but it has, as far as it goes, the same unity of style in the treatment of the legends, the same monotony; but a monotony which may have a pleasing effect in a series of short poems becomes rather a burden on the reader of five volumes. Other influences under which the *Earthly Paradise* was composed are indicated in the two final stanzas of the 'Envoi:'—

> Fearest thou, Book, what answer thou mayst gain
> Lest he★ should scorn thee, and thereof thou die?
> Nay, it shall not be.—Thou mayst toil in vain,
> And never draw the House of Fame anigh;
> Yet he and his shall know whereof we cry,
> Shall call it not ill done to strive to lay
> The ghosts that crowd around life's empty day.
>
> Then let the others go! and if indeed
> In some old garden thou and I have wrought,

★ Chaucer.

And made fresh flowers spring up from hoarded seed,
And fragrance of old days and deeds have brought
Back to folk weary; all was not for naught.
—No little part it was for me to play—
The idle singer of an empty day.

The melancholy refrain about the 'empty day' is the poetic expression of Morris's uncompromising pessimism, which could see nothing to admire and nothing to sympathise with in modern life. Everything was wrong—hopelessly wrong; an attitude of mind which, if we consider how much has really been done to ameliorate the condition of mankind since the beginning of the present century, and what immense steps have been made in our knowledge and grasp of the forces of Nature, is almost an indication of narrowness and despondency of temperament. This is not, unhappily, a great artistic age; but art is not everything, and in some respects the nineteenth century has been a remarkable and a very memorable one, as future generations will recognise; and it is a blind and a morbid philosophy which would preach to us that there is no interest in the life of this day, and nothing better to be done with it than take refuge in poetic revivals of ancient legends. Nor do we mean to say that Morris in his own life, and apart from poetry, took no more vigorous view of life than this. He was, in fact, better than his theories; but that is his poetic or literary attitude. In claiming to be a follower of Chaucer he was—whether he recognised the fact or not—only adopting as a model a certain side of Chaucer, and that not his most important side. Chaucer was not essentially a singer of old legends in rather melancholy and plaintive verse. He was essentially a man of vigorous and healthy nature, with a keen interest in life, an inexhaustible fund of humour, and a great power of dramatic characterisation. The central and real Chaucer is the Chaucer of the *Canterbury Tales*, not the Chaucer of the 'Legend of Good Women,' which is after all a very small portion of his work; and to speak of Morris as our modern Chaucer is merely to show misunderstanding of Chaucer, who, in his leading work, is one of the very last poets with whom Morris could have any right to be compared; in fact they are at opposite poles of poetry. Whether Morris himself was aware of this seems very doubtful, from the fact that in the illustrated and decorative edition of the *Canterbury Tales* which he had been engaged on for some time before his death the illustrations were to be furnished by Sir E. Burne-Jones, of all painters of genius the very last one to be chosen to illustrate such a work. The most prominent quality in the *Canterbury Tales* is dramatic and humorous delineation of varieties of human character. Sir E. Burne-Jones is a painter absolutely devoid of dramatic power, and whose figures have so strong a family resemblance in physical characteristics and expression that the name of any one of them would do for any other. To depute to such an artist, great though he be, the illustration of the *Canterbury Tales* was equivalent to confessing an entire misunderstanding of the spirit of the poem.

There is, in fact, nothing Chaucerian about the *Earthly Paradise*; and, on the other hand, so far as we can connect poetry with painting, it strikes us that there is in it a great deal of the influence of Burne-Jones, with whom Morris was on terms of long and continuous intimacy. As modern representations of ancient legend, the feeling of these poems is remarkably similar to that of Sir E. Burne-Jones's paintings. They have the same kind of merits and the same kind of defects. As in the pictures, so in the poems, the personages presented to us are but personages who fill a composition in a decorative manner; they all speak the same mild and measured language; the whole composition is unreal, it is a dream-world, where mild, grave figures move and act with a slow serenity which never disturbs the beauty, calm, and balance of the whole. Only in little details of nature, of the landscape amid which the action takes place, are there touches of reality, often very charming ones, showing Morris's love of nature and his quick perception both of aspects of landscape and of the little incidents of bird and flower life, as when he says in 'The Good Knight in Prison' (*Guenevere* volume):—

> Like one who paints with knitted brow
> The flowers and all things one by one,
> From the snail on the wall to the setting sun:

though there is none of the 'knitted brow' in his poems, everything seems to slip into its place easily and naturally. There is a beauty of its own no doubt in this calm and equable movement of the poem; but there are moments when one feels that the situation demands that this calm should be broken by something more strenuous; and it never comes. One of the most remarkable fancies in *Jason* is the conflict in which Orpheus and the Sirens contend in song, as it were, for the souls of the Argonaut crew; the Sirens singing from the shore and Orpheus answering from the ship. This was a splendidly suggestive idea, and the contrast between the Siren promises of enchanted bliss and the endeavour of Orpheus to recall his companions to the sense of the everyday beauties of common earth is up to a certain point finely carried out:—

THE SIRENS.

Shall we not rise with you at night,
Up through the shimmering green twilight,
That maketh there our changeless day,
Then, going through the moonlight grey,
Shall we not sit upon these sands,
To think upon the troublous lands
Long left behind, where once ye were,
When every day brought change and fear?
Then, with white arms about you twined,
And shuddering somewhat at the wind
That ye rejoiced erewhile to meet,
Be happy, while old stories sweet
Half understood, float round your ears,
And fill your eyes with happy tears.

[quotes next 38 lines]

This contrast between the healthy brown-clad maidens of earth and the deceitful Sirens of the 'pearly limbs' is finely imagined, and the whole is expressed in verse of unimpeachable smoothness and finish. Yet surely it hardly rises to 'the height of this great argument;' surely one feels that the protest of Orpheus is almost as sad and monotonous as the temptation of the Sirens; that a more strenuous and vigorous style was called for to express the glory of human action and strife and suffering as against the temptation to the bliss of indolent enjoyment.

Taken altogether, the *Earthly Paradise* is a series of (mostly) classic legends reproduced in a very lengthy form, with a great many charming incidents of decorative setting, but with a total lack of flesh-and-blood humanity in the personages; told in verse which is for the most part exceedingly equable and polished in style, but characterised by an intentional naïveté and antiquarianism both of thought and expression which sets it still further back from the plane of reality, and sometimes gives to the writing the air of a kind of studied childishness. That is the mistake that Spenser made, and which has stood so much in the way of the general acceptance of his great poem; as Pope observed:—

Spenser himself affects the obsolete,

whereas Chaucer wrote honestly in the best contemporary English of his day; and the literary affinities of Morris are really much more with

Spenser than with Chaucer. Spenser's richness and stateliness he has not; but Spenser's lengthiness, affected archaisms, and want of genuine humanity in his personages, Morris has reproduced, whether intending it or not, only too well. And the consequence is that with whatever pleasure parts of *Jason* and the *Earthly Paradise* may be read now, the reading of the whole work becomes tedious. 'Very few and very weary are those who are in at the death of the blatant beast,' said Macaulay of the *Faërie Queene*; and very few and very weary, too, must be those who have waded straight through from the Prologue to the Epilogue of the *Earthly Paradise*. The Prologue itself is one of the most interesting parts of the poem, as there is a real narrative interest in it, though of a rather Utopian character; there is less of acted naïveté in it than in the stories themselves, and it is sprinkled with reflective passages which are worth serious reading; this very fine one among them on the contrast between the first and the latter half of the life of man:—

> Two gates unto the road of life there are,
> And to the happy youth both seem afar,
> Both seem afar, so far the past one seems,
> The gate of birth, made dim with many dreams,
> Bright with remembered hopes, beset with flowers;
> So far it seems he cannot count the hours
> That to this midway path have led him on,
> Where every joy of life now seemeth won—
> So far, he thinks not of the other gate,
> Within whose shade the ghost of dead hopes wait
> To call upon him as he draws anear,
> Despoiled, alone, and dull with many a fear,
> 'Where is thy work? how little hast thou done,
> Where are thy friends, why art thou so alone?'

[quotes next 11 lines]

This may be said to be a new expression of an old thought, and a fine and pathetic one. But to come to the stories themselves; take what may be called a fairly representative one, 'The Man Born to be King'; this is agreeably and smoothly told, with very pretty touches of description here and there; but notwithstanding the beauty of the descriptive passages, one of which we have already quoted, people who take poetry seriously may surely find nearly one hundred pages of this poem rather too much. 'Cupid and Psyche' is, we believe, a favourite; the legend is so charming in itself that in almost any form it takes the fancy, and the verse for the most part is as sweet and melodious as could be wished; yet it may be questioned whether the poet has not injured rather than enhanced its effect by reducing it to an almost childish simplicity.

'The Watching of the Falcon' is a more powerful tale, with a certain degree of moral significance about it. 'The Story of Rhodope' is one of those which best repay careful reading; it is less naïve in style than many of the others, there is more interest in the unfolding of the narrative, and there is more of real human pathos and character in the figures—the ambitious, restless-minded maiden, stubbornly discontented with her lot, the poor old father who desires her love above all things, and at last shrinks silently from accompanying her to her life of grandeur, through a modest sense of his own unfitness. The close of this poem is really pathetic; under the influence of the last touching incident the author altogether forgets his decorative limits and his assumed naïveté, and writes powerfully and impressively; but such moments are too rare in the wide spaces we have to traverse. With all the frequent beauty of detail and incident, and the somewhat drowsy charm of a versification nearly always equable and musical, it is to be doubted whether such a book as this can survive as a living book of English poetry. That there should be so much verse, and so generally good, produced by one who in one sense was no 'idle singer,' but a very busy man, is no doubt in itself a remarkable feat, but 'more matter with less art' would have been more to the purpose for posterity.

We can only regret that a poet of distinctly original genius has to a great extent sacrificed his opportunities by allowing himself to be led astray, as by a kind of intellectual mirage, into the task of mediævalising Greek legend for modern readers, for that is what it comes to; the atmosphere of the *Earthly Paradise* is mediæval, not classic; and even the mediævalism is an assumed attitude. There is more of real impression, of ancient Greek feeling and atmosphere conveyed in Arnold's 'Strayed Reveller,' concentrated as it is, than in all the pages of *Jason*, 'Cupid and Psyche,' and the rest. Morris, for many reasons, will not be forgotten, and his longest poem will probably always fill a place in library shelves, but it will be less and less read as the phase of æsthetic feeling, which has made it attractive to one generation, begins to wane. Of his epic *Sigurd* we have spoken recently,* and a return to it confirms us in our former opinion that it is a most remarkable *tour de force*

* *Edinburgh Review*, October 1893, pp. 474, 475.

in poetic composition, but that for a poem which was to take a permanent and recognised place in modern poetic literature it needs
concentration. We suggested then that the author might still make a
great poem of it if he would rewrite it in a more concentrated form;
for that it is unhappily too late, nor in fact did we suppose that Morris
would be likely to accept or act upon advice of that kind either from
this or any other quarter. A vain man he certainly was not, but a man
more obstinately convinced in his own opinions probably never lived.
It is obvious that in *Sigurd* he dreamed of producing what should be
a modern Homeric epic on a mediæval subject; and it is so far a greater
success than the *Earthly Paradise* that the poet's mediævalised mind and
turn of thought and expression and imagery are more in accordance
with the mediæval character of the subject. But the fact is that the
Homeric epic is an anachronism now. It is not sufficient to relate a
national legend in verse with a good lilt in it; that kind of exploit
belongs to the youth of nations, when verse is not merely a literary
art but is the vehicle of historical or legendary records. A modern epic
must stand on its literary workmanship, and whatever facility in composition a poet may possess—and that of Morris seems to have been
really phenomenal—an epic which can claim permanent acceptance on
that footing is not a kind of essay which can be 'written in the intervals
of business.' Milton's great poem, while we have drifted far away
from the school of religious feeling and creed to which it appealed,
retains its hold on us by its pure literary grandeur; but years were
devoted entirely to it, and the poet considered twelve lines 'a good
morning's work.' It would be rather interesting to know how many
lines of *Sigurd* its author considered a good morning's work. *Sigurd*
is a remarkable monument of poetic facility in versification and construction, and contains many picturesque and striking lines; but few
people will ever read it straight through, because the modern mind
does not care for the retailing of the legend as such. The legend is
common property now; if a poet treats it at length, what we require
from him is that he should make it the vehicle for a poetical composition of which every portion will have a high literary value for
its perfection of expression; and this certainly cannot be said of *Sigurd*.
Morris's translation of the poem which he chose for some reason to
call the *Æneids* of Virgil has the same characteristics. It is very facile
and easily written, and keeps, as far as we have examined it, very close
to the meaning of the original; but as to any attempt to represent
Virgil's finish and delicacy of expression, there seems not a trace of

such a thing; it is Virgil done into the 'vulgar tongue,' that is all. Even
the most marked and palpable effects of the original are ignored, *e.g.*
the contrast of metrical effect in the two lines—

> Corripuere viam interea, qua semita monstrat.
> Jamque ascendebant collem, qui plurimus urbi
> Imminet.

which Morris translates:—

> But therewithal they speed their way as led the road along,
> And now they scale a spreading hill that o'er the town is hung.

But where is the expressive contrast between the dactylic and spondaic
line? Utterly gone. To convey any impression of the style of Virgil in
a translation would give the translator a long and difficult task, no
doubt, but such a work ought to be a long and difficult task. Morris
seems to have regarded it as something to be turned off easily as a
leisure occupation; that he should have been able to do it as well as
he has done in that kind of offhand way is in itself remarkable, but he
has only produced what may be called a readable popular translation
of the story. He might have produced something far beyond this if,
in his facility for verse-making, he had not underrated his task.

It is in the last volume, *Poems by the Way*, that we are brought back
again to what we consider to have been the real Morris—if only he
had known it. Here, as in the *Guenevere* volume, we find that the
author of the dream fancies of the *Earthly Paradise* had the power to
touch our hearts in poems of concentrated expression and passion. To
one or two of these we have referred in a previous article. Another to
be noticed is 'Mother and Son,' the reflections of a mother over her
infant; a poem as remarkable for its truth and pathos of feeling as for
its simple and perfectedly unaffected style. 'The Half of Life Gone' is
another of the same kind of merit; and we may quote the following
little poem as an instance how Morris could write when he could put
away his acted mediævalism:—

> Lo, when we wade the tangled wood,
> In haste and hurry to be there,
> Naught seem its leaves and blossoms good,
> For all that they be fashioned fair.

> But looking up, at last we see
> The glimmer of the open light,
> From o'er the place where we would be:
> Then grow the very brambles bright.

So now, amidst our day of strife,
With many a matter glad we play,
When once we see the light of life
Gleam through the tangle of to-day.

Considering the genuine ring both of style and feeling in some of these poems, one cannot but feel that Morris might have been a greater poet if he had written less, and would have secured a larger and more permanent place in the literature of his country had he given more scope to the power which he undoubtedly possessed of appealing in poetry to the deeper sympathies and passions of humanity, instead of spending himself, as 'the idle singer,' in volume upon volume of old-world legends the super-sweetness of which, seductive at first, proves at last rather tiring to the reader.

Of Morris the craftsman it is less difficult to speak, for here there can be little occasion for criticism or difference of opinion. The change which has taken place in the average public taste in this country in regard to the design of carpets, furniture, etc., and the general fitting up and decoration of dwelling houses, is something extraordinary, and can only be appreciated by those who can remember the general appearance of an ordinary 'well furnished' drawing room some forty years ago—the staring white marble chimney-piece with the gilt timepiece of debased Louis-Quinze aspect, the sprawling sofa-legs in double curves, the big knops of flowers on the carpet and hearthrug, and the terrible colours and realistic foliage of the wall papers. About the present furnishing taste there is no doubt often a certain amount of affectation; it is adopted as a mere fashion by some persons who would follow any fashion that was set them; but the fact remains that whereas some thirty or forty years ago the general taste in England in such matters was perhaps worse than that of any other country, it is now on the whole better than that of any other country, except the United States; and even the Americans learned from us lately in the first instance, though they have perhaps in some respects improved upon our lessons. Even in the ordinary work exposed for sale in furniture shops the effect of the change is manifest; tradesmen, it is true, care nothing about artistic style, but they have been compelled to do their best to follow the change in the public demand. And this improvement in household taste is the direct work of Morris more than of any one else. He set the example of designing furniture in accordance with the requirements and expression of structure (in which respect furniture properly follows much the same principles as architecture); of considering harmony of colour in the carpets, papering, and other decorations of a room; of treating designs based on natural foliage on true decorative principles, conventionalising the forms employed, and teaching his public the importance of beauty of line and of preserving the balance and spacing of decorative detail. He has been the means of revolutionising our taste in the design of textiles and wall papers, and of reviving the artistic employment of needlework and tapestry. More recently, no doubt, others have followed in his wake, and the work turned out from his own establishment was probably, in later years, rather influenced than designed by him; but he was himself a designer in the first instance, and subsequently collected round him a kind of school of workers, who were able to carry out work in the spirit which he had started. And Morris's perceptions in this class of work were not based on any mere dilettante preferences. They were the result of a close and unremitting study of the subject. It is said by those who knew him well that no man had such a thorough and exhaustive knowledge of the technical processes of old work, so far as we now have the means of knowing them. Design in all the decorative arts is, or should be, based upon or largely influenced by technique; it was the perception of this, and the knowledge of the technical requirements and possibilities in connection with each class of material, which led him to the right path in the treatment of design. There was no better example of his perception in this respect than the cheap chair, which used to be called the 'Morris chair,' which he designed many years ago. This was an attempt to show how an article of furniture could be made which, by simply following out the best lines of construction with plain materials, in the form most convenient for its practical purpose, would nevertheless have a distinctly artistic character. This chair, if we remember right, was originally sold for about ten shillings (the price has followed the general rise in prices of work since); it was an artistically designed chair for the million, but it would hardly look out of place in the mansion any more than in the cottage.

In regard to architecture, Morris's opinions as to the present time were as consistently pessimistic as his social opinions. His lecture on Architecture, delivered at the Arts and Crafts Exhibition some years ago, is a brilliant and interesting recapitulation of the history of architecture from his own standpoint, and contains some very suggestive remarks; but his view is a narrow one. His theory was that architecture could only be said to exist as a living art when it was the work of a co-operative guild of artificers, and Gothic architecture alone was supposed to fulfil this condition. He could not deny that there was a beauty of its own in Greek architecture, but he held the theory—once popular, but which few artists or students of art now hold—that the Greek temple was dependent for all its real beauty on the sculpture. Most people will say that the remains of the Parthenon, even in its present ruined state and divested of its sculpture, are a sufficient answer to this. And the guild theory of Gothic is rather delusive. In regard to details of mouldings and ornament, and the method of constructing the vaulting, the Gothic churches were no doubt the result of a kind of general consensus of habit and method of working among the artisans of a particular generation. But the west fronts, for instance, of Wells, Peterborough, and Ely, each constitute a distinct and original architectural conception, which must have been the conception of one individual mind, and could under no circumstances have arisen from the spontaneous and fortuitous concurrence of a number of working masons. There is really more *a priori* ground for supposing the Greek temples to have been the production of guilds of craftsmen, for they have a much closer family resemblance than the mediæval cathedrals; yet we know positively that there were special architects in Greece who enjoyed great consideration and commanded very high terms, and we derive the very word from Greece. The architect to whom the individual character and main design of a Gothic cathedral were due (and their individuality of character, even taking only the English cathedrals, is much greater than is generally recognised) did not command high terms, and was not called by a Greek name, but he was an architect or 'master builder' all the same. The blank denial of all beauty and interest to Renaissance or neo-classic architecture is mere bigotry, and hardly worth refutation; and to suppose that any building, as buildings are now required to be, can be adequately carried out on the 'guild' system is to suppose that we are to ignore planning, lighting, heating, and ventilation; in fact, to go back to the life of the Middle Ages. Architecture is an individual art now, and it is not likely to cease to be so, as far as we can predict, unless our habits of life relapse into comparative barbarism. Nor is there any reason why the artisan, under the modern system, should be a mere unintelligent machine; the more intelligent and educated he is, the greater will be his value on the work and the greater his interest in it. But to say that a building is to be evolved by the combined efforts of a guild of craftsmen (and that is what Morris's theory practically comes to) is about as reasonable, in the present day, as to expect that a book should

447

be the combined production of the 'companionship' of printers who set up the type.

The little volume in which the above-mentioned lecture on Architecture was issued was printed at the Kelmscott Press, and is in itself a kind of specimen of Morris's idea as to the make-up of a printed page. As a matter of decorative effect, it may be questioned whether the introduction of a little conventionalised black leaf design on the page to mark the close of each paragraph—a kind of glorified full-stop—does not produce a rather disagreeable 'spotty' effect. Speaking generally, however, the productions of the Kelmscott Press are models of fine workmanship, and Morris did good service, which may bear further fruit, in calling attention to the fine character of design of some of the old founts of type, as compared with the hard and meagre character of those most commonly employed nowadays. The designing of type is a matter of extreme delicacy, as the total effect is not realised till a whole page or so comes to be printed; and a difference in the designing of the extremities of the letters, for instance, so slight that it would be unnoticed if not looked for, may make all the difference in the appearance when we see the impression of a whole page together. Two points there were in Morris's theory and practice, however, to which we must demur. In reviving the old habit of leaving large margins towards the external side of the pages, and bringing the type close up to the centre stitching of the book, he maintained that the 'unit' of a printed book was the double page as presented when the book is spread open, and that therefore the type on the two pages should be concentrated towards the centre, so as to make one mass, or nearly so, to the eye. This we deny. A book is a series of pages, and the single page is the 'unit'; and the practical result of Morris's revived system is that in thick books it becomes difficult to read the inner portion of the page, owing to the curvature of the surface; and this is distinctly unpractical. We suspect that the real reason for the old habit of setting the type towards the centre and leaving a wide outer margin was to leave space for annotations, and the method might still have this value if we ever left ourselves time for annotations in these hard-reading days. Apart from that, a certain difference in the margins looks much better than a rigidly symmetrical margin all round; but it must not be carried so far as to inconvenience the reader. The other point against which we must protest strongly is the practice, in some of the more costly decorative books turned out from the Kelmscott Press, of printing poetry in continuous lines, as if it were prose, instead of in separate verses, in order to fill up the page in a more decorative manner. This is absurd; it is putting the make-up of the page before the matter. Poetry is literary expression in verse, and the printer has no right, for his own private ends, to transform it into the semblance of prose.

Behind these various crafts of poet, designer, and printer came Morris's general views as to the relation of Art to Life and our state in respect of this at the present time, a good deal of the pith of which may be supposed to be expressed in the five lectures published in 1882 under the title *Hopes and Fears for Art*. A strange kind of prophecy it is, and reminds one of the Hebrew prophet's denunciation, 'Woe unto you, ye rich men; weep and howl for the misery that shall come upon you.' To read it, one would suppose that modern life was a howling wilderness, without a joy to be found in it; a state of feeling from which a little of the sense of humour at least would have preserved the lecturer. He might also have credited his hearers and readers with a little more general knowledge of history than to believe, as they are repeatedly asked to believe, that there is no bane to art like wealth and luxury. He might have expected that we should remember the existence of Egyptian temples reared with forced labour; of the Taj Mahal, of the Alhambra, of wicked popes and princes of the Renaissance for whom the greatest artists were glad to work. It is useless to tell us, in the teeth of these and other stubborn facts, that art is only connected with simplicity, with morality, with honesty, poverty, and thrift. Splendour and costliness in our surroundings are not necessarily artistic, and where they are not they are vulgar and revolting; but wealth and luxury are no blight on art, as Morris sought to persuade his hearers—they may even be the means of fostering it. There is hardly a beautiful thing at South Kensington but has been made because some wealthy man wanted it or could purchase it. The artist must have enjoyed making it—there has never been any work of real art which did not interest the man who made it; but it was not made for that sole end—it was made to sell. Still, there are noble thoughts in these lectures, not less so because they are sometimes aspirations after the impossible. 'That which I understand by real art is the expression of man's pleasure in his labour. I do not think he can be happy in his labour without expressing that happiness; and especially is this so when he is at work at anything in which he excels.' This reminds one of George Herbert's—

> Who sweeps a room as to Thy laws,
> Makes that, and the action, fine.

449

though Herbert alluded rather to the moral than the æsthetic aspect of the subject. Morris enlarges on the beauty, almost the necessity, of man having pleasure in his work—'If a man has work to do which he despises, which does not satisfy his natural and rightful desire for pleasure, the greater part of his life must pass unhappily and without self-respect.' As to despising his work, George Herbert gives him the antidote to that; but as to joying in it, the fact is that the happiness of having work to do which is a source of pleasure and interest for its own sake is, and must be in this crowded life, the lot only of a fortunate minority; to expect otherwise is Utopian, though it is an ideal, no doubt, to aim at. That 'you cannot educate, you cannot civilise men, unless you give them a share in art,' is, in the highest and noblest sense of the word 'civilisation,' a wholesome and absolute truth, and one to be carefully borne in mind (and it is now not entirely overlooked) in connection with national education schemes. A more practical maximum, which Morris laid such stress upon that he repeats it twice in emphatic italics, is this: 'Have nothing in your houses that you do not know to be useful or believe to be beautiful.' That maxim is perhaps the best thing in the book, since it is absolutely true and universally applicable, and its mere application would at one sweep put an end to bad taste and vulgarity in the daily surroundings of our lives. The words form a very good summary of the kind of improvement in household taste which Morris did so much to initiate and carry out.

Bibliography

This short select bibliography is of works directly informative about William Morris's reputation in the nineteenth century.

FREDEMAN, W. E., *Pre-Raphaelitism, A Bibliocritical Study* (Cambridge, Mass., 1965): a valuable, though not exhaustive, list of early reviews is included.

LITZENBERG, K., 'William Morris and the reviews: a study in the fame of the poet', *Review of English Studies* (1936), xii: the only study, and valuable as far as it goes.

SCOTT, TEMPLE, *A Bibliography of the Works of William Morris* (London, 1897): Section VIII, 'Articles on the Man and his Work', contains references not available elsewhere. The complete bibliography is included in VALLANCE, AYMER, *The Art of William Morris. A Record* (London, 1897).

Index

The index is divided into four sections; I. William Morris: writings; II. Characteristics of Morris and aspects of his work and career; III. Persons; IV. Periodicals and newspapers.

I. WILLIAM MORRIS: WRITINGS

II. CHARACTERISTICS OF MORRIS AND ASPECTS OF HIS WORK AND CAREER

III. PERSONS

IV. PERIODICALS AND NEWSPAPERS

THE CRITICAL HERITAGE SERIES

GENERAL EDITOR: B. C. SOUTHAM

Volumes published and forthcoming

Continued